Ethics at a Standstill

You are not expected to complete the work
and yet you are not free to evade it.

— Ethics of the Fathers, 2:16

Ethics at a Standstill

History and Subjectivity in Levinas and the Frankfurt School

Asher Horowitz

DUQUESNE
UNIVERSITY
PRESS

PITTSBURGH, PA.

Published in the United States of America by
DUQUESNE UNIVERSITY PRESS
600 Forbes Avenue
Pittsburgh, Pennsylvania 15282

Library of Congress Cataloging-in-Publication Data

Horowitz, Asher, 1950–
    Ethics at a standstill : history and subjectivity in Lévinas and the Frankfurt School / by Asher Horowitz.
        p. cm.
    Summary: "Explores the philosophies of Lévinas and the critical theorists of the Frankfurt School, demonstrating the ways in which their works diverge from and complement each other, and arguing that both fall short of their own theoretical ambitions"—Provided by publisher.
    Includes bibliographical references (p.   ) and index.
    ISBN 978–0–8207–0407–4 (hardcover : alk. paper) — ISBN 978–0–8207–0408–1 (pbk. : alk. paper)
    1. Lévinas, Emmanuel. 2. Frankfurt school of sociology. I. Title.

    B2430.L484H67 2008
    194—dc22

                                                            2007041144

∞ Printed on acid-free paper.

Part of the research for this book was supported by a grant from the Social Sciences and Humanities Research Council of Canada. Mielle Chandler and Jonathan Short helped out with a bit of the research.

    A portion of chapter 2 was published earlier under the title "How Levinas Taught Me to Read Benjamin," *PhaenEx* 1 (Spring/Summer 2006): 164–97.

    Thanks go to Gad Horowitz for his patient commentary and the use of his stove to safeguard the manuscript.

    Apologies go to Marte Misiek for whatever ill humor its writing may have exposed her to, and thanks for her patience as well.

Contents

Abbreviations

Levinas

ET   "The Ego and the Totality." In *Collected Philosophical Papers,* translated by Alphonso Lingis, 25–45. Pittsburgh: Duquesne University Press, 1998.

INS   "Intentionality and Sensation." In *Discovering Existence with Husserl,* translated by Richard A. Cohen and Michael B. Smith, 135–50. Evanston: Northwestern University Press, 1998.

JR   "Judaism and Revolution." In *Nine Talmudic Readings,* translated by Annette Aronowicz, 94–119. Bloomington: Indiana University Press, 1994.

NI   "No Identity." In *Collected Philosophical Papers,* translated by Alphonso Lingis, 141–51. Pittsburgh: Duquesne University Press, 1998.

OTB   *Otherwise than Being, or Beyond Essence.* Translated by Alphonso Lingis. Pittsburgh: Duquesne University Press, 1981.

PT   "Philosophy and Transcendence." In *Alterity and Transcendence,* translated by Michael B. Smith, 3–37. New York: Columbia University Press, 1999.

RMRO   "The Rights of Man and the Rights of the Other." In *Outside the Subject,* translated by Michael B. Smith. Stanford: Stanford University Press, 1993, 116–125.

RPH   "Reflections on the Philosophy of Hitlerism." Translated by Sean Hand. *Critical Inquiry* 17 (Autumn 1990): 63–71.

TH   "Transcendence and Height." In *Emmanuel Levinas: Basic Philosophical Writings,* edited by Adriaan T. Peperzak, Simon Critchley, and Robert Bernasconi, 11–31. Bloomington: Indiana University Press, 1996.

TI   *Totality and Infinity: An Essay on Exteriority.* Translated by Alphonso Lingis. Pittsburgh: Duquesne University Press, 1969.

WEH   "The Work of Edmund Husserl." In *Discovering Existence with Husserl,* translated by Richard A. Cohen and Michael B. Smith, 47–87. Evanston: Northwestern University Press, 1998.

Adorno

AP   "The Actuality of Philosophy." *Telos,* no. 31 (Spring 1977): 120–33.

INH   "The Idea of Natural History." Translated by Robert Hullot-Kentor. *Telos,* no. 60 (1984): 11–124.

MM   *Minima Moralia: Reflections from Damaged Life.* Translated by E. F. N. Jephcott. London: New Left Books, 1974.

ND   *Negative Dialectics.* Translated by E. B. Ashton. New York: Seabury Press, 1979.

Adorno and Horkheimer

DE   *Dialectic of Enlightenment.* Translated by John Cumming. New York: Continuum, 1988.

Benjamin

N   "N [On the Theory of Knowledge, Theory of Progress]." In *The Arcades Project,* translated by Howard Eiland and Kevin McLaughlin. Cambridge: Harvard University Press, 2002.

TPH "Theses on the Philosophy of History." In *Illuminations,* edited by Hannah Arendt, 253–64. New York: Schocken Books, 1969.

S   "The Storyteller: Reflections on the Work of Nikolai Leskov." In *Illuminations,* edited by Hannah Arendt, 83–109. New York: Schocken Books, 1969.

SMB "On Some Motifs in Beaudelaire." In *Illuminations,* edited by Hannah Arendt, 155–200. New York: Schocken Books, 1969.

Marcuse

CRR *Counter-Revolution and Revolt.* Boston: Beacon Press: 1972.

EC *Eros and Civilization: A Philosophical Inquiry into Freud.* 2nd ed. Boston: Beacon Press, 1966.

ODM *One-Dimensional Man: Studies in the Ideology of Advanced Industrial Society.* Boston: Beacon Press, 1964.

SA   "A Study on Authority." In *Studies in Critical Philosophy,* translated by Joris de Bres, 51–155. Boston: Beacon Press, 1972.

Introduction

This essay grows out of the conviction that both the Frankfurt School and Levinas each fall short of their own theoretical ambitions, yet do so in ways that allow for the possibility of a mutual fecund embrace. Emmanuel Levinas's ethics as first philosophy is wanting in the promotion and orientation of the social critique his ethics actually calls for and requires. The social critique of the Frankfurt School remains deficient in perceiving and unearthing its own ethical substance. In allowing these lacunae, moreover, each has inadvertently opened itself to appropriations that either limit or belie their most fundamental truths. In Levinas's case, ethics as first philosophy, remained open to being assimilated to liberalism — a view that his philosophy is far from endorsing, if not essentially opposed. In refusing or being unable to unfold a positive ethical optic, the Frankfurt School ironically invited, in Habermas's theory of communicative action, its own historical succession by a renewed program, and dialectic, of liberal enlightenment. Yet each, by heeding the other, could have possibly taken several important steps further.

It is not uncommon today for Levinas's philosophy to be recognized as a radical departure in our understanding of the ethical relation and its subject, including a devastating critique of the rationalist ethics of Western ontology, as well as the irrationalist, naturalistic, and sentimentalist reactions to such ontologies. His work is increasingly being welcomed as one of those rare watershed moments in the development of Western thought where, once its import has been absorbed, it will be impossible to go back. It is a thought that, in the words of one of his eminent commentators, demands "nothing less than a fundamental reorientation of Western spirit — philosophy, logic, rhetoric, praxis, ontology, science, art, politics, religion — in the light of morality and justice."[1] Levinas evokes this demand through a nonidealist phenomenology exquisitely focused on the ethical relation, and on the subject that is not only *in* this relation but also *is* this relation, a relation that precedes and even constitutes the subjectivity responsible for all of these ontological activities, yet a relation binding subjects radically separated from any totality and from one another, therefore subjects with no identity, who escape ontology. The ethical exigency to which this radically embodied material subject will always already have been irretrievably summoned means that my ethical relation to the other includes an infinite responsibility that is unconditional, nonreciprocal, and asymmetrical, a responsibility that is also my freedom, *bien entendu*. Furthermore, Levinas also insists that the ethical relation cannot be restricted to the realm of the private or to relations of intimacy. My responsibility to the other brings with it the same and as much, indeed infinite responsibility to the third party, all the other others. The ethical relation is thus inseparable from the need and necessity to realize political justice, and justice as some form of law. But the very same law that the ethical relation brings with it or commands, also necessarily undermines that which makes the ethical relation ethical. Ethics requires law, and therefore objectifying distance, thematization, universality, comparison, calculation, measure, and symmetry. But ethics and the justice it commands also require that the law be simultaneously transcended in my singular response to the singularity of the absolutely other. Political and social critique is simultaneously emboldened and stymied in this impasse.

If Levinas's phenomenology of the ethical arrives at an impasse, the critical social theory of the Frankfurt School has had little or no issue. Its so-called second and even third generations are so far removed from its original sources of inspiration, its goals and its methods that they constitute altogether different, even antithetical, schools of thought. In Habermas, whose claim to be a legitimate successor to the critical theory of the Frankfurt School rests to a large extent on his effort to reground critique in a moral point of view itself rooted in a universal pragmatics of linguistic communication, there is an overriding impetus to assimilate the ethical relation to the universalizing trend expressive of and functional for the highly differentiated form of modern capitalist social structures. In Habermas's theory of communicative action and in communicative ethics there is a reduction of the moral plane to the development of rationalizable action coordination, where the normative is simultaneously more than instrumentality and part of it. Ironically, Habermas returns morality to instrumental reason because his model of intersubjectivity presupposes relations of formal reciprocity among abstractly identical cognitive subjects as the ultimate model of the social relation, and as the final basis for political justice. The other revealed in Saying would, according to Habermas, always be simply the sort of being making the same claims as I would, claims that arise from the needs of systems reproduction.[2]

One important reason for this lack of issue is that the Frankfurt School had to avoid any attempt to integrate an articulation of the ethical relation into their critiques of enlightenment and civilized class societies. Their commitment to negative dialectics and historical materialism necessarily eschewed an external, transcendent critique with all of the metaphysical baggage such a critique would carry. They focused instead on the ideological fate of moral doctrines and systems, occasionally speaking of a naturalized morality as socialized affect, as in Horkheimer's early evocation of a "new form of human interest" which would be neither self-interest nor duty, but a synthesis of both in the rational society.[3] Or else they referred the ethical to a transcendence of the subject of domination, but only as a virtually inarticulable not yet whose symbol was to be found in aesthetic experience. It is not that the social critique of the Frankfurt School does not involve ethical imperatives. After all, according to Adorno, negative dialectics, a dialectics that has fully come into its own in the self-reflexive repudiation of identity theory, would be the "morality of thought."[4] Yet Habermas turns out to be correct in pointing out that a dialectics of this sort cannot give "an account of its own normative foundations."[5] For Habermas this is simply because it recognizes that the great philosophical tradition in which ontic and normative claims are conflated has outlived its pretensions and also because, according to him, the Frankfurt School recognized no other rationality than instrumental, subjective reason. But this is not the ultimate reason why critical theory does not attempt to lay bare those foundations. More than that, it would be that the ethical relation, for Adorno especially, cannot be presented within what Levinas calls the terms of formal logic. The moral relation that is a transcendence of identity cannot be described in terms of the categories of immanence. In Critical Theory, the ethical relation is referred to negatively, in terms of those instances in which the logic of identity defeats itself. In addition to negative dialectics, art would contain instances of this defeated logic of identity.[6]

It remains true nonetheless, as Habermas accuses, that this is a lacuna, but in something other than the sense of a theoretical space that is to be filled with grounds, principles, procedures, or sociological necessities. Being unable to lay bare the ethical dimension of its social critique implies that the Frankfurt School lags behind its own ambition, the ambition to comprehend reification and the ambition to understand the possibility of abolishing reification as the ethical imperative. This is the exact point at which Levinas's phenomenology of the ethical relation can be adduced to articulate the very substance of critical theory without making that the grounds for a new version of objective reason. From Levinas's perspective the theoretical deficiency of the Frankfurt School would not in itself be a moral defect, since the ethical relation is prior to the rationality that can offer principles, procedures, logical inferences and sociological necessities. The ethical relation, in Levinas's construal, is prior even to the quest for certainty, and prior to the possibility of doubt for a cognizing, laboring, acting subject. The ethical relation is itself a precise violation of what Levinas calls formal logic and what Adorno recognizes as the logic of identity underlying all such grounds, principles, rules, or maxims.

If Levinas's insights into the ethical relation offer to critical theory a way out of the avoidance of articulating and understanding its own normative dimension, and perhaps a way of arriving at a fuller, less astringent premonition of freedom beyond what Marx would call *prehistory,* then it is also the case that critical theory is able to contribute to breaking the impasse in the relation between ethics and justice to which Levinas accedes. Levinas creates an impasse in relating the thinking of ethics to historical-critical social theory. Inasmuch as such a theory must also be a sociology, political economy, psychology, and a history — in other words, a science of the human — Levinas cannot approach social critique as anything but fatally susceptible to totalizing activity. A totalization that is at best ignorant of the ethical relation and ignorant of its ignorance, and at worst complicit in the destruction or obstruction of the ethical relation. Even at its most critical, historicizing critique will always tend to involve a reduction of the human to a part played in the whole. For Levinas, then, even radically critical social theories fall behind or have not yet caught up with an understanding of the ethical relation as the only relation in which the human is not a possible object or subject of power and domination. For the other human to be other and human, the ethical relation must be approached as outside all the categories and relations appropriate to the manifestation or monstration of being, or even the Being of beings. The critique of instrumental reason is not enough to indicate the human to human relation and neither are radically historicized, dynamic, processual ontologies, whether or not they are dialectical, capable of rendering the sense of the ethical relation. Yet without a relation to historical social critique, Levinas's thinking about the relation of ethics to politics continually slips back into the very impasse of liberalism which impasse he identifies as one — but only one — of those important moments in which the ethical appears in history, or even to history, and without being realized.

A part or avatar of this impasse in which ethics as first philosophy remains at a standstill is therefore to be found in the relation Levinas establishes between history and eschatology. The impasse of ethics and politics is doubled up in the impasse in the relationship between history and eschatology. Rather than conceive of the eschatological as either the predetermined outcome of some historical logic, as the telos of a secular or sacred history, or as the cancellation or renewal of history through an intervention, an act of grace on the part of a transcendent power susceptible to deification, Levinas presents the eschatological as the ethical relation itself. The eschatological speculations of theologies and philosophies now old, ugly and wizened are retrieved as mythical references to a dimension beyond the predations of universal history. The end of history does not appear at or as the end of time, but is always already beneath and within the history of ethical subjects who nonetheless can and do become allergic to one another, and in their allergy conceive of peace only as the rational peace of agreement in or submission to the laws of a totality alien to the human-to-human. This is not a dualism in which history and eschatology are external to one another, neither is it a reduction of eschatology to historical development. Either alternative would in fact violate the ethical relation itself. Rather, what is novel in this vision is that the eschatological, the ethical relation, both makes history possible and, at the same time, all but immune to its own condition of possibility. Levinas's thinking makes this relation steady and stable, virtually that which Adorno calls an invariant. It is therefore not adequate to the historical possibilities of the relation between history and eschatology. Yet on rare occasions, and usually if not exclusively outside of his phenomenological writings, Levinas can say that the "epoch of the Messiah can and must result from the political order that is allegedly indifferent to eschatology."[7]

What makes the critical-historical social theory of the Frankfurt school particularly appropriate to the problem of Levinas's impasse lies in the manner in which for Horkheimer, Adorno, and Marcuse history is related to what Levinas might call eschatology. It lies, that is, in their theories of the development of what Adorno calls "natural-history" and in their critiques of the ways in which human experience is, in such a history, progressively attenuated. In unfolding the concept and critique of natural history the Frankfurt School also rejects what Levinas rejects: not only dualistic, but also teleological understandings of the relation between history and eschatology, no matter how secularized or scientific. But, unlike the invariant relation of eschatology to history in Levinas, natural history is neither progress, nor does it *simply* repeat itself. It harbors its own possibilities for its own transcendence, and even amplifies or intensifies such possibilities as they remain frozen. What makes the Frankfurt School especially appropriate for the task of lending to Levinas an opening to social critique is that both perceive history to be one single catastrophe, yet for the former it is clear that catastrophe is not the final word. Such a conception of natural history would not have been possible without the leavening of historical materialism, which was brought to the Frankfurt School by Walter Benjamin.[8] The concept and critique of natural history open onto a critical theory that does not reduce the ethical relation to rational freedom, to some functional dimension of human survival or simply to eudaemonistic ends. The construal and critique of natural history demands a negative dialectics that is able to retain and refine an understanding of the variable and relative reifying forces of differing historical formations, yet in its critique of reification refrain from ontology and totalization.

This essay is not a comparative study of different thinkers in which their approaches and results are compared and contrasted.[9] It is not simply an interpretation of one and the other in relation to a particular problem or set of problems, even though it rests on and offers a fair amount of interpretive effort. It does not aim at or pretend to be anything like a comprehensive or systematic treatment of any of the five thinkers who are its foci.[10] Neither is it my intention here to blend or to synthesize thinkers with quite distinct aims and methods. Not only do their aims and methods differ, but also they operate much of the time at different, though not essentially separate, levels of analysis, and concentrate on substantially different dimensions of what might be thought of as the problem of reification. The goal is also not to accept or reject one or the other on the basis of the arguments of the one or the other.[11] Nor will I amend each to fit better with the other. Levinas and the Frankfurt School are not conceived of as two disjoined moments of a potential dialectical unity. They are not related, positively or negatively, by way of a third term of which each might be a privation or abstraction.[12] Bringing them into relation will not supply a whole or outline a system. The manner in which they are related to each other does resemble, up to a point, the notion of a supplement[13] except that, unlike the relata of supplementarity, each is not considered full in itself. It is not, as it is in supplementation, that one completes the other; instead it is that one speaks to the desire the other already exhibits, but in a manner in which that desire is half-forgotten, blocked, or muted. Thus the relata do not remain wholly in tact. They already tend toward each other. The manner in which Levinas and the Frankfurt School are here related to each other resembles even more closely Adorno's suggestion, or even program, for thinking in constellations. It aims not only to bring the relations between the particulars in question into view without making them instances of a higher universal but also, by circling both around the object each would like to unseal, it hopes that what they each approach "would fly open like the lock of a well-guarded safety deposit box: in response not to a single key or a single number, but to a combination of numbers" (ND, 163). Thus, in some sense, the constellated thoughts will also converge. But another thing that thinking in constellations allows and perhaps even requires (see chapter 2) is that each *point* in the constellation might stand in a critical as well as supplementary relation to the other points. To treat Levinas and the Frankfurt School in the form of a constellation will mean that, in order to avoid bringing both under a supervening master concept (and thereby also to avoid setting up false dichotomies that suggest positive syntheses), they will have to be treated micrologically. To a certain extent this means immersion in the details and particulars of the works under consideration. The argument being advanced relies on sometimes new interpretations of sometimes familiar works, and these interpretations rely on a level of exegetical engagement that would seem secondary in an analytical approach.

Chapter 1 unfolds the structure and implications of the political impasse into which Levinas's revolution in ethical philosophy leads his thinking. It does so through an examination of several different texts that belong to different stages in his development. It begins the process of separating and insulating ethics as first philosophy from its looming appropriation for liberalism. It ends with an examination of the first efforts made, more or less to date, to embark on a Levinasian politics beyond liberalism, pointing forward to the need to open the question of history in order to do so.

Chapter 2, through linked interpretations of several key texts of Benjamin and Adorno, attempts to outline the concept of natural history. And it presents this concept, together with its allied forms of the critique of natural history, as a necessary and better alternative to Levinas's formulation of the relation of history to ethical experience. What in Levinas remains an impasse, now begins to become not simply an aporia, but also, at least in principle, a problem. As a problem it does not circle endlessly around its own apparent necessity.

Chapter 3 further concretizes and expands the notion of natural history through an examination of how that notion plays a constitutive role in the historico-social critiques of Benjamin, Horkheimer and Adorno, and Marcuse. Together these critiques of natural history point to the possibility of the interruption of the reduced experience with which the natural-historical is intertwined, an interruption that would amount to the *sine qua non* for a concrete emancipation beyond the liberal state and capitalist economy.

Chapter 4 is an examination of Adorno's *Negative Dialectics* as his most mature and realized version of the conceptual and performative metatheory of the critique of natural history. On one level, as epistemology, it retrospectively underpins the substantive analyses by the Frankfurt School of natural history in the development of enlightenment and in late capitalism. However, at another level, as metacritique avowedly and purposely shadowing Kant's critical system, negative dialectics aims to keep open the possibility of a subject that, in being able to unravel its own activity of transcendental constitution can see beyond itself. As with Kant, the critique of reason here too is meant to preserve the possibility of a domain in which the subject is not bound only by necessity. But in order to achieve this Adorno must call for a new categorical imperative, which he cannot conceive except as privative in relation to the project of identification inherent in thought. Adorno thus misses or does not quite reach what Levinas calls "the surplus of the social," which is prior to identification. Critical theory, which does indeed depend on this surplus, thus responds to the ethical demand which, because it remains a critique of the subject, it cannot conceive.

Chapter 5 returns to Levinas to take up the thread which Adorno can pursue in negative dialectics and in the aesthetic, but only up to a point. In order to go beyond and at the same time ground the possibility of a negative dialectics that reaches towards a new categorical imperative beyond universalizing totalization, an understanding of the ethical relation is needed that is modeled neither on knowing nor simply on the self-negation, the dialectics, of identity. Such an account is central to both of Levinas's major works, but is achieved with sufficient clarity and force only in the second of these, *Otherwise than Being*. To get to the point that is reached there, the point at which he discloses the ethical relation as the sensible proximity of the subject in the radical passivity of saying, Levinas had needed to retain Husserl's phenomenological method and, at the same time, both move it beyond Husserlian idealism and distinguish his own departure from Heidegger's early and later engagements with that very idealism. In order to accomplish his distance from Heidegger, Levinas will recur to an unexploited potential in Husserl's phenomenologies of sense and time, setting him on the road of a certain transcendental sensualism. A good part of chapter 5 is therefore devoted to tracing how, over the course of his career, Levinas was himself able to place Husserl and Heidegger in a constellation that eventually propelled him, in *Otherwise than Being,* to transcend not only Husserl's phenomenological idealism, but also both Heidegger's earlier existential correction of that idealism, and what he calls Heidegger's later faint materialism. In doing so, Levinas opens up the possibility of a nonintentional consciousness diachronically sensitive to the trace of the other, which is in turn the basis for his radical redescription of ethical subjectivity as substitution and created freedom.

Although this trajectory allows and compels Levinas to raise the question of the propagation of substitution, it is not sufficient to indicate how its propagation might take place and in what sense it would differ from the propagation of power. Chapter 6 takes up this theme by following the Frankfurt School in their efforts to separate what in Levinas remains conflated, that is, the law of the third with the law of the few, or totalization with domination. It begins by following Horkheimer and Adorno in their analysis of the dialectic, the self-destruction, of enlightened morality. In subjecting Kantian morality to a natural-historical critique, they at least suggest that the law required by the third party is not to be equated with even the most enlightened version of rational peace.

It is left to Marcuse in *Eros and Civilization* to theorize the nonimpossibility of a law of the third, beyond surplus morality, that is not only the abrogation of the law of the few, but a law that therefore no longer subverts the ethical relation, but supports it. The propagation of ethics, of substitution becomes the potential work of a liberated eros, because, for Marcuse, beyond natural history, "agape is eros." This might seem to put him at odds with Levinas, for whom the ethical relation is irreducible to anything that might be conceivable as a force or drive. But Levinas had already linked agape and eros in his own analyses of eros and fecundity. It turns out that one could say that for Levinas eros is agape, inasmuch as the radical plurality of the ethical-social relation is fully expressible only in relations that have not removed themselves from the attachment of enjoyment, an attachment quite different from the common belonging within totality. Although they do not quite meet, critical theory and Levinas thus also converge. The last word is left to Benjamin who suggests that the profane order of happiness may assist the approach of messianic redemption. Such an approach includes the possibility of its actual arrival.

Totality, Ethics, and History

Justice Is Not the Solution

At the limits or on the horizon of ethics as first philosophy Levinas leaves thought with a conundrum and in an impasse. The ethical relation demands, or has inexorably laid upon it, contains — as though it were a condition of its own possibility — another relation that, while not quite negating ethics, betrays ethics, and in betraying it, strains ethics to the breaking point. Even though Levinas unfolds his analysis of ethics beginning always from the situation of a single and singular subjectivity in a relation to absolute alterity, to the other or the Face, before he breaks off the analysis it will in each case have become clear that what, for purposes of phenomenological clarity might have appeared to be a relation of *the* one for *the* other, was always *my* relation to an unlimited number of unique and incomparable others, each of whom is related to and for an unlimited number of other unique and incomparable others. This does not simply complicate the ethical relation, leave it the same while adding more instances to its first instance. Society is not composed, like an onion, of a finite or even infinite number of identical layers, each layer being the relation of me to an other. Rather, the "real society" as he says, does not add another, and another, ethical relation to the one from which I might have begun, in an indefinite and open-ended series. Much more than that, society alters the very nature of the relation, even turning the ethical relation against itself, consigning the ethical relation to the very domain from which it is also the *only* escape, the domain of being or totality.

The ethical relation, without reference to or abstracted from the social, signifies the unlimited responsibility of a singular sensibility to the height of the other, a responsibility and desire that can never be fulfilled and that increases as it is assumed. Such obligation is inordinate, beyond reciprocity and comparison, measure and calculation. It is not visible from the vantage of any third person perspective; it is an unbreakable bond, no matter how attenuated empirically, across an absolute distance between terms that, in themselves, are sufficient unto themselves. The proximity of the one to the other is an exception to the rational order: "It is both the relation and the term of the relation" (*OTB,* 85). Yet it is this very relation that enjoins what appears to be its negation. The multiplicity of singular others, their very relation to each other as singularities requires — but requires ethically, and not formally — the thematization and formalization of all relations within a totality. It requires the "comparison of incomparables" (158). Levinas states, "There must be a justice among incomparable ones. There must then be a comparison between incomparables and a synopsis, a togetherness and a contemporaneousness, there must be thematization, thought, history and inscription. But being must be understood on the basis of being's other" (16). There must be, in other words, the very relation which the ethical relation both subtends and transcends. Justice, law, the state, and politics are required, and required by the ethical relation, yet their very existence has the status of a paradox: "This conclusion is paradoxical; the certainty that the relation with a third party resembles neither my own intimacy with myself nor the love of a neighbor compromises...the very status of man as an irreplaceable singularity, which is, however, presupposed by every aspiration to innocence." This "priority" of law over charity (ET, 33) means that not only is the singularity of the subject compromised, the singularity of the other is compromised as well. It could not be otherwise.

The ethical relation of a singularity to the absolute alterity of the other thus becomes, but instantaneously, as a quantum leap without transition, the relation of a particular to a universal, or of a particular to other particulars of the same universal, identical bearers of symmetrical rights and reciprocal duties. But if the latter condition were all that obtained, then ethics, and with it justice, would be truly and simply impossible. The ethical relation is prior to justice, with a priority more temporal than logical. It is prior, but "not presupposed the way a principle is presupposed" (*OTB,* 160). Yet if one were, somehow and for some reason, to try to separate that relation from justice, the state and law; or if one were to propose the possibility, no matter how historically remote, of their abolition, or their withering away, Levinas would be compelled to greet the suggestion, not with an objection grounded in the cynicism of one who has unshakeable faith in and copious evidence for the inherent evil or selfishness of others and himself, but nonetheless with an objection, but coming from the opposite direction. It is the very goodness of humans, however much there is, that commands that "there must be" the state, law, and justice. In either case, there must be that which compromises that which above all, as we will see, must not be compromised. The difference announced seems to be in the reasonings that are meant to justify: "It is then not without importance to know if the egalitarian and just State in which man is fulfilled and (and which is to be set up, and especially to be maintained) proceeds from a war of all against all, or from the irreducible responsibility of the one for all" (159).

If Levinas were engaged in political theory, then knowing how to judge between these alternatives would indeed make an important difference. But Levinas, quite intentionally, even necessarily, stops short of such theory. The irreducible responsibility of the one for all is not to be understood as an ultimate principle from which lower order principles, then structures, then institutions might be derived. The irreducible responsibility is that which existentially animates whatever and however much social responsibility there is at any given point in time within history. Ethics itself is, and must be, prehistorical; it must belong to a memory older than memory, a diachrony that precedes all possible histories, depending as they must upon synchronizable time. Yet there will have been no history without the relation that has no history. Levinas is not engaged in political philosophy, but *against* it,[1] in revealing that which makes it possible, necessary, and impossible. Given what political philosophy must deal with, and what its currency must be, it cannot ever, in principle, be up to its task. Political philosophy must always, it seems, reproduce the very totality that both expresses and negates what animates it. That the just State follows from the responsibility of the one for all does, then, make all the difference, and, at the same time, it may make very little difference. Knowing that the just State follows from sensibility, proximity, and the substitution of the one for the other would be the *sine qua non* for a perspective beyond the logic of being, the logic of identity and self-preservation. But at the same time, because such knowledge is not prior in the way that a principle is prior, it must produce a perspective that both accepts and rejects whatever justice there is. The responsibility of the one for all is not an ought commanding "the infinite pursuit of an ideal" (*OTB,* 12). It cannot be approached asymptotically or achieved in an objective dialectic.

The State both Confirmed and Denied

The conundrum into which Levinas leads thought is thus an amphibology, or better, a double amphibology: the ethical relation ethically demands the just State which both expresses and defeats the ethical relation. The ethical relation is prior, but not exterior to or above its empirical instantiations and thus the ethical relation both confirms and denies its own instantiations. Before we follow this structure further into the network of master categories that necessitate it as the terminus (but not the telos) of his thinking, it can be outlined in miniature in one of his later and more political essays, "The Rights of Man and the Rights of the Other" of 1985. This essay could be read simply as, but is actually much more than, a muted and qualified celebration of the doctrine of individual human rights as it has developed in the modern West, and of the liberal state that exists to protect and enforce the exercise of such rights. It all but undermines the very state and the very model of individuality it purports to uphold.

Levinas begins by recognizing that what differentiates the modern doctrine of natural rights from anything analogous in traditional societies, is that they are not conferred: "That the rights of man...*does not proceed* from the sternness or the grace of God...has been, since the Renaissance, the trait that has characterized the rights of man" (RMRO, 118). Dispensing with the traditional or traditionalistic grounding of rights, Levinas asserts that there came into "a world that until then was felt to be doomed to an arbitrary play of forces that (natural or supposedly supernatural, individual and social) only counted in proportion to their power, in the obstinacy that Beings and institutions invest in persevering in their being and their traditions — there came the *a priori* of the rights of man understood as an intellectual *a priori,* and becoming in fact the measure of all law" (119). From such foundations in the spontaneous freedom of reason, technical-legal systems would develop and proliferate legal rules aimed at supplying the necessary conditions for the realization of the right to human dignity, life, liberty, and equality before the law: more and more rights "that are the necessary conditions for the actual exercise of those rights," up to and including "the right to oppose exploitation by capital (the right to unionize) and even the right to social advancement; the right (utopian or Messianic) to the refinement of the human condition...the right to fight for the full rights of man, and the right to ensure the necessary political conditions for that struggle" (120).

Yet it is clear that Levinas does not, like Grotius, Puffendorf, or even in some sense Montesquieu, ground human rights in an intellectual *a priori* — in the case of the former two, "an idea of law based on considerations similar to those of mathematics" (RMRO, 120). If rights are not conferred externally by the God of theology or by Nature (116–17); and if they are not to be deduced internally from the purely innate ideas of independent mind, in what, then are they based? For Levinas will say that they "are based on an original sense of the right — or the sense of an original right" (116). This curious reversal of terms, appearing in the first sentence, actually foreshadows the reversal Levinas will accomplish in the crux of the essay. An *original* sense, a meaning or idea of right, a clear and distinct idea of right innate to a mind that has achieved a distance from its circumstances in the production of a knowledge flowing from the possibilities of science and technology (119) will be replaced by the *sense of* an original right, a sense — a sensibility-to — the incomparable uniqueness of the other. The very non-conferrability of rights (for, after all, what kind of right is it that rests upon the will or grace of another or the belonging to a whole?), their *a prioricity* per se "may signify an ineluctable authority, older and higher than the one that is already split into will and reason...the authority that is *in* the respect for the rights of man itself" (117).

The basis for these rights, the authority upon which the idea rests, is thus not something dependent upon any absolute or axiomatic idea the knowing subject might have of such a right and subsequently assign to all identical instances of such a knowing subject. The authority is not in an original sense, but in the sense of an original, unconditional right. Rights assigned to a certain class of being do not command respect; the sense of respect, which is perhaps sense itself, commands rights. Prior to rights is the respect for rights, the sense of original right. Sense, or respect itself,

> express[es] the alterity or absolute of every person, the suspension of all *reference:* a violent tearing loose from the determining order of nature and the social structure…an alterity of the unique and incomparable, due to the belonging of each one to mankind, which *ipso facto and paradoxically,* is annulled, precisely to leave each man *the only one* of his kind…beyond the individuality of multiple individuals within their kind. A uniqueness not because of any distinctive sign that would serve as a specific or individuating difference…A uniqueness that is not forgotten, beneath all the constraints of Being, History, and the logical forms that hold it in their grip. (RMRO, 117)

The sense of original right calls for a phenomenology of the structure of the consciousness in which that sense takes shape (RMRO, 117). But this is not only a phenomenology of mind in its essence as universalizing. There is not only the

> form of *consciousness* rejecting contradiction, that would encompass the other things under concepts, disalienating them within the identity of the universal; it [the reasonable] also designates the ability of the individual, who initially appears to exist relatively to the extension of a concept — the species man, to posit himself as *the only one of his kind,* and thus as absolutely different from all others, but, in that difference, and without reconstituting the logical concept from which the *I* disengaged itself, to be non-in-different to the other. Non-indifference, or original sociality — goodness; peace or the wish for peace…. In which the *I* frees

itself from its 'return to self,' from its auto-affirmation, from its egotism of a being persevering in its being, *to answer for the other,* precisely to defend the rights of the other man. (RMRO, 124–25)

This exquisitely abbreviated phenomenology of the "reasonable being" has not simply placed the august neutrality of rationality *alongside* the nonindifference of an original sociality, as though there would be two competing principles or forces at work; it has also inextricably linked the original sociality to an ability to posit oneself as "the only one," as outside but not yet above the whole. Sense, then, the sense of original right, the nonindifference and wish for peace, which is the original sociality, depends upon a "violent tearing loose" from the form of consciousness that encompasses entities under concepts. But this very tearing loose is also not unrelated to the formation of the *indifference* of the logical concept. Thus the sense of original right, at the inception of the modern world, can be pronounced as the original sense of right and the sense of human rights as independent of any conferral can be (mis-)understood simply as a discovery of reason out of itself.

One could say then that the original sense of right betrays the sense of original right, expresses it, but also denies it, both at once. And it will be crucial to understand that betrayal is neither a translation nor is it a synthesis, nor is it the possibility of a synthesis. The idea of human rights, and the legal and political institutions that — at least ostensibly — promote them, *in pursuing also negate* the sense of original right that was always already the ineluctable authority upon which the original sense of human rights was based. The idea of human rights as nonconferred Levinas links inherently to the achievement of a radical independence on the part of reason (RMRO, 119). But this same reason will leach what there is of the sense of original right right out of the original sense of right. One way in which this takes place is in the "inhuman requirements" imposed by the very social techniques that are supposed to actualize the rights of human beings: "In a totally industrialized society...the rights of man are compromised by the very practices for which they supplied the motivation" (121). In another, but not unrelated way, human rights themselves, as expressing "the absolute of every person, the suspension of all *reference*" (117), open upon the requirement for a plurality of free wills negating each other and united by reason, which Levinas will link with Kant's model of "a just legality, in agreement with universal laws" (122). A universalizing legality, however, will be

> already a way of treating the person as an object...Whence the essential harshness of a law that offends, within the will, a dignity other than that which attaches to respect for universal laws....Thus limited by justice, does not the fundamental principle of the rights of man [the sense of original right] remain repressed...? A bad peace. Better, indeed, than a good war! But yet an abstract peace, seeking stability in the powers of the state, in politics, which insures obedience to the laws by force. (RMRO, 122–23)

Distance Mediates Ethics and Justice

It would be something of a travesty to read, or to criticize, this complex as simple acquiescence on Levinas's part to a gap between some utopian ideal and a limited human power to realize such an ideal. It is instead, in his hands, a structure that does not cease repeating itself as the double amphibology already mentioned. Not just the state, but even the just state must be confirmed and denied. And, at the same time, from the vantage point from which it is both confirmed and denied, all instances of it are, in some way, on a level. All empirical social instantiations of the ethical relation, although essential to it, have already betrayed it in the double sense of revealing and realizing it as well as obscuring it and delivering it to its enemies.

It is crucial in this regard to recall that the much-discussed transition from ethics to justice, as it is portrayed most forcefully in *Otherwise than Being,* is not a transition at all, not a transition from one empirical situation to another, or even an inference from one concept to another. The so-called "entry" of the third party is not an empirical fact by which the otherwise than being of unlimited responsibility is constrained by the force of things. On the contrary, "In the proximity of the other, all the others than the other obsess me, and already this obsession cries out for justice, demands measure and knowing, is consciousness" (*OTB,* 158). Thus, justice is not to be considered a "degradation" or a "degeneration" of proximity and substitution (159). Yet neither can justice be identified with the institutions of justice: "The one for the other of proximity is not a deforming abstraction... This means concretely or empirically that justice is not a legality regulating human masses, from which a technique of social equilibrium is drawn, harmonizing antagonistic forces. That would be a justification of the State delivered over to its own necessities" (159; see also 161). What the entry of the third signifies is simultaneously the justification of "the neutral notion of being" (158), a notion about which Levinas is elsewhere in his writings not so sanguine, and the justification of that justification as being just only on the basis of the dependence, the reducibility of the neutral, and with it consciousness, thought, comparison, calculation, measure, institutions, and so on to the horizon of ethical proximity. The neutral notion of being, the very foundation of the egotism of the I persevering in its being, is simultaneously the foundation of justice. What is primarily at issue here is the question of whether it is neutrality or sensibility that is prior, or in different terms, whether rational necessity has the status of an origin or if rational necessity "has a hither side," which is presupposed in some sense, but not like a principle (160).

The essential affinity between neutrality, justice, and comparison on the one side, and nonindifference, ethics, and proximity on the other side, is *distance*. Distance is that which mediates the two sides and makes them relatable, what allows for the phenomenological reduction of justice and the state to the ethical relation in a way parallel to the central methodological strategy and argument of *Otherwise than Being,* the reduction of the Said to the Saying. It is, according to Levinas, the other and the third *together,* as inseparable, that now "put distance between me and the other and the third" (*OTB,* 157). Were it not for the fact that the third were present from the beginning, there would be no problem: no consciousness and self-consciousness, no need for the beyond being to revert to being. It is therefore no accident "that the order of truth and essence...[are of] the first rank in Western philosophy" and that Levinas holds to this order (157). To be sure, there is a distance between the distance of the proximity of the ethical relation and the distance of the neutral notion of being. But it is by virtue of both distances still being distance that the double amphibology can take place. Both ethics and the neutral notion of being, which are otherwise irreconcilable opposites, can be seen to be lodged in a structure of betrayal by virtue of the fact that in each of them the distance of the subject is maintained. What is different here, in Levinas's later work, as represented by both *Otherwise than Being* and "The Rights of Man and the Rights of the Other," is that it is now the presence of the third party from the start that *introduces* distance, both the distance of consciousness, thought, intentionality, as well as the distance of sensibility, proximity and substitution.

In the earlier phase of his mature thought, as represented by "The Ego and the Totality" and by *Totality and Infinity,* the distance that is expressed in the ethical relation is *not* a function of the prior inclusion of the third party in that relation even though Levinas recognizes the presence of the third party from the start. The neutral notion of being and with it totality are instead put at a virtually unbridgeable distance from the distance that is maintained in the ethical relation. As a result, that which in the later work is expressed in the complex ambiguity of a betrayal of ethics in justice, in the double amphibology which both identifies and opposes the two, in the earlier work takes place as a movement toward the transcendence of totality seeking, but not finding a concrete and adequate instantiation in a social form other than a whole. Also as a result, Levinas's earlier work is closer (but perhaps only negatively) to the dimension of the historical. Let us, then, go behind Levinas's later formulation of the problem to see if earlier there might have been at least the hint of the possibility of something less than the conundrum and amphibology so far analyzed

The Real Society: On the Way to Betrayal

In "The Ego and the Totality" Levinas is looking for a way to characterize the social relation that will not reduce it either to nature or to reason or to some combination of both. The problem of the ego and the totality is to find a way of describing the moral conditions of thought (ET, 28). Although a living being as such has consciousness, its consciousness is thoughtless; lacking in exteriority, it has only an inner world whose centre it occupies, and "one cannot deduce thought from biological consciousness" (28). Thought, on the other hand, begins with a consciousness of particularity. Thought is not simply exteriority striking consciousness, but self-consciousness, the apprehension of *an exteriority which encloses*. To enclose is to include, but, in including, to permit the separate existence of the particular. If this structure is not to be found in biological consciousness, it is also not to be found in labor, which itself presupposes thought and is not its origin. It is rather human society alone that explains the possibility of the birth of thought. Society alone carries with it a "simultaneity of participation and non-participation" and it is this basic structure that thought requires: "It must on the one hand consist in the thinking individual positing himself in the totality…in acquiring his identity from what distinguishes him from the other parts with which he is compromised; but at the same time, it must consist in remaining outside, in not coinciding with his concept, acquiring his identity not from his place in the whole (from his character, work, or heritage), but from himself — in being me…its self-reference" (28).

Thus *society* "marks the advent" and is "the a priori proper to thought" (ET, 28). But thought will also diverge from its own a priori. It will become unable to express its own nonlogical basis or a priori in the terms essential to thought, in terms of the structure or operation Levinas will later call formal logic. It will, however, not only forget its social a priori but also in its forgetting, especially in the history of philosophy necessarily assimilate the social relation to the form of universality. Under the formal pattern of thought, in rational ontology, there is always a simultaneous union and distance of the terms related (*TI,* 110). In any conceptual judgment aiming at propositional truth, a universal both unites its particular instantiations by identifying what is common to them and simultaneously allows for their difference through an extension of the concept. What is then produced is a "numerical multiplicity" (*TI,* 120–21, 220ff.). Particulars still belonging to or falling under the universal, still united, will at the same time also be distanced by their participation in other universals or by their spatial or temporal location or both (ET, 36). Such numerical multiplicity is not, however, the "radical multiplicity" (*TI,* 220) of the social relation for it reduces all the terms under their concepts to their genus, to that which they have in common. Formal logic will not only fail to see radical multiplicity, it will even also see numerical multiplicity as a fall from the One, as the one in its privative condition (291). Thus, Western philosophy is drawn ever and again to a reduction of the social relation "to an impersonal relation in a universal order" (87–88) because it cannot think the simultaneity of participation and nonparticipation. The element of nonparticipation is (mis-)conceived in privative terms as a falling away from being as unity.

Yet at the social basis of thought, in the "simultaneity of participation and non-participation" in which nonparticipation is pure "self-reference," in the enclosing which must permit separate existence, there is also a different relation at work. This relation, nonformal, nonuniversalizable, is a relation that is an exception to the rational order (*OTB,* 85), being the unrepresentable excluded middle of formal logic (96, 169), an excluded middle that, because it cannot be represented (even though its structure is the basis of representation) brings into relation a radical multiplicity in a way that can and must be not-visible from the outside, not as a function of reflection on the relation, but is accomplished in depth from me to the other (*TI,* 120–21).

In "The Ego and the Totality," the social relation proper, a relation from me to the other is not yet linked inextricably to the immediate presence of all the others of the other, as it will be in *Otherwise than Being* and subsequently. Thus, the inclusion of all the others in the other is not yet that which "puts distance between me, the other and the third." But neither is it possible to say that the third party is excluded from the social relation (ET, 42, 37). In the 1954 essay Levinas does primarily relate radical social plurality to speech, which in its relational structure satisfies the requirements of a simultaneous participation and nonparticipation. The speech Levinas already has in mind is not simply rational communication mediated by systems of signs: "As a manifestation of reason, language awakens in me and in the other what is common to us. But in its expressive intention, it presupposes our alterity and our duality" (36). Language or discourse in its expressive function is addressed to and invokes an other "prior to community," "a being situated beyond every other," in an "encounter with a hard and substantial interlocutor, who is the origin of himself" (41). By not yet linking distance, and with it thought, comprehension, knowledge, theory, universalization and ontology directly to the presence of the third *in the other* Levinas here leaves open a much greater gap, and a different relation, between ethics and justice than the one which in *Otherwise than Being* is not closed, but rendered ambiguous in the double amphibology or the structure of betrayal. This gap is the gap between eschatology and history that will frame and motivate the argument of *Totality and Infinity*.

In "The Ego and the Totality," however, a decade before *Totality and Infinity*, Levinas will have the social relation bifurcate into two opposed possibilities, neither of which is satisfactory. In neither will the social relation find adequate concrete form nor, especially, ethical standing. The first possibility is that of the *intimate society*, a structure that historically finds a certain concretion perhaps in enclosed religious confessional groupings. In such societies, ruled by love, a pardon is possible that can cancel the guilt of an offending party. Levinas says, "The ego, in dialogue, would thus recover, be it only after the fact, through pardon, its solitary sovereignty" (ET, 30). But the intimate society is not a *real society* because in intimacy the agent is, by this pardon, freed from the weight of the consequences of the acts "which escape it and engage it, and through which...every will runs the risk of self alienation" (31). In a *true society*, on the other hand, "I act in a sense that escapes me. The objective meaning of my action overrides its intentional signification...I am objectively guilty, and my piety cannot cleanse me of this.... Love is only a pious intention, oblivious of the real evil" (31).

In a true society, then, there is an "ontological alienation" that "institutes history," an ontological alienation that is "the structure of creation" and the mark of a "created being." The possibility and necessity of an ontological alienation follows from the nature of the will productive of works. According to Levinas, "Through its work it involves an unforeseeable signification which others give it when they put the work, detached from its author, into a new context." The will in its works is thus radically different from the expressive function of speech, "in which the other personally presents himself." In separating itself from itself in work, the will enters into history as a freedom yet becomes a "plaything of a fate which transcends it." Along with the possibility of a conception of justice, comes the "evident injustice of that history," understood as exploitation. It follows that "The will productive of works is a freedom that betrays itself. Through this betrayal society...is possible. The ego's relationship with a totality is then essentially economic" (ET, 38–39). The role of the third party here is to be "delivered over to my power": "He is accessible in injustice. And that is why injustice...is possible, through gold which coerces and tempts...The injustice by virtue of which the ego lives in a totality is always economic injustice" (39). In the real society, then, as opposed to the intimate one, "fault is determined on the basis of a universal law, and consists in the wrong done, rather than in the disrespect. We are then not what we are conscious of being, but are the role we are playing in a drama where we are no longer the actors....Then no one can find the law for his action in the depth of his heart. The impasse of liberalism is in this exteriority of my consciousness to itself" (34). Whereas biological consciousness, in not relating to an exteriority, possesses innocence, and whereas the intimate society of love and pardon, ignoring history, remains a pious intention, real society knows a history of injustice, and therefore justice. But although it only knows justice because of the "absolute status of the interlocutor, a being and not...a truth about beings" (41), the justice it knows is nonetheless a paradox. This paradox is made explicit in money.

Economy, for Levinas, is that dimension of a real society in which "a will can have a hold on another without destroying it as a will" (ET, 44). Money is the medium of that dimension: *"It is thus the abstract element in which is brought about the generalization of that which has no concept, the equating of that which has no quantity...* an ambiguous medium where persons are integrated into the order of commodities, yet where they still remain persons, since the order of commodities (which is not equivalent to the order of nature) does presuppose persons" (45).[2] Levinas knows very well that money is also, better than the sword, the instrument of "true violence" which "conserves the freedom it coerces," that allows for "exploitation or slow death" to be "substituted for the passion of war." Yet, in presupposing persons, in being an element in which "the personal is maintained while being quantified," the "ambiguity" of money "points to a new justice," and allows for envisaging "a justice of redemption to be substituted for the infernal or vicious circle of vengeance or pardon." Nothing else but money, as the "category" for the common measure between men, allows for surmounting the "radical difference between men"; without such a common measure violence would endlessly reproduce itself. Neither vengeance nor pardon could interrupt this cycle, which "is the march of history." Vengeance calls for further vengeance, and the cycle of vengeance is evil engendering evil, while "pardon extended infinitely encourages it." Thus the "quantification of man" must be accepted as an essential condition for justice. Nonetheless quantification cannot be accepted: "We cannot attenuate the condemnation which from Amos 2:6 to the *Communist Manifesto* has fallen upon money, precisely because of its power to buy man" (45).

If one possibility of the social relation, in the form of the intimate society, is radically wanting, the other possibility, in the form of the real society, cannot be deemed adequate or final. With this confrontation between the necessity — for justice

— and the condemnation of money, "The Ego and the Totality" breaks off, leaving the problem neither solved nor unsolvable. Earlier in the essay, however, Levinas had also raised the possibility of yet a third way "between" sympathy or love in an intimate society detached from history, and that which, within history, "converts us to a singularization of the concept man, where an individual in the extension of that concept is subject to the legislation of an impersonal reason." This third way would understand society as a society "of egos which are without conceptual unity but in relationship with each other" (ET, 37). Language as discourse, speech in its expressive function, which will play such an important role in *Totality and Infinity,* is, however, in this essay the only way in which Levinas will offer a concrete structural instantiation of the third way. Whether this third way is something like an historical possibility is a subject not explicitly broached. The nature of works, the existence of an ontological alienation, works against the possibility. On the other hand, with the absolute status of the interlocutor having been established, a vantage point outside the totality has been gained. Thus, from within history, "justice…appears like a principle external to history.…The human world is a world in which one can judge history. It is not necessarily a rational world, but it is one where one can pass judgement" (40). The possibility of a judgment of history, from what appears external to it, thus opens the nonimpossibility of the third way as historical. Otherwise there would not be much point in Levinas saying "one can do anything with man. The will by virtue of its essence exposed to violence, can be emancipated only by building a world in which it suppresses the occasions for betrayal" (39). If, under the double amphibology that characterizes his later work, Levinas brings ethics and justice so close as to be virtually undifferentiated (while they remain at the antipodes of each other), in "The Ego and Totality" their differentiation at least tacitly opens the question of history. In *Totality and Infinity,* this question will be taken up in the form of an apparently (but only apparently) polar opposition between history and eschatology and will be answered in terms of the infinite time of fecundity.

History Betrays Eschatology

Totality and Infinity contains Levinas's most sustained reflections on historical being and on the relation of ethics to history. Far from being only incidental in this text, the challenge or provocation of historical being frames the entire attempt to recast ethics outside of the tradition of ontology, which attempt itself absolutely cannot avoid the activity of thematization or totalization. The announcement of the question to which *Totality and Infinity* as some sort of totality is the answer, takes place largely in the preface to that work. According to Levinas, the work as a whole will attempt to describe "a relation or an intentionality of a wholly different type" than the synoptic, objectifying and totalizing vision, the vision that is proper to representation. Representation is itself not original. And objectivity is neither the primordial nor the only form in which being imposes itself on consciousness (*TI,* 22–23). Nonetheless, philosophy has from the start proceeded from, and one might add reproduced, an experience calling for its rational representation as a totality — totality under the aspect of formal logic, a whole that allows for both the simultaneous union and distance of the terms included within it. This philosophical vision, born from the experience of history, is one that excludes eschatology. To philosophical thought, he says, obviously including the philosophy of history, "being reveals itself as war" (21). But "of peace there can only be an eschatology" (23).

One dimension of the problem at hand is therefore to find a way in which eschatology may be thoroughly secularized and brought into conformity with the demands of reason itself. Of course, Levinas will go even further than that, basing the very possibility of rational discourse upon the eschatological vision philosophy thinks it rationally refuses: a position summed up in the formula of "ethics as first philosophy." But, to begin with, under modern conditions, eschatology can only appear to be irrational. For philosophy it belongs at best to the realm of opinion. It will be perceived as a threat to the rational peace that can be summed up in a hierarchy of concepts revealing the unity and internal differentiation of the whole. Even worse, eschatology in the age of enlightenment must be taken to be a crude divination of the future, arbitrary and subjective, an idiopathic revelation presented without evidence — a completely untrustworthy and merely oracular representation of being as a future present. To entertain the eschatological vision would be a sacrifice of the intellect, and with it, of freedom (*TI, 22*).

Although Levinas does not explicitly refer to them, there have, of course, been attempts in the past to secularize and thus continue the work and experience traditionally communicated in religious eschatologies, Hegel's being the most important in this context. But Levinas is not aiming at something similar to that, as the young Hegelians including Marx still might have been. Levinas's debt to Rosenzweig's anti-Hegelianism is broad and deep, "too often present in this work," as he says, "to be cited" (*TI,* 28), and well marked by several commentators.[3] Levinas is intending a new eschatological vision that one might describe, in his terms, as atheist; a radical break with the onto-theo-logical tradition consummated in Hegelian absolute spirit. The "real import" of the eschatological vision is quite different: "It does not introduce a teleological system into the totality; it does not consist in teaching the orientation of history. Eschatology institutes a relation with being beyond the totality or beyond history, and not with being beyond the past and present" (22).

Levinas will neither substitute eschatology for philosophy nor try to find philosophical justification for eschatological truths. And this vision does not proceed from any attempt to represent or to disclose, to grasp the whole in its unity. It lives from another experience, the experience of a situation in which totality "breaks up" in the "gleam of exteriority or of transcendence in the Face of the Other" (23).

Eschatology, then, in either its traditional theological forms, and in Levinas's non-onto-theo-logical form, would refer to the objectified expression of an original experience, but essentially different from the experience of the mutual allergy of egoisms or war: "Of peace there can only be an eschatology"(23). Eschatology in this sense, then, as an experience that is a function of a wholly different intentionality or relation is nevertheless still a candidate for phenomenological description, a phenomenology that would be in some sense a metaphenomenology (rather than a fundamental ontology) describing, and giving evidence for, the very experience that makes both representation and the phenomenology of representation possible. As such, eschatological vision does not lend itself to the terms of experience understood as an adequation of thought and being (25). Thus, Levinas's avowal of a fundamental debt to Husserl's phenomenological method: the "search for the concrete," where what is essential "is the idea of the overflowing of objectifying thought by a forgotten experience by which it lives" (28). Eschatology, then, refers to a forgotten experience, an experience, in some way, of peace, of a nonallergic relation in which the other is neither repelled nor included with me in a whole, and is only recoverable at two removes: at a first remove from the experience of experience reported in rationalism and idealism; at a second remove, from the dominant experience of history, the experience of war domesticated as totality, which is the experience to which rationalism, idealism, and ontology are bound. As the recovery of a forgotten experience, eschatology must refer back to a forgotten subjectivity which is, at the same time, the subjectivity capable of its opposite: war and history.

Thus, *Totality and Infinity* announces a "defense of subjectivity": "We oppose to the objectivism of war a subjectivity born from the eschatological vision" (*TI,* 25). Such a subjectivity will not oppose to the totality a merely personal, egoistic protestation or even a personal salvation. In *Totality and Infinity* we will have left the notion of an intimate society behind at the very beginning. Such a subjectivity is an existent, rather than a truth about existence; it belongs to beings who "exist in relationship, but on the basis of themselves and not on the basis of the totality" (23). And such a subjectivity, born from the eschatological vision, which is a vision and not a prediction of a peace more than rational, will importantly not be modeled on the relation of knowledge, nor on what precedes knowledge as interiority and enjoyment, even though the latter do themselves stand outside the totality. Instead, eschatological vision will be modeled *against* the very cognitive relation captured and articulated by Husserlian phenomenology as the "intentionality where thought remains an *adequation*" and can always be referred back to a transcendental ego (27), and against that of Heideggerian phenomenology where consciousness always accomplishes events whose meaning is disclosure (28).

The meeting point of eschatology and experience at the level of the *knowing* subject is to be found in the idea of infinity, which is the philosophical term of art expressing the situation in which totality breaks up. The eschatological vision does not therefore depend on a discovery of the finitude of knowledge, but as idea it is pronounced in the idea of infinity, in which infinity as thought "overflows" thought (*TI,* 24). The idea of infinity is not a representation of something, nor does it point to nothingness (27). On the contrary, ontological vision itself is owed first of all to the experience named as infinition. It is not an accidental notion or a mere boundary term. Infinity is neither objective nor subjective: "Infinity does not first exist, and then reveal itself. Its infinition is produced as a revelation... in the improbable feat whereby a separated being fixed in its identity... nonetheless contains in itself what it can neither contain nor receive solely by virtue of its own identity" (26–27). The idea of infinity is presupposed by all knowledge, and refers to the experience of nonadequation (27). If experience is the adequation of thought and being, which is how the philosophical tradition generally construes it, then the relation with infinity can not be stated in the terms of experience. But if experience means precisely the relation with an absolutely other, then the relation with infinity accomplishes experience in its fullest sense (25).

But Infinity, no matter how important it is to Levinas in *Totality and Infinity* in helping to delineate the a-logical structure of the ethical relation is, in another sense, simply a spatialized representation of the original experience that can also and necessarily be broached as eschatology. Infinity works as a translation or transposition of a situation or experience beyond the totality from a language of spatio-temporality onto an other level, where eschatology can now be formulated in the terms of a set of more palpable experiences reaching their climax in the face to face encounter, in the erotic relation and in fecundity. And Levinas will, even in the preface to *Totality and Infinity,* quickly drop reference to the term eschatology in favor of the opposition of totality with infinity. This will allow him to attempt finally, at the end of the book, a translation of infinity back into temporal but not quite historical terms, as the infinite time of fecundity. The infinite time of fecundity would be the final and ultimate experience beyond time in time, and beyond history (which *is* totalized time) in history. But whether negotiated in terms of infinity or eschatology, the issue for his defense of subjectivity is always the possibility of an experience beyond totality. With reference to time and history, the beyond of totality is eschatology; with reference to objects and events encountered within time and history, the beyond of totality is infinity. Eschatology is infinite time rather than eternity, which is timelessness. Eschatology is beyond history; while history, at this level of extreme abstraction, is eternity in its privative condition, the retotalization of the (ultimate) One which has fallen into multiplicity, differentiation, antagonism, and flux.

For Levinas, however, this experience of transcendence beyond the totality, this metaphysical experience that is the ethical relation or goodness, is not simply to be approached in negative ways, and certainly not to be thought of as an achievement demanding specialized knowledge. It is the "common" experience of "common" human beings. Not philosophers, saints, heroes, or mystics. It *requires* no intellectual or "spiritual" equipment or training. It is already found in the "common moral experience" where what I can demand of the other I cannot compare to what I demand of myself (*TI,* 53). This common moral experience is the concrete starting point from which all the analyses of the possibility and significance of the ethical in *Totality and Infinity* will start and to which they will lead back. Eschatology/infinity, or relation with a surplus always exterior to totality, "*is reflected within the totality and history, within experience*" (23; emphasis added). But that the ethical relation exists and that the question of what it is must be approached through contrast with totality are together only half of the problem of *Totality and Infinity.* The other half of the problem, although it receives relatively little explicit foregrounding, is the question of the justification to the subject of its goodness within history, or the relation of eschatology to history. On the one side, eschatology, as in "The Ego and the Totality," allows for a human world: "The eschatological...draws beings out of the jurisdiction of history and the future.... Submitting history as a whole to judgement...it restores to each instant its full signification in that very instant" (23). In history, not merely in historiography, but in the real history of human society, individuals are reduced to being "bearers of forces that command them" behind their backs; the very meaning of their lives is derived from their function in the totality and "sacrificed" to the future. The eschatological vision detaches individuals from the history that bears them and it addresses them in their unicity (21–22).

Yet the totality and its history are not thereby simply exposed as an illusion. When Levinas asks, in the first paragraph of the book, whether lucidity does not mean "catching sight of the permanent possibility of war," this is not a merely rhetorical question to be answered in the negative. History, the history of violence and politics, is not to be denied, nor are transcendence and eschatology to be referred to a telos informing or directing history, or to a world beyond the world. If the eschatological vision means a morality that transcends the requirements of living within totality in order to be able to pass judgment on history as a whole, eschatology must nonetheless justify itself in terms that do not in any way reduce history to mere appearance or to the function of an education in the ways of providence. The first and overriding question of *Totality and Infinity,* the question "of the highest importance" concerns the necessity of knowing "whether we are not duped by morality" (21). If eschatology is essential to answering the question of what the morality is by which we may or may not be duped, the question of the relation of history to eschatology is vital to answering the question of whether in fact we are so duped. But in order to deal with the second aspect of the question, we need to know not only the what of morality/goodness/eschatology, we also need to know that, how and even to what extent it is at work in history: and what history is. "[T]he moral consciousness," says Levinas, "can sustain the mocking gaze of the political man only if the certitude of peace dominates the evidence of war....Morality will oppose politics in history and will have gone beyond the functions of prudence or the canons of the beautiful to proclaim itself unconditional and universal when the eschatology of messianic peace will have come to superpose itself upon the ontology of war" (22). Does this mean that Levinas could be suggesting, not a teleology, but something like a movement in history, the possibility, within history of an effect of eschatology? This cannot be ruled out. Yet, at the same time he says that "peace does not take place in the objective history disclosed by war, as the end of that war, or the end of that history" (23). History and eschatology are opposed, but this opposition is not an abstract negation, not a dualism. Yet they are also not identified. The identification of history with eschatology would be the teleology that Levinas quite explicitly rejects. The answer will ultimately depend on whether objective history is *entirely* disclosed by war.

And for Levinas it is not entirely so disclosed. For Levinas objective history, as it is for Hegel (and, by slight extension, for Marx), is also a struggle for the freedom of the particular, as well as the arena in which the election of the I takes place. In a sense the whole problem which Levinas raises, or perhaps reaches, would be found in the possibilities of the relation between election and freedom. What Levinas recognizes as Hegel's "great meditation on freedom" maintains that "the good will" without the means to realize itself is not a true freedom: "Freedom is not realized outside of social and political institutions...Apolitical freedom is to be explained as an illusion due to the fact that its partisans or its beneficiaries belong to an advanced stage of political evolution" (*TI*, 241). Yet the state, including the Hegelian State, is still only another inversion and antipode of the freedom of the person that it purports to realize. In its "virile judgement of history" it repeats the "virile judgement of 'pure reason'," which is "cruel" (243). Precisely within the state, whether Hegelian or liberal, "the will now knows another tyranny: that of works alienated, already foreign to man...a tyranny of the universal and impersonal, an order that is inhuman though distinct from the brutish" (242; see also 213–14). The freedom Hegel celebrates as the historical realization of objective spirit in the modern state cannot be the resolution of the antagonism of eschatology and history. It is, if anything, only the reduction of eschatology to history in its absolutely idealist form. Does this mean that a materialist translation of Hegelian history into the terms of the corporeal labor of subjectivity might prepare the ground for such a resolution? After all, materialism has its not unimportant share in "eternal truth," a share that lies "in the fact that the human will can be laid hold of in its works" (229). Materialism reveals, is aware of, and is a response (virtually *in toto*) to the dimension of corporeity according to which "the will…by its works [is] exposed to the Other" (226). Levinas continues, "Corporeity thus describes the ontological regime of a *primary self-alienation* contemporaneous with the very event by which the self ensures, against the unknown factor of the elements, its own independence" (226; emphasis added). This is the inescapable dimension of self-alienation Levinas had attached to the economic in "The Ego and the Totality," and here as there it is the dimension of a real society that institutes history. And here, in *Totality and Infinity,* as there, the nonimpossibility of a coincidence or meeting of eschatology and history is left open: "The mortal will can escape violence by driving violence and murder from the world" (242). And although it remains somewhat ambiguous, it seems that Levinas envisions this escape from violence as an escape from the infliction of violence as well as from subjection to violence.

Yet, for Levinas, this will not be the route taken in resolving the antagonism of history and eschatology, at least inasmuch as "history is not an eschatology. The animal fabricating tools frees itself from its animal condition when its momentum seems interrupted and broken, when instead of going of itself to its goal as an inviolable will it fabricates tools and fixes the power of its future action in transmissible and receivable things"

(*TI,* 241). Thus *"fate does not precede history; it follows it"* (228; emphasis added). The "primary self-alienation," the production of works beyond and alongside the expression of speech, introduces a dimension into human existence according to which although fate is not fundamental, history is fundamentally fated to be a history that contains (in the sense of holding within and restraining) eschatology. The subject as living body, even pursuing its dis-alienation, would be pursuing a course that, not unlike the irony of the Hegelian state, turns against itself: "spontaneity undergoes, turns into its contrary" (229). Materialism, as Levinas understands it in *Totality and Infinity,* is therefore, in *principle,* not the resolution of the antagonistic relation of eschatology to history. By upholding the *power* of spontaneity to become conscious of and to thereby undo its alienation by getting a grip over the event of history, materialism repeats the same logic that gives rise to history in the first place. If Hegelianism is the idealist reduction of eschatology to objective history understood in teleological terms, materialism would be the reduction of history to an eschatology still understood in teleological, purposive-instrumental terms.

It is vital for Levinas, by the end of *Totality and Infinity,* to return to the theme of temporality as history. This is required by the question of the status of morality, of whether we are duped by it. To withstand the mocking gaze of the political man, the lucid realist who catches sight of the permanent possibility of war and who is capable of rising to the notion of a rational peace, it is necessary that infinity, or the ethical relation, or goodness or morality not only take place in time, be experienced within history, but that they "superpose" themselves on "the ontology of war." Although much of *Totality and Infinity* is devoted to the analysis of the ethical relation, and its conditions, virtually all of the second half of the book, beginning with section 3, returns to this theme.

What Hegel and materialism both recognize, and this is why Levinas devotes strategic attention to them when he does, is the essentiality of historical time to the situation or horizon of the radically separate subject capable of goodness. However, what neither address, or what neither address adequately, is the situation of subjectivity as mortal. The inadequacy of both Hegelianism and materialism is to look for a response to death in the *works* of subjectivity. Not only are such works (for Hegel, the return from alienation in the achievement of the modern state, the Idea in its objective form; for Marx, the work of the returning of works from their alienation as power over the worker) fated in objective history to become their contraries; the more essential problem is that, for Levinas, to seek freedom in works is to have already submitted and succumbed to totalization. Such a subjectivity, losing itself in its works is already dead. Works, for Levinas, are on their way already, as works, to being dead things, merely candidates for totalization, as they are "merchandize" and thus "exchangeable." To seek life in works is already to have embraced the "capital of being" that precedes and makes possible the "capital of having" (NI, 150,n9). The discourse of history as the discourse of the work of the subject is already a "necrological discourse." Yet both Hegelianism and materialism, in seeking a recovery from the loss of subjectivity in the historical works of subjectivity, are also, but tacitly, acknowledging that death is actually perceived by subjectivity not the way the religious and philosophical traditions have always construed it (that is, exclusively as either nothingness or another world [*TI*, 232]), but as "the alienation of its powers" (247). "Mortality, Levinas asserts, "is the concrete and primary phenomenon. It forbids the positing of a for itself that would not be already delivered over to the Other and consequently be a thing" (235). The philosophies of history, then, supply at least a clue, beyond the traditional relation of eschatology to history, to what that relation is in truth. Subjectivity has access to, or rather lives a temporality that is not only that of objective history, even though both temporalities are responses to the negation of my powers (229, 232). Eschatological time, experienced within history, is not the time of the "willing of the living will [which] postpones…subjection, and accordingly wills against the Other and his threat" (227), thus enjoining war, politics, lucidity, ontology and rational peace. Although still involving a postponement, and therefore a distance and therefore time, subjectivity, faced by the Other, may also go beyond seeking its freedom in its will: "The will, already betrayal and alienation of itself but postponing this betrayal, on the way to death, but a death ever future, exposed to death, but not immediately, has time to be for the Other, and thus to recover meaning despite death" (236).

My relation to my mortality is an exceptional instance because "in life, it is the impossibility of every possibility, the stroke of a total passivity.…My relation with death is not the fear of nothingness, but the fear of violence — and thus it extends into the fear of the Other, of the absolutely unforeseeable" (*TI*, 235; see also 233–34). Yet Levinas's thought as a defense of subjectivity is not about being human as a being for death,[4] nor about a being beyond death, but about a being beyond being for death. Eschatology will answer the alienation of my powers, which appear in both mortality and history, not by their reassertion, producing more of the history of death, but in the ethical relation, in goodness: "Goodness consists in taking up a position in being such that the Other counts for more than myself…the possibility for the I that is exposed to the alienation of its powers by death to not be for death" (247).

The time of history follows from the ability of the subject (already in a social relation which, according to Levinas, is not just another relation among many that can be produced in being but its "ultimate event" [*TI*, 221])[5] to become separated from the domain of pure enjoyment and enter into the domain of works. In works, already presupposing a dwelling established through the face of the Other in its welcoming (feminine) aspect, subjectivity defers and deflects the uncertainty and treachery of the elemental. But in doing so subjectivity also establishes itself within a possible and actual history of exploitation, violence, and domination. It becomes ensnared in totality; it achieves an identity and identifies with its achievements. Ensnared in totality it comes eventually to project its freedom, still in the domain of the works of a spontaneous power, into a power against the power of history. But neither idealism nor materialism, as teleological eschatologies, are able to restore (even dialectically, at a higher level), the separation and unicity that subjectivity already unconsciously and primordially enjoyed in an enjoyment immersed in the elements. Objective history is the history of the constituting and constituted subject, but not the history of subjectivity per se; and in it there is no escape from the violence inherent in totalization. The time of eschatology, neither beyond time, nor the end of time, and issuing from the possibility of impossibility, requires a different possibility in relation to history; the time of eschatology is not eternal life, but an infinite time bearing the subject beyond death. This infinite time is again the time of a social relation, but one where "my future does not enter into the logical essence of the possible. The relation with such a future, irreducible to the power over possibles, we shall call fecundity" (*TI*, 267). This relation does not belong to the time of history and the state. Levinas finds its exemplary extant concrete instantiation in the relation to the child. The structure, meaning, and possibility of fecund being, a being of goodness, is something that will need further exposition (see chapter 6), in the discussion of what we can hope. But without the reality, within history, of such an infinite time, we would in fact, Levinas implies, be duped by morality. Without the infinite time of fecundity, "goodness would be folly" (280).

Is meaning despite death, a being beyond death that does not at all lessen its sting, sufficient to superpose messianic peace on the ontology of war? The separation of eschatology from history that Levinas accomplishes in this superposition is not an abstract negation of history by eschatology. It is not a dualism. Although history and eschatology must remain essentially separated, they also in some sense contain each other, perhaps in the sense that each is something like the transcendental condition, or paratranscendental condition, of the other. Eschatology is the condition of history in the sense that for Levinas in *Totality and Infinity,* the ethical relation of the other for me is the condition under which subjectivity can achieve the practical separation necessary to engage in dwelling, works, and thereby in history. And history is the condition of eschatology in the sense that without it, eschatology would necessarily refer merely to an illusory world beyond the world, a happy or unhappy eternity, heaven or hell; or to the unreal society of intimacy. Yet the relation *is like* a dualism. History and eschatology cannot *meet* each other. Like the relation of ethics and justice, the relation of history to eschatology is also not a nondualism. And this is because, "in the last instance," goodness, categorically and apodictically, cannot become a work, that is, some visible thing, to be integrated into the third-person perspective that establishes totalities: "The invisible must manifest itself if history is to lose its right to the last word.... But the manifestation of the invisible must not mean the passage of the invisible to the status of the visible" (*TI,* 243). It is as though the relation of eschatology to history had the same structure as that of the ethical relation itself, where each term of the relation is both utterly separate and completely relational. Such a structure is not dialectical because even though the terms are internally related to each other, they are not internally related simply or exclusively by negation. Because negation does not constitute their relation, they do not portend a synthesis.

Thus, in *Totality and Infinity,* where some sort of radical separation between history and eschatology is maintained, the state, law, and justice are not treated in quite the same way that they are in the later mature work. In the "Conclusions" Levinas asserts that even though the state destroys unicity it must take unicity "as its model." There is a subtle perhaps, yet notable difference between taking unicity as the model of the state and taking the state to be the betrayal, but not degeneration of ethics. This is especially marked in the conclusion" inasmuch as Levinas will maintain that it is *only* fecundity that will maintain the irreplaceable unicity of the I "against the State" (*TI,* 300–01), and that the peace, the messianic peace, which is the unity of a radical plurality belongs only to the infinite time of fecundity (306).

As a movement to move eschatology beyond onto-theo-logical frameworks, Levinas's work is in some ways unsurpassable because of the radical separation he establishes between eschatology and any teleology embodying the purposive will of an omnipotent Providence. Yet neither in his earlier nor later mature work is his thinking structurally capable of going beyond what he terms in "The Ego and the Totality" to be the impasse of liberalism, the very problem he set for himself in that essay. This structural deficiency, however, does not follow from any commitment to liberalism on his part. The concluding chapter of *Otherwise than Being* sets the problem once again in place: "The true problem for us Westerners is not so much to refuse violence as to question ourselves about a struggle against violence which, without blanching in non-resistance to evil, could avoid the institution of violence out of this very struggle" (*OTB,* 177). The betrayal of ethics in politics, which is Levinas's way of negotiating their relationship in *Otherwise than Being,* is thus not a resolution of this problem. It is the problem itself. Justice *is* the problem and not a halfway solution to the problem of the third. What seemed to be the beginning of a possible resolution in *Totality and Infinity,* the development of the thought of a dimension of social being that is neither the intimate society nor the society of economy and state, the fecund social relation that is instantiated in the structure of the familial, is in the later mature work dropped. But the problem itself remains in place, the problem of a third way. Levinas, to the end, thus displays a certain indirect sensitivity to the amphibology that his construal of the relation between ethics and politics sets up. And he does not celebrate it as an aporia or impossibility the recognition of which is what ultimately could carry us beyond totalization in the real society.

Amphibology and Ideology

In a 1981 interview, Levinas is returned by his interviewer to the question of eschatology and responds with an expression of his reservation about the term *"eschaton* [which] implies that there might exist a finality, an end (*fin*) to the historical relation of difference between man and the absolutely Other.... This is what Hegelian dialectics amounts to, a radical denial of the rupture between the ontological and the ethical." It has become mistakenly obvious to most readers of Levinas that his solution to the problem of the relation of ethics to politics is in a political form that requires a "perpetual duty of vigilance"[6] over itself; that an adequately or even ideally liberal openness to unending critique is itself the end and limit in earthly reality of the messianic relation with the other. Levinas's statements that ethics can only disturb the State, but in a radical way can much too easily be assimilated to the one-dimensional view that accepts this situation as final. But to think that unending critique by itself marks the end (either the goal or the limit, or both) is already to have abandoned the critique one is ostensibly espousing. When Levinas acknowledges that the "practicability of ethics in human society as we know it" is a "fundamental point" and "the great paradox of human existence; we must use the ontological for the sake of the other,"[7] this cannot be read as final acceptance of an ultimate form. This is so because the relationship of ontology to ethics simply as critique is every bit the "fixed and permanent state of affairs" that Levinas sees as the "danger of eschatology," when the *eschaton* is thought to be, à la Hegelian dialectics, "a finite fusion" with the infinite. Paradoxically, to accept the finality of the paradox that keeps the situation open, is to close the situation. To accept even the most radical liberalism as the best possible world would then truly be to "degrade the infinite relation to the other." Eternal vigilance should first be vigilant about itself. The danger of Levinas's double amphibology lies in part in this acceptance: the acceptance of the "perpetual duty of vigilance" as vigilance, as the ethical interruption of the political.[8]

The eternal vigilance of the ethical over the political is not eternal vigilance, as long as it leaves the political in place as the "art of foreseeing war and…winning it by every means" (*TI,* 21). Behind and above the art of foreseeing war there must be the vigilance of foreseeing peace, a foreseeing that goes beyond merely rational peace, beyond saying that only beings capable of war are also able to be at peace. Without the art of foreseeing peace, and foreseeing peace in the real society, the ethical relation that radically disturbs the state, but *only* disturbs it, continuously expanding rights in and against the eternal state, the eschatological vision necessarily implied by ethics, would be itself unethical. It would be unethical in opening itself to ideology in precisely the sense in which Adorno sees art being open to ideology: "If, in empirical reality everything has become fungible, art holds up to the world of everything-for-something else the image of what it itself would be if it were emancipated from the schemata of imposed identification. Yet art plays over into ideology in that, as the image of what lies beyond exchange, it suggests that not everything in the world is exchangeable."[9] In barring himself from being able to pursue a vision of peace that somehow belongs to the realm of history and the will, Levinas will run a risk he might not find as acceptable as the fine philosophical risk he is willing to run, the risk of saying that which cannot be said.

To too many of his readers, though not all, Levinas seems to offer a certain political quietism. And this is so despite having generated, using the very terms of rational ontology, an opening to the perspective that sees beyond what Adorno calls the schemata of imposed identification. The ethical assignation is precisely beyond the schemata of identification and beyond identity itself. In the reception of Levinas in relation to this problem, his interpreters and commentators could be ranged along a continuum from those who see in Levinas a refounding of liberalism, on the right, all the way to, on the left, those who go beyond Levinas in order to make "use of the ontological for the sake of the other."

The sketch that immediately follows does not attempt to provide anything like a comprehensive analysis of existing approaches to the problem of the relation between Levinas's ethics in general and either politics in general or Levinas's own political views. The latter question is especially a separate one. I will merely indicate that there are a number of ways of doing this that Levinas leaves open, not in spite of but by bringing ethics and politics into a difficult relation which contains the amphibology discussed earlier. The continuum suggested here is not strictly representative. It is meant to briefly situate and describe efforts from what might be called the Levinasian left, or left Levinasians, to move beyond this amphibology, and to indicate that ultimately this must involve the encounter with the historicity of experience and the history of experience explored by the Frankfurt School.[10]

On the Levinasian right there are those such as Richard Cohen who see in the priority of the ethical over the political a wholehearted endorsement of the liberal state.[11] Still to be ranged nearer to this end of the continuum would be others, perhaps surprised to find themselves here, such as Geoffrey Dudiak, for whom the principal import of the relation Levinas establishes between ethics and politics would lie in the necessity of continuous critique.[12] This reception tends to beg the question, not only of whether continuous critique is in any way sufficient to the problem of putting ontology to use for the sake of the other, but perhaps more to the point, especially when it comes to relating Levinas's relation of eschatology to history to that of the Frankfurt School, of whether the ethical resources of critique are themselves drying up, at least at the level of the real society, in the history of disenchantment as domination.

At the very border of the politically quietist reception, with a foot on either side, would stand someone like Adriaan Peperzak. In answering the question of whether Levinas has founded duties and rights in a new way, Peperzak, in an astute formulation of a centrist Levinasian orthodoxy, places the decisive difference between Levinas and the Western political tradition (as summed up in Kant and Hegel) on the *perspective* from which justice, social organization, politics, and the state are seen as necessary. Whereas for Hegel, they are the realization of the idea of freedom, for Levinas they are the necessary mediation between goodness and war. According to Peperzak, "Levinas accepts the order of inevitable counterviolence-against violence in the name of universal justice."[13] Yet Levinas, placing "the unpredictability of time above eternity," and thus going beyond the tragic wisdom of the Hegelian system, will point to a minimal margin between morality and universal history, a margin that is "no more than a line without any volume."[14] Although he acknowledges the pull of Levinasian Desire to leave the history of "Greece-inspired modernity" behind, Peperzak's counsel would be to "plunder it as much as we can before we leave it behind."[15] In what this plunder might consist is radically unclear.

Across the border of Levinasian orthodoxy would be the stance of Robert Bernasconi who, recognizing that Levinas's thought "cannot be assimilated to what passes as political philosophy," would nonetheless like to open a space in which ethics could find a political expression beyond liberalism. But Bernasconi restricts himself in this effort exclusively to Levinasian resources and can therefore bring this task no further than pointing out that Levinas "sought a way of focusing on [the relation of ethics and politics] as conflicting aspects of what he increasingly presented as a single structure."[16] In this structure, sometimes alluded to by Bernasconi as "fraternity" the role of the ethical remains limited to an interruption of the political; no direction of the political, but a challenge to "its sense that it embodies the ultimate wisdom of 'the bottom line.'"[17]

If Bernasconi's stance is one place where, on our continuum, the Levinasian left begins, its next phase would be found in perhaps the only effort to date to suggest the possibility of a systematic rapprochement between Levinas and Marx. For Robert Gibbs, Levinas, by the time of *Otherwise than Being,* has all but abandoned his earlier program for a refusal of totalizing views *inextricably joined with* a demand for economic justice. In "The Ego and Totality" Levinas had made ethics identical to economic justice, according to Gibbs. In *Totality and Infinity* Levinas had projected the beginning of a social program of sorts by elevating the fecundity of the family over the state. The family would represent a nontotalizing intermediate structure, a Rosenzweigian *aufhebung* of political society. However, in *Otherwise than Being,* "there is no liberation from politics, nor can ethics create its own institutions or realm."[18] Rather than end here, Gibbs suggests that Levinas, by recognizing his affinities with Marx, could have projected a liberation involving nontotalizing social structures for economic justice. Marx shares with Levinas a "social ethic" in which "one exists for others" and in which our nature is to become fully social.[19] Like Marx, freedom would be found through responsibility to others' needs. And like Levinas, there is in Marx, early on, a positive image of sociality in sexuality and the family, but later an attenuated recognition of the inescapability of the state, a Hegelian state becoming a nonstate. Thus, in Levinas, we miss the call for a refounding of society, while in Marx there is, along with the call for a revolutionary and violent founding of a new totality, an apparent insensibility to the reduction of responsibility in any totality. But Marx need not be totalizing,[20] and Levinas could have gone beyond his scattered critical and appreciative aperçus in relation to Marx in order to pursue a serious discussion of the sociality Marx proposed. Liberation would mean a restructuring of society to develop the originary responsibility.[21]

There is here the beginning of an attractive program for the Levinasian left.[22] But what it does not yet address, and what needs to be addressed by any relating of Marxian social theory and Levinasian ethics as first philosophy that seeks "a positive combination of the two" is the question of history.[23] The social relation has a temporal dimension, or rather two temporal dimensions that must themselves be related if something like this rapprochement is to take place. It is not simply a question of conceiving a nontotalizing form of responsible sociality, difficult and essential as this might be, but of conceiving and thinking the conditions of possibility of transcending the logic of the "primary alienation" that ultimately, for Levinas, inaugurates the history that does not cease for a moment its self-totalization. Something in history would need to give birth to the time of fecundity in history.

Furthest to the left on our continuum, and certainly to date by far the most fully achieved reflection on relating Marxian social theory with Levinas, is the liberation philosophy of Enrique Dussel, which deserves a fuller treatment than can even be indicated, let alone given here. What perhaps most importantly characterizes Dussel's work is the direct mapping of Levinas's ethical categories onto Marxian (and sometimes populist) ones, and vice versa. For Dussel the terms and relations of Levinas's ethical relation tend to become immediately collective political terms and relations. The relation of the Same to the Other is transposed directly into the relation of the center to the peripheral peoples. For Dussel the thought of liberation must start not where Levinas starts, in the situation of a singular subjectivity, itself not ready to recognize the very ethical relation that allows and transcends its imminent entry into the synchronizable time of history. Thought must instead start from the center/periphery, dominator/dominated, totality/exteriority dissymmetry.[24] Dussel states, "Philosophy of liberation knows that politics — the politics of the exploited — is the first philosophy because politics is the centre of ethics as metaphysics."[25] What this means, on the one hand, is that unlike Levinas, Dussel does not follow the trajectory leading to the impasse of liberalism, the merely rational peace of the Kantian-Hegelian state, to be confirmed and denied in ambivalence, to be eternally reiterated. But on the other hand it means that Dussel was able to avoid this only by drastically changing the reach and the meaning of the key Levinasian category of proximity. For Dussel, proximity is not a term describing the relation of singular subjectivity to an incomparable other with whom I have nothing in common; this is, rather, a European deformation and a mistaken individualization of "a collective personal experience." Rather than being reunified at the level of law and the state, the oppressed already constitute something like at least the beginning of a unified ethical plurality in the form of "the people,"[26] those who are oppressed by a political totality but maintain a cultural exteriority.[27] The people become the agency of the ethos of liberation, which is an ethos of commiseration, a placing oneself with someone in misery. And it is the oppressed who have unlimited commiseration of their equals.[28] "The people" become the origin of a fecundity within history. But in this construal, Levinas's eschatological experience within history is both collectivized and substantialized, and to a degree that seems to be commanded by the maieutics of Marx's Hegelian logic of transformation. History already contains eschatology, but in Dussel's hands it once again is on its way to becoming a teleological eschatology, and this in spite of the fact that Dussel would like to forbid fetishization of any future system.[29]

Dussel would at least be right, aside from all questions about misplaced faith in the unlimited commiseration of the oppressed, and against Levinas, in refusing to totalize all possible history as the ineluctable necessity of totalization, if that were in fact simply what Levinas is doing. And Levinas at least comes close to doing just that by radically separating works from expression for the Other. Works are always products of the will that render it self-conscious of its vulnerability to the threat of the other. But it could be that what Levinas is doing is also recognizing that history has been, as Benjamin put it, one single catastrophe. By refusing to make the *eschaton* a power within history, but instead an experience of the break-up of all systems of reference within history, Levinas establishes a beyond for the totalized historical. To repeal this catastrophe, to interrupt it and not start it over again, a radical distance from history is necessary. What Levinas cannot do is trace the historical experience of the ethical, this "experience *par excellence*" even to the point that history itself, as catastrophe, breaks up. This will be the impossible ambition of the Frankfurt School.

Two

On the Concept of Natural History

History, Freedom, and Embodied Interiority

The structure of the relation that Levinas unfolds between history and eschatology, like that between justice and ethics, and between subjectivity and the absolutely other, discloses an anterior posteriority. The end of history will have always already taken place. The end has already preceded its beginning. From within the ethical optic, a judgment on history will also therefore always already have been passed, no matter how tacitly. To look for an end of history as the *telos* of the historical is only to repeat an act of identification, itself antiethical, a cognitive power-project that nonetheless lives from the forgotten horizon of the ethical relation, the relation that is ultimately a material-transcendental condition of the subjectivity that is able to create a violence, not only against this or that other, but a structural violence that envelops all subjects. The endless repetition of the violence of the real society is not a result of a lack of strength in a moral will which can be reformed. Nor is it the result of a mere misunderstanding that beyond being and nonbeing there does not exist an otherwise-than-being. But there is also no movement in this relation between eschatology and history, or between the Same and responsibility to the other within subjectivity.

There is for Levinas, strictly speaking, no solution to this problem. This is where, for him, one truly meets an aporia. Such an aporia cannot be broken through, nor evaded. In Levinasian terms there can be no politics of generosity, not because this is analytically, semantically an oxymoron, but *because of the logic of the history of the real society*. This logic, resting upon the works of a separated being, must inexorably cover over its being-for-the-other, in the process concealing the holy with the sacred, betraying ethics with justice. Need does not, over time, disappear into Desire. Nor is Desire in any way a sublimation of need. Moreover, Levinas has effectively barred any and all attempts at a dialectical resolution of this problem.[1] He has done so by subtly and carefully constructing the relationship between history and eschatology in such a way that they are bound to each other neither as analytical nor dialectical opposites. From an analytical point of view, their opposition cannot be undone by reduction of the one to being the appearance or accident of the substance of the other. Analytically, their relation must remain paradoxical. From a positively dialectical point of view, they are not internally related to one another essentially simply through negation, and do not therefore admit of a synthesis.

If, therefore, there is to be anything like a rapprochement between Levinas and Marx (or the inheritance of Marx in contemporary historical materialism) it must first involve, from Levinas's point of view, a movement beyond Marxism's inheritance from Hegelian idealism of something like a teleological construal of the relation of history to eschatology. At the same time, such a rapprochement would have to mean at the very least a certain displacement of the Levinasian aporia. It might mean that the very difference between an aporia and a problem would itself become problematic, or aporetic.

Among all of Levinas's scattered remarks about Marx, those that have most bearing on this question have to do with Marx not having gone far enough in separating his materialism from the ontological imperialism of Western philosophy and from the subject of that ontology, whose freedom is always conceived as spontaneity, possibility, or power. In one of his very first essays, "Reflections on the Philosophy of Hitlerism," from 1934, Levinas at once underlines both the radicality of Marx's view of the human, summed up in the phrase that "being determines consciousness," and the continuity of Marx with the liberalism of European civilization which, by positing the sovereign freedom of reason, produces a world in which "man is not weighed down by a History in choosing his destiny." On the one hand, "absolute freedom...for the first time finds itself banished from the spirit's constitution." As a result, Marx "breaks the harmonious curve" of the development of European culture. On the other hand, the link that Marxism perceives the spirit to have to a "determined situation" is "in no way a radical one." The power of "individual consciousness" remains sufficient "to shake off the social bewitchment that then appears foreign to its essence" (*RPH,* 67).[2] Thus, Marx rejoins the European ontologies for which "man is absolutely free in his relations with the world.... Speaking absolutely, he has no history" (64). In order to truly break with the notion of absolute freedom it would be necessary to acknowledge that "the situation to which he was bound was not added to him but formed the very foundation of his being" (67). This would entail a view of the human-historical that would invert and undo the Western conception of freedom: "For history is the most profound limitation, the fundamental limitation. Time which is a condition of human existence, is above all a condition that is irreparable.... Beneath the melancholy of the eternal flow of things...there lies the tragedy of the irremovability of a past that cannot be erased, and that condemns any initiative to being just a continuation. True freedom, the true beginning would require a true present, which, always at the peak of a destiny, forever recommences that destiny" (65). The Germanic ideal that Levinas is analyzing in this essay, despite the terrible forebodings that he perceives in it, has the philosophical merit of being "the awakening of elementary feelings," the contorted expression of "an elementary force" (64).[3] It is this elementary force, recognizable in the "feeling of identity between self and body," (68) that Marxism will not have fully come to terms with. In not coming to terms with it, Marxism will threaten to repeat not only the absolute freedom of liberalism, but will also not have come any closer to a true notion of freedom as bound to the irremovable limitation that is time.

In 1962, with *Totality and Infinity* already having been published, Levinas will return to this theme in "Transcendence and Height." According to Levinas in this essay, the flaw in Marx is not that philosophically his thought is a realism but that, like Husserl's transcendental phenomenology or for that matter Heidegger's late thinking, the realism with which Marx is satisfied "is not sufficiently realist to overcome idealism" (TH, 15). Philosophy, which is virtually synonymous with idealism, is the event in which knowledge "seems to suppress multiplicity and consequently violence. Indeed violence comes from opposition, that is to say, from the scission of being into the Same and Other. Philosophy...assimilates every Other to Same" (13). The search for truth, even in philosophical realism, repeats the idealistic assimilation of the other into the same, and "idealism is found precisely in the philosophers who denounce it most harshly" (14). The idealism of Marx's materialism reveals itself not only in such a search but also in his conception of a socialist society, where the human is only "conceived of as an I or a citizen — but never in the irreducible originality of his alterity, which one cannot have access to through reciprocity and symmetry. Universality and egalitarian law result from the conflicts in which one egoism opposes another" (14). It is worth noting in passing that in this essay Marx is not being criticized for any illiberalism his socialism might bear, in contrast with a doctrine of the rights of man leading to limited constitutional government under the universal rule of law, but precisely for the similarity of socialism to that rule. Thus there are more than residues of idealism in Marx. A sufficient realism would mean "the recognition of an other than I…to be possible, [and that] it is necessary that I myself am not originally what I remain even in my explorations of the obscure or the unknown: the peaceful and sovereign identity of the self with itself and the source of the adequate idea" (15). The social relation still obscured within Marx's conception of socialism would be a bond that does not annihilate the I but "binds it to the other in an incomparable and unique way," a way that is utterly unlike the way in which matter is bound up or in the way an organ is bound up. Such "mechanical and organic solidarities would dissolve I into a totality" (17). One can go beyond the imperialism of the same only when the other has nothing in common with me (16). And, as though to head off in advance the notion that certain Habermasians might entertain that discourse ethics would be a cut above such solidarities, Levinas will note that such a bond, not being an initial act of reflection, is therefore anything but "the entry of the I into a suprapersonal, coherent and universal discourse" (18).[4]

The third instance of Levinas linking his criticisms of Marx to the latter's insufficient realism, that is — by implication — to a more than residual idealism which could underwrite a his-torico-teleological eschatology, takes place in the 1970 essay "No Identity." Written in response to the events of May 1968, Levinas is here concerned not so much with the problem of overcoming idealism as he is with the radically inhuman insufficiency of those movements of thought that have replaced idealism. His targets are the sciences of the human and Heideggerian antihumanism.

Although Levinas sees the critique of humanism espoused by both of these movements as tacitly including a defense of the human "understood as a defense of the man other than me" (NI, 150–51), they are united in that both contest the "inward world" (144) of vulnerability that responsibility presupposes. They have, therefore, in one way surpassed the humanism of Hegel and Marx. Such humanism was based upon the notion of the recovery of a world of unfulfilled and alienated intentions and was therefore linked back to a subjectivity the core of which was the identity of the ego with itself. For Marx, the deviations of the will not at home with the world of its intentions was traceable back to *social* alienation. But, for Levinas, this does not mean that Marx has overcome Hegel. Standing him on his feet does not undo the imperialism of the head. Instead it means that "by exalting socialist hopes, one paradoxically rendered transcendental idealism plausible!" (143). Marx has not yet abandoned the world of radical inwardness, but it is still conceived along idealist lines. For Levinas, "today's anxiety is more profound" (143). The revolutions gone bad — 1776 and 1789 along with 1917? — have led to a state in which "the disalienation itself is alienated" (143), a condition in which we are alienated from the very project of disalienation as the project of an ego ultimately at home with itself, of an ego that is ultimately the Same. Yet the antihumanisms contest the imperialist subjectivity of idealism at the cost of abolishing an "impossible inwardness…an impossibility we learn of neither from metaphysics or the end of metaphysics" (149). One important manifestation of such inwardness, which is itself the vulnerability and susceptibility of responsibility, lies however in the very memory of universal alienation: "The condition (or the uncondition) of being strangers in the land of Egypt brings man close to his neighbour. In their uncondition of being strangers men seek one another. No one is at home. The memory of this servitude assembles humanity" (149). The memory of this servitude implies that "no one can save himself without the others" (149). Between and beyond both the form of memory that belongs to universal history and the radical forgetting of inwardness which issues from antihumanism, there would therefore lie a memory of inwardness and an inwardness of memory, a memory of the human "made of responsibilities" she did not assume, a remembrance of a "debt...absorbed only by being increased" (149). The expression of this unassumed debt involves the experience of a time other than the time of universal history.

This theme is already present in *Totality and Infinity*. There Levinas, linking interiority inalienably to memory in the phenomenology of separation, conceives of mortal existence as already disqualifying the time of universal history as the measure of the reality of the subject. Mortal existence flows in a dimension of its own. Levinas says, "Interiority institutes an order different from historical time...an order where everything is pending, where what is no longer possible historically remains always possible" (*TI*, 55). The time of universal history, especially the "thesis of the *primacy* of history constitutes an option for the comprehension of being in which interiority is sacrificed" (57; emphasis added). Countering and resisting universal history, along with the synchronizable time upon which it depends, is the memory of mortality and of separation — a memory which, in "No Identity" becomes the uncondition of all being strangers. The memory, Levinas's memory of radical separation available universally out of mortality but forgotten in both the universal histories, in Hegel and Marx, and in the antihumanisms, becomes "the way of access to social reality starting with the separation of the I...not engulfed in universal history, in which only totalities appear" (58). Thus memory, at least a certain memory, will operate as eschatology. And as such the "eschatological...draws beings out of the jurisdiction of history and the future; it arouses them in and calls them forth to their full responsibility. Submitting history as a whole to judgement…it restores to each instant its full significance in that very instant" (23). The memory of servitude and estrangement, inseparable from radical separation and interiority, do not function to constitute the moments of universal history, but estrange the subject from that history which engulfs it, but is *not* ultimately its own. This calls not for a second alienation, an alienation from alienation, but an alienation from that which can alienate itself. Interiority, like eschatology, stands outside universal history: "Memory as an inversion of historical time is the essence of interiority" (56). Universal history belongs to the functional relatedness of works, including the work of the social fact itself, but the inverted historical time of interiority announces the possibility of a continuous act of breaking with the historical totality. Acts are not works, they are in fact radically distinct from works: "Each instant of historical time in which action commences is, in the last analysis, a birth, and hence breaks the continuous time of history, a time of works and not of wills" (58).

The continuous time of history is a time of works, which according to Levinas necessarily escape the intentions and meanings of their authors, as we have seen. And, in a sense, the whole of Levinas's work is an effort to invert historical time through the remembrance of an interiority that is older than what can be captured by universal history or ontology. Such an interiority is anything but the noumenal freedom of Kant's transcendental ego, or Hegelian Spirit, or class-consciousness working their way through history, or as history. Neither would interiority be the disclosure of Being, whose essence in Heidegger is for Levinas the unfolding of a "certain meaning, a certain peace that borrows nothing from a subject, expresses nothing that would be inside a soul" (*NI,* 143–44). The interiority that Levinas would oppose to the continuous time of history involves the breaking up of everything in the subject that would reinstitute the synchronous time of the Same. And therefore this absolutely separate and singular interiority would also have to be, but against all logic, a relation, a relation across an absolute distance, which is the form of the ethical relation, its phenomenological *eidos*. Marxism in bringing forward more than a residue of idealism into its effort to link interiority to a "determined situation" will either mistranslate interiority and separation into a not-yet-achieved-but-in-the-process-of-becoming-so absolute freedom, or else it will become another of the human sciences, with its own particular parcel of insight into the nature of the real society. Or perhaps it will manage to combine aspects of both.

Yet Levinas's justifiable criticisms of Marx do not lessen or necessarily justify the risk he runs, outlined in chapter 1, of producing both the impasse of the relation between ethics and justice, and the amphibology laminated to it. The inversion of historical time taking place within the memory of interiority and performed, in a sense, in ethical actions, rather than in works, leave history and totality in place, even if not entirely to their own devices. And more than that, ethical acts foster the illusion that since interiority, (although it can be misinterpreted as absolute freedom or even forgotten after the end of metaphysics) is always with us as the inexpungible subjectivity of the subject presupposed by all the efforts of being, there is meaning and freedom simply in *despite* of history.[5] The challenge, then, for a Marxian-Levinasian rapprochement would be to develop a relation of subjectivity to history that, while retaining an absolute separation of the subject distinct from the always synthesizable internal contradictions of totality, along with inwardness and its "eschatology of messianic peace" (*TI,* 22), could also, in pointing beyond history, leave history open to its own de-totalization.

On the Concept of History

Such a de-totalization of history in and as historical memory
is figured metaphorically in Walter Benjamin's "Theses on
the Concept of History." Although not carried through as was
intended in his unrealized *Arcades Project,* the "Theses" present something at least similar to a program for the recasting of
the writing of history that would satisfy or come very close to
satisfying the very stringent conditions of de-totalization required
by Levinas's "memory as an inversion of historical time" (*TI,*
56). In doing so, moreover, they suggest the nonimpossibility
of a messianic peace that would mean something more than the
meaning Levinas is able to wrest from the jaws of mortality and
totality. The "Theses" are certainly inadequate to do anything
like this by themselves, or even in conjunction with any of the
finished works Benjamin was able to bring forward. Yet something crucial in Benjamin's thinking did not simply die with
him in the Pyrenees, but had already perhaps found a certain
fecundity not only in Adorno's program for a "radical natural-
history," but also in the realizations of that program in other
works of the Frankfurt School. But before turning to the idea
of a natural-history and its vicissitudes (which will lead to its
own apparent aporia), we should look at the "Theses," and first
of all in light of its central concepts of "empty homogeneous
time" and "the time of the now."

The "Theses" are not the encoding in theological terms of
a method of secular historiography that would simply revise
Marx's scientific materialism and give it the power, as the
first thesis announces, "to win every time."[6] If anything, they
are methodically antimethodical. They are concerned with the
possibility of the suspension of method, inasmuch as method
already presupposes that which the "Theses" are attempting to
undo: experience as structured by empty homogeneous time. If
method comes from the Greek *met'hodos* and means "the way

through," the "Theses" investigate the way back behind the methodical and methodologizing subject. Empty homogeneous time bears a striking resemblance to, if not complete congruence with Kant's conception of time in the *Critique of Pure Reason,* where time is the aesthetic form for the intuition of an object. Benjamin, although he makes empty homogeneous time negatively fundamental to his opposition to historicism, does not here formally or intensively explicate this concept. Instead, what positive meaning it has in the "Theses" is to be gleaned at once from the aims, methods, and functions employed by historicism as well as from the contrast he is sketching with the experience given to the historical materialist, *bien entendu,* the experience of a "time of the now."

Empty homogeneous time is the subjective condition of an experience in which being appears as a world of distinct and differentiated, but related and synthesizeable or unifiable objects or events which, as such, are susceptible of being organized causally (TPH, 263) and in which therefore each event-object becomes a transition to the next (262). Under the form of empty homogeneity history can and will be grasped by historicism as a continuum, a series in which all objects are like "the beads of a rosary" (263). In a series the object before us is only related to other objects through the relation of posteriority *or* anteriority. Each of the objects is related to all the others, but only by its relative anteriority to some and posteriority to others. Although all the events are strung together and belong to a single continuum, each event can only be related to another in terms of its coming before or coming after. One cannot take one bead to *be* another. The whole rosary, the whole series, is nothing but this sum of discrete entities related to each other through a continuous thread of "a causal connection between various moments in history" (263). Events which are anterior are, from the point of view of those which are posterior, things that do not shift or change or re-arrange themselves in a new configuration. A, which was always A, led to B, which was always B and which led to C, and so on. Thus, historicism orients its task through the premise that "'The truth will not run away from us'" (255). To recognize "the way it really was" becomes the watchword of historical memory (255), which in turn seeks and finds "the 'eternal' image of the past" (255). The past becomes a past-present and historicist historiography "rightly culminates in universal history" which, lacking "theoretical armature" only has an additive method (256).

The historical memory associated with experience structured by empty homogeneous time carries with it, according to Benjamin, a certain specific mood: *acedia,* a sadness or "indolence of the heart" (256) which lies at the origin of historicist empathy. In order to empathize with, and thus fully experience a past-present, historicist historiographers "must blot out everything they know about the later course of history" (TPH, 256). The past-as-eternal, the past fully present requires this mood for its disclosure. And this mood will therefore also imply an empathy with the victors. Blotting out all subsequent history, the past-present appears as "cultural treasures…[which] without exception…have an origin which [the historical materialist] cannot contemplate without horror. They owe their existence not only to the great minds and talents who have created them, but also to the anonymous toil of their contemporaries. There is no document of civilization which is not at the same time a document of barbarism" (256). The fully historicist historian in the "Theses" plays the part of a logical exemplar of the workings of empty homogeneous time in the memory of a subject. But the historian is an ironical exemplar in the conformism he or she actually expresses. Inasmuch as historicists *aim* at leaving their own and all intervening times behind themselves in order to fully absorb and recreate a past present, really there for the re-presentation as an eternal image, they *should not* conform — at least to their own time. But inasmuch as they approach the image of the past as a past present which is an element, a bead, within empty homogeneous time, they constitute an object, a thing, which is complete and finished — a "cultural treasure," a piece of eternity. A historian's conformity is with the very power of victory and the victory of power, the evidence of power maintaining itself in being. A historian's empathy with the victors is not necessarily desired at the start, but something like a necessary structural effect of his imprisonment in the experiential form of empty homogeneous time. Empty homogeneous time is not the effect of the psychological desire to empathize with the victor. Empathy with the victor is the effect of the continuous operation of empty homogeneous time and, of course, of the lack of any reflexive ability to dissolve the latter or break it up.

Now, in the "Theses," the historicism of figures such as Ranke, Gottfried Keller, and Fustel de Coulanges is not Benjamin's only or even principal object of criticism. The principal criticism, along with his unmitigated scorn, is reserved for the conformism of Social Democracy. It is perhaps likely that Benjamin's attention to historicism was partly a warning to himself (and his successors) to avoid the trap of historicism in the search for an alternative to the philosophy of history taken up in Social Democratic theory and practice. Memory is at work in both historicism and in the Social Democratic theories of history as progress, and this memory is structured by empty homogeneous time. Benjamin states, "Social Democratic theory, and even more its practice, have been formed by a conception of progress which did not adhere to reality" (TPH, 260). The individual dogmatic tenets of the belief in progress are, according to Benjamin, open to criticism, but "When the chips are down, criticism must penetrate beyond these predicates and focus on something that they have in common. The concept of the historical progress of mankind cannot be sundered from the concept of its progression through a homogeneous, empty time. A critique of such a progression must be the basis of any criticism of the concept of progress itself" (261). The individual tenets that comprise the doctrine of progress are controversial and can be challenged in one way or another without reaching the doctrine of progress itself. But the *critique* of that concept[7] requires the identification and suspension of the form of empty homogeneous time. The task of the historical materialist will not be the recapture of a past-present à la historicism, as though that were an adequate step beyond all past concepts of and beliefs in progress. Nor will it be the totalization of the objective historical process issuing in a teleological eschatology. Social Democratic notions of progress are already modulations of such beliefs. Messianic redemption operates in history, but much more indirectly, much more quietly than in the majestic and terrible necessities seemingly uncovered in theories of objectively inevitable social transformation.

One might, at this point or on this score, have expected Benjamin, like Levinas, to include Marx among those subscribing to a teleological understanding of history. But there is no mention of Marx as a scientist of revolution, replacing inwardness with the externality of dialectical logic. Instead Marx is curiously enlisted, along with the Spartacists and Blanqui — both of whom from the Social Democratic perspective are at the very antipode to Marx — to indicate the mood that would be fitting for an uncorrupted concept of history. And this mood is variously described as anger, hatred, and vengeance. Marx is enlisted in attributing to the working class the role of "the last enslaved class, as the avenger that completes the task of liberation in the name of generations of the downtrodden" (TPH, 260). In other words, Benjamin says, "The Messiah comes not only as the redeemer, he comes as the subduer of Anti-Christ" (255). The name of Blanqui, moreover, was universally associated with not only conspiratorial coups d'état, but with explosions of anarchical violence. At this point one might be tempted to believe that Benjamin is at best calling down the jealous anger of a vengeful God upon present oppressors — however, the role of vengeance and hatred is actually somewhat different.

If *acedia* is the mood in which the attempt can be made to disclose a past-present, then hatred of what had been done to the dead, remembrance of "enslaved ancestors rather than liberated grandchildren" (TPH, 260) would be that which tears one away from empathy with the victors. It is the mood in which no attempt is needed for the self-disclosure of a *present-past,* since this present is only a past that "flits by" in the "instant when it can be recognized and is never seen again" (255). Without this interruption of the present on its way to the happier future, "even the dead will not be safe from the enemy if he wins. And this enemy has not ceased to be victorious" (255). Horkheimer had once objected emphatically and viscerally to this suggestion that the dead could be redeemed, because once dead they are truly dead — nothing more can be done for them (N, 471).[8] But Horkheimer seems to have been guilty of a certain literalism. The redemption of the dead is their posthumous removal from that homogeneous empty time of universal history (which was never their time to begin with) that is in turn part and parcel of my subjectivity as a progressive being. And we are each and all dead in this sense, as Levinas recognizes, as merely unique moments of the historical totality as opposed to meta-/infrahistorical singularities. The holding on to this memory as it comes of itself is "the attempt made anew ['in every era'] to wrest tradition away from a conformism that is about to overpower it" (TPH, 255). The historical materialist will have the task of brushing "history against the grain" (257) in this sense: not simply in terms of reinserting the losers into the position of eventual victors in a future-present belonging to a process "regarded as irresistible, something that automatically pursued a straight or spiral course" (260); and not, in the manner of historicism, through an empathic leap into the past of the victors. History brushed against the grain does not mean another interpretation of universal history, or a universal history of the victim or other, or the accumulation of tidbits of forgotten lore even if they did belong to the victims, but the continual openness for the recapture of exactly that which universal history as such cannot acknowledge: the absolute meaning in the expression of the hopeful suffering of the past. Benjamin states, "Only that historian will have the gift of fanning the spark of hope in the past who is firmly convinced that even the dead will not be safe" (255). Only a being capable of suffering is capable of hope.

The Social Democratic doctrine of progress has become conformism, a "tool of the ruling classes" (TPH, 255). It is a confirmation of labor as the exploitation of nature (in opposition to nature as the exploitation of labor) insofar as the form of empty homogeneous time underlying the notion of progress makes for the possibility of believing that the working class was "moving with the current," that technological development was "the fall of the stream with which it thought it was moving" (258). *Both* historicism and Social Democracy thus empathize with the victors. The Social Democrats, however, empathize with the future victors rather than the past or present victors. And none of the dead, including all those presently and even potentially alive are safe from that.

If empty homogeneous time were truly a transcendental condition *tout court* of subjective experience, then there could be no hope of redeeming the signification of the hopes of the past, of "fanning the spark of hope in the past," which is the "gift" of the historical materialist (TPH, 255). But there is precisely an inversion of the empty homogeneous time of universal history in the time of the now. The time of the now ought not to be read as an alternative form for the production of the experience of an object via the operations of a transcendental subject. The time of the now lies at the antipode to the idealist subject's temporalization of time. Nor should it be read as a mystical claim to an ineffable knowledge. This is the case even though Benjamin may be borrowing from both Kant and mysticism, dialectically secularizing the latter while simultaneously re-enchanting the former. According to Benjamin, historical materialism is based upon a "constructive principle" (262) and this may lead the reader to infer or assume that the historical materialist is engaged in an act of re-constitution, an alternative interpretation. But such materialists are actually involved in something that is both less and more than re-interpretation. Rather than constituting the object of historical understanding, the historical materialist is allowing that object to, or finding themselves in a situation where that object will, de-constitute them as constitutor. This is because the constructive principle informing the historical materialist is not another thought or, in terms of our rosary, another unifying thread linking events, each of which is a transition, in a causal series which has a beginning, middle, and end, or *eschaton*.

Rather than being the thought of an object like a rosary or one of its beads, the principle in question here, if it can be called that, belongs to a different kind of thought altogether. Benjamin says, "Thinking involves not only the flow of thoughts, but their arrest as well" (262). In the arrest of thoughts — which is still a thinking — there is a "sign of a messianic cessation of happening" (263). Is it the sign or the cessation which is messianic? Or is it both? The arrest of thought is the sign of a messianic cessation of happening. Not entirely unlike the phenomenological bracketing (*epoche* originally means "cessation" and is applied to the flow of categorization), the thinking within the arrest of the flow of thoughts is messianic because it is torn from happening. The arrest of thought is a messianic sign, a trace perhaps, because it awakens the dead to me.

Thus, there is the possibility of an entirely different historiography than that of either historicism or the theories of progress, and which does not belong to the subject both constituting and constituted by or in empty homogeneous time. According to Benjamin, "History is the subject of a structure whose site is not empty homogeneous time, but time filled by the presence of the now" (TPH, 261). Such a time of the now is not the re-presentation of a past as a past-present, but a time in which all time stands still, yet a still-standing which is not eternity, nor an all-knowing vision from the standpoint of eternity: "Historicism gives the 'eternal' image of the past; historical materialism supplies a unique experience with the past" (262). The "unique experience with the past" would be, from our normal third person perspective, that which could only be taking place in the present, or in a later transitional moment of a series — my moment of danger in the present whose causes can be traced to specific past events. What is supplied by historical materialism is the momentary capture of that other now as it comes to me in a time which is filled by its coming to me now. What I am therefore supplied with, what is given to me in the accusative (or perhaps the dative) is a "present which is not a transition" — this present is something a "historical materialist cannot do without" (262). Such a present which is not a transition is not strictly speaking open to conceptualization. It flits by as an image, and as an image cannot, like a concept, be placed within a continuum construable as some sort of logical, inferential chain, whether straight or spiral.

In this passing by of an image in the time of the now the measurable time of the clock is cancelled. The event from the past takes place both then and now: "Thus the calendars do not measure time as clocks do" (261). For in calendars, "basically it is the same day that keeps recurring in the guise of holidays, which are days of remembrance" (261). In the image constructed by the historical materialist out of the flow of such remembrance history *as a continuum* is exploded, its grain is experienced as something perhaps incidental, perhaps inimical to what the wood is all about. That which is re-experienced, which recurs in my memory but which is not the same, is "blasted...out of the continuum of history" (261). In the time of the now the historical materialist will resemble the chronicler "who recites events without distinguishing between major and minor ones," thus "acting in accordance with the following truth: nothing that has ever happened should be regarded as lost for history" (254). Outside of the structure of history as a synthesizable series, the normal criteria of causal relevance to subsequent events would not apply to the giving of some sort of shape to the remembering which is taking place now. Thus, Benjamin will say that "no fact that is a cause is for that very reason historical. It became historical posthumously, as it were, through events that may be separated from it by thousands of years" (263).

The shape that remembrance will assume, a shape which is not a unified construct or, strictly, even the result of a selective principle, is the effect of an arrest of thought itself. Benjamin writes, "Where thinking suddenly stops in a configuration pregnant with tensions, it gives that configuration a shock, by which it crystallizes into a monad. A historical materialist approaches a historical subject only where he encounters it as a monad. In this structure he recognizes the sign of a Messianic cessation of happening, or, put differently, a revolutionary chance in the fight for the oppressed past" (TPH, 262–63). Benjamin will never say that historians initiate an arrest of their own thought, but only that historical materialists do encounter their thought being arrested. The relative pronoun "it" in the first sentence quoted immediately above refers not to the historian as agent, but to the arrest of thought itself. It is the being-arrested that produces the monad, the dialectical image, the constellation that the historical materialist "grasps...which his era has formed with a definite earlier one" (263).

In the monad, which would be from the perspective of empty homogeneous time an "enormous abridgement," the historical materialist "takes cognizance" of a "Messianic cessation of happening" (TPH, 263). This is what allows him or her "to blast a specific era out of the homogeneous course of history — blasting a specific life out of the era or a specific work out of the lifework. As a result of this method the lifework is preserved in this work and at the same time cancelled; in the lifework the era and in the era the entire course of history" (263). What is to be noted about this succession of blasts is that it in fact ends up removing the work from the retrospective synopsis of the homogeneous course of history. The totality or context or horizon that would normally be employed or referred to in order to give the lifework meaning, which would first be the era, is that *from which* the lifework is blasted. The same takes place in the relation of the work to the lifework. No event, whether it is conceived as an atom within the series or whether it is conceived as itself a lesser series within a larger series is any longer meaningful by virtue of its position within the series. Seriality itself will have been interrupted. The upshot is that each work both preserves the lifework and at the same time cancels it. The enormous abridgment that takes place within the monad preserves each event and all of history inasmuch as the beads of the rosary have become unstrung. It is the course of history that gets cancelled, certainly not history itself. The redemptive-messianic act is not the entrance into history of a force alien to it, but the removal of the works of the others from the series that can be strung from beginning-point to end-point through empty homogeneous time; it is their reception as in each case singular, and of having had that singularity forgotten in their presence in a series. History assumes the shape of one single catastrophe in which each work can be read as its allegorical expression.

The standpoint of redemption is the perspective, or nonperspective, or optic of Benjamin's famous angel of history. He says,

> His face is turned toward the past. Where we perceive a chain of events, he sees one single catastrophe which keeps piling wreckage upon wreckage and hurls it in front of his feet. The angel would like to stay, awaken the dead, and make whole what has been smashed. But a storm is blowing from Paradise; it has got caught in his wings with such violence that he can no longer close them. This storm irresistibly propels him into the future to which his back is turned, while the pile of debris before him grows skyward. This storm is what we call progress. (TPH, 257–58)

One of the most compelling things about this image is the powerlessness of the angel. Such powerlessness is not momentary or accidental. Were the storm from Paradise over, the angel might be able to bring his wings together and move or even turn around, but his desire of making whole and awakening the dead would already have been fulfilled. His presence is called for only so long as the catastrophe grows at his feet. The angel does not have to remember. At the angelic level the catastrophe as catastrophe is always before him. But in addition to the angel, Benjamin mentions, as instances of human figures who do not experience time as empty homogeneity several others: the historical materialist, the revolutionary classes, the Jews, and the soothsayers. The first three will have some remembrance of history as a single catastrophe; the last, although they do not experience time as empty and homogeneous are, unlike the angel, turned to the future. Those who "turn to the soothsayers for enlightenment," the seers of the future as present, "succumb to the magic of the future" (TPH, 264). One must imagine that succumbing to the magic of the future means a false enlightenment in which the desire to resurrect the dead is gone and, along with it, awareness of the catastrophe. Those who listen to the soothsayers are ripe for repeating the catastrophe. They cannot even sense the state of emergency that "the tradition of the oppressed" teaches "is not the exception but the rule" (257). They are amazed that things like fascism are still possible in the twentieth century. It is the Jews, "prohibited from investigating the future," who are (theologically) brought into the practice of remembrance (264). It is the historical materialist who has secularized this practice of remembrance. And it is, for Benjamin, the "revolutionary classes at the moment of their action" who have the "awareness that they are about to make the continuum of history explode" (261), as evinced by the following event, an event inside and outside universal history: "In the July revolution an incident occurred which showed this consciousness still alive. On the first evening of fighting it turned out that the clocks in towers were being fired on simultaneously and independently from several places in Paris" (262). Unlike those who succumb to the voice of the soothsayers and the magic of the future, the others will have recognized that "their coming was expected on earth," that, like "every generation," they are endowed with "a weak messianic power" to which the past has "a claim that cannot be settled cheaply" (254).

But the weak messianic power, which for Benjamin includes the power of a remembrance that encounters me, to whose fleeting transit I can only respond with an image, and not the synthetic re-presentation of a past-present is, after all, a *messianic* power. It is not the weakened power of a more-than-human messiah who is in turn (mis-)conceived of as the projection of the power of the human agent. Its messianicity does not lie in any power to command the course of universal history, to return objectivity to its ostensible grounds in the subject. The messianicity in question here is "the retroactive force to call into question every past and present victory of the rulers," a calling into question which is of the essence of what is spiritual in the class struggle: "it is not in the form of spoils that fall to the victor that [spiritual things] make their presence felt in the class struggle. They manifest themselves in this struggle as courage, humor, cunning and fortitude" (TPH, 255). The spiritual things are not manifested as hatred and vengeance. A messianic power, however weak, could only be a power that redeems, the redemptive itself. And it seems that what is redeemed here are three things: first, the works of the past — each and every one — as the expressions of a life, now blasted out of the continuum, a life that always signifies more (or otherwise) than could be known through its location or role in universal history; second, the redemption of the redeemer himself (as a human agent), freed from the illusions of universal history ("from the snares in which the traitors have entrapped them" [258]; from the resurrection of the old Protestant ethic [258]; from the vulgar Marxist conception of labor [259]); third, surprisingly enough, the redemption of happiness. In what way does happiness need and find redemption? In our remembrance, the desire for the happiness of the past other removes happiness from the sphere of envy and selfishness: "The kind of happiness that could arouse envy in us exists only in the air we have breathed, among people we could have talked to, women who could have given themselves to us. In other words, our image of happiness is indissolubly bound up with the image of redemption" (254). Would it be too much to think that it is redemption in these senses that is won every time by the "puppet [that is] called historical materialism," when it enlists the services of a "wizened" and ugly old theology that must "keep out of sight" (253)? The possibilities of redemption strike those who remember (or are brought to remembrance) and in their remembering have responded with a desire to redeem the unheard of appeal of the dead. And redemption strikes the redeemer not by delivering the spoils of victory, but only as detaching the redeemer from the very structure underlying the possibility of universal history.

If at the heart of Levinas's objection to Marx lies the *immanent* criticism that Marx was not sufficiently realist to overcome idealism, then Benjamin's reworking (*umfunktionierung*) of historical materialist historiography had already moved in a strikingly similar direction. Empty homogeneous time, which is also the time for the working through of systems of objective contradictions, is nothing but the temporalization of the idealist subject. The time of the now experienced in remembrance ought to be understood as that "inversion of historical time" which for Levinas "is the essence of interiority" (*TI,* 56). Interiority or radical separation is the condition, above all, for the removal of the subject from his place in the totality and is for Levinas an essential condition of the ethical relation. Redemption, is for Benjamin, also just such a removal for both the dead and their redeemers, the effect of the weak messianic power. For Levinas, "Fate does not precede history; it follows it. Fate is the history of the historiographers, accounts of the survivors, who interpret, that is utilize the works of the dead.... Historiography recounts the way the survivors appropriate the works of the dead wills to themselves; it rests on the usurpation carried out by the conquerors, that is by the survivors; it recounts enslavement, forgetting the life that struggles against slavery" (228). For Levinas, the historiography of the victors, being a universal history constructed out of representations, already constitutes a forgetting inasmuch as forgetting is a function of representation itself: "At the very moment of representation the present is not *marked* by the past but *utilizes* it as a represented and objective element.... Representation is the force of such an illusion.... The positing of a pure present without even tangential ties with time is the marvel of representation. It is a void of time, interpreted as eternity" (125).[9] For Benjamin, the time of the now, unlike idealist time, does not admit of representation, let alone the thematization and theorization that would make progress meaningful. The dialectical image or constellation fashioned by the historiographer is not a representation inasmuch as, *qua* image, it is not itself a concept or a representation of logical (or even illogical) relationships within a system of referentialities. Nor is the dialectical image the symbol of a beyond.

For Levinas, eschatology is able to function as another name for the ethical relation because in the ethical relation history as a whole, as universal history or the history of the totality, is submitted to judgment. For Benjamin, the collapse of empty homogeneous time into the time of the now puts the historical materialist at least for an instant into the position of the angel of history, judging all of history as a catastrophe that demands rescue. The angel, though powerless, desires above all not to remain a bystander. For Levinas, because life is always also *enjoyment* and therefore much more than the cognitive operations of the Same, and even more than a possible future of nonalienated labor which comprises those cognitive operations, each instant is potentially a time of completion: "Torn up from all the implications, from all the prolongations thought offers, all the instants of our life can reach completion, precisely because life dispenses with the intellectual search for the unconditioned" (*TI,* 139). For Benjamin there is a similar completion in the "'time of the now' which is shot through with chips of messianic time" (TPH, 263).

But Benjamin goes farther than Levinas because for him the relationship between history and eschatology has a different structure. Because it has a different structure Benjamin will pursue a historiography that Levinas cannot imagine. Benjamin will at least allow for the bare possibility of a collective action that is in some way the historical de-totalization of universal history. The structure of the relation of history to eschatology that Levinas holds to is also radically novel, compared to the philosophical tradition, in that the eschatological level is maintained within history while remaining eschatological (it does not belong to, but resists the totality). The eschatological is not separated into a beyond, nor is it placed at the end of empty homogeneous time as its telos. Yet the eschatological cannot make any contact with the real society beyond the betrayal of ethics in justice, a betrayal that does not affect totalization as such or alter its course. Eschatology takes place despite history. For Benjamin, the messianic is both at an absolute distance from the real society and operative within it.

Benjamin, in the very brief "Theologico-Political Fragment," again employs the language of theology, but now to sketch the structure of the relation of the messianic to history. Also written quite late in his life, the "Fragment" was considered to be of crucial importance by both Adorno and Scholem.[10] In its exquisitely condensed abstractness it remains in some ways even more hermetic than the "Theses," yet suggests a number of things about the way in which Benjamin was trying to relate history and eschatology. Benjamin begins by separating historical action from the Messiah himself: "Nothing historical can relate itself on its own account to anything messianic. Therefore the Kingdom of God is not the *telos* of the historical dynamic; it cannot be set as a goal…and therefore theocracy has no political…meaning." "The order of the profane" has its own "idea," quite different but not antithetical to the messianic. Yet Benjamin will accept from "the philosophy of history" that this radical separation of the two orders, the messianic and the profane, contains a genuine problem and a genuine relation. He says, "The order of the profane should be erected on the idea of happiness."[11] And the implication is quite clear that the messianic cannot be erected on such an idea. The Messiah quite simply does not strive for happiness, but to redeem, to complete. The messianic addresses a "spiritual *restitutio in integrum,* which introduces immortality."[12] The messianic is not only beyond history, it is a-temporal. Yet the juxtaposition of the profane desire for happiness with the messianic, the way they cross each other, does not pit them against each other. According to Benjamin, this is a problem that can be represented figuratively. If one arrow points to the goal toward which the profane dynamic acts, and the other marks the direction of Messianic intensity, then certainly the quest of free humanity for happiness runs counter to the Messianic direction; but just as a force can, through acting, increase another that is acting in the opposite direction, so the order of the profane assists, through being profane, the coming of the Messianic Kingdom. The profane, therefore although not itself a category of this Kingdom, is a decisive category of its quietest approach.[13]

It might first be noted that Benjamin is all but tacitly making a distinction between a Divine Kingdom and the Messianic Kingdom. He is therefore not reverting to any theocratic or theological politics, but making a claim for a secular and profane redemption. The dynamic of the profane does not bring the Divine Kingdom closer, but only the Messianic one. And the assistance of the profane to the messianic is possible only through a linking of the idea of happiness to the idea of the transient: "For in happiness all that is earthly seeks its downfall, and only in good fortune is its downfall destined to find it."[14] As opposed to the "immediate Messianic intensity of the heart" that "passes through misfortune as suffering," there is (by implication) a mediate messianic intensity, to which "corresponds a worldly restitution that leads to the eternity of downfall, and the rhythm of this eternally transient worldly existence...the rhythm of Messianic nature, is happiness. For nature is Messianic by reason of its eternal and total passing away."[15]

There is far more suggested here than can be briefly, albeit speculatively, unpacked. What is of immediate relevance, however, is the notion, contra the structure Levinas sets up in the relation between history and eschatology, first that the historical may promote the quietest approach of the eschatological; but second, it would do so only insofar as happiness is divorced from the notion of permanence in favor of the downfall of all that is earthly *and* that this downfall and therefore happiness is only to be found in good fortune. Third, nature is taken to be the figure of this eternal and total passing away. Where the "Theses" deal primarily with historiography and the politics of remembrance, the "Fragment" speculates on the possibility of a relation between history and eschatology that involves neither of the alternatives rightly rejected by Levinas. History and eschatology are neither analytically or dialectically related, neither pure opposites, or unifiable through a dialectical synthesis.

Natural-History

Benjamin's suggestions, however, are still quite insufficient to actually effect a rapprochement between Levinas and Marx that would alter both substantially. In these writings Benjamin may have begun to go beyond the more than residual idealism in Marx's concept of history, but problems abound. There are, first of all, the many problems raised by the vague or obscure relation of these programmatic sketches to the rest of Benjamin's achieved and intended work. Certainly, when it comes to the "Theses" there is a fairly clear relation to the planned *Arcades Project,* and also to those various writings that were sketches of it or first drafts of a portion of it. But absent the finished project, it will be forever premature to pronounce with great assurance what was actually going on in the "Theses." Second, and more important, as many Marxists have pointed out, the "Theses" is not very good Marxism, if it is Marxism at all. By itself or even in conjunction with his other works, it is not adequate as a lever to push a de-idealized Marxian conception of history into that realm of realism where it could meet up with the sensibility and responsibility of the Levinasian subject. Rather than attempt to do this by Benjaminian means alone, it will be necessary to pick up one of Benjamin's central threads in the

"Theses" that Adorno picked up a number of years prior to the "Theses," near the beginning of his career in critical theory, and follow that thread through his later elaborations of it, primarily in the section of *Negative Dialectics* entitled "World Spirit and Natural History." This may allow a more clear understanding of how Levinas embroils himself in his peculiar impasse and amphibology, as well as illuminate the possible consequences. That thread is the allegorical one of history as a single catastrophe that can only be understood in terms of a change in perspective that involves thinking in constellations.

In 1931, when "The Idea of Natural History" was published, Adorno had been for perhaps four or five years under the spell of Benjamin's *The Origin of German Tragic Drama,* a work which he considered to be of the highest philosophical significance despite it being a work of literary-critical history, of aesthetics. "The Idea" was, however, more than an attempt to persuade his colleagues in the Institute for Social Research that Benjamin's *Origin* deserved careful consideration. It is also arguably a programmatic essay that in retrospect can be seen to foreshadow the substance and outline of Adorno's career as a philosopher. In it the germs of the *Dialectic of Enlightenment, Negative Dialectics,* and even his unfinished *Aesthetic Theory* are visible. In "The Idea" Benjamin's analysis of allegorical history stands as a clue, and more than a clue, to a program of recasting Marxian historiography as natural history.

Adorno begins from the presumption that current movements of thought, as represented by both the phenomenological movement (after Husserl through Scheler to Heidegger) and the Frankfurt project itself agree in their desire to overcome the "usual antithesis of nature and history" (INH, 111, 116), as inherited from subjective idealism from Kant to the neo-Kantians. It seems to be assumed, and indeed follows from the substance of the article, that the Hegelian route to a dialectical overcoming of this antithesis, itself idealist, is rejected from the outset. Although post-Husserlian phenomenology has moved behind the Husserlian prioritization and foundationalism of epistemology to become once more ontological, the dualism it wants to overcome has ended up repeating itself.[16] The basic idea of phenomenology is fundamentally "paradoxical": "the means with which the attempt is made to establish transsubjective being is none other than the same subjective reason that had earlier erected the infrastructure of critical idealism...an attempt to secure transsubjective being by means of autonomous reason and its language since other means and another language are not available" (112).

The most significant attempt to overcome the dualism remaining in the phenomenological project occurs with the Heidegger of *Being and Time*. Heidegger offers a "correction" of just this still "Platonically ontological" dualism. With Heidegger, "the tension disappears; the existing itself becomes meaning and a grounding of being beyond history is replaced by a project of being as historicity" (INH, 113). By fully renouncing Platonism and by "regarding [being] as life, false stasis and formalism have been eliminated....History itself, in its most extreme agitation, has become the basic ontological structure....This structure is responsible for there being any history in the first place without, however, that which history *is* being set up in opposition to it as a finished, fixed and foreign object" (114). It is difficult not to believe that Adorno takes Heidegger's correction of phenomenology to be of signal importance. The move from transcendental subjectivity to life understood as historicity is not something behind which Adorno and historical materialism would want to move. The problem with this Heideggerian correction of phenomenology is in two intimately related and stubborn inheritances from the very idealism that only seems, therefore, to be corrected.

To begin with, the correction, by its very nature, is too general. The structure of historicity cannot account for the facticity of particular historical occurences. And this amounts to much more than the simple complaint that what Adorno calls neo-ontology cannot generate an empirical historiography, cannot interpret this or that event with sufficient concreteness, although this simple complaint is also true: "All facticity that will not on its own, fit into the ontological project[17] is piled into one category, that of contingency, of the accidental, and this category is absorbed by the project as a determination of the historical" (INH, 115). Furthermore, connected essentially to this loss of particular-historical concreteness is the much more fatal flaw that signals the repetition of idealism within neo-ontology, what Adorno calls the element of tautology. Neo-ontology will always repeat an idealist schema when confronted with "the unreachability of the empirical" (115). It carries with it the implicit claim "that he who combines everything existing under this structure has the right and the power to know adequately the existing in itself and to absorb it into the form" (115–16). Although neo-ontology will have abandoned the notion of a systematic whole in the manner of the Hegelian unfolding of the relation between particularities and the encompassing whole including them, it retains as a characteristic of its idealist starting point, a definition of the whole as a structural unity or totality. That the whole is conceived as rooted in the structure of a historicity that is not reason but nonrational life does not exempt neo-ontology from owing a substantial debt to idealism.[18]

The second idealist element Adorno finds in Heidegger's correction of phenomenology's attempt to undo the dualism of history and nature is what he calls "the emphasis on possibility rather than reality" (INH, 116). In neo-ontology the "project [*Entwurf*] of being at least takes priority over the subsumed facticity" (116). What is repeated here is an antithesis of possibility and reality that echoes the relation Kant construes between "the categorical subjective structure and empirical multiplicity" within the critique of pure reason (116).

Thus, on the one hand, Heidegger has advanced to the point of "radically [demonstrating] the insuperable interwovenness of natural and historical elements" (INH, 117). On the other hand, his tautological tendency, linked as it is to the emphasis of possibility over reality, means that there is a "subsumption of a being that is historical by the subjective category of historicity." (116) What we have is therefore "a new camouflage of the old classical thesis of the identity of subject and object" (116). In neo-ontology, therefore we will find a movement toward "false absolutes" and a "false spiritualism" inasmuch as its camouflaged idealism excludes "natural stasis from the historical dynamic" (emphasis on possibility over reality) and isolates "the historical dynamic from the unsurpassably natural elements in it" (in the notion of a structural unity where the project subsumes all facticity by assigning the unencompassed to the category of contingency, the separation of the merely *existentielle* from the *existential*) (117).[19]

The idea of natural history, in which the duality produced in idealism would be overcome, cannot therefore find its direction from the starting point of neo-ontology or the phenomenology it corrects. As Adorno says, "the starting point itself would have to be revised" (INH, 116). There can be no chance at a solution unless it is possible "to comprehend historical being in its most extreme historical determinacy, where it is most historical, as natural being, or if it were possible to comprehend nature as an historical being where it seems to rest most deeply in itself as nature" (117). Adorno will therefore contrast natural history as a *concrete* unity with both the structural unity of subjective idealism and the systematic unity of objective idealism. Such a concrete unity of nature and history would not be modeled on the "antithesis of possible and real being" (116–17). Such an "ontological reorientation of the philosophy of history" would mean a "retransformation of concrete history into dialectical nature" (117).

It is at this point in the essay that one might have expected Adorno to find natural history already worked out in the philosophy of history of historical materialism, or at least in the latest historical materialism such as that of the very Hegelian Lukács of *History and Class Consciousness,* a work that at the time was in its radical novelty making enormous theoretical waves only seven years after its initial publication. And Adorno, at the close of his essay, even deigns to "submit [himself], so to speak, to the authority of the materialist dialectic. It could be demonstrated that what has been said here is only an interpretation of certain fundamental elements of the materialist dialectic" (INH, 124). Yet Adorno will find the starting point of the idea of natural history neither in Hegel, nor Marx, nor in Hegelian Marxism. He will find it instead in an obscure and failed work not of political economy, historical sociology, or of epistemology and ontology, a work that could not even earn its author a doctoral degree. He will find the idea of a natural history in an allegorical work on all-but-forgotten allegorical dramas. A ruin indeed.

Adorno had begun his essay with "a few words on terminology." He does not intend by "natural-history" anything that has to do with the objects of the natural or mathematical sciences. The sense of both the concepts of history and of nature are "vague" and "preliminary definitions" that in fact will never reach exactness, precisely because the intent is to push "these concepts to a point where they are mediated in their apparent difference." In "standard philosophical terminology," the concept of nature comes closest to that of myth: "what has always been, what as fatefully arranged predetermined being underlies history and appears in history." History, on the other hand, "is characterized by the appearance of the qualitatively new…a movement that does not play out in mere identity" (INH, 111).

The idea of natural history, in a sense that can encompass these preliminary definitions, has only begun to appear at the margins of theory, in works of a historico-philosophical character, themselves "till now above all on aesthetic material" (INH, 117).

The problem of a natural history is outlined by Lukács in his *Theory of the Novel*. The key suggestions for a philosophical solution to this problem Adorno takes from Benjamin's *The Origin of German Tragic Drama*. Benjamin's "decisive turning point in the formulation of the problem of natural-history" (119) will be the staging ground for Adorno's program for "radical natural-historical thought" (121), which will take natural history into a realm much broader than the aesthetic-critical.

Lukács's principle contribution to the formulation of the problem comes from his perception of the nature of second nature. Adorno takes what Lukács portrays as the world of convention to be *both* "a meaningful and a meaningless world" (INH, 117). Like the first nature, the meaningless nature of the natural sciences, the world of second nature, of human constructs, is "'the embodiment of well-known yet meaningless necessities,'" a world which is "'unknowable and ungraspable in its actual substance.'" The world of second nature "'is not mute, corporeal and foreign to the senses like first nature: it is a petrified estranged complex of meanings that is no longer able to awaken inwardness; it is a charnel house of rotted interiorities'" (Lukács, quoted in INH, 118). For Adorno, this conception of second nature already begins to go beyond the idealist conception of second nature in that it does not reduce the externality and objectivity of second nature to the loss of the constitutive activity of the subject. Second nature is instead both meaningful and meaningless: "Natural-history is not a synthesis of natural and historical methods, but a change of perspective" (118).

For Lukács, second nature brings with it the problem of reawakening. It calls for a reawakening, which is for Adorno also "the problem that determines what is here understood by natural-history" (INH, 188). Lukács, however, cannot envision a reawakening except in terms of a "theological resurrection." (118) Lukács's second nature "cannot be decoded, but encounters us as ciphers," whereas for Adorno the first question of the problem of natural-history is "how it is possible to know and interpret this alienated, reified dead world" (118). For idealism, second nature is always to be referred back to the spontaneity of spirit; everything that appears as second nature is interpretable as the first nature of spirit. Benjamin's decisive turning point has to do exactly with this question of interpreting second nature without idealist reduction. Unlike the theological resurrection the early Lukács hoped for, and unlike the idealist translation of divine intervention into the dualism allowing for the prioritization of the spirit, Benjamin "brought the resurrection of second nature out of infinite distance into infinite closeness" (119). Benjamin's turning point does not once again reverse the polarity of nature and history as do both idealism and objectivist materialism with respect to each other. Nature and history are conceived, or rather figured, as *both* polar opposites *and* as expressions of each other. In his deciphering of the apparent ciphers of the allegorical poets of the Baroque, Benjamin recognized that what *they* saw was both nature and history as transience, and that this insight could only be expressed through allegory. For Adorno, "the deepest point where history and nature converge lies precisely in this element of transience" (119). He continues, "According to Benjamin, nature as creation carries the mark of transience. Nature itself is transitory. Thus it includes the element of history" (120). To see, or experience and express nature as transience implies that one is able to see nature as history and history as nature, a concrete unity rather than a systematic (German Idealist) or structural (Heideggerian) totality: "all being or everything existing is to be conceived is to be grasped as the interweaving of historical and natural being" (121).

If attempts at the resurrection of the world of second nature out of infinite distance allies itself with either the theological or the idealist reduction of history and nature to the absolute freedom of spirit, the resurrection or reawakening of that world out of infinite closeness implies an allegorical vision. Infinite distance takes the side of symbolic figuration, which for Adorno and Benjamin is in turn closely allied to the concept. Both symbol and concept are modes of representation, and as representation they identify the disparate. They seek and find identity in a world of timeless freedom. Infinite closeness, on the other hand demands a modality that does not represent. And allegory does not represent but expresses. Adorno wholeheartedly accepts Benjamin's reworking of the allegorical away from being the poor cousin of the symbol, a mere "composite of…adventitious elements," an "accidental sign for an underlying content," an "abstract and accidental presentation of a concept as an image" (119). Instead, the allegorical, the infinite closeness of what presents itself as the dead and alien other, is in fact expression rather than representation. The allegorical sign is itself a constantly shifting expression of permanent transience and transient permanence, unlike the symbol which, if truly symbolic is fully adequate to its referent. In Levinas's terms, the allegorical would paradoxically be the Said Saying Saying itself. And what is expressed or rather that with which the observer is "confronted," according to Benjamin, is "the *facies hippocratica* ["the physiognomy of a person suffering from the worst"][20] of history that, from the beginning has been untimely, sorrowful, unsuccessful…expressed in a face — or rather in a death's head" (Benjamin, quoted in INH, 120). What is expressible, or that which takes place only in allegorical figuration as "signification," according to Adorno, is the absolute presence of transience. Unlike the symbol, allegorical expression or

> "Signification" means that the elements of nature and history are not fused with each other, rather they break apart and interweave at the same time.…All being, or at least all being that has been or become what it is, transforms itself into allegory; in these terms allegory is no longer merely a category of art history.…This allegorical relationship already encompasses the presentiment of a procedure that could succeed in interpreting

concrete history as nature and to make nature dialectical under the aspect of history. (INH, 121)

The interweaving and separation of nature and history that takes place in allegorical expression, or the expression of natural-history in allegory, is therefore for Adorno, the beginnings of a program for radical natural-historic thought in which, however, "*everything existing* transforms itself into ruins and fragments, into just such a charnel house where signification is discovered" (INH, 121; emphasis added). Natural history is a change in perspective radically eschewing the perspective of idealism that nonetheless takes in all of history, but without totalization or reduction. There will be no camouflage of any notion of the identity of subject and object, a philosophy of history that is neither totalization nor absolute flux.[21] At the same time, subject and object are not dissolved either into each other or into a third term. Instead, the first task of the subject will be to hear the object in its signifying.

Adorno will at this point in the essay turn to the first steps he thinks are required to pursue this program, and then rather abruptly break off. Three of these stand out, in terms of his later work. They are, first, the notion of analysis in terms of a constellation; second, the structure of history as thoroughly discontinuous; and third, the "difficult problem" that what is new in history actually presents itself as the archaic (INH, 120–24). We will not outline Adorno's first tentative steps in relation to the latter two features of natural history. But it is worth pausing a moment on his characterization of the constellation, inasmuch as it underlies his procedure in virtually all of his subsequent work, and especially in *Negative Dialectics*. According to Adorno the idea of a natural-history requires a radically different procedure/style/mode of expression than that of traditional philosophy, "an essentially different logical form from that of a scheme of thought based on a project whose foundation is constituted by a general conceptual structure" (120). A radical philosophy of natural-history will thus follow allegorical expression in its distance from the goal of totalizing representation, but it will not dispense with ideas, nor with any and all logic. The ideas of or in a constellation still cohere. Nonetheless the allegorical in the mode of the ideational will not engage in "clarifying concepts out of one another." (120) Nor are these ideas "invariants" in the manner that concepts must be: "the issue is not to define them, rather they gather round a concrete historical facticity that, in the context of these elements, will reveal itself in its uniqueness" (120). It is important in this connection to realize that constellation, like Benjamin's historical materialism is not a method to be applied, although it retrospectively lends itself to proceduralization. But then, everything lends itself retrospectively to proceduralization. Nor is it a method or even something like a procedure that can be applied to all objects or a large class of objects. The constellation is specific to the thinking of natural-history. It would be the unique way in which universal history could be thought, outside all idealism, as natural-history. And the constellation is — as the *thought of* natural-history,[22] as the mode of the reflexivity of natural history itself that does not repeat natural history in the form of projecting a subjectively constituted (even if alienated) second nature — the first moment of an awakening of or from natural-history. It would be a first moment of awakening because it moves beyond (but not behind) the goal of identity inherent in the concept while retaining something of the reflexive distance established in the concept. And, as a nontotality, as the thinking of the fracturing of totality within totality, it would be neither a structural nor systematic unity.

Natural-History and Critique

The constellation became crucially important to Adorno not as a way of replacing identity thinking in general with some new way of thinking in general. It does not supplant science or scientific history. The constellation is called for by any effort to think universal history as natural-history, or to think universal history without recourse to explicit or camouflaged idealism. At the same time, to think universal history as natural-history is also to place all that has occurred within its nonfinal perspective, and in that limited sense to relativize the universal. This would include, to name a few, material events, modes of production, art, science, and philosophy. Yet the idea of natural history is barely suggested in the early essay by that title and, in that essay, its connection with Marx is left more than unclear, despite Adorno's express wish to be able to derive it from Marx's historical materialism. Some thirty years later, however, Adorno returns explicitly to the theme of natural-history in *Negative Dialectics,* taking up once more the thread suggested to him, both early and late, by Benjamin, of history as a single catastrophe that can only be read allegorically. At this point, however, there has been a reckoning, in a sense, with both Benjamin and Marx. Benjaminian allegory will have found a certain correction in a Marxian dialectics stripped of its positive inheritance from absolute idealism. At the same time, the Marxian philosophy of history will have found a correction of its residual idealism precisely through the Benjaminian notion of catastrophic history as natural-history, as the natural-history of the identifying subject, the identifying social subject.[23]

The chapter of *Negative Dialectics* entitled "World Spirit and Natural History" presents itself upon first encounter mostly as another episode in Adorno's ongoing quarrel with Hegel, and with what is unacceptably Hegelian in Marx. And it is also that to be sure. But it can and should be read as a constellation of ideas aiming at a fuller and more developed idea of natural-history.

A Note on Constellations

It is because of the necessity, for Adorno, of presenting natural history in the form of a constellation, which is already tacitly idealized by its straightforward conceptual definition and analysis, that Adorno will need to proceed negatively. The idea of natural-history is in a sense produced privatively from the insufficiencies and contradictions of the other attitudes to or theories of universal history with which Adorno engages in this chapter. At the same time, natural-history is not comprehended, not reduced to a logic whose grasp would allow the autonomous subject in an infinite distance to assert freedom over it. Instead, the understanding of universal history is taken to be its reflected experience as natural history.

Allegory translated into constellation is, for Adorno, a new philosophical language, a language unlike the language of autonomous reason still employed, as the only one available, by phenomenology in its efforts to undo the dualism of nature and history. For Adorno, this language will be the one needed by a consistent materialism to shed its idealist residues. The logic of presentation here (as actually everywhere in Adorno's work) *is* the logic of discovery. Expression and discovery are not neutral with respect to each other. To accept the neutrality of presentation and discovery with respect to each other would already be to subscribe dogmatically to a certain metaphysics. And the logic of the constellation is not the logic of the concept, the logic of intensive definitions and necessary inferences. The logic of the constellation cannot therefore be formalized although it can to an extent be formally metaphorized. But because the constellation is neither pure image nor pure concept, because it is in between both worlds, of both and neither, its logic will not define in order to relate hierarchically and vertically, either arriving at or proceeding by classification; instead it will relate laterally in order to move toward a definition that "will never reach exactness." Constellations are at the antipode to the mathematical, but they are not founded upon simple or pure inductions. They are neither Platonic forms, nor the Hegelian absolute as the synthesis of all syntheses of the negative, nor are they Humean impressions or simply poetic symbols. They are at least intended as the concrete in its transitory voice.

What is related in the constellation is not only the constellation itself to its object, but also the ideas used, the points in the constellation, to each other. They have two axes, as it were, that mediate and effect each other: a vertical axis along which the constellation relates to its object, and a horizontal axis along which the ideas of the constellation, the ideas constellated, relate to one another. But these two axes cross each other at multiple junctions. And if it were possible to map the constellation in three-dimensional space, the two axes would have other lines of possible force that bend and twist each of these axes, lines that were derivable from the tension between the two axes. The ideas of the constellation may be concepts that are interpretable as images, as having more than one knows of the mimetic in them; and they may be images, that have more of the conceptual in them than is traditionally granted. But they are not haphazard, accidental, utterly disparate, arbitrary, or unconnected punctual attempts to get at the object. They cohere. Their coherence gets at the object in and by the relationships among their plural failure to actually reach the object. Each idea of the constellation both succeeds and fails in reaching the object. And each idea illuminates the success and failure of other ideas in the constellation. Also, the tension in relation to one another of the ideas in the constellation discloses something actually *of* the object, and in this way thinking in constellations does not go behind the discovery of intentionality in the phenomenological tradition and reinstitute an epistemological duality of subject and object. But such thinking also does not presume the methodological possibility of an ultimately direct and unmediated contact with the object on the part of an abstract cognitive subject schooled in the methods of the phenomenological reduction. Unlike the fulfillment of phenomenological evidence, a fulfillment still modeled on the apodictic course of conceptual inference, evidence is gained negatively and always imperfectly inasmuch as the noetic-noematic structure is itself always mediated by objective social subjectivity. In the formation of the constellation itself, evidence is gained in the experience of the inadequacy of any one of its ideational points as this inadequacy is mediated by the relative adequacy of the experience contained in the others. Thus, the ideas of the constellation may negate one another and display their own internal dialectic without the possibility of any negation of the negation arriving at a synthesis.

Critique here is not simply or purely immanent critique. Yet neither is it transcendent in the manner of the metaphysical tradition. If one were to search for a neologism for this, perhaps it could be characterized as *subtendant* critique. Thus for Adorno, a negative dialectics is not a *weltanschauung* or a philosophical position to be picked out from among others, but instead "a challenge from below" (*ND,* 303). Yet this challenge is not direct. The challenge from below is mediated through the negations and affirmations traceable among the ideas of the constellation. Constellations will therefore lend themselves to a presentation that appears as aphoristic. But this can be somewhat misleading. If an aphorism is a terse statement of a general idea, then the constellation is not simply a series of aphorisms presenting one general idea or a set of related ideas. It is, instead, a relation among aphoristic presentations that indicate the generality of their plural-collective rather than common idea.

One of the surprisingly obvious consequences of thinking in constellations is that in a sense Adorno will never present any new ideas. The constellation will work with, on and against received ideas, it will work with the language of a tradition against the tradition and from below. The idea of, or in, the constellation then, will be a decipherment of the tradition in its ruins, fragments and pieces, often enough torn from their usual contexts and rubbed against the grain. It will both present allegorically and decipher the allegory it presents. Consequently, in *Negative Dialectics* Adorno will not advance the idea of a natural history (or any other idea) by either defining it or producing a theory of it. Instead he will approach its definition through a sort of second-order operation, working through the relations among other approaches to the idea in question. In its relation to the tradition, negative dialectics is thus both continuous and discontinuous with it.

Universal History as Natural-History

Thinking in constellations in the domain of the philosophy of history requires, then, that Adorno engages with at least a significant range of interlocutors. Adorno's virtual interlocutors here are Hegel, positivism, Marx, Heidegger, and Benjamin. Each will contribute something to the idea of natural-history. Each will also indicate the deficiency or unacknowledged contradiction in one or more of the others' relation to the question of universal history.

Compared to the 1931 article, Adorno's position has changed somewhat. It is no longer a matter of moving abstractly beyond the tradition's duality of nature and history. Adorno will now hold that "the traditional antithesis of nature and history is both true and false — true insofar as it expresses what happened to the natural element; false insofar as, by means of conceptual reconstruction, it apologetically repeats the concealment of history's natural growth by history itself" (*ND,* 358). To the extent that the antithesis is both true and false this implies that the idea of universal history is not something that can either be cast aside as myth or can be accepted as rational and good. The outcome can be summed up in a formula: "Universal history must be construed and denied" (320). All of the ideas constellated in

"World Spirit and Natural History" can be referred back to this formula; each thinker who is brought to bear on the question of universal history will have either construed it, or denied it, or construed and denied it, but to varying degrees of success in its simultaneous construal/denial. Anything less than success in its simultaneous construal and denial will imply, according to Adorno, the re-installation of ideology.

The preponderance of the chapter is devoted to a critique of Hegel, but especially in relation to the positivism or nominalism that has replaced Hegelianism as the dominant theoretical outlook. Hegelian world spirit and the Marxist law of value, which takes up the objectivity of world spirit, are necessary correctives to the individualistic nominalism that straightforwardly denies universal history (*ND*, 324). But their status as correctives can be derived immanently from the truth of positivist nominalism itself. Positivist nominalism will deny the reality of the universal in favor of the reality of the isolated particulars whose unity is always perceived as at least relatively artificial. Thus for nominalism, universal history would be a pernicious myth, "a relic of metaphysical superstition" (319). But for Adorno this equally metaphysical mainstay of bourgeois liberalism is itself a socially necessary semblance. There is no experience of particularity that has not already been predigested and "a true preponderance of the particular would not be attainable except by changing the universal. Installing it [the particular] as purely and simply extant is a complementary ideology. It hides how much of the particular has come to be a function of the universal" (312–13). The apparent substantiality of the particular, the principle of individuation at the social level, along with the individual's narcissistic illusions concerning his ultimate sovereignty (312) are themselves functions of the social process of production. Thus, nominalism undergoes its own dialectic "because in the total functional context which requires the form of individuation, individuals are relegated to being mere executive organs of the universal" (343). The positivist nominalism that denies universal history is inadequate in that the weight of the universal returns behind its back and *inside* the particular. In the world of nominalism, despite the appearance of radical particularity that is supposed to characterize the social, "society and individual harmonize…as nowhere else. With society, ideology has so advanced that it no longer evolves into a socially necessary semblance and thus to an independent form, however brittle. All that it turns into is a form of glue, the false identity of subject and object" (348).

Positivist history, therefore, where the universal is denied, is itself denied or negated by the truncation or damage done to the experience it reports and reproduces. In purely denying the universal it remains under a spell in which ideology is no longer even needed, presupposing, as the latter does, the maintenance of both the reality of universality and a significant distance between subject and object, particular and universal. The particulars, by denying the universal, "on their own, a priori so to speak…act in line with the inevitable." This spell is hardly felt anymore "because hardly anything and hardly anyone escapes it far enough to make the difference show it" (*ND*, 344–45). But in acting in line with the inevitable, the particulars admit their actual universality.

As opposed to positivism, Hegel's philosophy of history expresses the construal of universal history without its denial. To the positivist the Hegelian philosophy of history would appear to be merely the hypostatization of a subjective logic that even fails at being logical. But for Adorno the objectivity of the Hegelian world spirit as the construal of universal history represents what would and should seem real to "an unleashed experience" (*ND*, 300). The universal is real inasmuch as it confronts its particulars as their negation. And its importance lies partially in the fact that it begins from an experience of irrationality, of the noncoincidence of subject and object. Universal history construed is therefore capable of functioning as an ideology rather than as part of the glue that merely asserts and maintains the rationality of the real. Adorno, to be sure, follows Marx who "in a stoutly nominalistic sense" criticized the notion for being an hypostatization and therefore a mystification. But for Adorno, this mystification, although ideological, is not pure illusion, but "equally a distorted sense of the real predominance of the whole... [which] has its empirical content in the heteronomous conditions in which human conditions faded from sight" (304). This, however, is of course not the sense in which it was developed by Hegel. For the latter, world spirit and universal history were to be the process in which universal and particular were to be reconciled in the form of freedom. For Adorno, what Hegel's logic will overlook is the antagonism of the universal and the particular, an antagonism that cannot be overcome by logic, but only by changing the universal into something else.

Adorno will go to some lengths in this chapter to demonstrate immanently the dialectic at work in Hegel's idea of such a reconciliation. Most of the details of this immanent critique do not concern us here, except for one which may be particularly germane to the critical distance Adorno will offer relative to the way Levinas relates ethics to justice, law and the state. The world spirit is read by Adorno (as by many others) as part of Hegel's secularization of theodicy. In Hegel's universal history, Divine omnipotence is transformed into "the principle that posits unity" and teleology, the "world plan," into "the relentlessness of what happens" (*ND,* 305). In doing this Hegel passes beyond a theoretical grasp of the reality of the universal over into ideological affirmation, if not worship of the facticity of social coercive power itself. The particular is identified with the universal, without the recognition that "their totality is their otherness at the same time.... The ideology of the idea's being-in-itself is so powerful because it is the truth, but it is the negative truth. What makes it ideology is its affirmative reversal. Once men have learned about the preponderance of the universal, it is all but inescapable for them to transfigure it into a spirit, as the higher being which they must propitiate. Coercion acquires meaning for them" (*ND,* 315). Hegel, that is, has from the start, as it were, ruled out the possibility of denying universal history. And for Adorno, this shows up most forcefully and immanently in Hegel's philosophy of law where, although it carries "the cult of the world's course to extremes," (309) there is also, by that extremity, a meeting on Hegel's part with the *negativity* of the relation between universal and particular. What Adorno will focus on is what might appear to be merely a slip of the pen in Hegel's assertion of the supremacy of law over conscience in the *Philosophy of Right.* Inside a longer passage which Adorno quotes from that text the following appears: "universality and distinctness — this, the law, is what that feeling that reserves its own discretion, that conscience that makes the right a matter of subjective conviction will *with good reason* consider most hostile to itself. The form of the right as of a duty and a law strikes it as a dead, cold letter and a shackle" (Hegel, quoted in *ND,* 310; emphasis added). Adorno is not concerned here to defend the opposite thesis: that subjective conscience is necessarily higher than the law, although his antinomianism in this section might suggest that.[24] He is, however, concerned to show that the paradox of Hegel's teaching shows through at such a moment, in such a slip of the pen as takes place in the italicized phrase above: that Hegel *is at the same time teaching and disavowing the reconcilement* of conscience and the legal norm. And this is no accidental detail or minor matter but the visible sign of a fundamental fissure in the system as a whole: "Hegel is thus conceding that the reconcilement whose demonstration makes out his philosophy does not take place" (310).

The draw and power of the Hegelian system, its ability to absorb everything into the idealist vortex, is only a proportional function of its ability to claim a certain realism, its recognition of the reality of the negative moment. Were it not at first to articulate negativity, the *opposition* of universal and particular, and do so in the extreme, its ascending reconciliations would simply not matter all that much (*ND,* 330). They would belong to another realm of timeless logic rather than the here and now. Hegelianism would be unable to be a philosophy of history, and it would be unable to construe universal history, that is, to reduce history to the self-realization through time of nature. Adorno astutely notes that for Hegel "contrary to the Kantian *chorismos,* philosophy is not supposed to make itself at home in the universal as a doctrine of forms; it is to penetrate the content itself…and this why in a grandiosely fatal *petitio principii,* reality is so arranged by philosophy that it will yield to the repressive identification with philosophy" (329–30). Everything in absolute idealism rests, in a sense, on its actual ability to demonstrate that the most antithetical opposites are only partial truths, moments of a synthesis whose truth will come to be known and known as already having been known. Thus for Adorno, one of the crucial and most promising characteristics of Hegelian dialectics is the philosophical call for "immersion in detail" (303). Hegel is to be taken seriously inasmuch as he represents, or claims to, a new departure in philosophy, one where it becomes, as Hegel says in the *Phenomenology,* "the science of the experience of consciousness" (307). But not only does the movement of history itself belie reconciliation, in passages such as the one above Hegel himself is driven into the admission of more than the fact that a reconciliation has not yet taken place, but of an irreconcilability. The other side of Hegel to that of phenomenological immersion is the tendency in the execution of his program to get caught in tautology (303).

"Tautology" here comprises more than its formal meaning. It indicates a forceful identification of identity and nonidentity in which negativity returns ever and again behind the back of the synthesis. Even though Adorno grants to Hegel (and to idealism tout court) that *even the particular and not only particularity* cannot be thought without the universal that differentiates the particular, Hegel in the execution of his program has forgotten that the fact that "dialectically one moment needs the other... reduces neither to a *me on*" (*ND,* 328). Were this not the case, were the moments not *also* in a sense each an absolute in their mutual mediation as the negative of one another, then Hegel would have had to stop with "the absolute, ontological validity of the logic of pure noncontradictoriness, which the dialectical demonstration of 'moments' had broken through" (328). Thus, the particular which was to have been grasped forever eludes its concept. Adorno writes, "His logic only deals with particularity, which is already conceptual" (328). In dealing only with the particularity of the particular, there are fatal consequences for a philosophy of history in which the universal is to be construed. Furthermore, "He who was set upon a transition of logic to time is now resigned to timeless logic" (331). Time, therefore, is itself "ontologized" and "turned from a subjective form into a structure of being as such, itself eternal" (331). Ironically like Kant here, Hegel exempts time as an *a priori* from time. Both subjective and objective idealism will agree in this glorification of "time as timeless, history as eternal — all for fear that history might begin" (331). And they will do so because "the basic stratum of both is the subject as a concept, devoid of its temporal content" (331).

Thus, the consistent construal of universal history would result in the impossibility of history itself, inasmuch as a subject actually empty of its temporal content cannot be said to be historical or have a history, and hence not be much of a subject either. Against such forceful identification of the subject, moreover, with what turns out to be its opposite, positivist individualism is right to protest: "the individual, the necessary phenomenon of the essence, the objective tendency, is right to turn against this tendency since he confronts it with its externality and fallibility" (*ND,* 325). Thus, in their one-sided construals and denials of universal history, both Hegel and positivism all but cancel themselves and each other out. But in doing so they nonetheless reveal something about universal history, about its character as natural-history. What they reveal without knowing it is precisely the character of natural-history in which that which is most historic is natural (Hegel) and that which is most natural is history (positivism). Together in the constellation they reveal the falseness of the traditional antithesis of nature and history. But they do not reveal the falseness and the truth of the traditional antithesis. The first important modern effort to do that will be taken up by Marx.

The simultaneous construal and denial of universal history does not have its first beginning with Marx. The theological tradition in the person of Augustine had already wrestled with this problem.[25] But Marx, in secularizing it, begins to bring the problem into its own. According to Adorno, the objectivity of the universal is a characteristic of natural-history and Marx, as opposed to Hegel, knew this "in the context of the universal that is realized over the subjects' heads" (*ND,* 354). Marx, that is, unlike Hegel, understood negativity or antagonism *as* the mediation of the universal with the particular — that is, with the Hegelian particular *as merely the particularity of the particular*. Hegel lacks or denies the sense of the mediation of the mediation of universal and particular by antagonism. With the Hegelian absolute present from the start, all such antagonisms are retrospectively and from the perspective of the totality to be understood as relatively illusory moments in the progress of Absolute Spirit. For Marx the unity of society and of history to this point has not ceased to have been realized through antagonism, the antagonism of the particulars to each other and the antagonism in the relation of the particulars to the whole. The class relationship cannot be understood but in these terms. Marx therefore grasps that the history of the socialization of society is one in which "unity is division" (317). The concept of natural history captures the fact that "history is the unity of continuity and discontinuity. Society stays alive, not despite its antagonism but by means of it: the profit interest and thus the class relationship make up the objective motor of the production process, which the life of all men hangs by" (320). Hegel will therefore become the apologist for, while Marx will be the critic of "the negative supremacy of the concept" (334).

Adorno quotes Marx from volume one of *Capital* to the effect that his theory comprehends "the development of society's economic formation of society as a process of natural history" (*ND*, 354). But it would be a perversion of Marxian motives, like the one performed in the official doctrines of dialectical materialism, "to falsify Marx's polemical concept of natural legality into a scientivistic doctrine of invariants" (355). Drawing upon the newly discovered *Grundrisse,* Adorno holds that there can no longer be any doubt that Marx's "view of natural history was critical in essence" (354). The law of capitalist accumulation is only a natural law "so-called":

> That law is natural because of its inevitable character under the prevailing conditions of production. Ideology is not superimposed as a detachable layer upon the being of society; it is inherent in that being. It [the being of society] rests upon abstraction, which is of the essence of the barter [commodity-exchange] process. Without disregard for living human beings there could be no swapping. What this implies in the real progress of life to this day is the necessity of social semblance. Its core is value as a thing-in-itself, value as 'nature.' The natural growth of capitalist society is real, and at the same time it is that semblance. That the assumption of natural laws is not to be taken *à la lettre* — that least of all is it to be ontologized in the sense of a design, whatever its kind, of so-called 'man' — this is confirmed by the strongest motive behind all Marxist theory: that those laws [of capitalist accumulation] can be abolished. The realm of freedom would no sooner begin than they would cease to apply. (*ND*, 354–55)

Thus, in simultaneously construing and denying universal history, or to the extent that he does so, Marx avoids the fate of Hegel — which is the fate of once more reproducing nature, and therefore history, as fatality (*ND,* 319), the very core of what had been taught by the Western myths of nature (356). According to Adorno, "In the midst of history, Hegel sides with its immutable element, with the ever same identity of the process whose totality is said to bring salvation. Quite unmetaphorically he can be charged with mythologizing history" (356).

But Marx does not only simultaneously construe and deny universal history. He also denies the denial of universal history and thus becomes fated, in a sense, to also construe it once more, in the manner of idealism. Thus, Adorno's critique of Marx converges with that of Levinas: Marx is not realistic enough. According to Adorno, Marx and Engels "whose idealism was hardly anywhere as pronounced as in relation to totality — would have rejected all doubts of the inevitability of totality....Economics is said to come before dominion, which must not be deduced otherwise than economically" (*ND,* 321). Yet the reason for this regression to totalization was a political motive aimed at the avoidance of the retotalization of society that they felt would follow merely political-reformist or doomed anarchistic attempts at revolution. The revolution they desired "was one of economic conditions in society as a whole, in the basic stratum of its self-preservation; it was not revolution as a change in society's political form, in the rules of the game of dominion....Marx and Engels were enemies of utopia for the sake of its realization" (322). They thus turned to the logic of the "accumulated objectivity of what had historically been stronger since time immemorial" (322). In doing so they rejoin Hegel by standing him on his feet: "It was a matter of deifying history, even to the atheistic Hegelians, Marx and Engels. The primacy of economics is to yield historically stringent reasons why the happy end is immanent in history...until the inevitable deliverance from the compulsion of economics" (322). As a result they could not foresee the continuation of domination into the planned economy. And in this way they ironically contributed to the ideology that derives domination from "allegedly inalienable forms of social organization" (322). More than that, even though Marx also "violates the presently universal taboo against doubting production as an end in itself" (307), they partially yielded to the brutality of the logic of productivity: "The unleashing of the productive forces, an act of spirit that controls nature, has an affinity to the violent domination of nature" (306).

Thus in both failing and succeeding in the simultaneous construal and denial of universal history Marx negatively reveals something crucial to the relation between theory and natural-history: "Theory cannot shift the huge weight of historic necessity unless the necessity has been recognized as realized appearance and historic determination is known as a metaphysical accident. Such cognition is frustrated by the metaphysics of history" (*ND,* 323). Natural-history requires thought "to see all nature and whatever would install itself as such, as history, and all history as nature" (359). But even though Adorno does not make it explicit, through the operation of the constellation in his thinking it begins to become clear that Marx's simultaneous success and failure in construing and denying universal history is not due simply to political circumstances (and certainly not simply to a personal flaw), but to the hold that idealism and the principle of identity still exercise over thought.

In his own way Marx, like Hegel — when Marx is like Hegel — brings the dialectic up short. He does so in not also pursuing Hegel's program for immersion in detail, for a science of the experience of consciousness to the point where idealism or identity thinking is itself in ruins. "The immanent critique of dialectics," says Adorno, "explodes Hegelian idealism" (*ND,* 329). But Marx's immanent critique, inasmuch as it reinstalls a metaphysics of history, does not appear to Adorno to carry a sufficient charge. This is because historical materialism in Marx still aims at the universal, whereas the explosion of idealism can be charged only to a thinking that aims at the particular: "Cognition aims at the particular, not at the universal. It seeks its true object in the possible determination of the difference of that particular — even from the universal, which it criticizes as nonetheless inalienable" (329). Adorno therefore brackets the constellation concerning natural history with references once more to Benjamin's program in the preface to the *Origins of German Tragic Drama*. References to this appear both near the beginning and near the end of the chapter in question. Benjamin's purpose there was to oppose the sort of tautology still operating behind Hegel's program, to oppose it with the intent "to save inductive reasoning. When Benjamin writes that the smallest cell of visualized reality outweighs the rest of the world, this line already attests to the self-consciousness of our present state of experience" (303). Although Marx did use Hegel's philosophy of mediation to expose the mediation of the absolute by its own disavowed negativity, and thus open a self-conscious perspective on natural history, he was not yet able to carry through that conception to the limit at which it can truly point to a transcendence of universal history. In other words, Marx had not produced a theory of universal history in which continuing catastrophe was seen, but not seen as carrying inevitability along with it, that is, seen as unnecessary necessity. Marx, via Hegel, is able to correct Benjamin's lack of mediation (or put positively, Benjamin's one-sided denial of universal history). But Benjamin's intent to rescue induction corrects the triumphalist progressivism that issues from Marx's residual idealism.

It is by way of this Benjaminian correction that Adorno proposes to reformulate historical materialism as natural-history: "The world spirit...would have to be defined as permanent catastrophe. Under the all-subjugating identity principle, whatever does not enter into identity, whatever eludes rational planning in the realm of means, turns into frightening retribution for the calamity which identity brought on the nonidentical. There is hardly another way to interpret history philosophically without enchanting it into an idea" (320). Marx, in this respect also still like Hegel, enchanted universal history into an idea. For Adorno, the central cognition of Benjamin's *Origins of German Tragic Drama* once again, as in "The Idea of Natural History," is that "the moment in which nature and history become commensurable with each other is the moment of passing," and thereby "natural history still remains the canon of interpretation for philosophers of history" (359). Any critique worthy of its name must engage in historico-philosophical interpretation inasmuch as "to strike out the latter as a relic of metaphysical superstition would spiritually consolidate pure facticity as the only thing to be known and therefore to be accepted" (319). Grand narratives — if natural or catastrophic history are grand, or narratives — are themselves not the problem. Natural-historical interpretation, however, will interpret without ideational enchantment only by virtue of being able to read its materials as allegorical signs — passing (because virtually interchangeable) traces of something that, because it is finite, passes away. For Adorno, even Hegel's grandest narrative of them all registers this possibility and his last word in this constellation (itself simply a passing convention) concerning World Spirit is this: "No recollection of transcendence is possible any more, save by way of perdition; eternity appears, not as such but diffracted through the most perishable. Where Hegelian metaphysics transfigures the absolute by equating it with the total passing of all finite things, it simultaneously looks a little beyond the mythical spell it captures and reinforces" (360). If, for Adorno, there is an absolute in "the total passing of all finite things" then the passing finite things are not only the particulars of the universal. Natural-history itself is a finite thing and therefore perishable.

Universal and Catastrophic History

We have been pursuing the notion that any rapprochement between Levinas and Marx will have to pass through a fundamental
reworking of the Marxist philosophy of history, bound as it is,
in its resurrection of the idealist subject, to a teleological eschatology in which the radical inwardness of ethical subjectivity is
lost. Levinas shies away from Marx not because he thinks that
liberalism is better, or the last word in historical development
(that would truly be ironic), or that there is some fated movement from Marx to Stalinist totalitarianism, but because Marx
falls short of his own ambition to be realist enough to overcome
idealism. The Marxist philosophy of history recognizes no other
time than the time of universal history, and as a result its time
lacks that memory of interiority, that memory of the human made
of vulnerability and responsibilities, that eschatology which can
submit history as a whole to judgment. Without this memory,
for Levinas, politics and the state would become merely a form
of rational peace, a form uninformed by the ambiguity and
nonfinality of the betrayal of ethics in justice.

Adorno's idea of natural history, on the other hand, indebted
both to Benjamin and to Marx, recognizes a beyond of synchronizable time. Although Adorno does not name it diachrony as
Levinas will, he approaches it negatively in his critique of the
eternalization of time, in his opposition to that exemption of time
from time that even (or especially) absolute idealism does not
fail to repeat. The time of universal history for Adorno, as for
Benjamin, is not final, but a perishable moment of natural-history. Consequently, in the idea of natural-history, the primacy of
universal history is not recognized. In its simultaneous construal
and denial universal history becomes the history of the very
real sacrifice of interiority, in both senses of the genitive "of":
interiority has from time immemorial been sacrificed to the universal; and, the universal itself is based upon the self-sacrifice of

interiority or, in Adorno's terms here, of the particular beyond particularity. It is because the particular is forever beyond particularity and the universal that Adorno will say that "the function of the individual is that of the functionless — of the spirit that does not agree with the universal and is therefore powerless to represent it [as its agent]" (*ND*, 343). Adorno indicates Levinasian interiority, vulnerability, and responsibility by way of a denunciation of its opposite, through the naming of what passes for humanity as reified consciousness, as "coldness." The spell of universal history is perpetuated "as coldness between men, without which the calamity could not recur. Anyone who is not cold, who does not chill himself…must feel condemned" (345). In the essay "Education After Auschwitz" Adorno returns to these linked themes of a reified consciousness and the coldness that it demands. Coldness here, accepted as a potentiality that may be inflicted on the human, is identified as the *sine qua non* of the death camps: "the coldness of the societal monad, the isolated competitor, was the precondition, as indifference to the fate of others, for the fact that only very few people reacted."[26] And the first task of thought is said to be to bring this coldness to a consciousness of itself, to the reasons why it arose.[27] In its functionlessness, the particular will, however, precisely not reinstitute totality: "The instants in which a particular frees itself, without in turn by its own particularity, confining others — these instants are anticipations of the unconfined" (*ND*, 306).

Adorno's particular or individual, or here "spirit" in its very un-Hegelian connotations, converges with Levinas's notion of responsibility, of the social relation as a noninstrumental gratuity, as neither means *nor even end-in-itself*. The very concept of ends becomes for Adorno questionable, implicated as it is in the logic of means, and the possibility of the dissolution of totality for him implies relations that can barely be conceived from within the universal history "leading from the slingshot to the megaton bomb" but not from "savagery to humanitarianism" (320):

> The concept of ends, to which reason rises for the sake of consistent self-preservation, ought to be emancipated from the idol in the mirror. An end would be whatever differs from the subject, which is a means.... The more enhanced the forces of production, the less will the perpetuation of life as an end in itself remain a matter of course. The end, as a prey to nature, *becomes questionable in itself* while the potential of something other is maturing inside it. Life gets ready to become a means for that otherness, however undefined and unknown it may be; yet the heteronomous constitution of life keeps inhibiting it. (*ND*, 349; emphasis added)

With the particular or individual or spirit thus conceived in the originality of his alterity outside reciprocity and symmetry, as called for by Levinas, Adorno will express no ambivalence with regard to the law, as the former does. For Adorno, "Law is the primal phenomenon of irrational rationality...it becomes the myth that survives amidst an only seemingly demythologized mankind" (*ND*, 309). He continues, "In large measure, the law is the medium in which evil wins out on account of its objectivity and acquires the appearance of good...in its extant forms its destructiveness shows undiminished, thanks to the destructive principal of violence. While a lawless society will succumb to pure license, the law in society is a preservative of terror, always ready to resort to terror with the aid of quotable statutes" (309). The idea of natural-history, of universal history as catastrophic history, thus submits history as a whole to judgment rather than judging everything that gets taken up by the universal from the perspective of the whole. And in so doing it rigorously eschews any teleology. Or this means that it understands teleology itself as having natural history as its transcendental condition of possibility. But this does not mean for Adorno, or the rest of the Frankfurt School, that there is not also an eschatology at work within it. The eschatological within universal history operates, however, as the permanent possibility of what can only appear from within that history as the possibility of the beginnings of sudden reversal. For Benjamin this is the awareness that the Messiah might enter at any moment. For Adorno in his construal of the idea of natural history it is the notion that in compressing and splintering the particular, the universal works against itself: "It is not altogether unlikely that the spell is thus breaking itself...total socialization objectively hatches its opposite, and there is no telling yet whether it will be a disaster or a liberation" (346).

Levinas's impasse and the amphibology that issues from it come down to the fact that he denies universal history and only appears to construe it, that is, he construes it as only to be denied. To a significant extent this follows from Levinas's attempt to break out of transcendental phenomenology from the inside, and using its methods. And in the process Levinas, ironically here like Marx, reinstalls a metaphysics of history. For Levinas meaning and freedom in relation to the totality are only to be had in despite of universal history. Levinas, from within the ethical optic, envisions only two alternatives. Either universal history is conceived of and lived as fate or it is denied in an ethical transcendence. In the first case, as fate, it matters little from Levinas's perspective whether the inevitability and necessity of fate is carried by onto-theological or economic-determinist teleologies or by the enrootedness of the subject in bodiliness, in the elements, or in soil and blood. Both will swallow up the unicity of ethical subjectivity. In the second case, where meaning and freedom are recovered in the ethical relation, in fecundity according to *Totality and Infinity,* and in the latter's substitute, "substitution," according to *Otherwise than Being,* that relation is what it is only by virtue of its strictest denial of universal history. But in order to ensure the strictest denial of universal history, while simultaneously preserving the ethical relation from a collapse into merely personal salvation (see *TI*, 305), universal history must be construed as the *antithesis* of ethical subjectivity. In order to ensure the antithesis of universal history and ethical subjectivity, the real society must be construed as necessarily always the same. These antitheticals meet in the impasse of the third, the state and the law where whatever justice there is is both rejected and accepted. Thus, for Levinas, history is a nature to be denied. But it is *not also the case* that nature is a history that is accidental, contingent, and unnecessary. In order to save subjectivity from its ontologization as the particularity of totality, he will reintroduce a metaphysics of history. Levinas will thus tend to rule out from the start any reconception of the real society in which the latter does not meet subjectivity as its negation.

In doing this Levinas ironically also both inverts and follows Heidegger whose atmosphere he would like to leave behind, as much as Adorno would like to do the same. According to Adorno, in Heidegger the "ontological claim to be beyond the divergence of nature and history is surreptitious [*sic*]. A historicity abstracted from historic existence glosses over the painful antithesis of nature and history, an antithesis which equally defies ontologization" (*ND*, 358–59). Levinas certainly recognizes the painful antithesis, but in the process of doing so he simultaneously ontologizes that antithesis.

One of Levinas's greatest philosophical strength here — his commitment to Husserlian phenomenology to the point where its idealism is inverted into what John Drabinski has called a transcendental materialism[28] — is also a methodological trap. Although he is exquisitely aware that "ontological imperialism" is even more visible in phenomenology (*TI*, 44), relentless phenomenological reduction also leads Levinas away from the idea of natural history, an idea of which he is on the edge of being able to be open to, one that could be folded into the "defense of subjectivity" that in *Totality and Infinity* he says he is attempting. In Levinas, the more or less exclusive pursuit of phenomenological method, despite his use of it to de-idealize the subject, also carries forward an idealist mode of understanding concrete subjectivity. The defense of subjectivity threatens to become the defense of an abstract potentiality. According to Adorno, "Man is a result, not an *eidos.*"[29] Although Levinas will grant this crucial point abstractly, the result of his reductions are always *eidetic,* even when they are developed out of the concrete.[30]

Thus, Levinas will tend to leave the transcendental ego of idealism reduced and dependent on the ethical relation, but always intact — once the ego has been aroused in its relations with the absolutely other. And the same is also true of the ontology that he is so much at pains to demote from the status given to it in Western philosophy from Parmenides to Heidegger. Even though the ethical relation itself should be thought of as prior to ontology and history (both ethically and existentially prior) the *thought* of, the recognition of, the priority of the ethical relation to thought and ontology is not prior. For Levinas, all that falls under the category of ontology is judged more or less to be on a par. Nor does the priority of the ethical in relation to ontology necessarily mean that ethical subjectivity ever exists unmediated by the history of the Same. Even if the ethical relation is in some sense an invariant for human history, this does not mean that the Same does not have a history. And to the degree that the Same does have a history, that history is essential to the subject's concrete ethicality. In abstracting methodically from the history of the Same, in treating the real society as essentially the always-the-same, Levinas's denial of universal history all but becomes its own opposite, an acceptance of the Same. "Whatever wants nothing to do with the trajectory of history," says Adorno, "belongs all the more truly to it. History promises no salvation and offers the possibility of hope only to the concept that follows history's path to the very extreme."[31]

Through the ethical optic Levinas is able to see history as a whole as nature. But by remaining purely or strictly phenomenological in his approach — even in his approach to the critique of phenomenology — Levinas does not also simultaneously see nature as history. Partly, there is a justifiable fear at work here, that in seeing nature as history one will end up in a historico-teleological eschatology that reduces the responsibility of subjectivity to the part it plays in the whole. But in not also seeing nature as history, Levinas despite his ambitions to remain above (or beneath) the political-ideological fray, while at the same time profoundly reorienting it, inadvertently opens his thought to ideological appropriation. Levinas does so by seeing both subjectivity and the relation between subjectivity and history as what Adorno calls an invariant. He thus lends credence to the notion (as Marx also did, ironically) that domination can always be derived from some permanent feature of society. In Levinas's case this permanent feature would be the fact of the primary alienation that takes place in works, works that are radically distinct from expression and are therefore "already merchandise" awaiting their assemblage within the totality according to the iron legality of comparison, calculation, and thematization.

For Levinas, not only does the Same eternally remain the same, but *the relation* of the Same to responsibility within the subject remains the same across all of history. But one can even accept that the former proposition is true without subscribing to the latter. Both the ethical relation and its antipode, the Same, can remain the same while their relations are historically mediated. In the context of natural history, this would mean that "along with his functions, the individual's own composition is subject to historical change" (*ND,* 343). For Levinas, the individual is never *only* his inwardness, vulnerability and responsibility. She is always also the Same, living from, (in or as) the body that can, (with) labor and work, (on the basis of) cognition and ontology, (moving through) eros and fecundity. Adornian natural-history would be, in Levinasian terms, the possibility of a history of the relation between the Same and its responsibility to the absolutely other in which that relation would not always necessarily be the same. We have been absorbed thus far in sketching the abstract idea of such a natural history. That idea is concretely executed in a number of other works by Adorno, Horkheimer, Marcuse, and Benjamin to which we now need to turn.

THREE

The Dialectic of Natural History

Ethics and the Crowd: Experience at a Standstill, or Baudelaire

Levinas's thinking, as a philosophy out of the concrete, is certainly not insensitive to what Adorno calls the *micrological*. Time and again Levinas refers to typical yet concrete, small but significant instances of the ethical relation out of which his phenomenological investigation will yield structures that break up and reverse the totalizing operations of the Same, shattering the rigid complacency of the idealist subject. The following frequently noted passage could be taken as a prime example: "It is through the condition of being hostage that there can be in the world pity, compassion, pardon and proximity — even the little there is, even the simple 'after you, sir.' The unconditionality of being hostage is not the limit case of solidarity, but the condition for all solidarity" (*OTB,* 117). Even this minimal act of *politesse* in which I defer to a stranger on a crowded sidewalk, perhaps the smallest possible unit of Desire, bears witness to that radical passivity in which the Infinite passes by, and which, as the very condition of possibility of a totalizing subjectivity, is not mightier than, but still so far beyond the reach of the Same that it carries with it a judgment encompassing universal history.

Levinas will go on to say that all "the transfers of feeling with which the theorists of original war and egoism explain the birth of generosity...would not succeed in being fixed in the ego if it were not with its whole being, or rather with its whole dis-interestedness, subjected not, like matter, to a category, but to the unlimited accusative of persecution" (118). Yet of pity, compassion, pardon, and proximity in the world Levinas will have said, simply, there is little.

This is too simple. The paucity of Desire that "there is" demands an aetiology of the forms of damaged life which take root in natural history. It calls for something like a phenomenological history of the modern subject, one that can diagnose the reification of consciousness reaching its height in modernity, unearthing the conditions of possibility of ethical indifference and anaesthesia. Once more it is Benjamin who offers the Frankfurt School a direction into this critical inquiry. Their inquiries, however, will once again go farther than Benjamin into the socio-historical mediations of Desire and make them more explicit. As Adorno complained often enough, Benjamin's Marxism was lacking precisely in the dialectical mediation of subjectivity and objectivity.

But to get to a sense of what makes Levinas's statement too simple, and of how natural-history will approach the problem of solidarity in the world, we can begin with an examination of the use Benjamin makes of Baudelaire's encounter with the crowd in "On Some Motifs in Baudelaire." In this essay, the subject of which was to be an important part of the *Arcades Project,* Benjamin rubs Baudelaire's work and life against the grain, among other things in order not only to illuminate and condemn a certain "increasing atrophy of experience" (SMB, 159), but also, in the figure of Baudelaire's relation to the crowd, communicate both the difficulty and the imperative of communicating the experience of that atrophy of experience. As the first real poet of modernity, Baudelaire's relation to the crowd already prefigures a "crisis of art" which is part of a crisis in perception itself (187), and therefore by extension a social and ethical crisis.

Levinas's "after you, sir," however small it might be, is a face to face relation. Benjamin will begin from other perceptions of such an encounter. One side of Baudelaire's relation and reaction to the crowd is similar to those of Engels, and of Poe in his story "The Man of the Crowd." Engels' "old-fashioned" reaction to the crowds of London is both aesthetic and moral, revealing, according to Benjamin, not only an "unshakeable moral integrity" but a certain premodern German provincialism: these faces reflect nothing to each other but "'brutal indifference, the unfeeling concentration of each person on his private business'" (Engels, quoted in SMB, 167). Poe's story similarly relays about the crowd "something menacing in the spectacle they presented" (172). According to Benjamin, "Poe's text makes us understand the true connection between wildness and discipline. His pedestrians act as if they had adapted themselves to the machines and could express themselves only automatically. Their behaviour is a reaction to shocks. 'If jostled, they bowed profusely to the jostlers'" (176). After you, sir.

The deference displayed to the passerby who jostles is associated not with my ethical response, but with the truth of the connection between wildness and discipline. Citing Valery, who "had a fine eye for the cluster of symptoms called civilization" (SMB, 174), Benjamin associates the isolation of the man of the crowd with savagery, with wildness. The automatic self-expression, the discipline which is the deference of the crowd to itself, is a function of the isolation of all its members. Inwardness and the social relation disappear together. These men of the crowd — these masses who are precisely not "collectives" or "classes" but "an amorphous crowd of passers-by" (165) — are not the *flâneurs* who, as gentlemen of leisure, precisely did *not* defer, but who, in their glacially relaxed perambulations, at times holding turtles on leashes, (165, n. 6) "demanded elbow room" (172). The composure of the *flâneur* gives way, with the crowd, to manic behavior in the continuous exposure to shock.

Baudelaire, however, is neither a man of the crowd nor is he a *flâneur*. On the one hand he shares a sense of the crowd's "essentially inhuman make-up," on the other, "he becomes their accomplice even as he dissociates himself from them. He becomes deeply involved with them, only to relegate them to oblivion with a single glance of contempt" (SMB, 172). Thus, Baudelaire's relation to the crowd is that of neither Engels nor of Poe. It is ambivalent, a "defensive reaction to their attraction and allure" (166). This defensive reaction, however, is not unconscious, but linked to a studied intent. What allows Baudelaire to become a lyric poet in the age of high capitalism is his intention to be historical and his plan to put the shock experience "at the very centre of his artistic work" (163). But such a project is problematical on several levels. Not only has lyric poetry never before issued from the experience of shock, it is entirely questionable whether it can possibly have "as its basis an experience for which the shock experience has become the norm" (162). Moreover, inasmuch as the poet must have readers, the training that the generalization of the shock experience gives, tends to cancel out a potential readership. Baudelaire is looking to speak to readers for whom "the reading of lyric poetry would present difficulties" because the metropolis of high capitalism has disciplined their tastes to avoid concentration and prefer sensual pleasures (155). He is looking for readers who have been subjected to "a change in the structure of their experience" (156).

But what is *the* shock *experience,* according to Benjamin? It is certainly more than sensitivity to external forces. And shock experience is not simply the "threat" of external energy stimuli that Benjamin notes as being central to Freud's analysis of the function of consciousness as being a protection against stimuli.

In fact, Benjamin makes the threat come from shock, rather than the shock come from a threat (SMB, 161). But Benjamin never defines the nature of the "shock factor" (163) abstractly. It is not that some experiences, belonging to a subcategory of experience in general, are threatening and therefore a shock, nor that experience in general is shocking and therefore a threat. Yet the automatic self-expression of the man of the crowd is clearly some kind of shock defense. In some form of experience, shock and threat are one. The shock experience is not even a function of an intensified rate of stimulation, or even an intensified rate of variability inside an intensified rate of stimulation. Shock experience is, instead, a function of subjective temporalities and allied forms of memory, which in turn are themselves functions of material practices.

The practice to which Benjamin first turns in order to elucidate the nature of the shock experience is the machine-technological practice of high capitalism. Only this practice is not a practice at all. It is instead a drill. In order to evoke, if not define practice, Benjamin emphasizes two terms in a passage from Marx that relate to practice rather than drill: "'each particular area of production finds its appropriate technical form in *experience* and *slowly* perfects it'" (Marx, quoted in SMB, 176; emphases are Benjamin's). It is not accidental or trivial that Benjamin emphasizes these two terms. Practice, in other words, has a rhythm, and a rhythm responsive to the being of that to which the practice relates. Practice is not discipline. In practice, so to speak, works are not "already merchandise." What essentially differentiates drill from practice is not that the former is faster, or even that it makes a harsher demand on the energy of the worker, or even that it is imposed by an external power. What differentiates drill is that it has virtually no rhythm, and therefore cannot qualify as an experience other than shock experience. Quoting again from Marx, this time in relation to the drill imposed by the machine, this is what

Benjamin selects: "with machines, workers learn to co-ordinate 'their own movements with the uniformly constant movement of an automaton'" (175). Uniformly constant movement is not yet a rhythm but the closest possible thing to an absence of rhythm in sound or sense, perhaps at best the degree zero of rhythm. Without rhythm there can be no poetry, or music, no human speech. No expression. Automatic self-expression. In Benjamin's construal of the shock experience, it is worth noting the difference it bears to the theory of alienation. It is not that machine, as an appendage of industrial commodity production, takes the worker's labor power and transforms it into a power over and against him, but that in doing so it begins to rid him of the possibility of that experience which could be the basis of solidarity. Shock experience will not produce solidarity but, eventually, impotent rage.

Baudelaire, however, was only, according to Benjamin, indirectly a student of the machine, in the form of the idler and especially the gambler. Whereas one might expect the gambler to represent a romantic experience outside of the humdrum of bourgeois everyday life, something anarchic, a symbol for a truer experience beyond routine, he in fact denotes the shock experience as well or better than even the unskilled worker "whose work has been sealed off from practice; his experience counts for nothing there" (SMB, 176). In his own quick movement of the hand, the gambler's experience is one of drudgery and futility, capable only of reflex no matter how much agitation he embodies. The drill of attending to "the ivory ball which rolls into the *next* compartment, the *next* card which lies on top" (179) consigns the gambler's experience to what Benjamin calls "time in hell," the "province of those who are not allowed to complete anything they have started" (179), the time of "inability to complete something which is inherent in the activity of a wage slave in a factory" (177). The "starting all over again" that is the "regulative idea" (179) of both gambling and wage-labor inaugurates the time of hell. Such activity, unrelated to experience as it is, does not even embody a wish, which is itself a form of experience.[1] The time of starting all over again belongs to those who "live their lives as automatons and resemble Bergson's fictitious characters who have completely liquidated their memories" (178).

The endless repetition of starting all over again in sympathetic adaptation to a uniform constant movement is an inexorable training, at the level of perception, in voluntary memory. It is also a simultaneous shrinkage of that involuntary memory without which experience atrophies, and along with it, not only lyric poetry but the possibilities of narration, of storytelling, and of the counsel and wisdom that the latter had woven into the fabric of tradition. In voluntary memory external impressions (stimuli as shocks in the objective sense of the term) are precisely registered as to time and place. Impressions are *defended against* by being screened, thus fixed as instances already predetermined in a schematism. Screened experiences are completely in line with empty homogeneous time. They belong to that limited area of experience (*Erlebnis*) where one is concerned with being able to start all over again. Voluntary memory is "an achievement of the intellect," a function of consciousness which is the more efficient "the less impressions enter into experience (*Erfahrung*)," but instead tend "to remain in the sphere of a certain hour of one's life" (SMB, 163). The shock defense of screening belongs to memory (*Errinerung*), as distinct from remembrance (*Gedächtnis*). Benjamin quotes Reik, wherein the function of memory is the disintegration of impressions, their destruction, while "'The function of remembrance...is the protection of impressions,'" their conservation (160). Freud's fundamental thought on the issue is that "'becoming conscious and leaving behind a memory trace are processes incompatible with each other within one and the same system'" (Freud, quoted in SMB, 160). The term "involuntary memory," however, belongs to Proust, and is in fact Proust's substitute for Bergson's "pure memory," which the latter thought of as available to the intellect but which Proust did not, consigning it instead to accident, and placing it in the realm of haphazard sensuous contact (158). But this does not mean that in either Proust's or Benjamin's usage, involuntary memory is to be identified with Freud's unconscious or dynamically repressed memory.

Voluntary memory or screening, according to Benjamin, takes place "at the cost of the integrity of its contents" of experience (SMB, 163). With involuntary memory, it is not as though the impressions are not met by the subject, but rather than being screened, they are "parried": "That the shock is thus cushioned, parried by consciousness, would lend the incident that occasions it the character of having been lived in the strict sense. If it were incorporated directly in the registry of conscious memory, it would sterilize this incident for poetic experience" (162). Drill makes use of voluntary memory; practice depends on involuntary memory. The "after you, Sir" of the man of the crowd is drill making use of voluntary memory. The interlocutor is screened by an intellectual achievement that actually destroys him for me. He has not been part of my experience. He has not left a (memory) trace.

The practice with which Benjamin is most centrally concerned in this essay, and in its companion "The Storyteller" (1936), is not lyric poetry per se. Baudelaire's lyric poetry, it turns out, belongs to the story of the demise of the story and in a certain sense tells that story, when rubbed against the grain. Proust, who figures large in the essay on Baudelaire, endures Herculean labors in the production of his eight volume work which was an effort to "restore the figure of the storyteller" (SMB, 159) in an attempt "to produce experience synthetically, as Bergson imagines it, under today's conditions" (157). And, for Benjamin at least, Bergson's conception of the nature of experience in the *durée,* that is undenatured experience, implies that "only a poet can be the adequate subject of such an experience" (157). Poet and storyteller merge in their relation to involuntary memory, which lies at the basis of both. Baudelaire "made it his business to parry the shocks, no matter where they might come from" (163), not to screen them.

The story, storytelling, narrative, and experience are for Benjamin involved in an infinite loop, a virtuous circle. They appear and disappear together. Experience (*Erfahrung*) is the source of the story (S, 84) and the story is the passing on of experience (SMB, 159). In the story, what is passed on is not simply information which has as its "prime requirement" that it "appear understandable in itself" (S, 89). The story, unlike information, "does not aim to convey the pure essence of the thing" (91). The newspaper brings us information every day from across the globe, but always already "shot through with explanation," whereas the story requires that it be left up to the listener to interpret and that it be "kept free from explanation" (89). Newspapers have it as their aim "to isolate what happens from the realm in which it could affect the experience of the reader" (SMB, 158–59). The story "requires a state of relaxation which is becoming rarer and rarer" (S, 91) inasmuch as, to cite Valéry again, "'the time is past in which time did not matter'" (93). The story as practice performs the *slow perfection* of one's relation to the contents of experience conserved by involuntary memory. Thus, rather than conveying information, storytelling is useful because it has "counsel" (86). And counsel is not the answer to a question, but "a proposal concerning the continuation of a story which is just unfolding" (86). The story presupposes, then, a community of listeners (91) and a community of tellers who are in an assymetrical relation, in and out of phase with each other at the same time, insofar as "to seek this counsel one would first have to be able to tell the story" (86). Because the orientation of the story is toward counsel over something practical, it aspires to wisdom, which is "counsel woven into the fabric of real life" (86–87). One can begin to see the organic connection that Benjamin frequently invokes among experience, memory, and narrative gradually accreting and agglutinating into tradition and ritual. Thus, in "On Some Motifs in Baudelaire," against Proust's reliance on individual accidents of sense objects opening the doors of involuntary memory, Benjamin will mention that involvement in rituals and festivals,[2] which can be taken to be the sedimented issue of countless stories told and retold, and in which the contents of the individual past merge with those of the collective past, to allow "voluntary and involuntary recollection [to] lose their mutual exclusiveness" (SMB, 159–60).

But in the crowd, as in uniform constant movement, there are no rituals or festivals: "The man who loses his experience feels as though he is dropped from the calendar. The big city dweller knows this feeling on Sundays" (SMB, 184). The atrophy of experience is the loss of the time for and therefore the (non-)time of involuntary memory, together with its dissociation from the voluntary. This has enormous and terrible consequences precisely in the realm of expression, in which we might include both art and the "after you, Sir," inasmuch as both will depend on the *aura*. According to Benjamin in this essay[3] the aura can be designated as "the associations which, at home in the *mémoire involuntaire,* tend to cluster around the object of a perception...[and] its analogue in the case of a utilitarian object is the experience which has left traces of the practiced hand" (186). Art that bears an aura to the observer is an object unique among objects, to the extent that it both affirms and defeats its status as an object: "The painting we look at reflects back at us that of which our eyes will never have their fill. What it contains that fulfills the original desire would be the very same stuff on which the desire continuously feeds" (187). Once more citing Valéry, Benjamin agrees to the following: "We recognize a work of art by the fact that no idea it inspires in us, no mode of behaviour that it suggests we adopt could exhaust it or dispose of it. We may inhale the smell of a flower...it is impossible to rid ourselves of the fragrance by which our senses have been aroused, and no recollection, no thought, no mode of behaviour can obliterate its effect or release us from the hold it has on us. He who has set himself the task of creating a work of art aims at the same effect" (Valéry, quoted in SMB, 186–87). The temporality of involuntary memory is at work here precisely in its conservative function, in its preservation of the endless stream of not yet screened and organized events for which the term "sense impressions" is a truncated overidentification. Thus, involuntary memory preserves a past that can never become fully present without destroying that which it brings forth. And the successful auratic work of art conjures up the beautiful "out of the womb of time" (187). It is the "image of the past" (187), not the historical past, but the remembrance of "pre-history" (182) that "prevents our delight in the beautiful from ever being satisfied" (187).

It is no accident that Benjamin's description of the aura of the art object recalls many of the very terms that Levinas uses to demarcate the human-ethical relation in its relation to the Same and totality, terms such as height, Desire, transcendence, asymmetry, and holiness; even the diachrony of sensibility and being hostage. This is because Benjamin himself sees the aura, and art, as a transposed memory of what is particularly a human relationship:

> The camera records our likeness without returning our gaze. But looking at someone carries the implicit expectation that our look will be returned by the object of our gaze. Where this expectation is met...there is an experience of the aura to the fullest extent.... Experience of the aura thus rests on the transposition of a response common in human relationships to the relationship between the inanimate or natural object and man.... To perceive

> the aura of an object we look at means to invest it with the ability to look at us in return. This experience corresponds to the data of *mémoire involuntaire*. (SMB, 188)

But what makes itself "felt" in Baudelaire's lyric poetry is the "disintegration of the aura" (SMB, 189).

It is no simple task to auratically express and convey the disintegration of aura to an audience dissociated from and unpracticed in involuntary memory. Baudelaire "describes eyes of which one is inclined to say that they have lost their ability to look" (SMB, 189). Such eyes, according to Benjamin, have a "smooth stare" and a "mirrorlike blankness" that displays "remoteness" rather than the "distance" from which a look back can be sensed (190). Such eyes are the eyes in the big city crowd (190–91). Yet what can be conveyed, though not necessarily received, or perhaps received only much later, like a message in a bottle, is, at this, Beaudelaire's point in time, the sense of expectation of the return of a gaze that could have been met but cannot be met. Thus, of all of Baudelaire's poems Benjamin devotes most attention to the sonnet "A une passante." This is his characterization of the poem:

> Mysteriously and mutely born along by the crowd, an unknown woman comes into the poet's field of vision. What this sonnet communicates is simply this: Far from experiencing the crowd as an opposed, antagonistic element, this very crowd brings to the city dweller the figure that fascinates. The delight of the urban poet is love — not at first sight, but at last sight. It is a farewell forever which coincides in the poem with the moment of enchantment. Thus the poem supplies the figure of shock, indeed of catastrophe. But the nature of the poet's emotions has been affected as well. What makes his body contract in a tremor... is not the rapture of a man whose every fiber is suffused with *eros;* it is, rather, like the kind of sexual shock that can beset a lonely man.... [These verses] reveal the stigmata which life in a metropolis inflicts upon love. (SMB, 169)

What Baudelaire as a man in but not quite of the crowd experiences as a sensation, is the shock of shock experience. And this is what permits Baudelaire the poet to convey the story of catastrophe. The aura appears here in its disappearance, negatively. But this is a story of catastrophe that is without counsel, a story, if there can be one, of desolation. The figure of desolation appears again, according to Benjamin, in a line from one of Baudelaire's *Spleen* poems from *Les Fleurs du Mâl:* "Le Printemps adorable a perdu son odeur." To Benjamin this expresses something extreme "with extreme discretion": "A scent may drown years in the odor it recalls. This gives a sense of measureless desolation to Baudelaire's verse. For someone who is past experiencing, there is no consolation. Yet it is this very inability to experience that lies at the heart of rage" (SMB, 184). According to Benjamin, Baudelaire paid a high price for bringing modernity and lyric poetry together. Not of the crowd, but drawn to it in its midst, he battled it "with the impotent rage of someone fighting the rain or the wind. This is the nature of something lived through (*Erlebnis*) to which Baudelaire has given the weight of experience (*Erfahrung*). He indicated the price for which the sensation of the modern may be had: the disintegration of the aura in the experience of shock. He paid dearly for this disintegration — but it is the law of his poetry" (194).

A good part of Benjamin's fascination with and shadowing of Baudelaire in the crowd lies in the way the latter is understood as an allegory for the catastrophic atrophy of experience in the modern world. And Benjamin makes it almost clear that it is a specifically capitalist modernity. And one of the things that makes Baudelaire so interesting is that unlike "Bergson the metaphysician" (SMB, 185), Baudelaire the poet was not "estranged from history" (185). Bergson "rejects any historical determination of memory" and himself shuts out the experience of large scale industrialism from which his own philosophy evolved (157). Baudelaire's superiority in this regard had also to do with his own sense of the "spleen time" which, for whatever it means,[4] indicated to Benjamin a "supernaturally keen" (184) perception of a time outside history, like that of involuntary memory, but one which "exposes the passing moment in all its nakedness. To his horror, the melancholy man sees the earth revert to a mere state of nature. No breath of prehistory surrounds it. There is no aura" (185). In comparison with Baudelaire's sense of history from out of spleen, Bergson's *durée,* "from which death has been eliminated, has the miserable endlessness of a scroll" (185). Although Levinas certainly does not eliminate death from the sense of time, and although neither diachrony nor fecundity have the miserable endlessness of a scroll, Levinas, like Bergson in this respect, does not allow for the historical determination of experience.

Natural History as One-Dimensional Experience

Levinas tends to think of experience in terms held over from dualism. He writes, "The relation with infinity will have to be stated in terms other than those of objective experience; but if experience precisely means a relation with the absolutely other...the relation with infinity accomplishes experience in the fullest sense of the word" (*TI,* 25). Either experience involves intentionality, in which thought remains adequation with the object, or, at a level of subjectivity more fundamental than intentionality, experience is that nonadequation which is the "common source of both activity and theory" (27). Or, as he puts it in *Otherwise than Being,* "Ethics is the breakup of transcendental apperception, that is, it is the beyond of experience" (*OTB,* 148). In dividing experience, usually quite strictly, into the ethical experience on the one hand, and the experience of ontology on the other, even though in some sense the latter is dependent on the former, Levinas will have methodologically abstracted from those realms, levels, or domains of experience in which there might have been something like the experience of the breakup of experience, the conscious or barely conscious afterimage of what Benjamin calls the aura or prehistory. Yet it is in this grey area, which is the domain of natural history, that totalization will forever recommence. By pursuing his analysis as though experience were either the one or the other Levinas will have systematically occluded the possibilities of any analysis of their relation that goes beyond the quasi-transcendental reduction of ontology to ethics. It could perhaps be argued that there is no other way to avoid the ontological misunderstanding of ethics attested to in the history of the philosophy of the West than to focus exclusively on "the difference between objectivity and transcendence" that Levinas attests "will serve as a general guideline for all of the analysis" in *Totality and Infinity* (49). Nonetheless, Levinas himself will recognize, if only tacitly, that this grey area not only exists, but is essential to the possibility of freedom, and of freedom in neither simply the senses of negative or positive freedoms, but of finite or created freedom as well. Thus, in "Freedom and Command" (1953) Levinas will describe the phenomenon of a "servile soul": "That one can create a servile soul is not only the most powerful experience of modern man, but perhaps the very refutation of human freedom." He continues that such a soul, a "true heteronomy, begins when obedience ceases to be obedient consciousness and becomes an inclination. The supreme violence is in that supreme gentleness.... The love for the master fills the soul to such an extent that the soul no longer takes its distances."[5] Rather than look, however, at the history of such servility, Levinas's concern will be to display and locate the "pacific opposition" of the face, "what resists me by its opposition and not what is opposed to me by its resistance"[6] as the ultimate source of any rational discourse which could support and legitimate a rational peace.[7]

Levinas's dilemma, which keeps recreating the impasse of liberalism, thus bypasses the realm of reduced experience, of damaged life, which is neither the pure breakup of totality in the ethical revelation of the face nor the triumphant (Hegel) or humble (Heidegger) march of ontology through the world. And this despite his apparent sensitivity at times to the existence of the historical determination of experience. Benjamin, on the other hand, although he is concerned with an archaeology of reduced experience, the unearthing of those layers of memory, perception, and expression whose atrophy, or its alternative, is a matter of historical determination, is like Baudelaire in expressing something extreme with extreme discretion. The something extreme that Benjamin barely names is the measureless desolation and rage of being past experience, and being past experience is exactly the experience of what Levinas might call the servile soul who is neither subject *to* the opposition of the face, nor the subject *of* labor, thought, expression, ontology, or even eros.

For the Frankfurt School, following and expanding upon Benjamin, but for whom Benjamin's discretion is too extreme, the experience of the breakup of totality is at a standstill. The historical determination of experience has arrived at a point where increasingly the soul cannot, as Levinas says, "take its distances," but paradoxically, only because the soul as free and rational subject has evolved to aspire to and claim absolute distance. Lacking in distance from the totality, it seems not only subject to intensified servility, but equally unable to generate solidarity. Marcuse, who supplies probably the most multilayered single account of the standstill of the breakup of totality in his natural history of the then present moment of "advanced industrial society," formulates this condition of "paralysis" as "one-dimensionality": "There is only one dimension, and it is everywhere and in all forms" (*ODM,* 10). The loss of multidimensionality is not only in the loss of the distinction between potentiality and actuality, a loss that occurs in many domains and at many levels of experience and thought, it is also, although he does not use the same terms as Levinas, a loss of "height," of the ethical relation. The Happy Consciousness prevails when the real is taken as the rational. The apparatus assumes the role of a moral agent. Conscience does not actually up and disappear, but lives, one is tempted to say, a sort of half-life or mere life. The call it still might hear is one from which it is effectively absolved by reification, by the general necessity of things (79). The Happy Consciousness, in combination with the assurance that things could not be essentially otherwise, facilitates acceptance of the misdeeds of this society (76). It is perhaps important, then, at least from the start not to presume that the denunciation of one-dimensionality takes place from a vantage point that simply invokes the potentiality of undeveloped capabilities. The need to be otherwise, or its absence, may have something essential to do with the (im-)possibility of an otherwise than being.

But it is precisely the achievement of capitalist society a century after Baudelaire confronted it in the crowd to have reduced experience to the point that not only otherwise than being but even being otherwise appears to be irrational. The whole of advanced industrial society appears to be the very embodiment of reason, yet this society is irrational as a whole (*ODM,* ix). The uniform constant motion of the machine has expanded to fill ever more of the space of interiority. Aside from its transformation of the essential modalities of social control, its distinctive features are its "need for the production and consumption of waste," its need for "stupefying" and unnecessary work, its need for forms of relaxation that prolong stupefying and unnecessary work and the maintenance of "deceptive liberties" (7). The power of advanced industrial society is great enough to make the "notion of alienation questionable" because "people recognize themselves in their commodities" (9). The distance of the soul from commodity fetishism shrinks. The commodity fetish cannot be experienced as a loss of self. The notion of the introjection of a superior power once different and opposed to the individual would then be outdated, to the extent that any interior private space has been absorbed. As with Adorno's sense of the spell becoming a form of glue, "The result is, not [the] adjustment" of the once-rebellious subject, but "an immediate identification of the individual with his society," a kind of "mimesis" (10). In other words, Levinas's "servile soul" now understood as the freedom created by late capitalism.

"All liberation," according to Marcuse, "depends upon a consciousness of servitude" (*ODM,* 7), and *a fortiori* an experience of servitude. Yet this experience is, in advanced industrial society, exactly what is blocked. Rather than social control being imposed through terror and justified by ideology, it is accomplished by overwhelming efficiency and ever-increasing satisfaction of certain ever-increasing needs. Its "most singular achievement" is to deprive critique of its basis in the experience of servitude (xii). Critique, when it manages to exist and be disseminated, plunges into a void of incomprehension and dismissal. And that it often does manage to exist does not alter the equation. All kinds of "transcending" and "protesting" deviations abound, yet they amount to "the ceremonial part of practical behaviorism" (14). Critical deviations lend credence to the idea of the continued existence and even spread of the old bourgeois freedoms (and today to the slow march of "human rights" across the globe on the heels of either oppressive neo-liberal trade regimes or the exportation of "freedom" through war, or both), but these freedoms lose their critical functions (7).[8] Even though the distinction between true and false consciousness, or as Levinas would put it, the distinction between truth and ideology, remains meaningful, such a distinction can be validated only to the extent that the nonsubjects of advanced industrial society live *in need* of changing their way of life, of refusing and denying the positive (xiii–xiv, 48–49).

The historical determination of experience will undercut both the consciousness of servitude and the need for its transcendence when the political needs of social domination have become the needs and aspirations of individuals. According to Marcuse, "The most effective and enduring form of warfare against liberation is the implanting of material and intellectual needs that perpetuate obsolete forms of the struggle for existence" (*ODM,* 4). Thus, at least to the extent that human needs are historical, and to the extent that possibilities exist for the "pacification of the struggle for existence" (227), a struggle within and among humans as well as between humans and nonhuman nature, it is possible to distinguish between true and false needs. At *any given* historical point in time, false needs are those that "perpetuate toil, aggressiveness, misery, and injustice" beyond what is imposed by external necessity (5). This is not a quantitative distinction, or a distinction between greed and abnegation. It is not as though in the past true needs were experienced because of absolute scarcity, but that with the technological plenty of advanced industrial society an absolute threshold was superceded by an extra margin of false needs. It is not as though true needs are first satisfied before false needs are generated. A false need is not a need for too much and a true need is not a need for just enough. All, or virtually all societies will have experienced both, to the extent that they were not capable of organizing and disposing of all their material, intellectual, organizational, and affective (or one might say spiritual) resources to minimize toil, aggressiveness, misery, and injustice.

According to Marcuse, "For any *consciousness and conscience, for any experience* which does not accept the prevailing societal interest as the supreme law of thought and behavior, the established universe of needs and satisfactions is a fact to be questioned…in terms of truth and falsehood" (5–6; emphasis added). Thus, the distinction between true and false needs, the absence of the experience of which would be the lynchpin of one-dimensional servitude, is fundamentally an ethical, and not an economic or even strictly political distinction. Marcuse makes this somewhat clearer later in *ODM* in his discussion of possible criteria for the "truth value of different historical projects" (219), by which he aims to distinguish the critical theory of society from historicist relativisms. A better historical project would be one not validated by success, (223) but one which offers greater hope for the pacification of existence in institutions that offer a better chance for the free development of human needs and faculties. For Marcuse, the very concept of reason originates in this "value judgement" (217–20). In a muted and still obscure way, it seems that for Marcuse ethics is first philosophy.

Thus, the "most vexing thing" about advanced industrial society is not its irrationality, but the *rationality* of its irrationality. In meeting true needs it simultaneously creates false ones on an ever expanding relative scale (9). And in "preconditioning" the subject to lose the distinction between the given and the possible, its transplantation of the societal needs required by domination into individual needs is so powerful "that the difference between them seems to be purely theoretical" (8). Thus, if there are true needs (the ethical need to reduce toil, aggressiveness, misery, and injustice), and if the distinction between the given and the possible is needed to experience such needs, and if that distinction is becoming increasingly difficult to maintain, or if, in other words, the possible is more and more the replication and repetition of the given, and — finally — if rationality has something to do with the meeting of needs, then the meeting of given needs is both rational and irrational. Or, according to Marcuse, "modern industrial society is the pervasive identity of...opposites. It is the whole that is in question" (xiv). Natural history is just such a pervasive identity of opposites.

The problem of false needs, then, does not originate as an individual-psychological problem, or even as an individual-ethical problem. It is instead an *ethical systemic problem* informing the totality. And the problem is not that the totality is riven by contradictions displaying its irrationality, but that it is in fact not fractured by its latent contradictions. Thus, one-dimensional society dissimulates both the presence *and* the absence of an outside or beyond. There appears to be a beyond, but it is the same. In the classical Marxian conception of qualitative social change, this outside or beyond was, as a beyond, inside the totality in the form of the objective and subjective alienation, and resistance to that alienation on the part of the working classes (*ODM,* 23, 100). But the historical determination of experience has caught up with and surpassed those contradictions.

This form of subalienation is traceable not at all simply to a rising standard of consumption (or as he puts it somewhere, a "high level of servitude") or to the penetration of the spheres of leisure and culture by the commodity form, although these are important features of advanced industrial society. Those features, as moments of mimetic identification, of Adorno's "glue," find their basis, however, in what Marcuse calls the new technological work world. The intensification and penetration of the uniform constant movement of the machine also means the reduction in the amount and intensity of physical labor. Mental fatigue and performance anxiety replace physical exhaustion while human beings as the indispensable bearers of tools disappear. Along with technologization of the productive apparatus comes an assimilating trend in occupational stratification that moves toward a cancellation of the Marxian notion of the organic composition of capital. As this progresses, it becomes increasingly difficult to refer the extraction of surplus value and its measurement to living human labor. The relative quantification of individual output becomes impossible.

The weakening of the negative position of the working class, its social and cultural integration into capitalism, is not then simply a change in consciousness. It is not a new interpretation of an old condition, but a change in the condition itself, in societal existence, in the being that determines thought. On the other side of the equation, domination is increasingly translated into administration. No longer a dialectical relation between master and slave, the administered world becomes a vicious circle that encloses both (*ODM,* 24–33). In this respect, Levinas's notion of a servile soul does not go far enough, inasmuch as it still refers to the servant's love of the master, rather than the love of the administered for their own administration, or for the power and rationality of administration per se. In Levinas's terms, the sacred absorbs into itself whatever traces of the holy it might ever have sheltered.

The administered world, however, is not the result of the corruption of the administered or even the administrators, who are also administered (48). Its state of unfreedom *proves* itself to be rational, continuously and tangibly demonstrates its reasonableness, in the possibility of realizing its possibilities, in the comfort and even the goodness of the life provided to those who do not refuse it (49). And how can it be refused when to refuse appears to go against the whole, against society and reason itself? Would that not be immoral? Actually to refuse it would mean to negate reality itself, not only one's own self-preservation, but the preservation of all. Yet this would be precisely what Marcuse recognizes as a "Great Refusal," the "protest against that which is" (63). It is in a sense no longer possible to truly refuse without refusing the whole. And not merely this or that whole, but perhaps what appears to be being itself, "that which is." At least the latter possibility is not excluded, or refused, by Marcuse. And any limited, partial, conditional refusals that do not reach that which is being itself would remain subordinated to their functioning in the whole. To have a conscience now would mean to at least risk going beyond "the general necessity of things" (79). Inasmuch as the administered life is the "pure form of domination," its negation appears to be, or appears in, the pure form of negation (255).

The pervasive identity of opposites, the latest avatar of natural history in Adorno's sense of the term, where unity is a function of antagonism, the rational irrationality on the way to consummation in advanced industrial society, are all for Marcuse characterized by a specific form of reason and rationality, one emerging from "the experience, transformation and organization of nature as the mere stuff of domination" (*ODM,* xvi). The technological rationality that produces and expresses one-dimensionality (145) is the function of a specific historical-social project (158–59). Although Marcuse in his account of the dialectic of scientific reason is telling a story that has become perhaps overly familiar, especially in its Heideggerian but also Husserlian versions, what is specifically natural-historic in his narrative is generally overlooked. He notes, but is not particularly concerned with what took place in the quantification of nature by early modern science: as reality was separated from inherent ends the true was separated from the good, as was science from ethics. This led to an inexorable subjectification of values. However high a dignity values might be granted, they were not real, inasmuch as they could not be verified by scientific method. What were once real but transcendent ideas become mere ideals, always in principle reducible to the purposeless play of immanent impersonal forces.

But, paradoxically, as science and the philosophical reflection guided by science advanced it became increasingly apparent that the objective world of quantifiable qualities was dependent in its objectivity on the subject.[9] The subject of science was necessarily a constituting subject (146–50). The science which begins with an elimination of independent substances eventually arrives at the "ideation of objectivity." But this is a very specific ideation in which the object "constitutes itself in a quite practical relation to the subject," specifically as a *possible* object of manipulation (155). The neutrality of matter as a possible object of manipulation is what relates objectivity to a specific historical subject and project (156), the other side of which is the relating of people to each other as units (or bearers of units) of abstract labor power, which in turn requires freeing them from all apparently "natural" hierarchies (as well as ideas of commutative or distributive justice) (157). Not only is scientific rationality inherently instrumentalist, and therefore *a priori* technological, it has as its specific *a priori* a form of social control and domination (157–58).

It has been noted often enough that Marcuse's account of technological rationality, if it does not owe a good deal to Heidegger's thought on being, certainly exhibits strong affinities. In agreement with Heidegger, and Bachelard, Marcuse affirms that "the science of nature develops under the technological a priori which projects nature as a potential instrumentality, stuff of control and organization. And the apprehension of nature as (hypothetical) instrumentality precedes the development of all particular technological organization" (*ODM,* 153). But unlike Heidegger, Marcuse does not refer the technological a priori back to the disclosure and self-disclosure of being. Nor would he be satisfied with a genetic epistemology of scientific method that would refer it back to a biological function that would be supra- or infrahistorical in the manner of Piaget (161–62). Instead, he turns to Husserl's later work, specifically *The Crisis of the European Sciences and Transcendental Phenomenology,* for the beginnings of a genetic epistemology that may be able to focus on the socio-historical character of the technical rationality of scientific reason. Husserl recognizes that modern Galilean science, in its theory and method, develops from and out of *Lebenswelt* projects of anticipation and projection. According to Marcuse, "The scientific abstraction from concreteness, the quantification of qualities which yield exactness as well as universal validity, involve a specific, concrete experience of the *Lebenswelt* — a specific mode of 'seeing' the world. And this 'seeing,' in spite of its 'pure,' disinterested character, is seeing within a purposive practical context. It is anticipating (*Voraussehen*) and project-ing (*Vorhaben*)" (164). What makes Husserl's reflections on the transcendental conditions of scientific rationality different from the invariance that would accompany a biologistic genetic epis-temology is that the *Lebenswelt* is itself, and even for Husserl, historic. The *Lebenswelt,* understood historically, would include not only the specific experiences of projection and anticipation that technological reason comes to abstract and refine, but the abstraction of abstraction itself and its results. Once the mathematization of nature is seen historically, as the absolute autonomization of a "specific method and technique for the *Lebenswelt*" (162), its horizon in a more general historico-social project of *domination* also becomes potentially visible.[10] Thus, Husserl is able to *suggest,* but not follow through on a grasp of what Marcuse calls the "inherent limit of the established science," and its "stabilizing, static, conservative function": Husserl realizes that "Even its most revolutionary achievements would only be construction and destruction in line with a specific experience and organization of reality. The continuous self-correction of science — the revolution of its hypotheses which is built into its method — itself propels and extends the same historical universe, the same basic experience" (165). Thus, technological rationality is both the product and agent of the experience of domination. The historical development of science turns out to be natural-historical, a repetition of the ever-same. In this sense there are no scientific revolutions. And at the same time, the nature apprehended by technological reason turns out to be historical and transient. One-dimensionality is natural history.

In this context, reduced experience is less and less capable of being experienced as reduced. Technological rationality would be the "most mature...form" of reification inasmuch as in it not only are relations between people actually "determined by objective qualities and laws," as they can be seen to be in the concept and in the context of commodity fetishism (*ODM,* 168–69), but that they are so determined is accepted as natural and necessary. There seem to be no relations possible that would not be the relations among things. Under what we might call simple commodity fetishism and in its concept there is as yet an experience of reduced experience — a repulsion for and a repugnance against the mystery of the relations among commodities taking over and replacing relations among human beings.[11] But, in the social functioning of technological rationality, under matured reification, the laws of attraction and repulsion among commodities lose their very character as mysterious and "appear as calculable manifestations of (scientific) rationality" (168–69). Relations between people no longer appear uncannily as relations among things. Instead, relations among things appear as and are relations among people. Therefore, "The world…become[s] the stuff of total administration" (169), in which the administrators are in control only so long as they repeat and reinforce the process of control. The *experience* of reification is itself reified. Reification dis-appears.

The Natural-Historical Experience of Culture

A good part of Marcuse's analysis in *One-Dimensional Man* is devoted to the ways in which increasingly dominant modes of thought relinquish the theoretical possibilities of transcendence. This occurs for such modes of thought in their abandonment of any transitive meaning in concepts as they instead refer meaning back exclusively to the concept's functioning within the context of a given whole (see *ODM,* 86ff, 203ff). Outside of the natural sciences, scientific thought tends either toward a pure self-contained formalism or toward a total empiricism — and between these two there is neither contact nor conflict. They share a "common denominator" in the principles of "non-contradiction and non-transcendence" (*ODM,* 169). It is therefore vital to Marcuse, and to the Frankfurt School in general, that the experience of thought include the experience of contradiction not only because without it critique becomes impossible, but because without a thinking that can register and include contradiction there can be no experience (or experience of the experience), of what Levinas would call the breakup of totality.

The structure of experience is never unmediated by existing conceptual or conceptualizable structures, even if those concepts — as images — are sensible aesthetic works. One might be tempted to think that this indicates an unbridgeable difference with Levinas, for whom experience par excellence is precisely nonconceptual and not to be modelled on the cognitive relation with an object. This would be to forget, however, that for Levinas, the approach of the other (and not simply the other-than) also cannot effectively do without mediation. In his terms, there would be no pure Saying that was not betrayed in a Said, or no expression that was not mediated by the terms of a discourse. One might even say that the sense of diachrony in which there is the trace of the other could not be felt unless synchronizable time were also in effect.

In the grey area of the historical determination of experience, to which Levinas remains open, there is ample space for experience to be preformed. According to Benjamin it would be a grievous error to ignore this preformation at the level of sensibility: "Technology has subjected the human sensorium to a complex kind of training" (SMB, 175). For Adorno and Horkheimer, a crucial part of this training takes place in those spheres of culture devoted to aesthetic expression and reception.

According to Horkheimer and Adorno in their analysis of the culture industry as mass deception in *Dialectic of Enlightenment,* "anyone who doubts the power of monotony is a fool" (*DE,* 148). What characterizes the fate of art under the culture industry is not the replacement of high aesthetic standards with the chaos following upon a leveling of such standards, as conservative cultural criticism complains. They write, "Culture now impresses the same stamp upon everything.... Even the aesthetic activities of political opposites are one in their enthusiastic obedience to the rhythm of the iron system" (120). Nor does the culture industry simply substitute the popular for the elitist, or even light for serious art (135). Or amusement for edification (142). What it effects fundamentally is the totalization of voluntary memory, a being past experiencing, and what it brings with it is a desolation and rage in the "bourgeois whose existence is split...[who,] at odds with himself and everybody else, is already virtually a Nazi, replete both with enthusiasm and abuse; or a modern city dweller who can now only imagine friendship as a 'social contact': that is, as being in social contact with others with whom he has no inward contact" (155). This achievement is not the necessary result of putatively pure technological imperatives (121), but of the commodification of cultural production. Although art *as* commodity is not a new notion, the admission that art *is* a commodity is new.[12] The purposelessness of the great modern work of art, reflected in the standards of idealist philosophical aesthetics — purposefulness without purpose — was initially an effect of the replacement of patronage systems by a market in works. But this purposelessness is reversed in commodification, as profit becomes the purpose of purposelessness (157–58). Commodification, bringing with it enormous power and profit for "those whose economic hold over society is the greatest," imposes "a technological rationale [that] is the rationale of domination itself" (121).

The soul, in its innermost inwardness as expression, becomes servile in becoming a moment in the circuit of capital. And capital, following its own law of expanded reproduction, requires a differentiated product that is always the same: "Mechanically differentiated products prove to be all alike in the end" (*DE,* 123, 133–34). The new itself is generated according to a formula to the extent that "realistic dissidence is the trademark of anyone who has a new idea in business" (132). Differentiation of products is based on the classifying, sorting, and labeling of consumer audiences, not on the subject matter, so that "Something is provided for all so that none may escape.... Everybody must behave (as if spontaneously) in accordance with his previously determined and indexed level and choose the category of mass product turned out for his type" (132; see 149–50). What is new in the culture industry is therefore actually the exclusion of the new, where the "universal triumph of the rhythm of mechanical production and reproduction promises that nothing changes and that nothing unsuitable will appear" (132). The ideologizing force of industrial culture in the culture industry is not in the content of any of the ideas that might be expressed but in the endlessness of the repetition of standardized differentiation — like a scroll. It is in that "omnipresence" that "the social power which the spectators worship shows itself more effectively" (136).

The universal triumph of mechanical reproduction means not more leisure for the increasingly homogeneous mass, where leisure had meant, since Aristotle, the basis for the freedom provided by contemplation, but the disappearance of the difference between leisure and work. The experiences of leisure are "inevitably afterimages of the work process itself" (137). As the afterimage of the work process the consumption of culture is not even diversion. There would be greater diversion outside of "this bloated pleasure apparatus [which] adds no dignity to man's lives [*sic*]" (139). It would not be missed for long, for "As soon as the very existence of these institutions no longer made it obligatory to use them, there would be no great urge to do so. Such closures would not be reactionary machine wrecking" (139). Nor is the culture of consumption one of amusement, which has as its consequence "relaxed self-surrender to all kinds of associations and happy non-sense." What passes for amusement in the culture industry is always "interrupted by a surrogate overall meaning," reorganizing the amused but self-dissolving ego (142–43). Such amusement is not "flight from a wretched reality, but from the last remaining thought of resistance" (144), which is flight itself. Such a training of the senses is an education in sensible insensibility, an insulation, a desensitization, a general anesthetic. Even though the public occasionally rebels against the culture industry, "it can only

muster the rebellion which the culture industry has inculcated
in it" (144). Its rebellions become the occasion for the same
old differentiation of the standard product: "What sinks in is the
automatic succession of standardized operations" (137). Resistance, as they say, is useless. Especially since "everyone can
be like this omnipotent society; everyone can be happy" if only
he capitulates and sacrifices his claim to happiness (153). And
the miraculous integration of the defenseless and unrebellious,
the "permanent act of grace by the authority who receives the
defenseless person — once he has swallowed his rebelliousness —
signifies Fascism" (154).

What is perhaps even more unnerving than the critique of
monotony as the reduction of the experience of the subject in
Horkheimer and Adorno's analysis of the culture industry is
the monotony of the critique itself. It is as though the mimetic
identification imposed in reduced experience could be re-experienced by the reader who obeys the iron rhythm of their
critique, which repeats over and over again the fact that the
culture industry is an allegorical expression of natural history,
the false identity of the universal and the particular. Something
extreme is here expressed without extreme discretion, but with
a discrete extremism, the extremism that "follows history's path
to the very extreme." An incomplete list of the moments of false
identity identified by Horkheimer and Adorno in the culture
industry would include the following: the false identity of the
needs of the audience with the supply of the industry; of style
with formula; of the individual with the whole; of leisure with
toil; of light with serious; of repression with sublimation; of
nonsense with sense; of rebellion with conformity; of purposelessness with purpose; of the work with the commodity form;
of art with advertising; of the power of the social totality with
freedom; of words with signs; of differentiation with uniformity.
But does this mean they are pursuing some form of true identity
that the culture industry lacks?

Nothing could be more misleading. What is at issue for them is not to be found in abstract questions of good or bad art, or even what makes a work aesthetic. What is at issue is the way, or the ways, in which all art is natural-historical. The ways in which taste, traditions, criticism, and philosophical aesthetics raise such questions, or even do not, is a part of the natural history of art as part of natural history. Cultural-industrial art is as much art as any. It also even has inferior and superior works. What differentiates it can, however, be seen only in retrospect, only by rubbing it against the grain. To that effect, the contrast Horkheimer and Adorno undertake with what they term great bourgeois art, a part of the art of the immediate past, can be instructive, as an ironically distanced critical foil, as Habermas says.

The standardization and mass production that must be pursued under the commodity form imply, above all, a progressive sacrifice of the distinction between the logic of the work and the logic of the social system (*DE,* 121). Tension or potential contradiction between the logic of the work and the logic of the social system belongs to all periods of art. Other periods, having had other variations on the logic of the social system, and other variations in the logic of the work (determined by, among other things, the development of technique), will have found other dispositions for this tension. What takes place in the period of the culture industry, however, can perhaps best be seen in the contrast between the style of great bourgeois works and the style of the industry. The problem with the industry is not that it lacks style, but that it has too much and too many. It is, in fact, by being all style — and all styles — the "negation of style" (129–30). It bears the technical power, and is subjected to the economic imperative, to differentiate and propagate a virtually infinite number of styles, new and old. But it must make everything new and old into a style. In this it has so far always remained successful. Standardization does not mean the

monotony of nondifferentiation. There are an infinite number of
standard unique styles. Enough to satisfy everybody, and more
every day. This way every unique need can be satisfied even
before it appears. And, with every satisfaction "the might of
industrial society is lodged in men's minds" (127). Each and
every product signals the reaction it can produce (137) and each
product "is a model of the huge economic machinery which has
always sustained the masses" (127).

What the industry cannot afford, however, is the failure of
style, which is exactly what, for Horkheimer and Adorno, is
"accomplished" by some of the "great" works of the past. What
made these artists great was not flawless style. Although style
was certainly of the essence, they were compelled at crucial
points to subordinate style to the "logic of the matter." What
is essential in style is the "*promesse* du bonheur." It promises
a reconciliation of the suffering particular with the social forms
in which that suffering is embedded by projecting a new form.
In its style the work holds out the promise "that it will create
truth by lending new shape to the conventional social forms"
(130). In holding open the promise of a reconciliation through
stylization it is able "to transcend reality." But stylization here
"does not consist of the harmony actually realized, of any
doubtful unity of form and content...it is to be found in those
features in which discrepancy appears: in the necessary failure
of the passionate striving for identity" (131). Thus, the culture
industry negates style by ceasing "to be anything but style,"
and in doing so "reveals the...secret [of imitation]: obedience
to the social hierarchy" (131). The logic of the work does not
turn out to be the logic of a style, but is instead lodged in the
discrepancy between the promise of style and those nonidenticals
that style seeks to reconcile. The logic of the social system, at
present, is the logic of an experience constituted through the
mediation of a transcendental schematism. But schematizing
is not the experience once promised or expressed in art. For

Kant, "there was a secret mechanism in the soul which prepared direct intuitions in such a way that they could be fitted into the system of pure reason." This is close enough to the logic of the social system. What the culture industry does is to transmit the power of the social totality to the customer by doing "his schematizing for him" (124).

Something of a test case for the ability of the culture industry to do the individual's schematizing for him is to be found in the way it absorbs the tragic into the system. To present life simply in terms of amusement and diversion would be for the industry to give itself the lie. Far from shrinking in the face of suffering the culture industry, then, looks it in the face proudly, "like a man." Pure amusement cannot by itself provide the substance without which the pure style of the industry might be revealed for what it is. It therefore borrows persistently from art its tragic substance. But in its disposition of the formula of tragedy it once more affirms the power of the social whole by turning the suffering in tragedy into mere punishment. It "assigns tragedy a fixed place in the routine. The well-known existence of the recipe is enough to allay any fear that there is no restraint on tragedy" (*DE,* 152). Freed from such a fear, it can become an instrument of cheap moral improvement: "The pathos of composure justifies the world which makes it necessary. That is life — very hard, but just because of that so wonderful" (152). Tragedy from the culture industry "comforts all with the thought that a tough, genuine human fate is still possible.... Life shows up all the more gloriously, powerfully and magnificently, the more it is redolent of necessary suffering" (152–53). Moral improvement within cultural-industrial tragedies becomes stoic acceptance and even glorifying in the punishment meted out: "In films, those permanently desparate situations which crush the spectator in ordinary life somehow can become a promise that one can go on living. One has only to recognize one's own nothingness, only to recognize defeat and one is at one with it all" (153). Tragedy, which once expressed the opposition of individual to society by bearing the "paradoxical significance" of "hopeless resistance to mythic destiny" (152–53), becomes the vehicle for the acceptance of mythic destiny as hopeful submission.[13] The liquidation of tragedy confirms the abolition of the individual who becomes merely the centre where the general tendencies meet (154). The disappearance of tragedy implies the disappearance of the aura, that is, the disappearance of the afterimage of the relation to the absolutely other across an unbridgeable distance.

The truth of art, the logic of the work, lies in the *necessary* failure of the passionate striving for identity, a necessary failure literally embodied in aesthetic stylization. And it might be worth noting that a necessary failure of identity implies the failure of necessity as the identity of the world or as its law. The repetition of styles in the culture industry, and the complete subordination of the rebellious detail or of the particular in style as formula, succeeds in formalizing the false identity in which such striving is extinguished. But it would be mistaken to assume that Horkheimer and Adorno are in any way calling for a return, aesthetically or politically, to that historical moment in which the individual took up some of the work of applying schematization to the object of experience.[14] For Horkheimer and Adorno, both Kant and the culture industry remain true to the same falsehood: that it is a *direct* intuition that is already prepared in the schema with which the individual can schematize (*DE,* 124).

The transcendental ego which might accomplish such an a priori preparation for its identification of and with the object already receives its transcendental status and its logic from out of the social. Even great bourgeois art is bourgeois great art. That they hold this to be the case becomes quite sufficiently clear later on, in one of Adorno's last essays, "Subject and Object." In his discussion there of the philosophical meaning of the term, Adorno links the idealist notion of the subject to a doubled meaning. The notion of transcendental subjectivity both reveals and conceals the constitutive function of the social in the reduction of experience. It reveals that function in actually being more real than the empirical or psychological ego:

> In a sense (although idealism would be the last to admit this) the transcendental subject is more real...more determinant for the real conduct of men and for the resulting society...than those psychological individuals from which the transcendental one was abstracted. They have little to say in the world....The living human individual, as he is forced to act in the role for which he has been marked internally as well, is the *homo oeconomicus* incarnate, closer to the transcendental subject than to the living individual for which he immediately cannot but take himself.... What shows up faithfully in the doctrine of the transcendental subject is the priority of the relations, abstractly rational ones, detached from the human individuals and their relationships — that have their model in exchange. If the exchange form is the standard social structure, its rationality constitutes people; what they are for themselves, what they seem to be to themselves, is secondary. They are deformed beforehand by the mechanism that has been philosophically transfigured as transcendental. The supposedly most evident of things, the empirical subject, would really have to be viewed as not yet in existence.[15]

On the other hand, the constitutive function of the social machine in the reduction of experience is concealed, but paradoxically, in the very claim of transcendental subjectivity to be first, to be constitutive of the experience, and the limits of the experience, that goes to the empirical/psychological ego: "That nothing can be true except the First — or, as Nietzsche critically phrased it, what has not come into being — is a *topos* of the entire Western tradition....There is no mistaking the ideological function of the thesis [of the priority of the transcendental subject]; The more individuals are really degraded to functions of the social totality...the more will man...as a principle with the attributes of creativity and absolute domination, be consoled by exaltation of his mind."[16] Correspondingly, Levinas will not be able to pursue his unseating of ontology, the prioritization of the ethical relation, without looking behind the transcendental ego to a self that is first of all not first, but sensibility, created being.

I will take Adorno literally at his word in the assertion that the empirical ego would have to be seen as not yet in existence. Instead it lives a half-life as the basis from which the transcendental ego may be abstracted. Natural history would then have to be seen not as something that happens to the individual or to society. Nor could it be seen any longer in terms of the alienation of a creative power. Yet natural history would allow no exit, there could be no weak messianic power, without the implication of subjectivity in it, without the collusion of the subject in its natural-historicity. These terms, implication, collusion, are simply ways of trying to indicate that neither natural history nor its subject should be taken to be the "first." The technological-rational reduction of experience is correlative with a natural-historical subject who might also be the not-yet-in-existence empirical subject.

The Subject of Natural History: The Experience of Sacrifice, or Odysseus

Horkheimer and Adorno offer an allegorical account of the subject of natural history in their famous excursus, "Odysseus, or Myth and Enlightenment." This excursus actually has two linked objects, the first being the pattern of Odyssean cunning as the birthplace of the subject of domination. The new Odyssean cunning is nonetheless a transformation and appropriation of the older mythical logic of sacrifice. The second, more tacit and discrete object of their analysis is the figure of Homer the storyteller, or the law of the Homeric poem as a figuration of the potential in art for escape. The wily Odysseus represents that subjectivity implicated in the expanded reproduction of natural history, the subject of a reduced experience. But inside the Homeric poem, Odysseus also represents sacrifice for the sake of the end of sacrifice (*DE,* 56), and the epic itself performs the beginnings of the escape from mythic repetition and inevitability that would lie at the basis of any "positive notion of enlightenment which will release it from entanglement in blind domination" (xvi). In tracing that entanglement so far back, Horkheimer and Adorno "offer the hope for a new release of the whole process" of enlightenment (45).

Odysseus belongs to a world that is already in the process of disenchantment. Homer describes "the retreat of the individual from the mythic powers" (*DE,* 46). But this is a tenuous and conditional achievement of a self that must be continuously reasserted. Taking on a form closer to the picaresque novel, the hero loses himself to find himself (47). Disenchantment is figured by a hero who will derive his unity from opposition to myth; the inner organization of the individual in the form of time is still relatively weak (*DE,* 48). The self here, escaping to become itself, to maintain its identity, is placing itself at, clearing for itself, a center point of experience around which the possibility of a synchronizable, linear, irreversible time might emerge. And its emergence in this form is a response to its physical weakness. Odysseus is always weaker than the physical powers with which he must contend. His strength will be the strength of mind, of the commander who organizes and can reverse or redirect the physical strength of others, including those powers that threaten his dissolution (56): "The opposition of enlightenment to myth is expressed in the opposition of the surviving individual ego to multifarious fate...and attaining self-realization only in self-consciousness" (46).

The secret of successful Odyssean cunning, together with his social predominance, lies in this self-consciousness, which is, in fact, precisely what the mythical powers he opposes do not possess. They express claims from prehistory. Each is a figure of repetition always programmed to do the same thing, a repetition-compulsion that "would come to an end should the repetition fail to occur" (*DE*, 57–58). Their "right... being that of the stronger, depends only upon the impossibility of fulfilling their statutes. If they are satisfied, then the myths right down to their most distant relations will suffer for it" (59). Releasing himself from the grip of mythical powers means he renders to nature what is nature's, and yet betrays it in the very process (57).

In order for the powers of mythical nature to be outwitted, deception as cunning must be moved to a higher level of self-consciousness. Odysseus's cunning is based upon a change in consciousness away from the mythical or magical identity of name and thing toward the distinction between name and object. Whereas in myth intention and expression interpenetrate, Odyssean cunning, as consciousness of the intention, allows for the exploitation of the difference between the two, for deceit (*DE*, 60). For Horkheimer and Adorno, sacrifice had always already included a moment of deceit, as a device to overthrow the gods by means of the system that honored them. It was already the magical form of rational exchange, whereas exchange would be the rational form of sacrifice (49). Yet pre-Homeric sacrifice seems simultaneously to have had the quality of an offering, a mimetic attempt, however false, to reestablish a "dislocated communication" (51). The prototype of Odysseus' cunning is in the abstraction and development of the *deception* in sacrifice, which is the only one of its elements elevated by Odysseus to self-consciousness (50).

In taking up the deceit within sacrifice (and self-sacrifice) by virtue of the distance he establishes between expression and intention, Odysseus is able to maintain his singleminded direction throughout his encounters with the dangerous temptations that threaten to remove the self from its logical course (*DE*, 47). Thus, Odysseus seems to escape the power of myth by turning its own powers of identification against it. But cunning is a false escape from myth that confirms the very same mythic logic of sacrifice from which Odysseus is aiming to distance himself. The mastery of nature that takes place here still takes place only through the identification of the subject with the very same powers that he sets out to deceive (56).

In discovering sacrificial deceit Odysseus has also discovered but, in that very discovery, betrayed nonidentity. The discrepancy between name and thing, implying nonidentity, in the form of formal equivalence allows the physically weaker party to obey, but also to go his own way. Odysseus can repeat the mythic commands but evade and escape them at the same time. But by obeying them in evading them, he transposes their logic into the very self he is now able to establish by having distanced himself from them. Nonidentity establishes itself here as identity through the *self-conscious* repetition of identity. The power of the mythical forces is nothing but repetition, identity, self-sameness, nature in the sense of *physis;* mythical power is that which has not come into being but is "first and always," the permanent, the eternal, the universal and necessary. Odysseus establishes mastery through adaptation, through a repetition of the very logic of the sacrifice that his self-conscious cunning allows him to recognize and manipulate. The deception of fateful power thus turns immediately into its repetition: "The ratio which supplants mimesis is not simply its counterpart. It is itself mimesis: mimesis unto death" (*DE,* 57).

In repeating sacrifice to evade sacrifice Odysseus inaugurates self-sacrifice, without which that evasion could not succeed because the mythical forces are also his own nature: "The self rescues itself from dissolution in blind nature, whose claim is constantly proclaimed in sacrifice. But it is still imprisoned in the natural context as an organism that tries to assert itself against the organic.... The identically persistent self which arises in the abrogation of sacrifice immediately becomes an unyielding, rigidified sacrificial ritual that man celebrates upon himself by opposing his consciousness to the natural order" (*DE,* 53–54). Odysseus is the allegorical sign of the subject of natural history. He represents "the inclusion of myth in civilization" (54) such that "the history of civilization is the introversion of sacrifice" (55). By virtue of this introversion of sacrifice, accomplished as the self-sacrifice demanded by mastery *as class history,*[17] the unyielding rigidity of subjectivity gains its apparent substantiality (54). And such a subjectivity, on its way to infinite remoteness from its own sensibility (its nature in that other sense), becomes the "germ cell of a proliferating mythic irrationality.... As soon as man discards his awareness that he himself is nature, all the aims for which he keeps himself alive...are nullified and the enthronement of means as an end, which under late capitalism is tantamount to open insanity, is already perceptible in the prehistory of subjectivity" (54).[18]

Odyssean subjectivity, through the possibility of evasion it discovers in formal identity, fatally enthrones the logic of sacrifice it attempts to abrogate, pointing forward to a natural history of proliferating rational irrationality. That subjectivity is a repetition of the "historic catastrophe" that is present in all sacrifice (*DE,* 51). But it does establish something that is in a sense new — the specific reduction in experience that allows subjectivity, while remaining subjectivity, to maintain its "logical course" (47). The Odyssean adventure is specifically not openness to the new or to the other. It is, since it is noble, masterful and strong, not so much risk averse, as unable to risk its self-preservative logic. Odysseus "gives way to each allurement as a new experience," but he is only "trying it out" and will soon retreat into the fixed identity of his self-preservation: "The knowing survivor is also the man who takes the greatest risks when death threatens, thus becoming strong and unyielding when life continues. That is the secret of the process between epic and myth; the self does not constitute the fixed antithesis to adventure, but in its rigidity molds itself only by way of that antithesis: being an entity only in the diversity of that which denies all unity" (47).

The *Odyssey,* however, is for Horkheimer and Adorno, not simply testimony to the repetition of the mythical in enlightenment. Odysseus himself is "also a sacrifice for the abrogation of sacrifice. His dominative renunciation, as a struggle with myth, represents a society that no longer needs renunciation and domination, which gains mastery over itself not in order to coerce itself and others, but in expiation" (*DE,* 56). On the one hand, "he satisfies the sentence of the law so that it loses its power over him, by conceding it this very power" (58). Yet he also opposes not only the mythical powers but the situation of "guilt as law" (58). Intimations of an escape from mythic guilt that is not its rational reproduction take place at a few key points in the *Odyssey.*

Despite its implication in the "female self-alienation in the patriarchal world" (*DE,* 74), the marriage of Penelope and Odysseus, for example, harbors one such moment: "Marriage does not signify merely the order that requites in life but also solidarity in facing death. Expiation develops in it round about subjection, as in history to date the humane has flourished only and precisely in the savagery that is veiled by humanity" (75). Another such ambiguous moment takes place in Odysseus' visit to Hades. Although he repeats there the logic of sacrifice by repulsing those shades who offer him no benefit "and will allow only those to approach...who will afford him knowledge of some utility for his life," nonetheless the Orphic theme "of the forcing of the gates of hell, the annulment of death, constitutes the core of all antimythological thinking" (76). A third intimation of what lies beyond myth is included in Teiresias' prophecy. The blind, hermaphroditic seer whom he encounters in Hades will prophecy for Odysseus an end to the wrath of Poseidon that has obstructed his journey home. But in order to appease Poseidon, Odysseus, in order to interrupt once and for all the cycle of guilt and retribution, will have to undertake a journey far from the sea carrying an oar. This will "make the fierce elemental god laugh, so that...his wrath will disappear." Even though such laughter "is still the sign of force, of the breaking out of blind and obdurate nature, it also contains the opposite element — the fact that through laughter blind nature becomes aware of itself as it is, and thereby surrenders itself to the power of destruction" (77). The possibility for the destruction of myth, sacrifice and retribution is assigned to nonsense, and therefore, in a way, to the failure of the passionate striving for identity.

Although these episodes symbolize or foretell the hoped for end of the powers of myth beyond its repetition in rational enlightenment, they do not represent for Horkheimer and Adorno the manner in which the Homeric epic, as art, opposes the mythlogical. In this respect what distinguishes Homer is the transition from "mythic song" to "eloquent discourse" (*DE,* 78). Homer's eloquence is "the cold distancing of narration" (78–79). It allows, on the one hand, the emotionlessness and the "inhuman composure," the "frigidity of anatomy and vivisection" exemplified in Homer's recounting of Telemachus' visitation of retributive justice by hanging, on the servant girls who in Odysseus' absence had turned to prostitution. With perfect eloquence, reticence and composure Homer compares them to birds caught in a net. He recounts the information that the row of their feet "'kicked out for a short while, but not for long'" (as quoted in *DE,* 79). The distanced cold narration here reassures its readers, distancing them from the brutality and suffering of the act. But at the same time it accomplishes something else: "But after the 'not for long' the inner flow of the narrative is arrested. *Not for long?* The device poses the question and belies the author's composure. By cutting short the account, Homer prevents us from forgetting the victims, and reveals the unutterable eternal agony of the few seconds in which the women struggle with death" (*DE,* 79–80). This something else is "the possibility of retaining in memory the disaster that has occurred...the law of Homeric escape" (78). This possibility for the retention of catastrophe is the perspective of Benjamin's angel of history. The civilized, eloquent and rational distance from the horror "allows the horror as such to appear for the first time," rather than to be taken for fate (*DE,* 79). Thus the Homeric epic takes up the achievements of enlightenment, and in turning them against natural history, stands beyond myth: "Reticence in narration...is the sudden break, the transformation of what is reported into something long past, by means of which the semblance of freedom glimmers that since then civilization has not wholly succeeded in putting out" (79).

Experience, the Concept, and the Principle of Immanence

Natural history is the very repetition, the expanded reproduction, and *not* the narration of something long past as long past, a narration a step removed from repetition and by virtue of which the fateful would be transformed into the catastrophic that appears as such, and appears therefore as not necessary, as not woven into the very fabric of being. Horkheimer and Adorno's Odysseus allegorizes the subject of domination who reproduces domination out of the very struggle against it. In his self-constitution and self-preservation, in his mutual embrace with the universal and inevitable, he signifies also the prototype for the truncation or atrophy of experience in the self that preserves itself as a technology of power that is able to schematize and screen and find its way back to its seat of power by virtue of a system of coordinates. But the Odyssean moment, the moment in which the subject becomes a subject in establishing his distance by accepting the law of equivalence and exchange in order to profit from his knowledge of it, in order to be able to manipulate its statutes, already presupposes not simply an apprehension of that unity which allows for equivalence and exchange but something like a capitulation before the necessity apprehended in unity itself. Enlightenment repeats myth only inasmuch as myth is already enlightenment.

For Horkheimer and Adorno the latest horrors (concerning which we are in no position to say that they are necessarily forever the worst) — fascism, late capitalism, the totally administered society, the reification of consciousness — are to be read as symptoms of a natural history, a dialectic of enlightenment, a "disease of reason."[19] Every attempt at its interruption has not yet ceased to become embroiled in it again. But natural history, even before but certainly once it has been identified, calls for its own abolition, for an awakening. The diagnosis and aetiology of natural history are not only inseparable but are to be pursued to the very extremes of history and prehistory.

In *Dialectic of Enlightenment* the natural-historical is traced back to the inception and formation of the concept — as far back as mythic fear. In the introduction to that work the authors set as their goal nothing less than explaining why humankind, "instead of entering into a truly human condition, is sinking into a new kind of barbarism" (*DE,* xi). The work aims to approach this task by attending to that which enlightenment, in its long degeneration into pure positivism, has come progressively to shrink away from, that is: a thinking about thought (25). Yet this thinking about thought is to be neither epistemology nor sociology of knowledge, although it will refer to and borrow from both. It might be possible to style it as a form of dialectical phenomenology, but only if it is understood that this dialectic differs essentially from the Hegelian version, in that dialectic is here encountered as something akin to Benjamin's monad in its form as arrested, rather than completed through a retrospective process of synthesis via negation. They have not, as they take

Hegel to have done, taken the process to be "decided from the start" (24). There is no presumption of a something that has not come into being because it is only being becoming itself which, one might say in reference to Hegel, is there from the start in the process of consciousness itself, as negation leading up to the final synthesis of that which has made negation possible. *Dialectic of Enlightenment,* more beholden to Benjamin than it makes explicit, is an analysis of dialectics at a standstill that is itself dialectical and at a standstill.

That the analysis of enlightenment as natural history takes on or perhaps mimics, or even parodies, the shape of a dialectical phenomenology is to be seen in the structure of the chapter entitled "The Concept of Enlightenment." The subject matter is both enlightenment's concept or idea of itself and the form of ideation, the concept developed in the social process of enlightenment. The starting point is not an abstract definition, but an historical-phenomenological definition of enlightenment, that is, enlightenment's self-definition. What we have at first is the "simple being" of enlightenment. But the phenomenological working through of this self-understanding, its self-examination, the thinking about this thought, will arrive at its negation: enlightenment is not what it simply appears to be. It negates itself. It turns out to possess a ground beyond and before itself which appears to be more real and to which it relates as appearance to essence. From simple being we move to the stage of consciousness of essence, and this essence is also the negation of being as appearance. But since the essence must have already included its appearance before essence could be rediscovered in appearance, essence is inherently unstable, that is, temporal. In a Hegelian, or positive dialectical phenomenology, the final form in which enlightenment should find itself would be one in which its appearance and essence, which negate each other, could be synthesized in retrospect and its essence come to finally coincide with its appearances. A final unity would have appeared through negation — and as already present at the start. This would be the notion of enlightenment in the Hegelian sense. But this will be exactly the point at which Horkheimer and Adorno will leave Hegelian dialectic behind as being itself mythological. There will be no notion of enlightenment to be known as one can know a perfected unity. In the end there will be no concept of enlightenment beyond the very inability of enlightenment to coincide with itself, its nonidentity with its object, a nonidentity which is revealed historically in the persistence, despite enlightenment, of those relations to its object which are unenlightened: art, metaphysics, religion.

The working, initial definition of enlightenment is enlightenment's self-definition as the opposite and negation of myth. Enlightenment sees itself as the dissolution of myth, as a process of progressive disenchantment whose knowledge will provide a liberation from the fear of multifarious, hidden, inscrutable, and fateful forces, but forces that have the character of wills and wills that enact retribution. In enlightenment "there is to be no mystery" and "no wish to reveal mystery" (*DE,* 3–5). The way out, the escape from what enlightenment takes to be the hellish circle of retribution and guilt that governs myth will be through "the extirpation of animism," a project at least as old as Xenophanes (5). In its more recent phase of development in the West, enlightenment, after Bacon and Galileo, becomes aware of its own previous repetition of animism in the guise of metaphysical ideas and essences. It recognizes the old gods in the metaphysical categories and learns that "all the equivocal multitude of mythical demons were intellectualized in the pure form of ontological essences." It opposes as superstition the notion "that truth is predicable of universal" concepts. And thus, "From now on, matter would at last be mastered without any illusion of ruling or inherent powers, of hidden qualities" (6). The metaphysical ideas, which in modernity it begins to see are still entangled in myth, are now taken to be themselves an anthropomorphic projection of the animate upon the inanimate, the very object of the critique of myth by metaphysics. This is its stereotypical, ever-repeated critique of animism — Oedipus's answer to the riddle: "It is man" (6). In its relentless pursuit of the logic of disenchantment the modern enlightenment will secure itself against the return of myth through an "anticipatory identification of the wholly conceived and mathematized world with truth" thus confounding thought and mathematics (25).[20] Horkheimer and Adorno go on to quote Husserl at some length in order to draw out the consequences of this anticipatory identification:

> An infinite world, in this case a world of idealities, is conceived as one whose objects do not accede singly, imperfectly, and as if by chance to our cognition, but are attained by a rational, systematically unified method — in a process of infinite progression — so that each object is ultimately apparent according to its full inherent being.... In the Galilean mathematization of the world, however, *this selfness* is idealized under the guidance of the new mathematics: in modern terms it becomes itself a mathematical multiplicity. (quoted in *DE,* 25)

A world of infinite, unforeseeable complexity in which objects "singly, imperfectly and as if by chance" come to us — but still come to us — is apprehended, but only in unity. The objects are "attained" as mathematical multiplicities, as the unity of that multiplicity has now been "made into an absolute instance" (*DE,* 25).

In its infinite progress toward pure mathematization, enlightenment confirms that it recognizes only what can be apprehended in unity. Its ideal is always the ideal of the system, from which all and everything follows. Even rationalism and empiricism are united in this pursuit (*DE,* 7). But the thoroughgoing extirpation of animism, the radical separation of the animate and the inanimate, does not turn out to be that liberation through empowerment sought by enlightenment. As magical illusion fades, repetition —

the cycle whose disenchanted, objectified form now takes on the character of natural law, knowledge of which would be the basis of action for a free subject — this very repetition now returns, more relentlessly than ever. This is so inasmuch as enlightenment and myth share a fundamental principle: "The principle of immanence, the explanation of every event as repetition, that the Enlightenment upholds against mythic imagination, is the principle of myth itself" (12). The essence of enlightenment turns out to be myth. And mythic power does not cease to reproduce itself: "The more the machinery of thought subjects existence to itself, the more blind its resignation in reproducing existence. Hence enlightenment returns to mythology, which it never really new how to elude. For in its figures mythology had the essence of the status quo: cycle, fate and domination of the world reflected as the truth and deprived of hope" (27). Although Horkheimer and Adorno devote a good part of this chapter to the irony of the fate of the enlightened subject, to the characterization of the march toward world domination of the subject as its liquidation (26, 28–31), we have already seen this reversal at work in the effects of the culture industry and in one-dimensionality.

In general, in the enlightened world myth has not been eliminated. It has instead entered into the profane. The disenchanted reality acquires the numinous quality, the "general necessity of things" that the ancient world had assigned to gods and demons (28). That numinous quality, it should be said, is analogous to the reification of the experience of reification which Marcuse's argument in *One-Dimensional Man* approaches. There is a reanimation of the inanimate under runaway enlightenment that goes above and beyond commodity fetishism. If the perspective of enlightenment begins in the distantiation of the subject who rejects myth because myth compounds the animate with the inanimate, the same perspective carries with it, at the terminus of its logical course, a compounding of the inanimate with the animate in which subjectivity tends toward pure objecthood, pure being. As pure objects, subjects are the more guiltlessly disposed of: "Hence the course of European civilization. Abstraction, the tool of enlightenment, treats its objects as did fate, the notion of which it rejects: it liquidates them" (13).

The myths enlightenment destroyed are in fact *not* destroyed *because* enlightenment *does not recognize myth as having been from the start its own product*. Rather, "Myth intended report, naming, the narration of the Beginning; but also presentation, confirmation, explanation" (*DE*, 8). The rituals associated with mythic interactions have within them "the idea of activity as a determined process" (8). Not only are the myths organized into "heaven and its hierarchy," more importantly the deities "are no longer directly identical with elements, but signify them." Myth already carries with it the activity making possible conceptual identification: "The gods are distinguished from material elements as their quintessential concepts. From now on, being divides into the *logos*... and into the mass of all things and creatures without. This single distinction between existence proper and reality engulfs all others" (8). If mythic fatality is open to dissolution, or if natural history is open to the interruption that might issue in redemption, then enlightened thought will have to go back behind this principle of immanence that is its essence.

For Horkheimer and Adorno there is or has been an apperception or experience which, though still mediated by the concept, does not express only apprehension in unity. In their chapter on "The Concept of Enlightenment" the allegorical figure for this experience is variously named either magic or *pre-animism* or *the primitive*. But this reconstruction of experience prior to the principle of immanence must not be taken as an appeal to any primitivism. As in Adorno's "The Idea of Natural History," here the historically new appears as "the most archaic." Although magic, like science, pursues aims, it does so not by "progressive distantiation," but by mimesis, by what one might think of as a certain progressive de-distantiation (*DE*, 11). Magic, unlike myth, does not presuppose, create and recreate a self-identical, transcendental subject, even though in it there is already a certain distance from the transcendent, from the object, in the mimetic itself. Mimesis is not pure unity but a striving to become the object, and perhaps conversely the feeling that the object has the power to invest the self. But this investment of the self would not be experienced as a mortal threat to an integrity as identity which the self as yet does not claim or perhaps need to claim. Unlike the mimesis in myth, "Magic was not ordered by one identical spirit: it changed like the cultic masks which were supposed to accord with the various spirits. Magic is utterly untrue, yet in it domination is not yet negated by transforming itself into the pure truth and acting as the very ground of the world that has become subject to it" (9). Magic thus still corresponds to what is experienced in "the primitive," that is the "intricacy of nature," a nature already "in contrast to the individual." Yet the latter "is not a spiritual as opposed to a material substance" (15). The magical self is not yet on its way to the assertion of that spontaneity and freedom as the idealist subject who can function as, or in its knowledge imitate, that which has not come into being. Consequently, "The magician never interprets himself as the image of the invisible power; yet this is the very image in which man attains to the identity of self that cannot disappear through identification with another" (10).

Within the magical relation there is representation. But magical representation is "specific representation," unlike both mythical and enlightened representation. For the former the scientific perspective substitutes "the specimen": "Representation is exchanged for the fungible — universal interchangeability. An atom is smashed not in representation but as a specimen of matter, and the rabbit does not represent but, as a mere example, is ignored by the zeal of the laboratory" (*DE*, 10). And the mythical, being already a product of enlightenment that enlightenment tries to reject, prepares the ground for ever further abstraction in enlightenment: "Substitution in the course of sacrifice marks a step towards discursive logic. Even though the hind offered up for the daughter...still had to have specific qualities, [it] already represented the species. They already exhibited the non-specificity of the example" (10). With the perfection of enlightenment "the multitudinous affinities between existents are suppressed by the single relation between the subject who bestows meaning and the meaningless object, between rational significance and the chance vehicle of signification" (10). With the scientific development of the enlightened mythical, nature as the substratum of domination is revealed as "the always-the-same." Therefore, "This identity constitutes the unity of nature" (9).

If magical representation remains specific representation it would be by virtue of the fact that the structure of experience in pre-animism includes both separation and nonseparation, both identity and nonidentity. Horkheimer and Adorno will illustrate this notion in their brief but essential characterization of the pre-animism that precedes myth, where separation arises but has not yet turned into that process of identification without which both Auschwitz and the megaton bomb would be unthinkable and impossible: "When the tree is no longer approached as merely tree, but as evidence for an Other, as the location of mana, language expresses the contradiction that something is itself and at one and the same time other than itself, identical and nonidentical" (*DE,* 15). This experience of identity and nonidentity at once is a linguistically and conceptually mediated experience, however figurative the language, however much concept and image are intertwined. And Horkheimer and Adorno take such experience to be the birth of the concept. *The inception of the concept is in a dialectical judgment correlative with an experience of the absolutely other in the same.* The concept is for them, not originarily the analytic concept, itself the basis for the principle of immanence, not the identity of the self-same: "The concept, which some would see as the sign-unit for whatever is comprised under it, has from the beginning been instead the product of dialectical thinking in which everything is always that which it is, only because it becomes that which it is not" (15). Nonetheless they also see in this "the first lines of the separation of subject and object" (15), that radical separation which will eventually result in the world domination by a subject which, by virtue of its having nothing left within it "but that eternally same I think" will advance its own self-liquidation (26).

Natural history begins, and in a sense always begins again, insofar as this experiential-dialectical logic is truncated or cut short, in the moment it is brought to a standstill. And it is cut short in the moment in which weakness and fear are transposed into the logic of self-preservation, that logic according to which social domination finds in the principle of immanence the unconscious strategy by which it preserves itself and society by demanding and instilling the very same principle in its subjects. Here "terror" is fixed "as sacredness": "The dualization of nature as appearance and sequence, effort and power, which first makes possible both myth and science, originates in human fear, the expression of which becomes explanation…*mana,* the moving spirit, is no projection but the echo of the real supremacy of nature" (*DE,* 15). The separation and prioritization of the logic of identity demanded by social self-preservation, the abstraction of the analytic concept from the dialectical judgment, the priority of the principle of immanence, the inception of the process of enlightenment in myth, develops from "the cry of terror, which is the duplication, the tautology of terror itself" (16). And this terror is not a specific fear, but in a sense the absolute fear where "nothing at all may remain outside, because the mere idea of outsideness is the very source of fear" (16).

As with Odysseus with his selective abstraction of the element of deceit in sacrifice taking a crucial step in the acceleration of enlightened subjecthood, so here what takes place in the differentiation of myth and enlightenment together out of magic is an abstraction of the moment of identity in the dialectical logic figured by magical pre-animism. But this abstraction is not itself (at least not once and for all) the consequence of a determined or predetermined logical course. It is the product of social domination, of an at best now-outdated survival strategy.

The self-preservation of societies and their individuals in the form of domination cannot do without the principle of immanence, which in turn requires and develops the universal rule of the principle of equivalence, that is, the rule of the universal, the analytical concept. The analytic concept is in turn the basis of that "formal logic" which "provided the Enlightenment thinkers with the schema of the calculability of the world." This is the logic of bourgeois society, which is "ruled by equivalence... which makes the dissimilar comparable by reducing it to abstract quantities" (*DE,* 7). The principle of equivalence "excises the incommensurable," and in doing so "men are brought to actual conformity. The blessing that the market does not inquire after one's birth is paid for by the barterer, in that he models the potentialities that are his by birth on the production of the commodities that can be bought in the market" (12–13). In this modeling of potentialities on the production of commodities, it is not simply that one subjects oneself to specialization and functional coordination within the economic totality, but that the potentiality of birth, the potentiality, one might say, of a created being to relate to the absolutely other, is reduced to the (apparent, but false) reciprocity of the exchange relation. In the process subjectivity is modeled on the abstract relations of transcendental egos to one another. The empirical subject is not yet in existence, or it is living a deformed existence as the basis from which the transcendental subject can be abstracted. The rejection of myth only reproduces the subject as myth, thus, "Animism spiritualized the object, whereas industrialism objectifies the spirits of men" (28). In this self-definition as a thing, success or failure are measurable and measured, and measured "by the yardstick of self-preservation." But for Horkheimer and Adorno "this represents the true quality of men as little as value represents the things which he consumes" (28).

Natural History and the Same

In Horkheimer and Adorno's construal of the atrophy of experience, what Levinas will call the Same — that which must be broken up in the ethical relation — is a function of the contingent development of social systems of domination. Like Durkheim here, they will recognize the social character of the categories of thought. But unlike Durkheim, this social character is not taken to be

> an expression of social solidarity, but evidence of the inscrutable unity of society and domination. Domination lends increased consistency and force to the social whole in which it establishes itself. The division of labor to which domination tends serves the dominated whole for the end of self-preservation. But then the whole as whole, the manifestation of its immanent reason, necessarily leads to the execution of the particular....What is done to all by the few, always occurs as subjection of individuals by the many: social repression always exhibits the masks of repression by a collective. It is this unity of collectivity and domination, and not direct social universality, solidarity, which is expressed in thought forms. (*DE,* 21–22)

In this analysis, it is not the Same, as the operation of the laboring, cognitive, ontological, disclosive subject that effects or is the basis for the totalization that will eventually conceive and execute universal history. And neither is universal history conceived in terms of a teleological eschatology. It is instead natural history, history unfolding as the repetition of nature as the always-the-same, itself established on the basis of a contingent social domination, that develops and reproduces the Same. For Horkheimer and Adorno, therefore, "The universality of ideas as developed by discursive logic, domination in the conceptual sphere, is raised up on the basis of actual domination" (*DE,* 14).

This is not altogether alien to Levinas's thinking, at least in "The Ego and Totality," where he sees that it is society, in its structure of simultaneous participation and nonparticipation, that "marks the advent" and is the "*a priori* proper to thought." But Levinas will stop before the notion that it is social domination that diverts thought from its own *a priori,* that is, from the simultaneity of participation and nonparticipation which is the ethical relation. Thought and the Same seem to operate on their own. Social domination is instead treated by him, both in that essay and subsequently, as an error, an erring that takes place in Western philosophy. Levinas thus abstracts society and thought from the natural history of domination in which society, and thought, are formed. And in doing so he ironically opens himself to criticisms like the one Marx makes of "perceptual materialism" in the ninth of the "Theses on Feuerbach": "The highest point attained by perceptual materialism, that is materialism that does not comprehend sensuousness as practical activity, is the view of separate individuals and civil society."[21] Although Levinas is not a perceptual materialist like the figures of the post-Lockian enlightenment, in his construal of the real society, and in his analyses of the consequences of the presence of the third party, despite the objectivity granted them, their objectivity seems to be referred back to individual wills, without the formation of those wills, and the concrete and historical forms of subjectivity upon which the will might be based, *also* being referred to their preformation in the objective universal. Levinas will still think about the state, justice and law as though they were simply or ultimately the creation, the decisions of separate individuals forming civil society. This has implications for Levinas's treatment of the consequences of the involvement of the third party in the ethical relation.

The impasse into which Levinas falls in his treatment of the consequences of the third party's presence is itself a consequence of the fact that he is unwilling to treat justice, law, comparison, and calculation as not simply or only called for — and which then assume the shape of a totalization — out of either the ethical relation itself, or out of the necessities of being, but also out of the requirements of domination. Instead, domination seems to arise spontaneously from the totalizations effected by the Same, totalizations that are needed to establish the justice demanded by the ethical relation. Those consequences also, from Horkheimer and Adorno's perspective, belong to the abstraction of the analytical concept from out of the dialectical judgment due to the hold that domination has progressively assumed over society and the self in the course of its own natural history. That there is little "pity, compassion, pardon and proximity" in the world can then not be taken to be the final word. The "little there is" cannot be taken to indicate an antithetical relation, in Levinas's terms, between objectivity and transcendence, even though the two may need to be radically distinguished. Levinas's construal of the relation between ethics and the just state as a betrayal is itself an effort to avoid just such an antithesis while preserving the tension between and the priority of the ethical over the political. One may grant, welcome and even enthuse over the distinction between the poietic, pragmatic, erotic, cognitive, ontological, disclosive, gnoseological relations and the ethical relation without consigning what remains in the end at most perhaps a necessary analytical distinction to the *status* of an ontological divide between experience and experience par excellence. When the consequences of the third party and the real society are historically inflected, the possibility is opened, however immediate or remote it might be at any moment, however impossible, of a withering away of the law, justice, comparison, and calculation. But for this possibility to be seen, let alone acted upon, it would be necessary to experience the reduction and atrophy of experience.

In one way, Levinas's whole philosophical art is directed at producing just such an experience of the atrophy of the experience of the ethical relation as a break-up of the experience of the Same — but only as it takes place in the philosophy of the West. His language carries with it little in the way of rational demonstration or proof. It is itself not even the frankness of ethical expression that he contrasts with rhetoric, but is poetic in the sense that Marcuse quotes Valery as predicating of poetry: poetic verses "'ne parlent jamais que de chose absentes.'" Poetic expression is "'le travail qui fait vivre en nous ce qui n'existe pas'" (quoted in *ODM,* 67–68). But in another sense Levinas stops short in his contestation of reduced experience, and falls short of his own ambition, by reducing his analysis to the description of a permanent structure prior to the origins of Western thought with the Greeks, the structure of an original radical plurality of existents unencompassable in the One or in representation. Because this original structure not only defies representation, but is systematically belied by the latter, Levinas will unfortunately also prematurely give up on or even abjure the possibility of an historical critique, a critique of natural history, that aims at the very reduced experience whose reduction he above all wants to undo.

For Levinas the social relation as the ethical relation is something systematically and inherently denied in social-theoretical and political-philosophical discourse. And he is right to foreground this absence in the political thought of the West. The social relation is "a field of research hardly glimpsed at (where more often than not we confine ourselves to a few formal categories whose content would be but 'psychology')" (*TI,* 79). He is first of all (but also exclusively) concerned with "disengaging" the "holiness" of the Other human from the "tragic and cynical accents" that mark the human sciences and from their "indifference with regard to the human" (*OTB*, 59). Anthropology, including Hegelianism, by which I take him to mean also or especially historical anthropology, is anything but the privileged philosophical discipline in this respect, according to Levinas. Even though, or precisely because, Hegelianism, dialectical thinking, leads us to thinking in distrust of the immediate data of consciousness, it leads to the notion that there cannot be truth in evidence acquired by myself (58). But the appeal of the Other would require or signify exactly that — a self-evidence evident to me that all the frameworks of possible objectivity could not recognize as possible. Thus, for the human sciences "truth is taken to result from the effacing of the living man behind the mathematical structures that think themselves out in him" (58). But the (meta)phenomenological investigations of subjectivity he undertakes, by contrast "lead to extreme and irreducible conceptual possibilities...that go beyond the limits of a description, even if it is dialectical, of order and being, lead to the extraordinary, to what is beyond the possible...substitution of one for another, the immemorable past that has not crossed the present, the positing of the self as a deposing of the ego" (58). Thus for Levinas, "We do not need this knowledge in the relationship in which the other is a neighbor, and in which before being an individuation of the genus *man,* a *rational animal,* a free will or any essence whatever...he is the persecuted one for whom I am responsible to the point of being of being a hostage for him" (58). The human sciences are capable of describing, perhaps explaining the "influences, complexes and dissimulation that cover over the human." But for Levinas it will be enough to demonstrate that no such distortions alter my relation of being hostage to that human because they "do not alter his holiness, but sanction the struggle for the exploited man" (58). Such an ethical struggle for the other is to go on, therefore, despite whatever "complexes, influences and dissimulation" cover over the human in the other to whom I remain hostage. His reduced experience, his indifference to me and even his indifference to the other others in no way absolve me from the struggle for him and all the others.

But why is it that Levinas also says that this means that one "is not obliged to subordinate to these possibilities the truth of the [human] sciences which bear on material or formal being or on being's essence"? Why is it that ethics and the human sciences should be kept at such a distance from each other, especially if Levinas also holds that one "must use ontology for the sake of the other"? Should not the struggle for the other human require precisely such a subordination of the human sciences, bending them somehow, without canceling their claim to truth(s), in the direction of revealing the possibilities of the human and the ethical relation?

Levinas's critique of Marx is the statement of the claim to a more thoroughgoing realism, one which does not, even tacitly, raise up the power of an idealist subject at the end of a dialectical history of progress. His realism, in the form of the radical passivity of subjectivity, will challenge the priority of transcendental subjectivity root and branch by reducing that priority phenomenologically to the ethical relation, to a radical social plurality. This phenomenological reduction of subjectivity and the Same is its reduction to a social relation that itself cannot be grasped in the terms of the Same, cannot be represented in any terms structured by formal logic. Behind and before the intentionality of consciousness, by virtue of which time itself appears, there will have been the response of the subject to the absolute other, to its diachronic trace. It is on the basis of such a realism, an otherwise than being and not only a being that precedes consciousness, that Levinas suggests what is in fact the possibility of an immanent critique of Marx. But he does not suggest the transformation of social critique that should follow. Yet, even if Levinas is correct concerning the ethical relation as both prior to and a breaking up of the Same or of ontology, this does not mean that he should deny the historical and social formation of concrete subjectivity *in its experience of, and nonexperience of, and reduced experience of the breakup of experience,* that is, the ethical relation. This is so because concrete subjectivity, out of which he is philosophizing, will always involve not only the Same and its breakup in being for the other, but the relation of natural history, and perhaps history, to the formation and intensity of the Same. The Same is not always the same Same, and therefore neither is concrete, worldly subjectivity.

For Horkheimer and Adorno, and for Marcuse, if there is to be a breakup of totality beyond and better than the betrayal of ethics in the state it is necessary to trace the possibilities of the breakup of Adorno's spell, that is to see the falsity of the identity of universal and particular, which means to see history as catastrophic *and* catastrophe as neither necessity nor fate. Critique must serve the purpose not only of revealing the contingency *of* as well as within natural history, but, in experience, must serve the purpose of breaking up schematizations that occlude the experience of the atrophy or the reduction of the experience of transcendence. In *Dialectic of Enlightenment* Horkheimer and Adorno indicate several modalities of representation in which this breakup has been kept alive, if only at the margins of representation: art, metaphysics, "religion" in the form of the Judaic ban on the name, the ban on invoking the infinite as finite (*DE,* 17–19, 23). Each of these share with the unreduced dialectical judgment an affirmation of nonidentity in identity, a beyond of the possibilities of the Same. If in reality natural history is to be transcended, it will not be possible without critique as determinate negation, as a negative dialectics that borrows from art, metaphysics, and religion. Negative dialectics would then be the form of critique specific to natural history as opposed to teleological history. But whether any negative dialectics or nonidealist subjectivity is possible that does not already presuppose the radical passivity of the ethical relation remains the tacit question that Levinas puts to the Frankfurt School.

FOUR

Negative Dialectics and Ethics

The Same, Critique, and Dialectics

Adorno begins *Negative Dialectics* with the arresting claim that "philosophy...lives on because the moment to realize it was missed" (*ND*, 3). Much too easily this can be taken to imply that Adorno intends somehow to either restore philosophy to its traditional functions of grounding and synthesizing a comprehensive knowledge, à la Hegel, perhaps with a new degree of modesty about reason's limits, à la Kant, or that he has in mind some future historical realization of its past aims, à la the young Marx. None of these are at all the case. If he promises anything, it is a "changed philosophy" (13) whose promise is not to formulate goals to be realized by the thinker or as universal history. Philosophy cannot be realized as cognition of the totality coming to itself or as the translation of this into the agency of the proletariat as a unified subject-object bringing about the end of prehistory. One can perhaps succeed or fail at negative dialectics, but negative dialectics itself can neither fail nor succeed in the purposive achievement of a positive end. To look at *Negative Dialectics* as an attempt at a new version of objective reason is to misunderstand radically what is taking place in it. If there is an analogous — but merely analogous — precedent for this project, Adorno finds it himself in Kant's search for the possibility of metaphysics after his own critique of rationalism made metaphysics impossible. The changed philosophy has as its animating question the problem of how any philosophy at all is possible now that Hegel's has fallen because the latter failed "to use philosophical concepts for coping with all that is heterogeneous to those concepts" (4). There are for philosophy only three possible extant choices: either it is to be simply the methodology of the special sciences, as positivism would have it; or in its search for substantiality it is to revert in one form or another to Hegel's bad identitarianism; or, finally, it may, from within the idealistically formulated notion of dialectics use "experiences contrary to the Hegelian emphasis" on the primacy of the subject for "re-opening the case of dialectics" (7–8).[1] Thus for Adorno, "the critical path is the only one still open,"[2] and "philosophy is obliged ruthlessly to criticize itself" (*ND*, 3). Negative dialectics, then, will be critique. But, after Hegel, it will have "regained the right to think substantively instead of being put off with the analysis of cognitive forms that were empty and, in an emphatic sense, null and void" (7). Thinking substantively, here, will not mean, however, identifying the substance it thinks. It will mean instead "full, unreduced experience in the medium of conceptual reflection" (13). And this unreduced experience will be "the world agony raised to a concept" (6). Where idealist dialectics was inherently tied, as its exposition, to a historico-teleological eschatology, negative dialectics is analogously tied to natural history as the necessary but insufficient precondition for an escape from that natural history. The teleo-eschatological construal of history is, on the other hand, only one of the symptoms of a history that is still natural-historical.

The dialectical critique that Adorno develops, which is more and less than a methodology and metatheory for a critical human science, which is in fact its philosophical subordination to the possibility of a transcendence of natural history, can, according to him "only be achieved negatively. Dialectics unfolds the difference between the particular and the universal, dictated by the universal" (*ND,* 6). Negation is inescapable: "Thought as such, before all contents, is an act of negation, of resistance to that which is forced upon it; this is what thought has inherited from its archetype, the relation between labour and material" (19). What Adorno borrows above all from Hegel is the moment of negativity, the "sense of negativity of the dialectical logic he is expounding" as exemplified in the introduction to the *Phenomenology of Mind* (156) but now relieved of the systematics of identity. The transcendence of the natural-historical reduction of experience by a different species of thinking will depend entirely on the negativity still contained even within such reduced experience, albeit tacitly. Thus, Adorno does not conceive of negative dialectics as a program of knowledge, at least nothing resembling positive knowledge (159–60).

Although he seems to be thinking largely, if not exclusively, of Hegel, Levinas will contest exactly the adequacy of negativity for transcendence, or for "metaphysics," which is "the relation between the same and the other...where the same, gathered up in its ipseity as an 'I,' as a particular existent, unique and autocthonous, leaves itself" (*TI,* 39). Negation and, we may infer, all that which follows from it — differentiation, discrimination, separation, dynamism, becoming, reflexivity, resistance, contradiction, transformation, and so on — are for Levinas insufficient to effect a de-totalization or carry the subject outside of itself. This would be due to the fundamental codependence, within the I, of negation and the Same. Even in negating itself, let alone an other, the Same remains the Same, even if not the same Same. Thus, for Levinas, identity cannot be transcended simply through the negative, reflexive operations of disidentifying, autonegating thought: "The I is not a being that always remains the same, but is the being whose existing consists in identifying itself, in recovering its identity throughout all that happens to it. It is the primal identity, the primordial work of identification" (36). Despite the fact that the I with its needs meets a world that can be hostile and alien, and that the logic of such an encounter seems to demand an alteration in the I, it will be able to recollect itself in all such encounters inasmuch as the world "offers itself to or resists possession" (38). "The way of the same" lies not in the actuality but in the possibility of possession (38). The I dwells in the world by maintaining itself as the body that can hold itself up and that can (37). The transformation of the world effected by the negativity of labor, and even the transformation of the relation of the Same to the world it transforms, does not effect transcendence because the labor that transforms the world "is sustained by the world it transforms" (40). Negator and negated thus "form a system, that is, a totality" (41). While it is the case that "the I is identical in its very alterations.... [and] represents them to itself" (36), the metaphysical relation with the other proves quite different. The Same remaining the Same in all its alterations leaves itself in relation to the other and thus is neither a representation as the work of identification, nor the reverse of identity as the result of external resistance to the Same and its identifying operations. The metaphysical relation must instead be prior to every initiative of the Same, even if that initiative is reflexive (38–39).

For transcendence, the negativity that flows from a discontent that refuses an established condition is not enough (40) because in fact "negativity is incapable of transcendence. Transcendence designates a relation with a reality infinitely distant from my own reality, yet without the distance destroying the relation and without this relation destroying this distance" (41). Thus, there is no thought, no matter how reflexive, that of itself is capable of undoing the identification it operates to be thought. "The breach of the totality is not an operation of thought," but can take place only when thought finds itself "faced" with an other "refractory to categories." Levinas continues, "The same is essentially identification within the diverse, or history or system. It is not I who resist the system, as Kierkegaard thought, it is the other" (40). Because negative dialectics relies on negativity for the transcendence of identification it will run up against the problem of its own insufficiency for effecting the transcendence of identification which it seeks. This will have consequences for the relation of critique to morality, ethics, and solidarity, and for the relation of the relation between critique and morality to liberation, the redemption of the utopian hopes of the past and the repair of the catastrophe of natural history.

Nonetheless, despite the stringency of Levinas's critique of critical negativity he reserves for it a place that is quite distinct from the place given to ontology, theory, knowledge, or comprehension. If, as Levinas avers, *Totality and Infinity*'s analysis of the ethical relation and the argument for its priority over ontology depends on the unfolding of a single distinction between objectivity and transcendence (*TI*, 49), this does not mean that critique either falls within one or the other category, or that it is the synthesis of both. It may in some sense be the intersection of both. To know ontologically means, according to Levinas, to remove an existent from its alterity while all the while acknowledging that alterity. Whether such knowledge is directed at the human or the nonhuman (or even, we could add, something that is neither) "ontology consists in apprehending the individual (which alone exists) not in its individuality, but in its generality (of which alone there is science). The relation with the other is here accomplished *only* through a third term which I find in myself" (44; emphasis added). Knowing ontologically involves both respect and what we might call denigration or domination. It promotes the freedom of the same, that is, the identification of the same, its not allowing itself to be alienated by the other (42; see also 46). It is on the one hand a relation with being that respects its alterity, such that the known is allowed to be manifest as such and does not get marked in any way by the relation. Knowledge to be knowledge must give a certain priority to its object. But on the other hand, ontology, knowledge, and theory also involve comprehension, which is a way of approaching the object such that "its alterity...vanishes" (42). Comprehension is thought of here as radical inclusion. This relation of simultaneous respect and its opposite requires a third, neutral term that is itself not a being; and this third, neutral term may be a concept, or a sensation or Being distinguished from the existent. Knowledge, to be knowledge, must involve a certain identificatory activity on the part of a subject. In the activity of comprehension by way of a neutral third term found within the subject "the shock of the encounter of the same with the other is deadened" (42). According to Levinas such ontological imperialism is not less, but even more visible in phenomenology, even the phenomenology of Heidegger insofar as *Being and Time* "has argued perhaps one sole thesis: Being is inseperable from the comprehension of Being (which unfolds as time); Being is already an appeal to subjectivity" (45).

But in relation to either the ethical relation or to ontological knowledge and theory, Levinas will grant that critique is not only another quite distinct structure, but a structure "essential for metaphysics." Critique, as critique, and presumably not critique as the preparation of the proper ground for knowledge or theory (as it remains in both Kant and Hegel) is "a calling into question of the same — which cannot occur within the egoist spontaneity of the same." By calling into question the freedom of the exercise of ontology the critical intention leads beyond theory and ontology. However, it does so only by a "further exercise of the same freedom" (*TI,* 43). In establishing itself as critique by turning the freedom of ontology against itself it has not, however, in its own past at least, as yet been able to grasp itself, as Levinas in *Totality and Infinity* grasps it, as dependent on an exteriority (of an existent) or on an infinity that belongs to no possible object and to no Being. Critique by itself is unable to grasp that it "is brought about by the other. We name this calling into question of my spontaneity by the presence of the other ethics" (43).

This unawareness, or the dogmatic slumber on the part of critical negativity itself of its own preconditions is reflected in social critique to the extent that it has not yet found a way to avoid a reproduction of violence in the very struggle against it. Not only in its reductive but substantive teleologies, but also in its liquification of every independent substantiality, social critique, inasmuch as it remains comprehension in the above sense, as it proceeds, erases that which separates it from ontology. It ironically, even imperceptibly, turns the judgment over power from which it begins into a judgment of or by a greater or more original power. But if there is to be a judgment over power it will not be able to proceed out of the power of being. Social critique that, having renounced transcendent universals, inverts essences into absolute flux or into pluralistic agonism does not renounce power but reproduces it. It is subject to its own dialectic:

> The concern of contemporary philosophy to liberate human beings from the categories adapted uniquely to things cannot therefore content itself with notions of dynamism, duration, transcendence or freedom, as opposed to the inert, the determined, as a description of the human essence. In order to say what is human nature, it is not so much a matter of opposing one essence to another. It is above all a matter of finding a place where the human no longer concerns us from the perspective of the horizon of being, that is to say no longer offers itself to our powers.[3]

Critique could not then go far enough to dissolve natural history if there were not already a relation beyond critique, a relation that makes possible the dialectical judgment out of which, under the principle of domination, identification could itself then be progressively abstracted, but a relation possibly largely or even entirely unknown to critique itself. Thus for Levinas, "All reflective self-critique already takes place after responsibility" (TH, 21).

The point for critique therefore would not be to renounce or abandon the categories of dynamism, to systematize, statically totalize, to revert to a new conception of human identity, but somehow in its activity to infinitely maintain, in its experience of experience, the sense of responsibility that will not allow for either immanence or dynamism to be adopted for their power, or as higher, more inclusive perspectives. The problem with reflection is not in the possibility of infinite regress forever frustrating the demands of formal logic for unity, but in its possible orientation toward infinity as infinite power. If it is not taken to extremes, reflexivity reproduces the power of immanence; but when it is taken to extremes, reflexivity may reflect only the power of a negation negatively bound to the immanence it rejects:

> It is, to be sure, the role of reflection to reduce meanings to their subjective, subconscious, social or verbal sources, to draw up a transcendental inventory of them. But the method, though legitimate to destroy many false reputations, already prejudges an essential result: it forbids in advance any transcendent aim in meaning. Before the research, every Other is already converted by it into the Same, but in its purifying work Reflection will itself use these notions [of responsibility, infinity, etc.], if only the notion of a beyond with respect to which immanence is situated.[4]

The question concerning negative dialectics is the way in which and the extent to which it might be inhibited by either its ignorance of, confusion about, or its reticence with respect to what makes it possible.

Negative Dialectics as Critical Constellation

Negative dialectics includes *and* criticizes the critique which Levinas criticizes as insufficient, but at the same time strives and knows that it strives to go beyond critique into a relation with the object which can only be described as metaphysical or as ethical. One fruitful way of tracing the moment of unity and coherence in *Negative Dialectics,* the *esprit systématique* that Adorno distinguishes from the *esprit de système* in idealisms, would be to read it as a second-order reflection on the relation of subject and object that is, as conceptualization, nonetheless itself nonidentifying. It is a second-order reflection because it takes as its starting point first-order reflections that assign to a knowing or laboring subject a constitutive role for objectivity (Kant, Hegel, Marx). Adorno will describe this variously as metacritique, as a reversal of the subjective reduction which does not restore the object to the status of being first, or as an axial turn within dialectics.

Metacritique versus Sociology of Knowledge

Within this second-order reflection maintaining nonidentity, the distinction between subject and object is neither cancelled by way of the identification of either side with the other via logical, phenomenological, or sociological reduction, nor is there the hypostatization of the separation of subject and object into a duality that would abstractly affirm or posit nonidentity as identical. At the same time, although the relation of subject and object is through such means rendered historical and temporal to the point where negative dialectics itself envisions and calls for its own disappearance (*ND,* 141), time and history cannot themselves be identified as totalities realizing a logic of progressive approximation to, or a (positive) dialectical logic culminating in, the telos of differentiated unity.

Thus, negative dialectics is differentiated from any and all sociologies of knowledge whether they are economistic, evolutionary, systems-theoretical, communicative, psychologistic in the manner of Weber's "ideal interests," or even if they are Nietzschean genealogies of power. Sociology of knowledge which, broadly speaking, reduces the subject to objective dynamics, substitutes for the concern of philosophy with the truth content of the idea an identification of its social functioning and conditioning by interests. Adorno takes such an approach to be powerless against philosophy because it refrains from a critique of that content itself in terms of its possible, or the extent of its actual, truth or falsity. The factors it brings to bear are not mediations but externalities brought up from the outside. Sociology of knowledge therefore fails as a critique of ideology inasmuch as the concept of ideology only makes sense with reference to the truth or untruth of that to which it refers.

Dialectics or materialism, on the other hand, is bound to be an immanent critique, "even if in the end it negates the whole sphere it moves in" (*ND,* 197). Dialectics, as materialism or immanent critique, will judge both "the subjective and objective shares and their dynamics" (197). It will negate the "false objectivity of concept fetishism" by reducing such external factors to their social *subjectivity,* thus further relativizing what sociology of knowledge brings in from the outside in order, as sociology first, to relativize. It performs a second-order relativization that reintroduces the question of truth/untruth by destabilizing the inside/outside frame of reference necessarily though usually tacitly employed by the sociology of knowledge. And at the same time, dialectics will do this by including the very truth — in the Hegelian sense of result — of the sociology of knowledge, the now destabilized inside/outside, in order to deny false Subjectivity, "the veiled claim that all being lies in the mind" (197–98). This second-order relativization is not at all to be taken to be an endorsement of relativism, even if it "shields no primacy, harbors no certainty" (34). Negative dialectics will, in fact, "give offense" just because it "concedes so little to relativism" (34). It opposes relativism as strictly as it opposes absolutism, but not by seeking any middle ground — instead it "convicts them of untruth by their own ideas" (35).

In differentiating itself from sociologies of knowledge and in opposing relativism, negative dialectics will nonetheless incorporate the negative moments included within those critiques, now stripped of their identifying propensities. Thus, Adorno will introduce a fundamental kinship between the identity principle itself and what he calls the "barter [exchange] principle" (*ND,* 146). Or he will, quite in the spirit of sociological reduction, criticize Kant for hypostatizing, as the categories of all possible objective experience, those scientific concepts that are the products of bourgeois society (387–88). He will go so far as to raise the possibility of an eventual restoration of metaphysical knowledge on the basis of its blockage to date by virtue of "the natural-historic cares we share with beetles" (389). And he will assign to Nietzsche credit for "the liberating act" that enables a negative dialectics to break through idealist foundations, systematics, and drives to unity, by seeing such things as sublimations of "the pre-mental, the animal life of the species" (22). Thus, for Adorno, "The system is the belly turned mind, and rage is the mark of each and every idealism" (23).

Inasmuch as the identifying propensities of sociological theories are negated in their disavowal of the problem of objective truth, thus restoring the philosophical aims they aim to undercut, the problem of truth itself, as identity of subject and object, is not eliminated by the reducibility of truths and truth to their functions and interests within some prior whole or prior flux. What marks both idealist systems and relativizing critiques of those systems, however, is their commitment to or entanglement within the principle of identity. Sociologies of knowledge will always tend to be reductions of the concept to identifiable and more or less dynamic social objectivities. In its infinite contestation of identity negative dialectics, as materialism, will retain their negation of the priority of the subject. But it will not retain their identification of the subject as object. That is not what granting priority to the object will mean for Adorno.[5] The mediation of the subject by the object is not the dogmatic hypostatization of the latter. Objective mediation can only be known "as it entwines with subjectivity" (*ND,* 186), the very subjectivity that seeks to identify. Sociologies of knowledge do not dissipate the truncation of experience that takes place in idealism. They even tend to reproduce it.

Unreduced Experience and Contradiction

At the heart of negative dialectics is a critique of the idealist concept of experience, a concept that is not undone, and an experience that is not opened out to transcendence by the sociology of knowledge, no matter how dynamic the latter makes the objectivities it identifies as constitutive. What especially marks the idealist concept of experience is the constitutive role granted to subjective forms in the cognition of the real. And in a very real sense negative dialectics begins with the possibility of the experience, the sense of the insufficiency of this formal constitution: "The forms of subjectivity are not cognitive ultimates, as Kant taught; as its experience progresses, cognition can break through them" (*ND,* 187). Thus for Adorno, matters that were not of interest to idealist metaphysics are of true philosophical interest now: nonconceptuality, particularity, individuality. Consequently, "A matter of urgency to the concept would be what it fails to cover, what its abstractionist mechanism eliminates, what is not already a case of the concept" (8). The challenge of philosophy would be "to counter Wittgenstein by uttering the unutterable" (9).

Negative dialectics begins, then, with the sense of contradiction, which sense however depends upon the very claim of the concept to adequacy with that object; it depends on the aspiration exemplified in idealism to the identity of concept and object and depends therefore on the identity of the concept. While for Adorno, "the ideal of identity is not to be discarded" (*ND,*

150), the ideal of identity, in Levinas's terms, would include the moment of respect for the alterity of the object. It is, for Adorno, necessity that compels philosophy to operate with concepts. But this same necessity does not necessitate identifying the necessity of identities "with the virtue of their priority" (11). And the necessity of operating with concepts does not simply spell out an inherent, invariant urge to dominate the object. It is not, or not simply a pragmatic necessity, a necessity of instrumental success. Concepts are recognized as moments of the very reality that requires their formulation. The changed philosophy is not non- or antiphilosophy.

Systematics and Speculation

The drive still inherent in identity for adequacy with the object also implies that philosophy "cannot do without speculation," that it cannot remain content with phenomenal knowledge (*ND,* 15). But the speculation in question is to be "without an idealistic substructure" (18). It is the idealistic substructure, granting priority to the concept and to the formal logic that is the only way of maintaining the identity of the concept, which shows up in the unity of idealistic systems and in the search for foundations, the search for a first philosophy that will cement the relation of priority of the concept to its object. Traditional speculation aims at a synthesis of the diversity that it prejudges as otherwise chaotic. And in its relentless pursuit of identity it is "forced to take exaggerated steps.... Great philosophy was accompanied by a paranoid zeal to tolerate nothing else" (22). To repeat, "The system is belly turned mind, and rage is the mark of each and every idealism" (*ND,* 23). This would be true even of the highest points of Kantian humanism: "The august inexorability of the moral law was this kind of rationalized rage at non-identity" (23). Although the idealist philosophical system, in its pursuit of unity and unanimity, is also the oblique projection of relations that are pacific and nonantagonistic, it is primarily an expression of the drive to identify, of the principle of immanence inherent in and made prior by the structure of social domination: "The system, the form of presenting a totality to which nothing remains extraneous absolutizes the thought against each of its contents and evaporates the contents in the thought" (24). The absolutization of thought is not avoided when systems are rendered dynamic and developmental. Thus, the Hegelian system was not a true becoming inasmuch as, from the start, all of its differentiated moments were to be conceived as deriving from the absolute idea.

Material dialectics, on the other hand, would no longer be able to comprehend its objects on the basis of a pregiven or foreordained meaning. Therefore, "Unconsciously, so to speak, consciousness would have to immerse itself in the phenomena on which it takes a stand. This would, of course, effect a qualitative change in dialectics. Systematic unity would crumble. The phenomenon would not remain a case of the concept" (27). In this situation the justified aim included within speculation, the aim of dissolving the apparent immediacy and necessity of the given, would have to be taken up by negation alone: "The speculative power to break down the gates of the insoluble is the power of negation. The systematic trend lives on in negation alone. The categories of a critique of systems are at the same time the categories in which the particular is understood" (28). Negative dialectics is also therefore a translation into the terms and framework of philosophical inquiry of the Benjaminian materialist imperative to brush objects against the grain and blast particulars out of the continuum of history, to extricate them from totalities and at the same time, in doing so, to perceive their own "monadic insistence" (162).

Philosophical systematics therefore has a double meaning. On the one hand, in its expression of the principles of immanence, identity, and unity it dominates the particulars that it aims to include. In Levinas's terms, system reduces the alterity of the other to the freedom of the Same. On the other hand, it is only the very same drive to identity that makes possible the speculative moment which transcends the phenomenon as given. *It is only identity that makes nonidentity possible.* In Levinas's terms, only a radically separated being will be capable of transcendence. Another way of putting this is to say that the "essence" of idealism, as exemplary of (and for) identifying thought, is an "antinomy of totality and infinity" (*ND,* 26).[6] For Adorno, this double meaning of the principle of identity "leaves no choice but to transpose the power of thought, once delivered from the systems, into the open realm of definition by individual moments" (24–25). Within idealism such "definition by individual moments" is a nonpossibility. But it is not because of the identity of the concept *per se* that idealism is bound so strongly to totality. It is not even subjective constitution or subjective mediation of the object that suffices to impose totalization. It is because of the *priority* granted to subjective constitution in all consistent idealisms that they end in a closed system, a positive infinity (27). Thus, idealisms, like Hegel's, may include "microanalysis" — the notion of letting "each concept pass into its otherness without regard to overlay from above" (25). But, as idealisms, what they cannot relinquish is the priority of the concept.

Thus, negative dialectics will not be the abstract negation of either idealism or its systematics.[7] To relinquish the speculative power would be to abandon the particulars themselves to a totalized judgment of absolute nonrelation. The abstract negation of systems and "a-systematic thought" both succumb to superficiality; so would negative dialectics in its critique of idealism, unless it were able "to release the cohesive force which the idealistic systems had signed over to the transcendental subject" (*ND,* 26). The retention and development of the cohesive force, the positive cognitive moment of negative dialectics, becomes the function of a negation that cannot proceed outside of identity thinking itself. Thus, for Adorno, "the speculative power to break down the gates of the insoluble is the power of negation. The systematic trend lives on in the power of negation alone" (28). This does not mean that "negation alone" provides only a poor remnant of the speculative power, but that whatever there is that is objective in the speculative power can live only by a negation not already in the service of a unity to be affirmed. Negative dialectics is dialectical rather than simply negative inasmuch as it retains from positive dialectics the requirement (as old as Plato) to understand the particular from out of the totality of its relations, and therefore also retains the distinction between essence and appearance. But it is negative rather than simply being dialectical inasmuch as those relations among particulars are not to be grasped as reducible to a higher unity, that is, ultimately as instances of the concept.

Nonidentity, Logic, and Contradiction

The problem, then, becomes one of using identity, but without identifying. The work of philosophical reflection for the changed philosophy is one of "unraveling [the] paradox" of uttering the unutterable (*ND,* 9). This cannot be approached save through a negation that takes place in the form of a sense of nonidentity. Consequently, "whatever truth the concepts cover beyond their abstract range can have no other stage than what the concepts suppress, disparage and discard. The cognitive utopia would be to use concepts to unseal the non-conceptual with concepts, without making it their equal" (9–10). Identifying thought is that thought "which depreciates a thing to a mere sample of its kind or species, only to convince us that we have the thing as such, without subjective addition" (146). Nonidentifying thought, a negative dialectics which is still thought while simultaneously definable as the ability to "think against our thought" (141), "is the consistent sense of non-identity. It does not begin by taking a standpoint. My thought is driven to it by its own insufficiency, by my guilt of what I am thinking" (5). Because there can be no nonidentity without identity, no nonconceptual to avoid equating with the concept without the concept, the consistent sense of nonidentity must show up as contradiction (or, more strictly, as either contradiction or total incoherence). Contradiction is necessary to express the nonidentical inasmuch as the moment of subjectivity is not to be (and cannot be) eliminated and inasmuch as "the appearance of identity is inherent in thought itself, in its pure form. To think is to identify. Conceptual order is content to screen what thinking seeks to comprehend" (5).

In the purely logical form of thought there is a striving for unity, a principle of immanence, that is evinced in the simultaneous identity of a given concept with itself and with its negation of others, expressed in the law of the excluded middle. To the extent that priority is assigned to the conceptual, the same logic will, in pursuit of the unity of the various conceptual unities, yield a totality, a differentiated unity that may be assembled through a progressive ascent from species to genus. Under the operation, therefore, of the identity principle, the nonidentical can only show up as contradiction: "Since...totality is structured to accord with logic, however, whose core is the principle of the excluded middle, whatever will not fit this principle, whatever differs in quality, comes to be designated as contradiction. Contradiction is non-identity under the aspect of identity" (*ND*, 5). Thus for Adorno, contradiction does not indicate actual existential impossibility or nonbeing, but instead it "indicates the untruth of identity, the fact that the concept does not exhaust the thing conceived." It indicates that "objects do not go into their concepts without leaving a remainder" (5). Thus, in negative dialectics neither identity nor contradiction are to be thought of as essential to the object; nor can they be combined in a positive dialectical logic in which, for all intents and purposes, contradiction becomes the motor of identity. It is important to realize that for Adorno, "Contradiction is not what Hegel's absolute idealism was bound to transfigure it into: it is

not of the essence in a Heraclitean sense" (5). The recurrence
of contradiction, which is in a sense what idealism both discovers and cannot abide, is not the essence of objective being,
but is a function of the natural-historic subjective principle of
identity. If there is no nonidentity without identity, there is also
no contradiction without identity. And there is no "sense of
contradiction" without identity.

Even though, but also because idealism will not countenance
contradiction, it will register, though indirectly, the subjective and
historic origins of the principles of identity and dominion: "The
pedantries of all systems, down to the architectonic complexities
of Kant — and even of Hegel, despite the latter's program —
are the marks of an a priori inescapable failure, noted with
incomparable honesty in the fractures of the Kantian system"
(*ND*, 21–22). This means that "the coercive state of reality,
which idealism had projected into the region of the subject and
mind, must be retranslated from that region. What remains of
idealism is that society, the objective determinant of mind, is
as much an epitome of subjects, as it is their negation" (10).
Contradiction cannot be absolved of its social history.

Objectivity of Contradiction

But to say that contradiction is a function of the subjective
principle of identity is not to indicate that that principle is either
invariant or that it is natural. It is only to say that it is natural-
historic. The principle of identity, although subjective, is not
the operation of an (individual) transcendental subjectivity or
of the world-mind. The principle of identity is itself an historic
function of *social* subjectivity that eventually, in the abstraction
of the analytic judgment from the dialectical one, establishes
the principle of dominion: "The principle of dominion, which
antagonistically rends human society, is the same principle,
which spiritualized, causes the difference between the concept
and its subject matter; and that difference assumes the logical

form of contradiction because, measured by the principle of dominion, whatever will not bow to its unity will not appear as something different and indifferent to the principle, but as a violation of logic" (*ND,* 48). Thus, although contradiction is not of the essence in a Heraclitean sense, the major premise of *Negative Dialectics,* explicitly avowed as a premise by Adorno, is that the object of mental experience is an antagonistic system in itself (10). But this objective antagonistic system must be understood as the natural-historic activity of social individuals. Without this premise, the sense of contradiction and nonidentity would once more either refer to an essence or merely to a simple illusion rather than a real illusion. Beyond natural history, the real cannot be said to be either a static or dynamic totality or their opposite, a "chaotic" infinite flow of atoms indifferent to one another (see 158). Thus, "What we differentiate will appear divergent, dissonant, negative for just as long as the structure of our consciousness obliges it to strive for unity. As long as its demand for totality will be its measure for what is not identical with it" (5–6). This law, Adorno says, is not simply cogitative: "It is real" (6). Although contradiction was once the vehicle of total identification, negative dialectics must retain the sense of real contradiction from out of a different direction: "Instead it is up to dialectical cognition to pursue the inadequacy of thought and thing, to experience it in the thing. Dialectic need not fear the charge of being obsessed with the fixed idea of objective conflict in a thing already pacified; no single thing is at peace in the unpacified whole. The aporetical concepts of philosophy are marks of what is objectively, not just cogitatively unresolved" (153).

Negative dialectics, is then, not Adorno's invention. Its anti-subjectivism already "lies under the crackling shell of absolute idealism; it stirs in the tendency to unseal current issues by resorting to the way they came to be" (*ND,* 26). Adorno's contribution will be to take on all the guilt of what he is thinking and follow through in the effort to change the goal rather than the substance of thinking: "The mistake in traditional thinking is that identity is taken for the goal" (149). Adorno will claim not only that identity thinking has nonidentity as its "secret telos," but also that "living in the rebuke that the thing is not identical with the concept is the concept's longing to become identical with the thing. This is how the sense of non-identity contains identity" (149). Negative dialectic will therefore always comprise two moments that cannot be abstracted from one another and yet cannot be synthesized into a unity. The first moment is destructive, dynamic, processual, and reflexive; the second moment is redemptive, immediate, mimetic, and utopian. Neither can take place without the other, yet they cannot be added together to form a whole.

Contradiction and Disintegration

The reflective, negative, and destructive moment of negative dialectics is necessary to effect a reversal of the traditional aim of philosophy, the aim of unity and identity projected and exemplified in the enunciation of a systematic whole of propositions encompassing being. But the destructive moment does not take place out of an act of will, but from the insight, according to Adorno, that conceptual knowledge is not the absolute, an insight that in fact follows from the nature of the concept itself:

> To refer to non-conceptualities...is characteristic of the concept, and so is the contrary: that as the abstract unit of noumena subsumed thereunder it will depart from the noumenal. To change this direction of conceptuality, to give it a turn towards non-identity is the hinge of negative dialectics. Insight into the constitutive character of the non-conceptual in the concept would end the compulsive identification which the concept brings unless halted by such reflection. Reflection on the concept's own meaning is the way out of the concept's being-in-itself as a unit of meaning. (*ND*, 11–12)

Such reflection would amount to a "disenchantment of the concept" that would provide "the antidote of philosophy." The changed philosophy's aim would therefore not be to reduce things to a minimum of propositions. Such a change in function is already, however, to be found in idealism, though in corrupted form, in the idea of infinity. As opposed to idealism, in negative dialectics, infinity will take another form: it will mean canceling the aim of capturing the infinite in the finite: "If it were delicately understood, the changed philosophy itself would be infinite in the sense of scorning solidification in an enumerable body of theorems" (*ND,* 13).

Out of this infinition would follow a change in the character and presentation of philosophy. In recognizing its affinity to art, it would come more to resemble art, without borrowing from art. The aesthetic, though no excuse for lack of cogency, is not accidental to philosophy. As a result, "Both keep faith with their own substance through their opposites: art by making itself resistant to meanings; philosophy by refusing to clutch at any immediate thing" (*ND,* 15). The changed philosophy will take place in fragmented form (28), will abjure timelessness, the "idol of a pure present," and eschew the notion of a pure beginning. Thus, recognizing that it "rests on the texts it criticizes" it will mind the tradition and avoid the dehistoricization of thought (53–55). It will avow its linguistic nature which at present the ideal of method "leads it to deny in vain" and "attempt a critical rescue of the rhetorical element, a mutual approximation of thing and expression, to the point the difference fades" (56). Its linguistic nature already by itself points to "how one should think instead." Rather than following the ideal of comprehensive classification in a system of stable meanings, the changed philosophy "instead has its distant and vague archetype in the various languages, in the names which do not categorically cover the thing, albeit at the cost of their cognitive function" (52). It will veer sharply away from the dominant ideal of scientific objectivity taken up by philosophy, whose quantifying tendency "was a reduction of the knower to a purely logical universal without qualities" (44). Instead, it will grant a new privilege to subjective experience: "The objectivity of dialectical cognition needs not less subjectivity, but more. Philosophical experience withers otherwise" (40). But this is for the sake of the objectivity of dialectical cognition, that is, the transcendence of the subject: "As more of the subject's reactions are tabooed as allegedly merely subjective, more qualitative differences of the object will escape cognition" (44). The infinition of the desire for the nonidentical in the changed philosophy would still yield truth, but a truth that "is suspended and frail due to its temporal substance" (34). But again, this "fragility of truth" is for the sake of truth: "By dissociating thought from primacy and solidity, however, we do not absolutize it as in free suspense. The very dissociation fastens it to that which it is not. It removes the illusion of the autarky of thought" (34).

The reflexive and negative side of negative dialectics would therefore involve what Adorno calls a logic of disintegration. Negative dialectics "is suspicious of all identity. Its logic is one of disintegration: of a disintegration of the prepared and objectified form of the concepts which the cognitive subject faces, primarily and directly. Their identity with the subject is untrue. With this untruth, the subjective pre-formation of the phenomenon moves in front of the non-identical in the phenomenon, in front of the *individuum ineffabile*" (*ND,* 145). The logic of disintegration however does not involve a flat denial of subjectivity, but instead a reversal of the subjective reduction in philosophy (176), and a dialectics of subject and object. A dialectics of subject and object, in its rejection of monism, is not to be taken as a dualism. As between subject and object there is no ultimate duality. Nor is their differentiation a "screen hiding" their "ultimate unity." It is rather the case that "They constitute one another as much as — by virtue of such constitution — they depart from one another" (174). Both, as abstractions, are thought products. Rather than setting either subject or object up as substance, as the ultimate source of unity, for Adorno, "the only possible course is definite negation of the individual moments whereby subject and object are turned into absolute opposites, and precisely thus are identified with each other" (175). They are thus identified with each other as identities. If neither subject nor object is to be an identity, then neither monism nor dualism apply to their relation to each other.

Beyond Subjective Reduction

A subject-object dialectics then, as a negative dialectics, implies first of all a "reversal of the subjective reduction" in philosophy (*ND,* 176). And such a reversal implies a "preponderance of the object" (183). Adorno writes, "Carried through, the critique of identity is a groping for the preponderance of the object.... [It] does not bring subject and object into a balance, nor does it raise the concept of function to an exclusively dominant role in philosophy; even when we merely limit the subject, we put an end to its power.... A minimum will do to spoil it as a whole, because it pretends to be the whole" (183). The categories of experience activated and operated by the subject are themselves subject to negation in the object of which the subject takes itself to be constitutive: "As its experience progresses, cognition can break through them" (187).

Empiricism registered something of the preponderance of the object in spite of "its sensualistic reduction of things" (187). Thus, for Adorno, "The object is more than pure factuality; at the same time, the fact that factuality is irremovable forbids contentment with its [factuality's] abstract concept and with the dregs of factuality, the recorded sense data" (188). However, the object is, according to Adorno, not "a datum or affection" of the subject (186). The realism of the empiricist tradition remained "rudimentary," substituting for the concrete object "a kind of minimum object into the direct data." But this definition of the object by progressive abstraction from subjective additions still subscribes to a "delusion of *prima philosphia*": "That the definitions that make the object concrete are merely imposed upon it — this rule applies only where the faith in the primacy of subjectivity remains unshaken" (187). The factuality of the empiricist tradition is merely opposed, perhaps tacitly, to the assumed fact of the pure spontaneity of the subject's identifying activity.

Thus, if empiricism is not realistic enough by itself to break through the primacy of subjectivity, this is because, for negative dialectics "neither the concept nor factuality is an addition to its complement" (*ND,* 188). Hegel's Absolute idealism, having dispensed with the form-substance dualism of Kant, supplies a better clue to the reversal of the subjective reduction: "Hegel's presupposition that the subject might yield purely, unreservedly to the object, to the thing itself, since the process would show the thing to be what it already is in itself: a subject — this presupposition is presumptively idealistic; but it does take note, against idealism, of a truth about the subject's mode of cogitative conduct. Because the subject does not make the object, it can really only 'look on,' and the cogitative maxim is to assist in that process" (188). To assist in the process of allowing the subject to only look on, for the sake of objectivity, the reversal of the subjective reduction also implies a reduction of the subjective reduction to its social objectivity (see 170).

Thus, the transcendental, free, and constitutive subject, the agent of Kant's Copernican revolution in philosophy, "can be deciphered as a society unaware of itself" (*ND,* 177). According to Adorno, "The centristic identity of the I is acquired at the expense of what idealism will then attribute to it [that is, spontaneity]. The constitutive subject of philosophy is more of a thing than the specific psychological content which it excreted as naturalistic and reified. The more autocratically the I rises above entity, the greater its imperceptible objectification and ironic retraction of its constitutive role" (176–77). There is a fundamental kinship of the principle of identity with the "barter [exchange] principle" (146). The identifying role of transcendental subjectivity thus brings it close to the truth of the commodity-exchange society: "The transcendental generality is no mere narcissist self-exaltation of the I…Its reality lies in the domination that prevails and perpetuates itself by means of the principle of equivalence. The process of abstraction — which philosophy transfigures and which it ascribes to the knowing subject alone — is taking place in the factual barter society" (178). If absolute idealism, however, only aims at, without accomplishing a yielding to the object, this would be because such idealism ends up, from the start, making the object only the alienated form of subjectivity as spirit. Its claim to "mental omnipotence" can be experienced as the negative echo of the subject's "real impotence": "The ego principle imitates its negation. It is not true that the object is a subject, as idealism has been drilling into us for thousands of years, but it is true that the subject is an object" (179). Self-reflection by the subject on its own objectivity, in this sense, opens the way for it to become aware of its own nonidentity — and, at the same time, by implication the nonidentity of the object which, if it remains prior, itself now resists being identified as identity. In this process, which elsewhere Adorno calls a second Copernican turn in philosophy, "thinking breaks the supremacy of thinking over its otherness, because it always is otherness already, within itself" (201). It is otherness within itself by virtue of three things: first, its mimetic relation to the object; second, the very reflexive activity it needs in order to be a subject; and third, the reflexive recognition of its own mimetic objectivity.

If the object is not a subject, as idealism would have it, and if this means that the subject is therefore an object, such objectivity — now, after the second reflection — is objectivity *not*

constituted any longer by the identifying power of the subject,
then objectivity would no longer be identified according to the
principle of immanence. The object would no longer be external
to the subject, because it would no longer be constituted by
the concept as identical. The principle of immanence would no
longer be necessity; in Levinas's terms, "Parmenidean being"
would not be the mark of reality, but the sign for human beings
of their "imprisonment in their survival mechanism" (*ND*, 180).
Thus, the reversal of the subjective reduction does not mean
placing the object "on the orphaned royal throne once occupied
by the subject." The purpose of such a reversal is, instead, "to
abolish the hierarchy" (181). The classifying, abstracting subject
of empiricism, in the cunning of its Odyssean weakness, is not
capable of this.[8] The identity and therefore the immutability,
power, priority, and necessity of anything are due to the operation
of the concept, when abstracted from the dialectical judgment.
It is the ambition of first philosophy that makes dualism and
hierarchy possible (137). Therefore, canceling the claim of the
subject to be "first" also rids whatever appeared "second" of
being subordinate (138). Subject and object "reciprocally perme-
ate each other" (139). The preponderance of the object is not
the reverse of the priority of the subject. The materialism that
grants priority to the object does not cancel subjectivity: "The
line that consciousness depends on being was not a metaphysics
in reverse; it was pointed at the delusion that mind is in itself,
that it lies beyond the total process in which it finds itself as a
moment" (200). Thus, to engage in "controversy about the priority of mind and body is a predialectical proceeding. It carries
on the question of a 'first,'" whereas both body and mind are
"abstractions of their experience" (202). Consequently, "The fact
that thinking is mediated by objectivity does not negate thinking" (181). Objectivity, far from being something immediate, is
"a moment in dialectics…articulated in dialectics" (184). Thus
"The object's preponderance is solely attainable for subjective
reflection, and for reflection on the subject" (185).

Dialectical Constellations

The dialectic of subject and object, and the passage to materialism that comes along with it, not only unravels the "image theory" of Marxism,[9] it also raises the question, by virtue of its logic of disintegration, its infinite disenchantment of the concept, of whether the philosophy that lives on is even possible. It might now seem that not only does all that was solid melt into air, but that the air itself is insubstantial. "Such a concept of dialectics," says Adorno, "makes us doubt its possibility" (*ND*, 10). On the one hand, moving *always* in contradictions makes negative dialectics seem to be a "mental totality," the very identity thesis it wishes to discard (10). On the other hand, a dialectics that is in fact no longer "glued" to identity will induce reactions of vertigo and bottomlessness (31).

With regard to the first possibility of impossibility, namely, that negative dialectics seems to imply a negative totality, a *system* of contradictions, a tacit identity, Adorno has two things to say: first, as was already mentioned, Adorno is consciously making use of the premise that natural history is "an antagonistic system in itself," but that as natural history, this system is inherently transient. (Not that transience is a function of contradiction; but that contradiction, as a function of identity, is itself transient.) Thus, second, that "dialectics is the ontology of the wrong state of things. The right state of things would be free of it [i.e. free of dialectics]: neither a system nor a contradiction" (*ND*, 11). Thus, a consistently negative dialectics becomes reflexive with respect to the temporality of its own reflexivity and historicity, a reflexivity that bears on the transience of the contradiction-system pair. Thus for Adorno,

> Dialectics is the self-consciousness of the objective context of delusion; it does not mean to have escaped from that context. Its objective goal is to break out of that context from within.... By means of logic dialectics grasps the coercive character of logic, hoping that it [logic] may yield — for that coercion

itself is the mythical delusion, the compulsory identity. But the absolute, as it hovers before metaphysics, would be the non-identical that refuses to emerge until the compulsion of identity has dissolved. Without a thesis of identity, dialectics is not the whole; but neither will it be a cardinal sin to depart from it in a dialectical step. (*ND*, 406)

About the second possibility of impossibility, the disorientation that might be felt, Adorno also has two things to say: the first is that negative dialectics is "not without anything solid, no more than is Hegel. But it no longer confers primacy on it" (*ND*, 37). It retains the theory of second nature [but without a first nature] and therefore "assumes…the abrupt immediacy, the formations which society and its evolution present to our thought; and it does this so that analysis may bare its [immediacy's] mediations to the extent of the immanent difference between phenomena and that which they claim to be in themselves" (38), Thus, negative dialectics, unlike Nietzsche, will also maintain the distinction between essence and appearance. Only the "directional tendency" of the distinction will be reversed: "Essence can no longer be hypostatized as the pure spiritual being-in-itself. Rather essence passes into that which lies concealed beneath the façade of immediacy…. It comes to be the law of doom thus far obeyed by history" (167). And what lies beneath the façade of immediacy is no longer to be taken to be self-identical. The second thing he has to say with regard to the vertigo that comes with "always moving in contradictions" is that behind the worry about the solidity, timelessness, and immutability of truth "lies mostly pure aggression and, a desire to take hold of it the way the historical schools used to devour each other" (32). Identity thinking will necessarily sacrifice the thing to a stable frame of reference "if only each [thing] can be localized, and if unframed thoughts are kept out. But a cognition that is to bear fruit will throw itself to the objects *a fond perdu*. The vertigo which this causes is an *index veri;* the shock of inconclusiveness, the negative as which it cannot help appearing in the frame-covered, never-changing realm, is true for untruth only" (33).

Thus, the second moment of negative dialectics is, without being positive knowledge, still a fruitful cognition, whose truth is to be indicated in a sort of shock, the shock of the dizzying, decentered, non- or more-than-inferential, truthful relations it registers among and internal to the *relata,* relations which are excised by the identifying functions of the concept. That which is uncovered by the logic of the disintegration that undoes the prepared and fixed conceptual identities, neither noumenon nor phenomenon, is not to be covered over again in new categories or a new frame of reference. If the object is in part to be redeemed it will only be through a thinking in constellations, where a constellation involves as much a reference for the frame as frame for the referent. The constellation substitutes for the perfect identity, timelessness, necessity, and immanence of the dominating concept and the system, the imperfected relations, historicity, insistence, and transcendence of the object, one might almost say, "as it flits by."

Thus, thinking in constellations redeems the speculative moment in idealist systematics not by abstractly negating but by secularizing and disenchanting the binding force of identity contained in the concept. Such speculation is an antisystematic freedom to interpret (*ND,* 20). But this freedom of interpretation is not freedom from the object, but for the object: "If the thought really yielded to the object, if its attention were on the object, not its category, the very objects would start talking under the lingering eye" (27–28). The cohesive force in the object, signed over by idealism to the transcendental subject, is not, in the constellation, the cohesion of logical inference. But neither is it the mere contiguity and association held together by the abstracting and classifying activity of the empiricist subject. Adorno writes, "Dialectically, cognition of non-identity lies also in the fact that this very cognition identifies — that it identifies to a greater extent, and in other ways than identitarian thinking. This cognition seeks to say what something is, while identitarian thinking says what something comes under.... Under its critique, identity does not vanish, but undergoes a qualitative change. Elements of affinity — of the object itself to the thought of it — come to live in identity" (149). The constellation does not therefore imply an abstract denial of all actual relation of conceptual identification to the object, and "the self-reflection of Enlightenment is not its revocation" (158). This is so inasmuch as "The non-identical would be the things own identity against its identifications" (161).

Dialectical thought taking place in constellations obeys the object, "even where the object does not heed the rules of thinking" (*ND,* 141). Thinking in constellations does not depend on logical inferences for its unifying moment: "The unifying moment survives without a negation of the negation.... Instead the concepts enter into a constellation. The constellation illuminates the specific side of the object, the side which to a classifying procedure is either a matter of indifference or a burden" (162). Thus, the antinomy of totality and infinity, latent in idealism, is made conscious in the constellation, which therefore takes "the *conduct* of language" (emphasis added) as its model. Such conduct, that seeks to say what something is without ever firmly defining its signifiers, is more than a mere system of signs each assigned enduring one-to-one reference with the signified. The conduct of language "defines" its object by the relations into which it puts the concepts, "centered about a thing." Within the constellation the thing is like the Hegelian concrete — the thing itself is its context, not a pure selfhood (162). Thus, "The most enduring result of Hegel's logic is that the individual is not flatly for himself. In himself, he is his otherness and linked with others.... What is, is more than it is. This 'more' is not imposed upon it but remains immanent to it, as that which has been pushed out of it" (161). Within the conceptual constellation the thing becomes its own nonidentity with itself, thus open to awareness of the process of its becoming. And so, "Cognition of the object in its constellation is cognition of the process stored in the object. As a constellation, theoretical thought circles the concept it would like to unseal, hoping that it may fly open like the lock of a well-guarded safety deposit box: in response not to a single key or a single number, but to a combination of numbers" (163). Outside the conduct of language as model for thinking in constellations, other instances of such thinking are not to be sought in philosophy, but in "important scientific investigations," which often "ran ahead" of their "philosophical comprehension" (164). In the social sciences, an example of the constellation might be found in a thinker of "so positivistic a bent as Max Weber, who did...understand 'ideal types' as aids in approaching the object devoid of any inherent substantiality and capable of being reliquified at will" (164).

Thinking in constellations is thus concretely a thinking against thought in which the ideal of identity is not discarded, but where the force of identity (in its retention of the possibility of negation) is turned against itself. Within the constellation the object is not subjected to classification or brought under a covering law; nor is it grasped as the appearance of essence; nor is it reduced to being a moment, no matter how individuated, within a coherent totality. Yet, although its comprehension would be infinite, and thus not comprehension *strictu sensu,* the object is to be infinitely comprehended, but out of itself. Therefore, "To comprehend a thing itself, is nothing but to perceive the individual moment in its immanent connection with others" (*ND,* 26). And this is a perception that can or must take place infinitely, but just as much against the concept as with the concept; never under the concept. Always being more and other than the finite concept, the object around which the constellation "circles" will be a "particular puzzle" which, as it is solved will be, *like* a monad is, that is,[10] "the ever elusive entirety in itself" (14). Within negative dialectics, the "object opens itself to a monadological insistence, to a sense of the constellation within which it stands" (162).

Mimesis, Metaphysics, and Morality

As the redemptive moment of negative dialectics, thinking in constellations is the bridge from critique to metaphysics, metaphysics in the sense of the subject going beyond itself. For Adorno, following Benjamin's footsteps "The interpretive eye which sees more in a phenomenon than it is — and solely because of what it is — secularizes metaphysics. Only a philosophy in fragment form would give their proper place to the monads.... They would be conceptions, in the particular, of the totality that is inconceivable as such" (*ND,* 28). Metaphysics is secularized inasmuch as the now disenchanted concepts still at work in the constellation allow the subject to only look on from within an infinite process of endless intricacy, looking out beyond the confines of an experience reduced by the exigencies of (abstract) identity. For Adorno, this possibility is still, though obscurely, contained within the concept itself, although not exclusively in the concept. Rather, the concept presupposes it. The possibility of a metaphysical relation to the object is so contained, comprised within the concept, because of what he calls "the qualitative moment within rationality." Rationality is not merely a *"syn-agoge,"* a gathering together into one. Reason is not "merely...an ascent from the scattered phenomena to the concept of their species, it calls just as much for an ability to discriminate. To aggregate what is alike is to discriminate what is different. But what is different is the qualitative" (43). Discrimination of the qualitative is not something that enlightenment can dispense with "if the process is not to annul itself. Even in the conception of rational knowledge, devoid of all affinity, there survives a groping for that concordance which the magical delusion placed beyond doubt. If this moment were extinguished it would be flatly incomprehensible that a subject can know an object; the unleashed rationality would be irrational" (45). For the rationality of the concept to operate at all, for there to be identity thinking, the postulate must obtain that the subject has a capacity to experience the object, and in this experience maintain, however minimally, its relation with "the infinitesimal that escapes the concept" (45). The capacity to discriminate conceptually thus harbors and suppresses and presupposes the mimetic affinity of subject and object. The ideal of discrimination (without which enlightened rationality could not function) is thus a "haven" within knowledge for the mimetic element, "for the element of elective affinity between the knower and the known" (45).

Thus, Adorno emphatically does not negate the necessity of "primary" or "immediate" experience, even though, dialectically, "immediacy does not maintain its immediate pose. Instead of becoming the ground, it becomes a moment. At the opposite pole, the same thing happens to the invariants of pure thought" (*ND,* 40). They become moments, rather than ground. Thus, "not every experience that appears as primary can be denied point-blank.... Whichever parts of the object exceeds the definitions imposed on it by thinking will face the subject first of all, as immediacy" (39). Adorno will therefore not abstractly negate Husserlian phenomenology, but in his critique charge it primarily, due to its inheritances from idealism, with a falling short of its own ambition to get back to the things themselves. From the perspective of negative dialectics, Husserl is right, against both the positivist scientific mentality and against Hegel, to insist that "there actually is a mental experience — fallible indeed, but immediate — of the essential and the unessential" (169). In Husserl's "most effective writings," the doctrine of "essence perception" gave "distorted expression to an anti-idealistic motive: to discontent with the thesis of the thinking subject's universal rule" (167). Thus, Husserl was able "to sharply distinguish the mode of apprehending the essence from generalizing abstraction — what he had in mind was a specific mental experience capable of experiencing the essence in the particular" (9). The inheritance from idealism, however, inclines Husserl to ascribe the experience of essence, even in the particular, to the transcendental activity of the I. According to Adorno, "because Husserl, like the idealists, put all mediations on the noetic side, on the side of the subject's [sic], he could not conceive the objective moment in the concept as anything but an immediacy sui generis" (167–68). Thus, Husserl rejects the Hegelian insight, transferable from idealism to materialism that the "essence categories…are evolved," even though not, as Hegel would have it, evolved "in the unity of the producing and produced mind" (168). Husserl's attempt to break out of idealism was therefore, like Bergson's, unsuccessful to the extent that each remained attached to the priority of the subject. In Bergson's case, according to Adorno, that priority shows through in that "Bergson's bearings, like those of his positivistic arch-enemies, came from the *données immédiates de la conscience;* Husserl's came in similar fashion from phenomena of the stream of consciousness. Both men stay within the range of immanent subjectivity" (9). The moment of primary or immediate experience of which Adorno speaks would not fall within the ultimately subjectivist frameworks of either Bergson's "cult of irrational immediacy" (8) or Husserl's "hypertrophied" idealism (167).

Whatever fallible experience there can be, for Adorno, of the essential in the particular (and not experience of the essence to which the particular belongs or comes under), and, therefore whatever experience there can be of the range of possible discrimination of particulars — and the range of their infinitely intricate, but unreducible relations within a constellation — will depend upon understanding that the mimetic moment is like neither the transcendental constitution of the object in idealism (whether it is Kantian or Husserlian), nor like the immediacy of the supposedly unmediated and irreducible sense data available to the subject and for abstraction, as in empiricism or positivism. The mimetic relation is not the imitation by an already existing subject of an already existing object, but the relation to that which, from a third-person perspective only, is deemed a subject, from or by, that which is from a third-person perspective only, deemed an object. The mimetic relation would therefore be a relation which, dialectically, that is, from a perspective that reflexively desubstantializes, decenters, or deobjectifies the third-person perspective, could be grasped as neither internal nor external. And, simultaneously, as both. The capacity to discriminate presupposed by all rationality presupposes the mimetic moment in experience. And the mimetic moment itself presupposes a relation to "outsideness as such." As strange as it may sound, mimesis, although it takes place in the subject, as much comes from the object as it does from the subject. The reversal of the subjective reduction, the groping for the preponderance of the object is, or is like, an inversion of Kant's Copernican revolution. In place of the constitution of possible experience through the agency of a constitutive transcendental subject, we get the constitution of the (potentially) rational subject (rational because cognizant of the real) through the experience of the object's transcendence, a priority of transcendental sensibility. Although mimesis might, from a third-person perspective aim at identity, this very aim presupposes an infinite nonidentity which mimesis registers. It is this outsideness as such that "modernist" philosophies (Adorno's term) like those of Bergson and Husserl would each in their own way both register and aim to resolve back into the subject.

Thus, according to Adorno, immanent critique, in both aiming at and in presupposing the exterior it aims at, has its limits. Consequently, "No immanent critique can serve its purpose wholly without outside knowledge — without a moment of immediacy, if you will, a bonus from the subjective thought that looks beyond the dialectical structure" (*ND,* 182). Thus, dialectics is only a moment of an experience other than or larger than the confines of dialectical experience itself. Thus, "our sense of dialectics makes us restrict dialectics" (182). Immanent critique works only by showing how the laws of a specific context, by their own logic, come to negate themselves. And in working this way it remains barred from identifying that from which it draws its ability to disenchant, that is, the identifying concept. Immanent critique therefore is better thought of not as an independent activity carried out by a purely knowing subject. Breaking out of the subjective context of delusion requires something beyond the operation of the subject, even when those operations are aimed at dismantling its own operations. The registration of even a minimum of the thing outside the subject presupposes the mimetic moment of rationality and presupposes therefore the relation to absolute exteriority that mimesis tacitly registers.

In registering the moment of absolute exteriority, mimesis holds open the possibility in the subject for the experience of transcendence that Adorno calls metaphysical. And such experience has a moral import. As with Kant's critical philosophy, which plays a crucial role as both foil and inspiration in *Negative Dialectics,* Adorno is not merely concerned with the critical rescue of a scientific reason facing the challenge of a radical empiricism. As much as Kant, Adorno is concerned with the critical redemption of metaphysics. Even the architectonic structure of the text of *Negative Dialectics* itself, as Frederic Jameson once pointed out,[11] is modeled on the *Critique of Pure Reason.* The last chapter of *Negative Dialectics,* "Meditations on Metaphysics," is thus not an incidental addendum to what precedes it, nor is it simply intended as a bridge to aesthetic theory. It is a monad within the critical constellation of *Negative Dialectics.* Metaphysics turns out to be essential for the "new categorical imperative," for the materialism now "forced upon traditional metaphysics" (*ND*, 365). Thus, negative dialectics is also a critical rescue of the critical rescue of metaphysics attempted by Kant. The changed philosophy will also necessarily change the critical rescue of the metaphysical relation. For one thing, *Negative Dialectics* is no longer the rescue of the theoretical theses of the existence of God, freedom, and immortality through a demonstration that the nonexistence of the latter cannot be demonstrated, no more than their existence can be demonstrated. It is not the construction of a rational faith in the manner of Kant's subjective idealism, but — perhaps — of a faithful reason. More importantly, the changed philosophy, by turning thought against its identitarian aims, rescues metaphysics, the knowledge of an absolute, from its traditional commitment to the absolute as the eternal. That is, negative dialectics aims to rescue metaphysics from the principle of immanence, and in doing so it places the object of metaphysical experience within the domain of material and historical relations where the absolute can be a living being, or in Levinas's terms an existent rather than the neutralized Being of beings. Thus, Adorno begins this final chapter with the observation, hearkening back to the main thesis of "The Idea of Natural History," and following upon the disenchantment of the concept, that we can no longer say that the immutable is the true and that the transitory is mere appearance. The relinquishment of the principle of immanence changes in turn the direction and the meaning of metaphysical experience: "One of the mystical impulses secularized in dialectics was the doctrine that the intramundane and historic is relevant to what traditional metaphysics distinguished as the transcendant" (361).

The problem of metaphysics in the changed philosophy takes up the question, after the second reflection leading to the preponderance of the object — a reflection made possible by the priority of the mimetic bond of object and subject — of what the cognitive relation with that object can be, beyond its constitution in "subjective" (and social) categories: "Metaphysics deals with an objectivity without being free to dispense with subjective reflection. The subjects are embedded in themselves, in their 'constitution': what metaphysics has to ponder is the extent to which they are nonetheless able to see beyond themselves.... Philosophemes that relieve themselves of this task are disqualified as counsel" (*ND,* 376). The absolute that traditional metaphysics pursued and claimed to capture, in one way or another under the principle of immanence, is, however, in the changed philosophy the nonidentical that "refuses to emerge until the compulsion of identity has dissolved" (406). At the "approach of the mind," for which approach identification is indispensable, the absolute, according to Adorno, "flees from the mind," because identifications of the absolute are anthropomorphisms, as progressive enlightenment has demonstrated (406).

Negative Dialectics does not go behind progressive enlightenment but, as enlightenment *in extremis,* carries the latter to its own *terminus ad quem* by reflection on enlightenment's own conditions of possibility. The flight of the absolute in the face of identification being the case, it seems that even a changed metaphysics is of questionable possibility for the changed philosophy. But it also seems that without a changed metaphysics, there would be no way of thinking the appearance of hope, the question with which the chapter on metaphysics begins (361). Negative dialectics would disqualify itself as counsel. Moreover, since for Adorno, metaphysical cognition is not simply mediated by universal and timeless categories, but by historical and social ones, it seems that the metaphysical cognition that could, in some nontotalizing manner offer hope, would have to follow temporally the realization of the hope it offers: "It is only in the right society that chances for the right life will arise" (396). "The ego must have been historically strengthened if, beyond the immediacy of the reality principle, it is to conceive the idea of what is more than an entity" (397), that is, if it is to have some relation to the absolute that is in some way a conception. "Metaphysics cannot rise again...but it may originate only with the realization of what has been thought in its sign [that is, hope]" (*ND,* 404).

Thus, Adorno consciously finds himself in a position similar to that of Kant, who "registered the constellation of the human and the transcendent as no philosopher beside him" (*ND,* 397). Like Kant, Adorno bears the "urge to rescue metaphysics as it is crushed" (384) by the expanding metaphysical indifference of enlightened modernity (395). Adorno shares this urge because without the urge hope would be impossible and despair would triumph. Kantian philosophy goes far beyond being simply the epistemology of that limited experience of the object suitable to instrumental-scientific objectivity by virtue of the fact that the "secret of his philosophy is the unthinkability of despair" (384). Kant's attempt, for example, to rationally derive a postulate of immortality speaks immediately to such unthinkability: "That no reforms within the world suffice to do justice to the dead, that none of them touched upon the wrong of death — this is what moves Kantian reason to hope against reason" (384). Yet throughout the critical system Kant also and simultaneously institutes a block against his own rescuing urge. Although Adorno attributes a moment of truth to Kant's block against the rescue of metaphysics, inasmuch as it "forestalls a myth of the concept" (389), he questions the ultimate validity of such a block by virtue of the unconscious social foundations of Kant's thought. And by doing so Adorno is able to move to the suggestion that in fact the critical rescue of metaphysics, a rescue necessary for morality, may be figured in art and that the task of aesthetics should be the rescue of that rescue.

Kant's self-suspension between a rescuing urge and a block to metaphysics is already upset, according to Adorno, by Hegel's critique of the dichotomy of form and content, his rending of the phenomenal veil (*ND,* 386). But Hegel's absolute knowledge, as it is expounded in the *Phenomenology,* is not the sought-for substitute since it is "nothing but the train of thought of *Phenomenology* itself, and thus in no way a transcending" (386). Kant's denial of the possibility of metaphysics is based upon his subjection of metaphysics to the criteria of a scientific cognition that takes the universality and necessity of mathematics to be the touchstone of both meaningfulness and validity: "Cognitions which have no scientific sanction — in other words, which are not necessary and not universal — are second-rate" (387).

Kant's block on metaphysics, a block supposedly against the identification of the absolute, is actually therefore — or dialectically — an identification, or as Adorno has it, a "rudiment" of identifying theory. And this rudiment indicates its own falsity by the "fact…that the rudiment does so little justice to the living experience which cognition is…that it is incapable of doing what it sets out to do, namely, to provide a basis for experience. For such a rigid and invariant basis for experience contradicts that which experience tells us about itself, about the change that occurs constantly in the forms of experience…. To be incapable of this change is to be incapable of experience" (387–88). Thus, Kant's version of the block on metaphysics does not maintain the rescue of the metaphysical urge it nonetheless harbors. Instead, it falsely presupposes another tacit but false "metaphysics": the universality and necessity of the very bourgeois society from which it emerges and which it expresses. The science that Kant takes as the measure of possibly valid knowledge

> is a product of bourgeois society. The rigidly dualistic basic structure of Kant's model for criticizing reason duplicates the structure of a production process where the merchandise drops out of the machines as his phenomena drop out of the cognitive mechanism, and where the material and its own definition are matters of indifference vis-à-vis the profit, much as appearance is a matter of indifference to Kant. The final product with its exchange value is like the Kantian objects, which are made subjectively, but accepted as objects. (*ND,* 387)

The Kantian block, for all of its value in denying the "myth of the concept," therefore does not succeed in the transcendence of myth. Still belonging to the world of myth in its repetition of natural history, it performs "the self-maiming of reason," a self-mutilation "inflicted upon itself as a rite of initiation into its own scientific character. Hence the scantiness of what happens in Kant as cognition, compared with the experience of the living" (*ND,* 388).[12]

Yet despite the falsity of Kant's block, which has the genealogy of its underlying dualism in the division of labor and instrumental rationality of social domination (*ND,* 389), Adorno will not simply assert the actual possibility of a changed metaphysics, right now, under current conditions, within natural history. The moment of validity he ascribes to the block renders the urge for rescue less than potentially complete within natural history. In his *Critique of Practical Reason,* Kant had envisioned the necessity, or the necessary postulation of an "intelligible world" in order to make possible the subject's ability to make moral changes in the world of empirical necessities, even though as a "'faculty of freedom...outside the world'" such a faculty would be "'an object not given to any possible perception'" (Kant, quoted by Adorno, *ND,* 390). This intelligible realm, for Adorno, although on the one hand a symptom of the contradictions in which Kant's subjective idealism (which aims to also be an empirical realism) must come to find itself enmeshed, nonetheless carries in it something negatively positive. Thus it turns out that "The concept of the intelligible is the self-negation of the finite mind" (*ND,* 392). In thus negating itself, the finite mind of theoretical reason takes a step beyond itself. In such self-negation by a finite entity "mere entity becomes aware of its deficiency; *the departure from an existence obdurate in itself* is the source of what separates the mind from its nature-controlling principle" (392; emphasis added). In such self-negation, by way of the postulation of an intelligible world, the "mind thinks what would be beyond it." Or it comes to know that "the finiteness that is its like does not exhaust it." Thus, negative dialectics, by thinking "in negations alone," without the postulation of a realm beyond, can properly take up what is there to be rescued of the functions of "the intelligible" (392). In the end, for Adorno, "Such metaphysical experience is the inspiration of Kantian philosophy, once that philosophy is drawn out of the armor of its method. The question whether metaphysics is still possible at all must reflect the negation of the finite which finiteness requires" (*ND,* 392).

To conceive of an intelligible world is therefore not to indicate the concept "of a reality, nor is it a concept of something imaginary. It is aporetical rather" (*ND,* 391). It would be "the concept of something which is not, and yet it is not a pure non-being" (393). Such a departure from itself, from its own identity as identity, from "an existence obdurate in itself," would bring the subject into the metaphysical relation with its object, and in some substantial sense give a positive answer to the question of metaphysics, which is the question "whether metaphysics as a knowledge of the absolute is at all possible without the construction of an absolute knowledge" (405). However, in order to effect this, something other than philosophy, even the changed philosophy of negative dialectics, is, for Adorno himself, necessary. Negative dialectics itself remains bound to the necessity of that identity it questions. Even as a thought "fully aware of what it is doing" that "recognizes something which is downright incommensurable with it, but which it thinks anyway," negative dialectics will find that "the only shelter it will find lies in the dogmatic tradition" (405). It remains the case that "Although dialectics allows us to think the absolute, the absolute *as transmitted by dialectics* remains in bondage to conditioned thinking." (405; emphasis added). Yet the point of the urge to rescue metaphysics is to escape identity, and "otherwise than by stealth" (406). But negative dialectics, even the changed philosophy "destroys the claim of identity by testing and honoring it; therefore it can reach no farther than that claim. The claim is a magic circle that stamps critique with the appearance of absolute knowledge" (406).

There is, however, a relation to the absolute exterior, which is neither identity thinking nor negative dialectics, and this relation is one in which the metaphysical experience finds a certain refuge and where it might remain a sign of that hope which identity thinking has always already negated in the principle of immanence. If the metaphysical experience is the subject's relation to something which is not, yet is not a pure nonbeing, then that to which the subject relates metaphysically (where it itself leaves itself, seeing outside of its own constitution) — the object of such experience would, under the principle of identity, be identified as semblance. Adorno notes that in the *Critique of Pure Reason,* Kant assigned the status of semblance to the domain of transcendental dialectics, that area of nonknowledge in which pure reason finds itself entangled in impossible antinomies, due to its overextension to a sphere beyond all possible experience in space and time. Yet semblance is neither falsehood nor truth; neither being nor nonbeing. And "reflection is not cut short by the verdict on semblance. Once made conscious the verdict is no longer the same. What finite beings say about transcendence is the semblance of transcendence; but as Kant well knew it is a necessary semblance. Hence the incomparable metaphysical relevance of the rescue of semblance, the object of esthetics" (*ND,* 393). Here, in referring to aesthetics, Adorno does not intend the philosophical discipline, but the experience of art itself, an experience in which the subject's relation to the object as absolutely exterior is maintained "beyond the mechanisms of identification" (406). Hence the solidarity between art, metaphysics "at the time of its fall," and "micrological thought" or negative dialectics inasmuch as all three in different ways recognize that the absolute explodes the identity of the concept, all three explode "the delusion that it [the object] is but a specimen" (408).

It would be mistaken to suppose that for Adorno art is a species of knowledge or even, by itself, the harbinger of a future form of knowledge. Adorno's utopia is not one where knowledge will become art, or where all labor will accord with the Kantian laws of beauty. The "affinity" of negative dialectics, and of philosophy, to art "does not entitle it to borrow from art" (*ND,* 15). What they have in common is a "mode of conduct" that "forbids pseudomorphosis," false formation (15). What both register, or attest to, is the unthinkability of despair. Art may even now, with difficulty, still anticipate the hope that had in the past been thought under the sign of metaphysics (404). In the semblance art produces it does not represent the point furthest from the absolute, as the Platonic doctrine of the forms supposed, but a point closest to a "knowledge of the absolute which is not absolute knowledge," which should not, in turn, be mistaken for a point closest to the absolute itself. One important place that hope takes place in art is precisely in its inconclusiveness: "The world's course is not absolutely conclusive, nor is absolute despair; rather despair is its conclusiveness. However void every trace of otherness in it, however much all happiness is marred by revocability: in the breaks that belie identity, entity is still pervaded by the ever-broken pledges of that otherness" (404). The semblance in which art trades is such a break that belies identity, at least where art manages somehow to avoid entanglement in immanence through its ossification by style, whether such ossification is imposed by the habits and rules of a rigid tradition or by art's commodification. The semblance rescued by art is the aura, one could say, of the middle excluded by the logic of identity.

> Art is semblance even at its highest peaks; but its semblance, the irresistible part of it, is given to it by what is not semblance. What art...says in refraining from judgments is that

> everything is not just nothing. If it were, whatever is would be
> pale, colourless, indifferent. No light falls on men and things
> without reflecting transcendence. Indelible from the resistance
> to the fungible world of barter is the resistance of the eye that
> does not want the colours of the world to fade. Semblance is a
> promise of non-semblance. (*ND*, 404)

By virtue of its production of semblance, art is not knowledge.
But by that same virtue art may relate to the absolute in a
manner that neither traditional philosophies of identity, nor the
changed philosophy can accomplish, inasmuch as even negative
dialectics, by honoring and testing the claim of identity, remains
bound to that claim.

For Adorno, therefore, art may maintain a promise of hope
otherwise and better than knowledge of any sort, because in
art hope is not maintained under the sign of identity. In this
way, art is even closer to that "total self-relinquishment" that he
announces is the aim of negative dialectics (*ND*, 13). But both
art and negative dialectics, in their infinition, in their abandonment of the claim of capturing the infinite in the finite, register
a different hope than the hope registered by what Adorno calls
the "dogmatic tradition." The tradition, inasmuch as it operated
under the sign of identity, determined hope in one way or another
by means of theodicy. In identity theory hope characteristically
appeared in the form of the ultimate goodness of the totality, a
totality which itself could be identified as divine or under the
direction of a benevolent but inscrutable divine will. But, for
Adorno, the identity theory that produces theodicy is radically
at fault in two ways: first, as Voltaire recognized, it justified
the course of the world. It reduced the unspeakable suffering of
innocents (and even noninnocents) ultimately to being "specimens
of the concept." Second, as Voltaire did not recognize, the very
identity theory underlying a theodicy of whatever kind is itself
implicated in — by virtue of the dialectic of enlightenment — or
at the very least complicit with, the production of that "social

disaster" that makes Voltaire's Lisbon earthquake "insignificant in comparison" (361).

Negative dialectics, if it is to be able to rise to the level of counsel, must be able to offer hope. But it cannot offer hope in the form of an identity ultimately transcending but including a fallen multiplicity. The hope of any theodicy at all would bespeak "the indifference of each individual life that is the direction of history" (*ND*, 362). This indifference has been brought home not by "philosophy," but by an experience, one that makes negative dialectics necessary, the experience that "in the concentration camps it was no longer an individual who died, but a specimen — this is a fact bound to affect the dying of those who escaped administrative measures....Genocide is absolute integration....Auschwitz confirmed the philosopheme of pure identity as death" (362). Auschwitz is not of extraordinary significance for Adorno because it was directed against Jews, gypsies, communists, homosexuals, or Slavs, or because it was an expression of murderous hatred or intolerance, or even because it was so successful on a large scale, but *because it was not even murder,* because it was the administratively rational and economical elimination of specimens. The history of bureaucracy is the march of identity through the world. It is of extraordinary significance in part because "[a]fter Auschwitz our feelings resist any claim of the positivity of existence as sanctimonious, as wronging the victims; they balk at squeezing any kind of sense, however bleached, out of the victim's fate" (361). Instead of a hope that would restore the feeling of the positivity of existence, hope must come in a different form, a form without sense, but a form that is not simply the reversal of positivity either.

The clue to the possibility of hope, *after* Auschwitz now lies not in a postulate of immortality, or in a doctrine of progress, whether liberal or socialist, but for Adorno, in "guilt," (*Schuld:* "guilt," "debt," and "responsibility"), in the weak feeling perhaps sometimes strong enough to transport the subject beyond his own identifications and identity, unlike empathy. Without this guilt, the changed philosophy would not even be possible (see 364). Thus, "If thought is not measured by the extremity that eludes the concept, it is from the outset in the nature of the musical accompaniment with which the SS liked to drown out the screams of its victims" (365). This guilt coalesces around the awareness, for even the potential victim who was a survivor, who merely escaped by accident, that he was already complicit in the disaster. "His mere survival calls for the coldness, the basic principle of bourgeois subjectivity, without which there could have been no Auschwitz" (363). Such is not a specific guilt, a limited liability, open to being weighed and measured, conditional upon some reciprocity, but "the guilt of a life which purely as a fact will strangle other life" (364). Such is an extraordinary, a "drastic" guilt that may lead one who experiences it to be "plagued by dreams," dreams of substitution for the victim, "such as that he is no longer living at all, that he was sent to the ovens in 1944" (363).

What sort of hope is it that manifests itself as this drastic guilt? Surely hope refers to my existence (along with the others, of course; at least some of them) in a better place, a better future or even in "fulfilled moments" within a "fullness of life" (*ND,* 378). But Adorno, quoting Benjamin paraphrasing Kafka, will have it that "for the sake of the hopeless only are we given hope" (378). Beyond the principle of identity, which is that beyond to which metaphysics, art, and the changed philosophy strive, hope must be drastic guilt because it is not a hope for me but a being for the other. Nothing less will be weak enough to break the hold of the totality. Thus, it is that "a new categorical imperative has been imposed by Hitler upon an unfree mankind: to arrange their thoughts and actions so that Auschwitz will not repeat itself, so that nothing similar will happen" (365). Auschwitz is of extraordinary significance to Adorno because it brings to mind my visceral, physical, somatic sense of my infinite responsibility to, my drastic guilt for, the absolutely other, who is no specimen, no instance of any concept at all, who has no identity. If in Kantian philosophy aesthetic beauty becomes the symbol for morality (and not its substance), so for Adorno, a bit, a taste of this drastic guilt may find its symbol in aesthetic experience.

From Knowledge to Sensibility

Negative Dialectics, composed over a long period and published late in Adorno's life, is the metatheory and methodology of a form of social-theoretical critique that is to be wholly immanent critique. At a less abstract level, negatively dialectical critical works had already been produced, and a few more would be, by himself and other members of the Frankfurt School. But as the metatheory of a purely immanent critique, *Negative Dialectics* recognizes and responds to the necessity of reflection on its own conditions of possibility. Such conditions cannot be found simply in objective history. It thus becomes the immanent critique not only of the knowing subject and of subjective reason, but also of the *critically* knowing subject; it becomes its own definite negation. In looking for its own conditions of possibility it must look beyond itself to metaphysics, to a relation with absolute exteriority that cannot be figured in the still cognitive, identifying terms of critique. Thinking in negations alone does not lead to a new positivity (implicitly always there from the start), or simply to the endless repetition of thinking in negations alone, but *implicitly* to a different relation than the knowledge relation. Art, as it produces the semblance of transcendence, becomes the symbol, or perhaps it would be better to say the allegorical sign of such a relation — a relation responded to in the new categorical imperative: that all our thoughts and actions be so arranged that nothing similar to the elimination of the possibility of murder would happen again. The implication is quite clear, in this work and others, that the elimination of the possibility of murder is due to the instrumental rationality produced over time by the principle of identity in social domination and that the new categorical imperative is therefore an injunction "to change the world." This is Adorno's recourse to what one might call "demonstration by Hitler."

But it is worth noting that it is not negative dialectics that produces this injunction. It is this injunction that ultimately makes a negative dialectics possible. Negative dialectics is possible only to the extent that the object is recognized as an exteriority to all identity, a recognition the possibility of which is included in identity or the concept, but historically not recognized. The new categorical imperative is therefore not even like the activity of a pure reason considered from its practical side. The moral imperative is not, as Kant had it, the activity of a purely good will, good and pure because of its disinterestedness, because of its free ability, as reason, because of its self-referential imperative to legislate universally, thus comprising itself in a totality, and, by virtue of that self-inclusion in a higher unity separating itself from "external" determinations, even when these determinations were feelings of compassion, love, generosity, and so on. This is why Adorno has it that the new categorical imperative is imposed upon an unfree mankind — not because he means that we are unfree to carry through upon the new categorical imperative, but because we have no choice but to do so — while remaining mankind. For Adorno, "Signs that not everything is futile come from sympathy with the human, from the subject's natural side; it is only in experiencing its own naturalness that genius soars above nature" (*ND,* 397). As with Kant, this imperative must remain categorical; but unlike Kant, it is not a spontaneous and free imperative of pure reason. Yet Adorno has too little, if nothing, to say about experiencing this natural side of the subject, about the possibility of the ethical relation. Negative dialectics, "the world's agony raised to a concept," the thinking that recognizes that "a condition of all truth" is "the need to lend a voice to suffering" (17) recognizes that in the imperative to cancel itself it admits to falling short of the metaphysical experience that Adorno sees as the ethical experience beyond reason. It also admits to being unable, as critique, to see what *allows* the subject to see beyond the subject.

This is the point at which negative dialectics most closely converges with, but cannot reach, Levinas's ethics as first philosophy; it is the point at which the exposition of an otherwise than being, of the ethical relation as open to some sort of material-phenomenological disclosure becomes necessary for negative dialectics itself. Levinas makes a distinction between two types, or perhaps moments, of critique, one of weakness and one of unworthiness. The first he says involves a discovery of weakness. The critique of weakness, predominant in the tradition of European thought, "subordinates unworthiness to failure"; it's concern is with the "necessities of objective thought" over and above moral generosity. In the critique of weakness there is a critique of spontaneity "engendered by failure," a critique that is nevertheless able to question the "central place the I occupies in the world." However, in the critique of weakness, "the spontaneity of freedom is not called into question; its limitation alone is held to be tragic and to constitute a scandal" (*TI,* 83). The critique of failure "implies," according to Levinas, "a power to reflect on its failure and on the totality." But the failure and knowledge recognized are merely theoretical. Thus, the critique of weakness cannot itself found theory or truth. It already presupposes them. The consciousness of unworthiness, on the other hand, can found truth and theory themselves because in it the critique of spontaneity "precedes the consideration of the whole, and does not imply the sublimation of the I in the universal" (83). It is a subordination not to fact but to the Other (83). The moral consciousness, by being "before" the whole delivers the subject "beyond" the whole within which, or by reference to which consideration of facts, questions of truth, might arise. According to Levinas, the absolute, by preceding consideration of the whole, does not impinge on the subject in the same way that knowledge impinges. As a result "the manifestation of the invisible cannot mean the passage of the invisible to the status of the visible" (243). Art may represent morality, but as simply semblance of the beyond it betrays transcendence.

Adorno registers a similar ambivalence with respect to dialectic in bringing it, by the end of *Negative Dialectics,* to the point of its self-reflection and self-cancellation without its subsumption in a new positivity. The allegorical relation of art to the hope previously inscribed also in metaphysics is not a new positivity. It is simply, for him, a salutary displacement of a relation to "outsideness as such" that is higher than traditional metaphysics or theology because art expresses hope more powerfully than they do (*ND,* 397). In *Minima Moralia,* moreover, Adorno was more direct and forthcoming with regard to the ambiguity of dialectic than he was in *Negative Dialectics.* In those earlier reflections, which are themselves earlier forms of thinking in constellations, Adorno ends the book with two long aphorisms on the subject of dialectics. In the first, number 152, he takes pains to point out that dialectics is necessarily subject to use and misuse. Its misuse shows through in its use as a formal method of proving oneself in the right. In its misuse dialectic carries with it a "restorative" function. Dialectics will tend to substitute the "bad old order for the non-existent alternative" (*MM,* 245). The tendency toward this "restorative, apologetic element" is something against which "an enlightened dialectic needs to guard incessantly" (246). However, as the subsequent and final section demonstrates, there is no method and no guarantee by which dialectics alone can guard against the possibilities of misuse built into it.

> *Finale* — The only philosophy which can be responsibly practised in the face of despair is the attempt to contemplate all things as they would present themselves in the light of redemption. Knowledge has no light but that shed on the world by redemption: all else is reconstruction, mere technique. Perspectives must be fashioned that displace and estrange the world, reveal it to be, with its rifts and crevices, as indigent and distorted as it will appear one day in the messianic light. To gain such perspectives without velleity or violence, entirely from felt contact with its objects — this alone is the task of thought. It is the simplest of all things, because the situation calls imperatively for such knowledge, indeed because consummate negativity, once squarely faced, delineates the mirror-image of its opposite. But it is also the utterly impossible thing because it presupposes a standpoint removed, even by a hair's breadth from the scope of existence, whereas we well know that any possible knowledge must not only be first wrested from what is, if it shall hold good, but is also marked, for this very reason, by the same distortion and indigence which it seeks to escape. The more passionately thought denies its conditionality for the sake of the unconditional, the more unconsciously, and so calamitously, it is delivered up to the world. Even its own impossibility it must at last comprehend for the sake of the possible. But beside the demand thus placed on thought, the question of the reality or unreality of redemption itself hardly matters. (*MM,* 247)

Thus, Adorno agrees implicitly and in advance with Levinas when the latter says that "negation carries with it the dust of the being that it rejects."[13] According to Levinas, Hegel's great discovery as a dialectician was to realize that to negate was to accept the terrain upon which both positive and negative are based, allowing him to unfold a positivity stronger than negativity. For all its critical force, therefore, negativity will not suffice to indicate the otherwise than being (*OTB,* 9).

Adorno's "Finale" to *Minima Moralia* indicates, among other things, that although dialectic — no matter how bad its material conditions of existence — is always possible, its possibility is also the impossibility of its reaching that standpoint of redemption to which it, in sympathy with metaphysics, aspires and which, in its misuse, it reads as having been accomplished. *Negative* dialectics, by continuous recourse to "felt contact with its objects" attempts to keep open the displacement and estrangement of the world. Thus for Adorno, the possibility of negative dialectics implies that, as he puts it in *Minima Moralia,* "true intentions would only be possible by renouncing intentions" (*MM,* 142). Or, as he makes clear in *Negative Dialectics,* what is demanded is a throwing oneself to the object *à fond perdu;* or, again in *Minima Moralia,* that "he alone who could situate utopia in blind somatic pleasure, which, satisfying the ultimate intention, is intentioneless, has a stable and valid idea of truth" (61). Thus, against the logic of identity Adorno will, in the search for that felt contact needed to maintain the displacement of the world visible under the light of redemption, regard such contact as "a distanced nearness" (89). In the introduction to *Negative Dialectics,* he announces that its aim is "total self-relinquishment" (*ND,* 13). But *the felt contact, the mimetic relation* that both preexists and that might open out further from the sense of nonidentity, and thus maintain estrangement, the experience of reduced experience, *is itself neither the messianic light nor the standpoint of redemption.* Knowledge, as negative dialectics, is given the difficult but not impossible task of keeping things open to the messianic light of redemption by estranging them, by displaying their indigence and distortion — something it *can* do by virtue of negation, by virtue of the reversal of the very power against which it strives, the power of the unsatisfiable claim of identity.

However, neither knowledge nor dialectics is the standpoint of redemption itself. The task of thought is to gain a perspective from which the indigence and distortion of things in natural history may be seen *as it would be if they were seen in the messianic light* — which they are not, at least not now. What prevents knowledge from *being* the standpoint of redemption is that the felt contact it needs, in order to be knowledge, is contact with that indigence and distortion, the dust of the being it rejects. Thought must remain within the "scope of existence," at least of that existence given to it. (And what other existence is there?) This is why, in order to maintain its *relation* to redemption, thought must, as it were, face away from redemption, backwards, toward the mounting catastrophe. But to see what it has contact with as a catastrophe, to see what is catastrophic in the natural history repelling it, the light of redemption must have already been cast from a source that it, as knowledge, cannot see. The truth of the object, limited and partial, but emphatically truth, is seen only when the light and the source of light itself are not seen.

Thus, the question of whether or not negative dialectics "belongs" to the critique of weakness or the critique of unworthiness is, strictly speaking, absolutely undecideable. Perhaps it could be said that negative dialectics is the critique of weakness itself criticizing strength and success themselves, but without being able to say why even success should be judged a weakness. Surely it dwells insistently on the failure of knowledge to achieve the identity which as knowledge it must aim at, but it criticizes this knowledge not only for failure, but for its failure to be able to see its own unworthiness. Yet negative dialectics, by itself, fails to say in what this unworthiness consists, at least beyond the criteria of truth, which are inadequate as criteria of unworthiness. But, on the other hand, it supplies good and valid reasons why it itself *should* not report on the light (reflected as indigent objects) which it sees that it cannot see. In different terms, it adopts the ban on the Name. Negative dialectics demonstrates that it is possible, contra Levinas, to subordinate the truth of the human sciences to the extraordinary, extreme, and irreducible conceptual possibilities of the ethical relation: substitution, being hostage, infinite responsibility, and so on.

What else might the new categorical imperative mean? But, as an attempt to break out of the context of delusion from within, it cannot, but negatively, delineate what ultimately justifies just such an attempt, and what makes it possible. This is so to the extent that Adorno cannot or will not distinguish between the object and the absolutely other. They remain conflated within the project of negative dialectics.

Levinas was barely aware of the existence of Adorno's work and seems not to have read any of it. But, in "The Thinking of Being and the Question of the Other" he offers a criticism of Derrida and deconstruction that also pertains to the limitations of negative dialectics. According to Levinas, deconstruction, like Kant's critical philosophy, represents a watershed behind which philosophy is unable to retreat. In its ceaseless pursuit of "the dissimulative essence of the symbol"; in its awareness that, and tracing of how, the signified is forever postponed; in its power to demonstrate that the immediate is not simply a call to mediation but the construction of mediation, a function of "linguistic signs creating the texture" of the "apparent presence" of "lived experience," deconstruction not only puts in question the world behind the world that has been put in question since Kant, but demonstrates the continual escape "of the world spread out before us." Deconstruction does not represent for Levinas, however, an awakening sufficient to move beyond the crisis of representation. In its war on the privilege of presence it lives from presence itself, which then comes to be taken as the norm. Deconstruction, then, remains faithful to "the gnoseological significance of meaning."[14]

To a significant degree, Adorno would be subject to the same criticism. In not distinguishing between the object and the absolutely other, the relation with exteriority as such is still grasped as the inability to grasp. The meaning of the object/other is relative to its gnoseological significance, and therefore to the question of whether, for me, it is a being to be known or not known. Even as it is deemed not knowable, its relation to me is framed in terms of being a possible or impossible object of my knowledge. With Adorno, negative dialectics, as self-reflexivity leading to the realization that reflexivity cannot rest in itself, that negative dialectics cannot come to rest and remain in itself, becomes a turning of dialectics against itself (*ND*, 406) and an aspiration to exteriority. The aspiration to exteriority is figured, given the semblance which is neither being nor nonbeing, in the aesthetic relation to the object, which in turn becomes allegorical for a moral relation beyond identity. Yet this moral meaning cannot be put in terms other than negatively gnoseological ones: the moral impossibility of the annulment of the possibility of murder is disclosed as the *knowledge* that the object cannot be simply a specimen of the concept. My relation with the other remains here my relation to an object, albeit a relation which, on my side, has extinguished the claim of identity, giving me a knowledge of the absolute that is not an absolute knowledge. In conflating the object and the absolutely other, by not stepping beyond the gnoseological significance of meaning, Adorno has not reduced the other to the object, nor has he anthropomorphized the object into another subject; but he has also has not been able to (negative dialectics is structurally unable to) describe the relation with exteriority in terms other than those that frame it as a cognitive relation. Thus, in spite of the undecideability of the question whether negative dialectics is a critique of weakness or unworthiness, it could be said that this very undecideability weakens it in its aspiration to be *both* a critique of weakness and a critique of unworthiness.

As the dust of the being it rejects, there is therefore in negative dialectics a trace of the idealism against which that dialectics is aimed. And this trace of idealism shows up ironically in the notion of mimesis. Negative dialectics recognizes that beyond a point it is not possible to broaden the concept of comprehension to include within it the relation to exteriority as such. Adorno thinks of identity thinking as something that has branched off from the mimetic relation (which is not simply a relation of comprehension), but which in its branching off has not only developed and sublimated mimesis but has truncated it as well. Identity thinking has developed and sublimated mimesis by means of the negation that identifying presupposes. And negation is the establishment of a distance in the relation of subject and object that *potentially* also might allow the object to be itself. Otherwise there would be no sense to the notion of negative dialectics existing for the sake of rescuing and expressing the mute suffering of the object. But the same development of identity thinking has truncated mimesis in that identity elides the absolute exteriority of that which it aims to identify. In the pure mimetic moment, in the dialectical judgment alluded to in *Dialectic of Enlightenment*'s discussion of the tree as *mana,* mimesis includes both the expressed desire of being the object *and* the object's absolute exteriority. In the purely mimetic there is, then, already something of a response to the absolute otherness of the other.

But there is also, as yet, no differentiation into what Levinas might have called the saming of the other, its comprehension by means of a third term to be found in both subject and object, and the mimetor's being for the other, or its Desire. Mimesis does not simply include saming and being for the other; it is both. Mimesis is not Levinas's Same, but neither does it transcend the Same. It is not a neutral third term, like the concept, sensation or Being as distinguished from the existent. It precedes the subject-object distinction in the subject. But at the same time mimesis objectively tends toward a destruction of the absolute distance between the same and the other that the ethical relation maintains. Thus, although the reestablishment of the mimetic moment within rationality may be necessary to allow for the critique of identifications, it is not sufficient to produce or to figure or conceive that intentionlessness, that extinction of identity that is required for the subject to leave itself. When Adorno departs from the identity of the concept to a relation more fundamental, it is to the mimetic that he recurs. In moving to the mimetic he refers to a relation that does not distinguish saming, comprehension and identification from the metaphysical relation with an absolutely other, or exteriority as such. The trace of idealism lies in that nondistinction.

A trace of idealism also shows up in Adorno's treatment of sense. Because of the nondistinction between other and object, the role Adorno assigns to sense, sensation, sensibility within negative dialectics also does not assume the meaning it needs to for the new categorical imperative to replace the old. The new categorical imperative is clearly not an operation of thought. It comes as feeling, as a being-affected and shows itself as a sense of the contradiction between identification as such and what is right, what the object forbids. It is a sense of the wrongness of identification. It is a sense of absolute exteriority. But as much as negative dialectics requires that sense be more than information about the object, that is not what his critique of empiricism leads to. Empiricism made a contribution to the critique of idealism, but Adorno's critique of empiricism as a sensualistic reduction of things leaves intact the character of sense as information; this, despite his identification of the somatic or physical body as irreducible and, as such, dethroning the guiding idea of epistemology — seeing the body as constituted mentally, as being the law linking sensations and acts (*ND,* 193–94). Even information referring to the preponderance of the object is not the sensibility that Levinas establishes as necessary for a critique that tries to break out of the context of delusion from within. Sensibility which is not information is, as Levinas puts it "a shuddering of the human" quite different from cognition (*OTB,* 89).

What would be required, therefore, is a shift from the plane of knowledge and the critique of knowledge to a different plane.

On this plane it is not something, even something of ultimate mystery, but someone who is absolutely external, who does not oppose me by resistance, but resists me by opposition. On the plane of knowledge and the critique of knowledge what can be maintained, according to Levinas, is a Great Refusal. In his version of the Great Refusal, discontent confuses transcendence with a negativity that refuses an established condition. But what is needed to effect transcendence, which takes place on a social plane, is a Great Reversal, which means a reversal of the priority of the Same to the priority of the Other (*TI,* 40). Because Adorno conflates other and object his great refusal, as he recognizes, "needs to guard incessantly" against a restorative, apologetic element. It therefore needs to cancel itself. And it also needs to reach to the allegory of the aesthetic to indicate, among other things, its own insufficiency. Because conflating object and other tends to mean comprising the other within the object, Adorno both registers the need for a great reversal and expresses the inability of negative dialectics to express the meaning of such a reversal.[15] What Adorno cannot say within negative dialectics, but which needs to be said to get it off the ground, is something central to ethics as first philosophy: the realization that the "breakup of identity... is the subject's subjectivity, or its subjection to everything, its susceptibility, its vulnerability, i.e. its sensibility" (*OTB,* 14). For Adorno, the breakup of identity and the preponderance of the object are co-relative to each other. But the dialectic of subject and object that leads to that breakup is a logical operation, a "grasp of the coercive character of logic by means of logic" (*ND,* 406), as Levinas points out, a "further exercise of the same freedom" (*TI,* 43).

And yet, latent in Adorno's defense of more subjectivity for the sake of philosophy, or in his appeal to contact with the object *à fond perdu,* or in his avowal that it is "the physical moment that tells us that suffering ought not to be, that things should be different" (*ND,* 203), or in his attribution of the new categorical imperative to an "unfree" humankind, in other things as well, Adorno testifies to, without being able to describe, just such a subjectivity. In his figuration of dialectics as drawing its negative power by depending upon the light of redemption, and for the sake of a redemption it cannot, as knowledge, reach, Adorno further testifies that, as Levinas puts it, "conscience is a conceptless experience" (*TI,* 101).

But negative dialectics cannot go far enough, nor can the aesthetic allegory of transcendence go far enough along the conceptual route to satisfy even the changed philosophy that transcendence in some sense exists. Negative dialectics tries to know the impossibility of total knowing, and draws the implications for a knowing otherwise, by means of demonstrating the impossibility of that which totalization demands, that is, the priority of the subject. But it remains ambiguous about whether the reversal of the priority of the subject comes from the finitude of the subject or from something like the appeal and command of the absolutely external. It makes a substantial connection between itself and conscience by conceiving itself as "the morality of thought," but cannot describe that morality as anything other than a suspension of the concept. Levinas will demonstrate that "the impossibility of total reflection must not be posited negatively — as the finitude of a knowing subject who, being mortal and already engaged in the world, does not reach truth — but rather as the *surplus* of the social relation" (221). The surplus of the social relation does not take place on the plane of knowledge, but on that of sensibility. The knowledge of this nonknowledge will be the gift that Levinas can offer to critical theory.

FIVE

The Preponderance of the Ethical

The Known, the Not-Known, and the Ethical

Adorno's changed philosophy represents not simply a change in the methods that might be employed in achieving inherited aims, but a refusal of, or an axial shift in those aims themselves. But if the performance of negative dialectics means to think against thought, this reflexive reversal does and must make use of that which it works against. For Adorno, to think is to identify. But the undoing of identification, which is the *via negativa* directed at the subject's self-transcendence, itself the condition *sine qua non* for the cancellation of the dialectic of enlightenment, lives from identity. This is why, for Adorno, idealism, especially German Idealism, is most worthy of critique. Culminating in Hegel, it goes the distance in identification. In order for identity thinking to be transcended, however, a gesture, an indicative reference or the mere name of the nonidentical is not enough. Identity itself must be shown to depend on a relation with nonidentity that is itself neither identity nor its opposite, but without which identity would not be possible. Such a relation, one which in making the sensuous discrimination of qualities possible presupposes contact before there are possible separate terms like Subject and Object to come into contact, is a part or a moment of mimesis. The mimetic opens onto "the infinitesimal that escapes the concept," which, according to Adorno should in principle be enough to spoil the claims of identity and idealism, and to remove the illusion of the autarky of thought. This is why for Adorno matters not of interest to idealism are of true philosophical interest now (*ND,* 8).

But mimesis is not simply contact; it must be remembered that mimesis is also the precursor and interior of the identity of the concept itself. The self-transcendence of the subject of the dialectic of enlightenment is therefore conceived or prefigured by Adorno in terms that are privative with reference to absolute knowledge, to perfected identity that includes the nonidentical. Thus, for Adorno self-transcendence is figured in aesthetic comportment. The semblance in art, which is a semblance of the absolute, here acquires its cognitive significance with respect to the self-transcending subject, the subject of a new categorical imperative, as much by its resemblance to as its difference from identifying knowledge.

For Levinas as well, "to think is to identify" (WEH, 60). This is not simply a postulate that he attributes to Husserl's analysis of intentionality, but something incontrovertible that Husserl's phenomenological reductions illuminated in a radically new way, by *attributing identification to intentionality prior to predicative judgments.* Levinas agrees with Husserl that identification already precedes what Adorno calls the concept. If the ethical relation is not to be a species of identification then it must be found somewhere beyond either knowledge or comportments understood privatively with respect to knowledge, such as art. Levinas will not depart from Husserl, or from many of Husserl's offspring, all that much. But where he does depart from Husserl, or where he draws from some of Husserl's analyses a significance unrecognizable to idealism, he will inadvertently also be supplementing negative dialectics. Levinas's critique of Husserlian idealism, as it becomes a metaphenomenology of the ethical-social relation, also supplies Adorno's negative dialectics (and by extension all of the critical theory of Horkheimer and Marcuse as well) with a view of the ethical relation which could both underlie identity and not be identity, not repeat identification in the way mimesis does, not even have its character constituted in a privative relation to identity, as does aesthetic comportment, a comportment which develops and refines mimesis differently than rational knowledge of the object but is still bound to identity negatively.[1]

It is consequently of the utmost importance to Levinas, and to our understanding of Levinas, that the social relation, the ethical relation, not be derived from or confused or conflated with knowledge, even when knowledge or ontology are rightly conceived as the utmost and purest respect for the exteriority of being. The formula that being is exteriority, essential to knowledge, is, according to Levinas, entirely justified as the basis for the denunciation of the illusions of subjectivity and of arbitrary thinking. But "objective forms" alone are not enough, either to describe the subject's relation to the absolutely other (*TI,* 290) or to reverse or undo the operation of the Same in our concept of the subject. In the knowledge relation the relation to exteriority is always a seeking for the interiorization of exteriority, if only as the not-yet-known: "The surplus of the in itself over my knowledge is progressively absorbed by knowledge" (295). Moreover, even a determinate demarcation of the unknowable marks the *identity* of exteriority in terms of the (im)possibility of its absorption. That which the knowing subject merely cannot absorb into its knowledge has thereby no ingress into the subject. In relation to the known unknowable the knowing subject must remain indifferent, curious, or merely indulge itself with speculation (see also *OTB,* 154).

This essential differentiation of ethics or society from knowledge, totality or ontology, or the differentiation of transcendence from objectivity, runs like a red thread through both of Levinas's major works, if not through all his works. In *Totality and Infinity,* in what at first seems like, but is emphatically not an aside, he states that "the difference between objectivity and transcendence will serve as a general guideline for all the analyses of this work" (*TI,* 49). And a good deal of that work is devoted to simultaneously elaborating these differences and reversing the derivation of transcendence from, or its conflation with, knowledge or objectivity, a derivation and/or conflation that permeates the philosophical tradition of the West. It is true that, as Socrates and Plato were unable to prove, it is better to suffer than to commit injustice. But it is not true, as they also held, that virtue is knowledge.

Totality and Infinity seeks to describe the experience of morality, an experience that is not objectifying and totalizing, not synoptic, but a "vision without image" (23). And this experience is not the experience available for knowledge; it is not, as we shall see, the intentionality upon which Husserl focused, even though in some of his analyses that experience manages to hover at the margins, almost within the horizon of the object at issue, waiting to be brought to attention. The experience of absolute exteriority is, instead, "a relation or an intentionality of a wholly different type" (23). It is the sense of his "whole effort," Levinas says, "to contest the ineradicable conviction of every philosophy that objective knowledge is the ultimate relation of transcendence, that the Other (though he be different from things) must be known objectively" (89). Levinas will in that text, therefore, work back from the existence of thematizing cognition and show that its possibility presupposes the relation with the Other. In *this* respect, *Totality and Infinity*'s movement "resembles the transcendental method" (24). In this respect it appears to contain a series of logical, even developmental steps that, as steps or stages, themselves presuppose the operation of essences or identities that can be interrelated in terms of categories capable of bearing inferential relations such as cause and effect, substance and attribute, essence and accident. But in another respect *Totality and Infinity* requires a coming to know that which is not knowledge; not merely knowing that the Other "forever escapes knowing," but *that* "justice," or goodness or ethics, the ethical relation of the subject to the absolutely other, is not "a noesis correlative of a noema" (89).

The knowing of the ethical relation as a not-a-knowing (as distinct from an unknowable) would thus go beyond the negative capacities of dialectics as finite thought which by thinking its finitude, abandons the claim to autarky. The trouble with, or limitation of, negative dialectics is not that it is a philosophy of the subject, but that the subjectivity it criticizes from within remains monological, simply affected and limited in the social; both mono- and logical, its sociality still tends to be conceived as its finitude, and the recognition of the finitude of its identifying becomes the key to its sociality, its morality. Levinas, however, will not counter this with a philosophy of dialogue alongside the I-It, or with a philosophy of communicatively rational intersubjectivity (along either the lines of either Buber or Habermas). He will instead radically revise the meaning of subjectivity by recourse to a step beyond the phenomenology of, and behind, the intentional act/relation. His analyses will therefore yield neither a pure spontaneity nor a finitude but a singular positivity; they will disclose a relation beyond disclosure, refer to a beyond of the amphibology of Being and beings. Thus, "the impossibility of total reflection must not be posited negatively — as the finitude of a knowing subject who, being mortal and already engaged in the world, does not reach truth — but rather as the *surplus* of the social relation.... The social relation is not just another relation, one among so many others that can be produced in being, but is its ultimate event" (*TI,* 221; emphasis added).

The thread of the difference between objectivity and transcendence, cognition and ethics is, if anything, more pronounced in *Otherwise than Being. Totality and Infinity,* in its argument and structure, was to a significant degree devoted to something like an explanation of the possibility of representational thought, alongside its description of ethics as both the transcendence *and* precondition of such thought. *Otherwise than Being* begins from the unaccounted-for existence of representation (in the Said) together with the question of whether the transcendence of/for the subject of representation means disclosure of the Being of beings, itself a mode of being, *or* an "otherwise than being" — that impossible and "artificially elliptical turn of phrase" (*OTB*, 4).

Where *Totality and Infinity* negatively mirrors the path of an existential analytic other than Heidegger's[2] in order to argue with Rosenzweig primarily against Hegelian and Husserlian idealisms, *Otherwise than Being* extends the difference between cognition and ethics, being and transcendence, to the Heideggerian disclosure of Being (as a verb correlative with a noun). If Heideggerian disclosure, after the turn, extends cognition into poetic thinking, broadening the notion of comprehension to include the thinking of Being beyond beings,[3] *Otherwise than Being* will continue the argument of and for subjectivity as a "radical break between subjectivity and the knowable," a radical break that both Hegel and Heidegger deny. The subject, says Levinas, resists ontologization when conceived as "saying" (18). This ontologization has a dual meaning: the subject cannot be reduced to an essence, a being, a noun; but neither can the subject be reduced even to an essential role (a verb) in the disclosure of essence (in the sense of essence as a verb, Be-ing, "être").

For Levinas, "The pathos of the philosophy of existence directed against the intellectualism of reflexive philosophy was due to the discovery of a psyche irreducible to knowing. Was there in this opposition, enough energy to resist the return of the intellectualist models?" (80). Heidegger's progressive abandonment of existential philosophy, although it probably took him

beyond fascist alternatives to liberal rationalisms and human-
isms, was regressive, Levinas suggests, in its reassimilation of
subjectivity into a (now broadened) notion of comprehension.
But the question arises: does Adorno have the energy needed
to resist the return of intellectualism with respect to the psyche
irreducible to knowing? Adorno, Horkheimer, and Marcuse had
a quite justified fear for what was concretely and socially happening to reason. And perhaps in their desire to identify and
analyze the disease of reason they were deflected away from
the notion of the psyche irreducible to knowing.

Thus, Heidegger's philosophy, both early and late, would
miss the essence (both verb and noun) of subjectivity, ethics,
the social relation (virtually interchangeable terms), which above
all, for Levinas in *Otherwise than Being,* is "a modality not
of a knowing, but of an obsession, a shuddering of the human
quite different from cognition. Knowing is always convertible
into creation and annihilation; its object lends itself to a concept, is a result. Through suppression of the singular, through
generalization, is idealism" (*OTB,* 87). To model subjectivity on
a knowing, and to conceive of sense, corporeality, embodiment,
and materiality as privation from or limitation on the ideal of/
in the cognitive relation, the ideal of identity, is to distort and
deface spirituality: "In conformity with the whole tradition of
the West, knowing, in its thirst and its gratification [idealism
as belly turned mind], remains the norm of the spiritual, and
transcendence is excluded both from intelligibility and philosophy.... Spirituality is sense, and sense is not a simple penury of
being. Spirituality is no longer to be understood on the basis of
knowing" (96; see also 99). If to think, in the broadest sense
of the term, means to identify an object of possible experience,
then thinking, including the thinking not only in theoretical
consciousness but in labor, action, and affect as well, is always
traceable back to some form of transcendental constitution, or
noesis correlative with a noema, or meaning summarizable in

identity. But "ethics is the breakup of transcendental apperception, that is, it is the beyond of experience" (148).

In *Totality and Infinity* ethics also figures as the breakup of transcendental apperception, as the breakup of the Same that occurs in the face to face, in the simultaneous prohibition of and recognition of the possibility of murder. And even though Levinas is at pains in that work to attempt to show that the face to face is prior to the activities of the Same, prior to the cognitive side of subjectivity, resulting in the curious temporal anomaly of anterior posteriority, *Totality and Infinity* still lends itself to misreadings of the ethical relation as a relation between or among subjects which, as subjects of knowledge, can too easily take on the character of substances. Consequently, in *Totality and Infinity* he is at pains to radically distinguish the separation of the subject in enjoyment and dwelling from the independence of a spontaneously free subject, conceived along the lines of a substance, the eponymous subject of liberalism. In *Otherwise than Being,* however, the task proper to a philosophy of existence, the task of showing the rise of representation in the horizon of more fundamental existential relations, is taken up in a different way, and changed.

What is needed now, says Levinas, is " a notion of subjectivity independent of the adventure of cognition" (*OTB,* 78). It would be too simple to understand this as a desideratum that applies only to the tradition, but not also to Levinas's previous critical relation to that tradition in *Totality and Infinity*. The question of how identification and representation arise is, in *Otherwise than Being,* no longer front and center; and when the question of representation does arise, it is dealt with not by an existential analysis that can be confused with an empirical developmental psychology, but by referring representation and ontology back to the requirements of the social relation as including the third party. By putting aside, virtually bracketing that question, Levinas is, in *Otherwise than Being,* able to attend precisely to subjectivity independent of the adventure of cognition, and therefore to subjectivity that, because it can now be understood as sensibility, has as for its proper modality neither being a being, nor being the servant of Being, nor being nothing, but being the otherwise than being, responsibility.

The Husserl-Heidegger Constellation

In order to produce a philosophical notion of subjectivity independent of the adventure of cognition, Levinas needs to venture not only beyond traditional idealisms (from Plato to Hegel), but also beyond the phenomenological idealism, but not all of the phenomenology, of Husserl. For such a venture to yield a description of subjectivity that is, on the other hand, not ultimately the negation of the freedom claimed by the idealist subject, Levinas also recognizes the need to take *un pas au dela* with respect to Heideggerian existential analysis inasmuch as the latter terminates in a dangerously particularized responsibility to what is *my* ownmost — my *Volk* in its historical destiny and my ownmost destiny in my historical *Volk*. In doing so, however, it must also avoid the return of a certain repressed intellectualism in a broadening of cognition in ontology. In rebounding from Heidegger, Levinas does not fall back into the arms of Husserl. Neither of these requirements, moreover, cancel either the value of phenomenology as philosophical method nor the value of the correction of that method in existential analysis. The latter removes itself from the claims of idealist subjectivity to the radical freedom of a spontaneous substance. But Levinas in the end does not synthesize them. He uses both to see beyond both. He is, albeit tacitly, thinking in constellations. Levinas's curious status as both a major figure of phenomenology, and as a thinker who breaks with it, is perhaps traceable to the constellation in which he places Husserl and Heidegger as inheritors of the principles and problems of an entire civilization.

Absolute Historicity, Self, and Body

The need to move beyond both, and what they represent, is not something that comes to Levinas late in his career. It is already a powerful subtext in his "Reflections on the Philosophy of Hitlerism" of 1934.[4] It reappears strongly in the 1940 article "The Work of Edmund Husserl," and is confirmed in both *Totality and Infinity* and *Otherwise than Being* (and other works) and reappears in extremely condensed, but pointed form in the 1990 prefatory note to the English translation of the "Hitlerism" essay, only a few years before his death.[5]

One of the most striking things about "Reflections on the Philosophy of Hitlerism," lies well beyond its prescient linking of "racist particularism" (RPH, 64) to a logic of the expansive propagation of a physical force. In contrast to the propagation of a universalizing idea, a physical force does not "disappear among those who submit to it," but is "attached to the personality or society exerting it, enlarging that person or society while subordinating the rest" (70). It is no great feat, Levinas suggests, to contrast universalisms (whether Christian or liberal) with racist particularism, but a return to "well-known truths" (70). But a mere logical contradiction of universalism and particularism is insufficient to judge "a concrete event." In order to judge the meaning of that contradiction one must go back to the "source," the "intuition" that makes possible the appearing of the two ideas in contradiction (64). What is important enough in this racist particularism to make Levinas assert that it brings into question "the very humanity of man" (71) and what cannot simply be dismissed because it is a "simplistic" notion expressed in "wretched phraseology," are the "elementary feelings" that "harbor a philosophy" (64). These elementary feelings that the philosophy of Hitlerism departs from, that it in a sense betrays, have to do with the "feeling of identity between self and body." These are the links, prior to any intelligence, or any "blossoming of the Self that claims to be separate from the body" that "withstand every test" and are incontrovertible. In the "impasse of physical pain" the sufferer "experiences the indivisible simplicity of his being." To rebel against this suffering does not free the sufferer who remains "ineluctably locked within pain." Thus, "the body is not only a happy or unhappy accident that relates us to the implacable world of matter. *Its adherence to the Self is of value in itself.* It is an adherence that *one does not escape* and that no metaphor can confuse with the presence of an external object. It is a union that does not in any way alter the tragic character of finality" (68).

On the other hand the "spirit" of Western civilization carries in it "a conception of human destiny" in which "man is absolutely free in his relations with the world and the possibilities that solicit action from him" (64). Such a spirit not only invites philosophical dualisms, but in producing such dualisms places not only the body but history, the history in the body, in the position of being an obstacle to be overcome (65, 67) Such a spirit "has never wished to content itself" with the "importance attributed to this feeling for the body" (69). In the Western tradition, the human being "speaking absolutely...has no history" (64). In order to assert freedom, then, the West from the mystical drama of Christianity, through the liberalism "of the last few centuries," in fact "the whole philosophical and political thought of modern times tends to place the human spirit on a plane that is superior to reality, and so creates a gulf between man and the world," locating "the ultimate foundation of the spirit outside the brutal world and the implacable history of concrete existence." In all of the manifestations of this spirit, including the (metaphysically) materialist one underlying modern science — which simply collapsed self into "body" conceived as extension and which thereby paid the price of a "pure and simple negation of the spirit" (68) — history is conceived as accidental to a self that is understood as a freedom "which is infinite with regard to any attachment and through which no attachment is ultimately definitive" (65). Therefore Levinas asserts that "In the world of liberalism, man is not weighed down by a History in choosing his destiny" (66). Rather than seeing possibilities as powers already given to and within him, "they are only logical possibilities that present themselves to a dispassionate reason that makes choices while forever keeping its distance" (66). Even Marxism, which was "opposed to the whole of idealist liberalism" and which "breaks the harmonious curve" of the development of European culture, in the final analysis does not make the break definitive. It does not perceive the radical link between spirit and a determined situation. It proposes a becoming conscious of the social situation sufficient "to free oneself from the fatalism of that situation" (67). Thus, even Marxism does not recognize the profoundest limitation, the "fundamental limitation" in history. And this limitation is "Time, which is a condition of human existence, is above all a condition that is irreparable. The fait accompli, swept along by a fleeing present, forever evades man's control" (65). The revolution does not feel the need to redeem the sufferings of dead generations.

Only one view of the spirit, and it could not be a view that would reassert the spirit as a freedom detached from bodily subjective time, could do justice to the elementary feelings, the intuition underlying the irruption of Hitlerism. The evidence of the self's adherence to body, to the body's determined and ineluctable past, requires that "the situation to which he was bound was not added to him but formed the very foundation of his being" (RPH, 67). Hitlerism, together with the Germanic conservatism which was its nexus and to which the middle Heidegger also belonged,[6] are not the sole possible expressions or developments of this break with that Western tradition which, in disavowing the self's radical adherence to body, finds the human "free and alone in the face of this world…free to the point of being able…not to make a choice" (69). But in the philosophy of Hitlerism proper the being bound to a situation that forms the very basis of one's being is bodily in the sense of being biological. Biological inevitability becomes the heart of spiritual life. "The mysterious urgings of the blood, the appeals of heredity and of the past for which the body serves as an enigmatic vehicle," are not the chains against which a "sovereignly free self" asserts its claims to freedom as radical distance. Such bondage, as blood, Volk and history, and the radical acceptance of such bonds, radical because the self itself is ineluctably bound to them, is now taken to be the only way of achieving an authentic existence, a being truly oneself that knowingly rejects the liberal distance that can too easily become a "game," a "deceit," a "lack of conviction," an insincerity, a "degenerate form" of the "true ideal of freedom" (69–70). Consequently, "Truth is no longer for him the contemplation of a foreign spectacle; instead it consists in a drama in which man himself is the actor" (70).

It is only *this translation* of the elementary feeling, this elaboration of the intuition of the body as radically bound to the self, an intuition disavowed and defended against by the West's religious and philosophical culture, that propels Hitlerism into a racism which, even as racism, cannot give up "the formal nature of truth and cease to be universal." When racism also translates universality into the terms of biology, its universality must take on the character of the expansion of a force rather than the propagation of an idea, the expansion of a force in which universal order "constitutes the unity of a world of masters and slaves" (RPH, 70–71). Liberalism will read Levinas's critique of Hitlerism as an acceptance of and recommitment to the idea of self and freedom traditional to the West. In doing so liberalism will overlook the distinction that Levinas is extremely careful to make in this essay between the meanings Hitlerism draws from those elementary feelings and those feelings themselves, that intuition itself, that "physical pain can reveal an absolute position" (68).[7] This absolute position, the adherence of the self to a situation that forms the very basis of the self, is not what Levinas is arguing against here. It is the unacknowledged truth that Hitlerism betrays.

Since this might not be clear enough, especially in the atmosphere of 1990, half a century after its composition (when the essay was being published for the first time in English), and during the most triumphalist moment of liberalism since 1848, Levinas will, in his prefatory note to the English translation, indicate once more that the essay's analysis of the "source of the bloody barbarism of National Socialism" is not an endorsement of liberalism (63). What the note indicates is rather that Levinas still believes that liberalism is in fact implicated in that bloody barbarism by the history of its rejection of the intuition that Hitlerism betrays.[8] He announces that the article "expresses the conviction" that the "source" of the bloody barbarism of Nazism

> stems from the essential possibility of *elemental evil* into which we can be led by logic and against which Western philosophy had not sufficiently insured itself. This possibility is inscribed within the ontology of a being concerned with being....Such a possibility still threatens the subject correlative with being...that famous subject of transcendental idealism that before all else wishes to be free and thinks itself free. We must ask ourselves if liberalism is all we need to achieve an authentic dignity for the human subject. Does the subject arrive at the human condition prior to assuming responsibility for the other man? (RPH, 63)

It is not biologistic racism here that is the source of the bloody barbarism, but rather the *logic* that may lead us into the possibility of elemental evil by endorsing the possibility of a subject whose transcendence is an absolute distance, a wish above all else to be free from a world to which he is bound even before distance is a possibility. By 1990 it is extremely clear to Levinas that responsibility for the other human would precede freedom, as the situation to which the self is bound not as an addition to the self, but as its very foundation, and as the condition of whatever intellectual distance the self may gain from the given.

Phenomenological Idealism, Historicity, and Heidegger

But in 1934 Levinas is still beginning the process of articulating the problematic that is coming to concern him after the Heideggerian revolution in phenomenology. In "Reflections," it is clear that Levinas, although he has not mentioned Husserl once in the course of that article's treatment of the West's philosophy of freedom, has become more than a little discontented with liberalism and idealism, including Husserl's, and with their concepts of freedom and subjectivity from which all else would follow. Yet the philosophy of Hitlerism seems to have persuaded him that a phenomenology that embraces the founding of a subjectivity without any recourse to a transcendence beyond its authenticity and sincerity, beyond the history as destiny into which it is thrown (even if that history would not be one of "blood and soil") will not be the requisite correction. In 1940, in the course of an article he writes on Husserl, these misgivings about *both* transcendental phenomenology and existential phenomenology, are percolating just below the surface of what seems simply to be an expository and interpretive essay. As an expository essay tracing the path and the substance of Husserl's published writings into the late 1930s, "The Work of Edmund Husserl" is probably unsurpassed. But what it sets up to be surpassed, and surpassed by an extension of what Levinas takes to be most original in Husserl's thought, is the conundrum of freedom and historicity within which the transcendence of the self is conceived as either the freedom of theoretical insight, or as submerged in historicity.

Perhaps the single most important discovery which Levinas finds in the inauguration and development of the phenomenological enterprise lies in Husserl's separation of meaning from objectivity, representation, and explanation, a discovery according to which meaning, and with it "mentation," are now broader than the notion of the representation of individual objects (WEH, 86). This is already implied in the notion of intentionality. Husserl does not start out from the existence of a separate object and subject and then inquire into their relation, and meaning for him does not necessarily announce the presence of a spatio-temporal object to be represented (56). A perspective is thus opened onto the objects of science that could never be the perspective of science itself. Consciousness can no longer be conceived as a pure and simple reality; it always intends or leads toward something. Its situation is not that of a body in motion, nor that of a symbol. There is thus a "dialectic of exteriority and interiority [that] determines the very notion of mind" (53). For Husserl, according to Levinas, "Intentionality is the way for thought to contain ideally something other than itself… [and] is essentially the act of bestowing meaning" (59). Intentionality goes beyond the traditional opposition between the activity and passivity of knowledge, inasmuch as the sense of world constitution by the subject is "the work of self-evidence" (62).

Self-evidence is not like the constitutive work of the subject of prephenomenological idealism, nor is it the feeling accompanying comprehension. In Husserl, "Self-evidence itself is the penetration of the truth; the notion of reason is defined by it" (WEH, 58). Self-evidence that is not the naïve assurance of common sense but the result of phenomenological reflection, is "not connected to the empirical constitution of our minds but to the structure peculiar to the object" (67). Knowledge is then ultimately to be founded upon an intuition of essence. But the ideality of the essences intuited or made self-evident, through the suspension of the natural attitude in bracketing and through the phenomenological reduction (see 72–74), or the essences given meaning "ideally," "are not formal like the objects of logic. They have a material content with a necessary structure, a structure which justifies certain relations between objects" (57). Intuited essences are thus a priori, but in another sense than that of Kant (57). Although essences are the a priori conditions for objects, the field of synthetic a priori judgments is infinitely broader than Kant supposed.

Unlike Kant, meaning is not restricted to the objects of possible experience in space and time (WEH, 51). Each object, whether it is of perception or of judgment, can only be reached by a specific type of thought, by an intention of a different kind (64). Each domain of being has its own way of being intended; and it has its own particular type of self-evidence (67). As a result, Husserl is against the model of a single truth and diverse approximations. The supposed lack of certainty belonging to certain kinds of knowledge can therefore be seen as something positive and as characteristic of the mode of revelation of their proper objects (47–48). The adequation of thought and its object will not be in the judgment (a posteriori or a priori) that connects two concepts, but in the intention that (more or less) grasps the object; truth will be in the confirmation of a symbolic intention by an intuitive intention. Truth is thus closer to perception than it is to judgment and judgment, presupposing intuition and self-evidence, becomes secondary (63). Since the perception of a thing is an infinite process founded upon sensuous perception, the intellectual intuition can never be taken for an absolute; the intellectual is incomprehensible without its concrete basis (65–66).

Inversely, inasmuch as meaning is broader than representation and explanation, intentionality does not belong exclusively to representational thought. The intentions in feeling, desiring, in will, in affectivity and activity, have gnoseological value (WEH, 60, 68). For Levinas, this is probably "the most fecund idea contributed by phenomenology" (60). But the other side of this broadening of comprehension by Husserl, which becomes the basis for Heidegger's transformation of phenomenology and revival of existential philosophy, will also portend Levinas's break with Husserl. Levinas's break from both, however, comes in reference to what they will share: the recognition that because meaning is broader than representation and objectivity, that representation and identification are prior to and within *both* the concept *and* action or feeling (60). Nontheoretical, nonconceptual meanings are also *like* representations. The relation of meaning and representation is reversible. This is so because for both Husserl, and for Heidegger, *meaning is characterized by "the phenomenon of identity."* For both, "The identity of unity across multiplicity represents the fundamental event of all thought.... To think is to identify" (60; emphasis added). "Thought" here includes nonintellectual, practical, affective intentions. Each intention, he says, is an objectifying act or is supported by one. Thus, "Intentions cannot subsist by themselves" (60, 61).

Thus, even though mentation and meaning are broader than representation, for Husserl, all mental life "participates in representation" (WEH, 59) in the sense that it all is involved with the identification of a unity across multiplicity. This gives Husserl's phenomenology it's unique character, but as an idealism. It is right, Levinas says, to see in phenomenology "a protest against an idealism that would absorb things into consciousness" (86). But this protest does not extend as far as idealism itself. Husserl's idealism is unlike the sensationalist idealism of Berkeley (69)[9] and is unlike modern and German idealism in that the correlation of noesis and noema is not the activity of a thinking substance (INS, 136). In phenomenological idealism knowledge of an object can in no way be compared to its production or to its being apprehended by a thought capable of grasping any object in the same way (136). In Husserl's idealism it is at each moment possible to define in what sense an object's *existence* is open to verification (WEH, 69),[10] Such idealism is committed to a correlation of "meanings that are thought & the thoughts — noeses — that think them" (INS, 136). Intentional presence presupposes a correspondence between the ways of "making appear" and the "appearing meaning" which "does not resemble a simple state of fact" (136). As a result, "The exteriority of objects proceeds from the absolute respect given to the interiority of its [exteriority's] constitution" (WEH, 86). Thus, Husserl's idealism "is the affirmation that every object, the pole of a synthesis of identifications, is permeable to the mind; or conversely that the mind can encounter nothing without comprehending it. Being can never shock the mind; the shock itself is a way of comprehending" (68). One could say that "in the case of self-evidence the mind, while receiving something foreign, is also the origin of what it receives" (61).

Being also the origin of what it receives, the subject is free, but not free in the sense that it *produces* the world, or *legislates* a world, but because, in its essential openness for the identification of meaning it is prior to the world whose meanings it identifies. Idealism is already in Husserlian intentionality because intentionality "has already been conceived as intending an ideal object" (INS, 136). The object, even when sensible and individual, will always be for Husserl *what* is identified through a multiplicity of intentions (136). Thus, bracketing, although close to the theory of Cartesian doubt, is un-Cartesian in that it is not provisional (WEH, 73–74). The mentation that remains after the suspension of every judgment does not play the role of a first axiom. The object of *each* thought, as an object of thought, instead belongs to a sphere of certainty that "characterizes the situation of a mind that instead of behaving like a being among beings finds itself at the moment when it neutralizes all of its relations with the outside" (82). Thus for Husserl, mentation is essentially free and the subject is in a certain sense a "monad": "In its inner recesses, the subject can account for the universe.

Every relation with another thing is established in self-evidence, and consequently has its origins in the subject" (82). This implies that, "Precisely as a thought, I am a monad...I am always in the process of going towards the whole in which I am, for I am always outside, entrenched in my thought" (84). For such a thought, for the transcendental ego which is a "concrete possibility in each one of us" (75), there is no superior force that dominates thought prior to its exercise (83).

The bracketing that characterizes both the steps from the natural attitude to the phenomenological reduction and from the phenomenological to the transcendental reduction is not therefore a "provisional procedure" but an "inner revolution," a return to, or toward, the freedom of self-evidence, a freedom "in which the resistant, the foreign object appears as springing from the mind, because it is understood by it.... Conscious of everything...[mind] does not have an existence of the same kind as the excluded being.... Its mode of existing does not consist in operating on a constituted world and engaging itself in it, but in being conscious of it in self-evidence" (WEH, 74). It is free in that it is "relative to nothing" (74). Or, in other words, "The fact of having meaning is the very manifestation of freedom. The opposition between activity and theory is eliminated by Husserl in his conception of self-evidence...Intentionality is nothing but the very accomplishment of freedom" (76; see also 79–80). In phenomenological idealism mind is essentially open to the world, yet without such openness implying any sacrifice of freedom. Yet although mind is openness, for Husserl the truth means turning these involvements of openness back into thoughts. A freedom tantamount to the freedom of a spontaneous substance is therefore asserted by the discovery, *in* involvements, of the spontaneity of a nonengaged mind in the play of self-evidence *of which such involvements are made.* Behavior, action, relation are ways of "understanding, positing, and identifying" (85).

These essential links among truth, self-evidence, openness to exteriority, and spontaneity mean, according to Levinas, that for Husserl mind in the enlarged sense, and therefore the subject, is essentially foreign to history (WEH, 71). The primacy of theory in Husserl is therefore linked by Levinas "to a liberal inspiration. The light of self evidence is the sole tie with being that posits us as an origin of being, that is, as freedom" (61). The process of identification can come in myriad forms, and it can be infinite, but it is concluded for Husserl in the self-evidence of the essence that accomplishes the aspiration of identification, and thereby in freedom. (61) But the fecundity of Husserl's founding reflection, the separation of meaning from objectivity, also allows Heidegger to pose a radical opposition (61) specifically to Husserl's liberalism and his a-historicism with respect to the subject.

The Heideggerian subject, the being who in his being is concerned with being, whose being is a being-involved, is neither free nor absolute. It is instead dominated and overwhelmed by history, by its origin. For Heidegger, my life is not "*un jeu* played for a thought." Instead, "the way in which I am involved in existence has an original meaning irreducible to a noema correlative to a noesis" (WEH, 84). Although Heidegger, because his thinking relies on the separation of the meaning of an object from representation, remains tributary to Husserl, he opens a path which diverges profoundly (87) because the distinction between meaning and objectivity is worked out in a distinct way. For Heidegger, each *situation* constitutes a way of understanding. Thus, "To understand is not to represent to oneself." It is in a sense to accept all of one's involvements in becoming progressively more aware of their depth. What Heidegger contributes that is new is an interpretation of existence "in its least intellectual forms" (86–87). Thus, for Heidegger meaning is essentially conditioned by history, by something that already has been. And authentic modes of mind's existence are not clarity and constitution; instead "the drama of existence, prior to light, is the essential part of spirituality" (87).

But does Heidegger's break with the harmonious curve of Western civilization, in his radical attachment of the subject to the latter's origins, its historicity from which it does not escape in its "thrownness" — does it also break with thinking as identification? Is it still the case for Heidegger, that to think is to identify? Does Heidegger's existential phenomenology imply that to identify, in the sense of relating to things through the structure of care — does it rather not simply invert the equation? Is it not that for Heidegger to practically identify is to think? And that in this prerepresentative thinking determined by historical involvements prerepresentative identifications are just the same always necessarily going on? That a "unity across multiplicity" is native not only to representations, and to reflectively fulfilled transcendental-phenomenological intuitions, but also to the least intellectual involvements? Levinas distinguishes Husserl and Heidegger by their concepts of meaning, but phenomenology has, for both, already broadened meaning sufficiently so that not only representations but all intentions, including the intentions of/in affect, mood, behaviors, involvements, and so on, could be seen to have an identifying function. Levinas's Heidegger of 1940 would thus, like the Germanic conservatism that helped spawn the philosophy of Hitlerism, in the end not escape involvement in the fundamental flaws of identification essential to the very liberalism he so vigorously and perceptively opposes.

Another Husserl: Sense, Diachrony, and Nonintentional Consciousness

It is as though between 1934 and 1940, and until some time just after Auschwitz, Levinas is standing on the sidelines, unable or unwilling to commit himself. The choice of phenomenologies seems to be one between a history without freedom or a freedom without history. In the middle of this dilemma there is the subjection of the body, the self, to irreversible time, which does not allow for either escape via idealism or transcendence through the philosophy of existence. But the break that does occur and that issues in a lateral movement in which this conundrum becomes a new relation, a hopeful, but not happy relation between eschatological vision and created or finite freedom, does not occur all at once.[11] And when it does take place, it will have been enabled not by Heidegger's ontology, not by the thinking of being which comes to be perceived as actually a new twist on idealism, but by the resources of Husserl's method of searching for the concrete, for what Adorno calls the infinitesimal that escapes the concept.

For Levinas, the rejection of Heidegger does not issue from any late reconversion to Husserlian idealism. Certainly Heidegger's main contribution to Levinas's thought is to wean him forever from that — if indeed he needed weaning — and perhaps to instigate a search behind the transcendental ego for an involvement that would not be a domination of or by subjectivity, but subjectivity's self-transcendence of identity and therefore also its transcendence of historicity as given to it. His rejection of Heidegger comes in what can only be described as a dialectical reversal, a certain dialectic of disenlightenment, in which Heidegger, both middle and late, is rejoined to the idealism and rationalism from which the latter believes he is escaping. According to *Totality and Infinity*, the Heidegger of *Being and Time* offers no escape from, but repeats the essential "self-sufficiency" (*TI*, 44) of the Same. The comprehension in which alterity vanishes and that takes place in ontology as prereflective involvements, involves as its third term, not a concept or a sensation, but Being distinguished from existents (42). "Ontological imperialism" (44) is even more visible in even Heidegger's phenomenology than in Husserl inasmuch as "Being is inseparable from the comprehension of Being (which unfolds as time); Being is already an appeal to subjectivity."

Consequently existential phenomenology subordinates the relation with someone to a relation with the Being of existents, "which, impersonal, permits the apprehension, the domination of existents (a relation of knowing), subordinates justice to freedom" (45). If, for Husserl, the "whole of mental life [is conceived] on the model of light" (WEH, 61), the nature of Heideggerian existential involvements, as well as the thinking of Being, only repeat this structure of vision. Therefore, "In the light of generality that does not exist is established the relation with the individual. For Heidegger an openness upon Being, which is not a being, which is not a 'something,' is necessary in order that, in general, a 'something' manifest itself.... To comprehend the particular being is to apprehend it out of an illuminated site that it does not fill" (*TI*, 189–90). But the illuminated site in which beings appear is itself a something seen in turn (*TI*, 190). And the vision enabled by the illuminated space "moves into grasp." The hand that grasps the object and refers it to other objects also identifies, "clothes with significance" by reference to other objects. Thus, "vision is not a transcendence.... It opens nothing that, beyond the same, would be absolutely other, i.e. in itself." Such an illuminated space, "instead of transporting beyond, simply ensures *the condition for the lateral signification of things within the same*" (191).

From the perspective of ethics as first philosophy, it would in fact be irresponsible to make too much of Heidegger's famous turn when in both versions, Heidegger's Being of the existent does not in fact make a break with the "philosophy of the Neuter." Such philosophies

> exalt the obedience that no face commands. Desire in the spell of the Neuter, said to have been revealed to the pre-Socratics, or desire interpreted as need, and thus bound to the essential violence of action, dismisses philosophy and is gratified only in art or in politics. The exaltation of the neuter may present itself as the anteriority of the We with respect to the I, of the situation with respect to the beings in the situation.... Heidegger's

> late philosophy becomes this faint materialism. It posits the
> revelation of Being in human inhabitation between Heaven and
> Earth, in the expectation of gods and in the company of men,
> and sets up the landscape or the 'still life' as the origin of the
> human. (*TI,* 298–99)

It would be a mistake to think that the materialism that Levinas here attributes to Heidegger is the opposite of or beyond idealism. What Levinas means by materialism here is not the "discovery of the primordial function of sensibility" but is instead the "primacy of the Neuter" (*TI,* 298), light itself.

In *Otherwise than Being,* the dialectical connection between Heidegger and Husserlian light, and thereby with rationalist idealism, is, if anything, made even stronger. In the first chapter of that work, "The Argument," Heidegger is put together in an unusual pair, with Hegel. Both, according to Levinas, by reintroducing time into being identify subjectivity with essence. They distinguish themselves from other idealisms, each in their own way, by making being temporal, but what unites them is that in doing so the correlation of the other and the subject is converted into "a modality of being." In Heidegger, this takes place both early and late: early, in that the subjectivity derived from *Dasein* (that is, from its temporalization of time) already belongs to essence, as the mode in which essence manifests itself; late, inasmuch as the manifestation of essence is what is essential in essence. Thus, in the late Heidegger, every overcoming or revaluing of Being in the subject would still be a case of Being's essence (*OTB,* 17). According to Levinas, the later Heidegger, whatever the intentions of *Being and Time* might have been, maintains "the founding primacy of cognition." This is the case because being's essence is, by its very withdrawal, the condition for the entry of light. Being "manifests its own mystery by the disclosure of entities" (65). The role of the subject in the thinking of being thus ironically enunciates its "absorption by Being," its being at "the Service of the System." Even when disclosure is not of attributes it is a "grouping" or a "co-presence" (132).

This means that "Dissolving into this intelligibility of structures [the subject] continually sees itself to be at the service of this intelligibility, equivalent to the very appearing of being. This is *rational theoretical consciousness in its purity*" (133; emphasis added). Although Levinas accepts that the subject is implicated in the way being "carries on," it remains for Heidegger that "as other than the true being…subjectivity is nothing.…The veracity of the subject would have no other signification than this effacing before presence, this representation" (134). In his turning away from existential phenomenology Heidegger ironically returns to rational theoretical consciousness in its purity, as wholly subjected to the mysterious substance of which its is a function. It is the miracle of Heidegger's later thought that rational theoretical consciousness can thus be resurrected, but purged of its Husserlian and liberal implications.

As important as it is for Levinas in *Totality and Infinity* to distinguish the intentionality of enjoyment, as the body's affirmation of exteriority beyond all constitution, from Heidegger's notions of the nontheoretical as thrownness and care (*TI*, 127–29), Levinas will not try to find a way beyond the dilemma already marked out in "Reflections" by recourse to an intentionality older than, prior to, or foundational for the freedom Husserl assigns to the transcendental ego. As suggestive as is the amphibology of beings and Being with regard to a relation that would be primordial, a disclosure older than that which is disclosed in representation, Levinas will, in *Otherwise than Being,* sidestep the relation and language of disclosure altogether, inasmuch as they repeat the neutralizations of the structure of cognition. The notion of the subject as the representative of the agency of the withdrawal of Being is still on the same plane as the notion of the subject as free agent of representation (*OTB*, 23–24). Rather than follow Heidegger's "pathways" beyond transcendental phenomenology into ontology, Levinas will both maintain a certain adherence to what he takes to be absolutely central to phenomenological method, and take a step beyond method, by following Husserl to his own limits, but then not stopping and retreating into idealism, even phenomenological idealism, as Husserl had stopped and retreated.[12] If Marx was not realistic enough in his historical phenomenology of consciousness, neither in the end was Heidegger.

The borderland to which Husserl leads, but does not enter is, according to Levinas, the "time structure of sensibility" (*OTB*, 34), as this structure all but appears in the relation Husserl establishes between hyletic data and the originary impression. The "most remarkable point" about Husserlian phenomenology, a philosophy in which intentionality "constitutes the universe," is that in rigorously pursuing its own course it finds that "the originary impression, 'non-modified,' self-identical, but without retention…precede[s] every protension, and thus precede[s] its own possibility" (33). In *Otherwise than Being,* Levinas has little more to say concerning this most remarkable point about Husserl. But in "Intentionality and Sensation," published in 1965, after *Totality and Infinity* but well before *Otherwise than Being,* he expands at some length on the challenge that Husserl's pursuit ever further of his own method poses to the latter's own idealism. Levinas notes that the grasp of intentionality *should have* freed Husserl from the notion of sensation. After all, in intentionality the empiricist sensation, which is closed in on itself, becomes a "sensed correlation" (INS, 138); sensing would be the noetic-noematic structure itself rather than the empiricist reception of meaningless, unreliable, and incoherent information, the Kantian rhapsody or the Humean booming, buzzing confusion, needing to be synthesized and categorized before it could be tested and verified. Unlike empiricism or the Kantian response to it, in Husserl's notion of intentionality the object is not a "judicative construct using sensible materials," sensation not an "embryonic object" or a "brute fact requiring interpretation" (140).

But sensation does *not* in fact get absorbed by Husserl into sensed correlation. Sensation occupies a more and more important role in Husserl, and as it does so it becomes clearer to the latter that sensation involves more than qualities of objects that are intended or which are attained by a transcendental intention: "It now turns out that a sensible content is necessary for such [an intentional meaning] to be thought. The presence of the object is not thought as such; it results from the materiality of sensations, from the non-thought that is lived" (INS, 139). Consequently, "The intentive act is at once intention thinking a presence and the indispensable presence of a content in the subject" (140). Thus, at the basis of intentionality there are hyletic data. Intentions are not "pure openings" but are "contents filling a duration," acts extended in time. That there is a temporal reality to the intentional act means that the consciousness that makes objects present to us is "felt and lived" first (138), before the "climb back" to transcendental consciousness. According to Levinas what this implies, beyond Husserl's commitment to self-evidence and the intellectualism of reason,[13] is that *there are "states of consciousness that are not consciousness of anything."* Such a state of consciousness not of anything would be lived experience. Moreover, "Consciousness that is not consciousness of the object is non-objective consciousness of itself. It lives itself.... The intention is *Erlebnis*" (139).

Already, then, with the notion of hyletic data, there is on Husserl's part, according to Levinas, an awareness of the temporal reality of the intention. In his *Phenomenology of Internal Time Consciousness,* Husserl will give a different interpretation to sensible content than being the matter of sense impressions. The upshot of Levinas's treatment of Husserl's analysis of internal time consciousness is *that time is not only the form* that houses sensations, *"but is also the "sensing of sensation,"* which sensing is *also* an intentionality and therefore also a "universal distance between the sensing and the sensed" (INS, 142;

emphasis added). Because it is a *sensing* of the sensed, time-consciousness for Husserl is therefore not a reflection upon time, but temporalization itself; time does not arise for a disengaged subject by contrast to an immobile eternity, and constitution of the object, unlike in idealism, is not a thought, but an event. And knowledge and event here, in the *sensing* of sensation, are not negation, but modification. "Consciousness is not negativity," at least not at this level where "absolute subjectivity" is deeper than objectifying intentionality and prior to language. It is rather that "The proto-impression, the absolutely non-modified, is the source of all consciousness and all being" (141). The flux of internal time-consciousness, where the duality of consciousness and event is surpassed, "no longer has any constitution; it conditions all constitution and idealization. Divergence is retention and retention is divergence" (142).

In the protoimpression, that is, in the flux of internal time consciousness where there is a sensing of sensation, Husserl has discovered, virtually unbeknownst to himself, that there is an affectivity that is *not an information*. He "imperceptibly" introduces an element into intentionality that is different from pure thematization, a desire that is outside of simple consciousness of, and radically different from the theoretical aim, but still an intention (*OTB*, 65). According to "Intentionality and Sensation," "the flux is only the modification of the proto-impression that ceases to coincide with itself…for only noncoincidence with itself — transition — is perceptual consciousness in the strict sense…but the proto-impression is non-ideality par excellence" (INS, 142). It is nonideality inasmuch as, preceding or being a priori with respect to temporalization as form, the sensing of sensation will always already have escaped the very beginnings of identification that takes place in the system of protensions and retentions. Thus for Levinas, although not quite for Husserl, "The object of intention is already older than the intention." And this allows Levinas to ask rhetorically: "Is there diachrony within intentionality?" (142) Such diachrony, an alongside of time, or literally a "through time," an "in time" (hence not an eternity) penetrating time from beyond *time as the form of lived experience* is already, for Levinas in 1964, "wholly passivity, receptivity of an 'other' penetrating the same, life not thought" (142). But for Husserl the protoimpression simply allows for a further broadening of cognition, for a "climb back to transcendental consciousness" (149–50).

By the time of *Otherwise than Being* the diachrony, the transcendental sensualism[14] that Levinas had discovered[15] in and through Husserl's phenomenology of internal time consciousness is both central to his argument there and even more clearly *un pas au dela* with respect to Husserl, but not with respect to Heidegger. Husserl offers the resource, but not the orientation, needed to go beyond both Husserl and Heidegger. Heidegger has asked the questions about the ultimacy and substantial freedom of transcendental consciousness, as had the philosophy of Hitlerism, that bestir the orientation already there in Levinas. The discovery of diachrony within the sensing of the sensed will make his movement fully beyond Heidegger possible by enabling the central theoretical-phenomenological step of *Otherwise than Being* to take place: the reduction of the Saying-Said correlation to the Saying in proximity. With the notion of the originary impression it is *Husserl,* according to Levinas, who liberates the psyche from the primacy of the theoretical, but not in the manner of Heidegger: not via the order of know-how with equipment and not via a thinking of Being different from the metaphysics of entities. Neither does Husserl recur to any "axiological emotion" to step outside the primacy of the theoretical. Yet Husserl himself slips back from a "consciousness…produced outside of all negativity in being" (*OTB,* 33). In the end his "analysis of time comes down to expressing time in terms of presence and simultaneity — as if time were reducible to its way of making itself known, or its manner of conforming to the requirements of its manifestation" (PT, 12). In *Otherwise than Being* Levinas puts it this way: "In Husserl the time structure of sensibility is a time of what can be recuperated. The thesis that...nothing can break the thread of consciousness, excludes from time the irreducible diachrony whose meaning the present study means to bring to light, behind the exhibition of being" (*OTB,* 34). Thus, with Husserl the "non-intentionality of the primal impression," which in *Totality and Infinity* is called an intentionality of a wholly different sort, gets "fitted back in the normal order, not leading back to the hither side of the same, or of the origin. Nothing enters incognito into the same, to interrupt the flow of time and interrupt the consciousness...produced in the form of this flow" (33).

If Levinas, as he puts it in the 1990 prefatory note, meant all along to insure against the possibility of elemental evil, of the wrong meaning appearing in the essential adherence of self to the body, a meaning into which we can be led by logic and by the subject of transcendental idealism, how does the diachrony discovered through and beyond phenomenology contribute to such an aim? In what way does it remove at least our thinking, philosophy in the West, from the conundrum that is not an aporia, of a freedom without history or a history without freedom? In *Otherwise than Being* Levinas will begin the analysis of an ethical subjectivity, of a subjectivity *independent* of the adventure of cognition, by making a distinction between subjectivity and consciousness. According to this distinction, consciousness is always correlative with a theme, always involves a present represented, is always the *consciousness-of* the one who looks and in looking asks the question "what?" In asking what, in seeking the true identity of the identified, in thinking, consciousness makes its quest entirely ontological, entirely within being. But *even in asking what, in seeking or awaiting* its manifestation, the manifestation of any what at all is "progressive" and "discontinuous." There is thus already, in or alongside consciousness, "an interval between the same and the other." It is this interval that "leads us to surprise the Who that is looking…as the crux of a diachronic plot between the same and the other" (*OTB,* 24–25). Diachrony, given in the sensing of the sensed, indicates that "the same has to do with the other, before the other appears in any way to a consciousness" (25). Both consciousness and subjectivity are therefore structured as "the other in the same," but in radically different ways. Whereas consciousness is correlative with a theme and takes place in the act of identification (whether theoretical or practical), subjectivity, at the level of diachrony which temporalization presupposes, is also the other in the same, but not as cognition, knowledge, thematization, not even as "the presence to one another of interlocutors in dialogue," but as the "restlessness of the same disturbed by the other" that implies "an allegiance to the other imposed before any exhibition of the other" (25). This allegiance cannot be an allegiance to the freedom that takes place in the transcendence of/by my transcendental ego. Nor is it an allegiance to those involvements that make me what I am. The plot of diachrony refers not to a conspiracy, but to a narrative of sorts, a history, but not one that could be the opposite of the freedom to which it gives rise. But neither is my freedom any longer the freedom of a substance, that is, of something relative to nothing, the freedom of Husserl's transcendental ego in its allegiance to liberalism. Neither is this lateral movement a dialectical synthesis of history and freedom or a dialectical history of the development of freedom, either positive or negative.

Some eight years later, in 1989, Levinas will return to this theme, but in different terms, terms that more explicitly link my imposed allegiance to the other in diachrony to a history which is and is not "my own" past. In "Philosophy and Transcendence," after a brief review of the major phases of Western thought, in which thought becomes freedom as a "besiegement" of an alterity, he asserts that a phenomenologically reduced consciousness does not yield only self-mastery and therefore confirmation of self-consciousness and absolute being. After the reduction of consciousness there also "remains, as if supplementarily, non-intentional consciousness of itself, without any voluntary aim; non-intentional consciousness acting as knowledge, unbeknownst to itself, of the active I that represents the world and objects to itself" (PT, 18).

Nonintentional consciousness is consciousness of itself not in the sense of belonging to an active I, not as one of its powers, or even one of its attributes, but "supplementing" the active I. Aware of the active I, but beside it, it is "lived in the margins of the intentional" (PT, 19), a "consciousness of consciousness, indirect and implicit without any initiative proceeding from an I, without aim" (18). It would therefore not be a negation of the active I, nor even a modification of itself. It is therefore not an act in any sense, but "pure passivity" (19), "a 'consciousness' that rather than signifying a knowledge of self is a self-effacement or discretion of presence" (20). It is not to be confused with any *pre*-intentional consciousness, or with prepredicative, tacit knowledge because it has nothing to do with information or identification. As immediate, it is to be distinguished from reflection, but it is not simply prereflective. It should not be thought of as a stage in consciousness-of in which knowledge is implicit or which gives a confused representation (18–19).

But in answer to his own question — "What goes on in that non-reflective consciousness that is taken only to be pre-reflective and that implicitly accompanies intentional consciousness?" (PT, 19) — Levinas moves from the negative to the positive. Although not an act or an initiative, pure passivity "does" something, or perhaps rather, positively *means* something. A nondoing that means something, but not as an act of omission. Nonintentional consciousness "signifies" as a nonintervention or a being-without-insistence, "without the protective mask of the individual (personnage) contemplating himself in the mirror of the world, reassured and striking a pose, without name, situation or titles" (20). Precisely in the *passivity* of the nonintentional consciousness, which does not have in it the noesis-noema structure, nor awareness of the opening or clearing-to-light that makes that structure possible and possibly visible, it is "the very justice of being posited in being put into question," a "having to answer for its right to be" (22). Positively, nonintentional consciousness "is also like the suspension (like the *epoche*) of the eternal and irrevocable return of the identical to itself, and of the inviolability of its logical and ontological priority" (27). This is not simply a bracketing of the natural attitude on the way to transcendental freedom, but both a bracketing of the natural attitude and a bracketing of that bracketing, that both in a sense *and in sense* "accompanies all my representations," as Kant would say. Neither identity, nor a deficiency of identity, thus not a privation from identity, therefore not mimetic (which is the simultaneity of identity and its deficiency), nonintentional consciousness is a "responsibility that is not the privation of the knowledge that comprehends and grasps, but the excellence of ethical proximity in its sociality.... *The human is the return to the interiority of non-intentional consciousness*" (29; emphasis added).

In this passage from the emptiness of nonintentional consciousness, which in a sense is so empty that it is not even an empty form, all the way through to the positivities of responsibility, ethical proximity in sociality and the human, it must be kept in mind that nonintentional consciousness, diachrony, and the time structure of sensibility are different names indicating the same something beyond the Same, the otherwise than being. Nonintentional consciousness is not a thing, another substance alongside the substance the ego takes itself to be, but diachrony itself and therefore the time structure of sensibility, the "temporality of time escaping, *a limine* by virtue of its lapse, all activity of representation" (PT, 20). In the responsibility that is diachrony, which is in turn the human social relation, *bien entendu,* "here I am cast backwards towards something that was never my fault...towards something that does not come back to me from memory....My non-intentional participation in the history of humanity, in the past of others, who are my business" (32). Nonintentional consciousness, diachrony, the time structure of sensibility, together as moments of otherwise than being, would therefore be, though Levinas never had occasion to say so, the very conditions of possibility of Benjamin's historical materialism, the responsibility to return to both the natural history in which the Others are gripped and to their imaginings against and beyond it, the messianic perspective of the angel of history. Diachrony would also place me in relation to a different narrative than the history into which I am thrown, and be quite different than the narrative of the comings and goings of Being.

The Reduction of the Said/Saying to Saying in Proximity

In "Philosophy and Transcendence," Levinas also describes nonintentional consciousness, familiarly to his readers, as subjection to an obedience that precedes the hearing of the order (PT, 32), that which in *Totality and Infinity* he calls the prophetic voice or refers to as anterior posteriority. But he also asks whether this is "just insanity" or "an absurd anachronism." His claim will be that it is not; that instead it is a "description of the paradoxical modality of inspiration breaking precisely with the intellectualism of knowledge" (34). But in that quite late essay (1989) Levinas does not perform the reduction of consciousness which is required in order to establish that this nonintentional consciousness accompanies all my representations, that there is an otherwise than being to be somehow described in addition to the representing ego. That essential task is, however, performed in chapter 3 of *Otherwise than Being,* in sections 1 through 4b of that chapter. After that point, based upon the reduction, *Otherwise than Being* will devote itself to drawing out the implications of the view of subjectivity yielded by the reduction.

Central as it is to Levinas's project in *Otherwise than Being,* it is curious that the reduction itself has not been the object of very much scrutiny within the burgeoning discussion of Levinas's ethics. Part of this has to do with the density and obscurity in his discussion of language, of verb and noun, of Saying and the Said that leads up to the reduction. This has led most readers of *Otherwise than Being* in a sense to begin, I think, with the first *results* of the reduction, with the notions of proximity and sensibility, which in turn might convey or sustain the impression that the subjectivity Levinas is describing in *Otherwise than Being* is something like an empirical description of the human subject, when it is in fact intended to go beyond not only empirical description but also beyond the going beyond the empirical of transcendental-phenomenological, existential-phenomenological and fundamental-ontological descriptions of the human subject as well. But Levinas is at the same time making use of the terms of natural language, of empirical description — yet the concepts he uses and the way he uses them are carefully tailored to be out of phase with their common meanings, which are nonetheless also employed. Also, and perhaps more important, the reduction in *Otherwise than Being* is intended to reveal subjectivity — as distinct from consciousness — *as* diachrony, behind the exhibition of being, which itself would be behind any transcendental ego, which itself would be behind any empirical ego, therefore, immediately, as the meaning of sense without information. Diachrony refers to the subjective as a modality of the other in the same that is different from the modality of the other in the same in knowing (*OTB,* 25–26).

Now, however, rather than try to describe subjectivity, in this sense, as diachrony, as the sensing of the sensed, as nonintentional consciousness, Levinas attempts to get to, to "expose" (*OTB,* 26) this modality of the other in the same, to expose subjectivity through the "notion of the saying without the said." But why this abrupt, even arbitrary-seeming shift from the reduction of temporality to diachrony (more strictly, to the temporality-diachrony relation as the horizon of temporalization and representation) over to the reduction of the Saying-Said? And why this transposition? Levinas in the first chapter, "The Argument," has already signaled that there will be no getting at subjectivity outside consciousness-of, no getting at an otherwise than being that is neither being nor nothing except through the notion of diachrony (9, 11) and will later on assert that "the subject said as properly as possible (for the ground of saying is never properly said) is not in time, but is diachrony itself." (57; see also 53, 88–89)?

There seem to be three not unrelated reasons for this transposition. One is that the transposition of a possible reduction of subjective temporality to a reduction of the Saying-Said goes along with a shift of the phenomenological focus from a monological subject-object relation, with its inherent negativity, to the sociality that adheres to the self, every bit as much as the body adheres to the self. Diachrony might otherwise too easily be taken to indicate simply a negative relation to an unknowable, a limitation of a finite power, rather than what in *Totality and Infinity* he had called "the surplus of the social relation." To expose subjectivity through the reduction of the Saying and the Said is to expose it immediately as not only relation, but as social relation.

Another reason is that, since the reduction of Saying and Said itself depends for its force on diachrony, the very structure of diachrony is itself revealed not only in the result of the reduction, but in the way the result has "self-evidence." That is, in order to go behind the saying-said co-relation, to perceive "the pre-original saying" (*OTB,* 6) somehow outside the said, in its self-evidence, is to be able to perceive that the "truth of what does not enter a theme…is produced out of time or in two times without entering into either one of them, as an endless critique, or as skepticism…. The said, contesting the abdication of the saying that everywhere occurs in this said, thus maintains the diachrony in which, holding its breath, the spirit hears the echo of the otherwise" (44). The particular said that *contests* what inevitably happens in the said, that is, the abdication of saying — which also happens in the said that contests that inevitability — must refer the truth-value of its contestation to a different time than the time of the said in which the contestation takes place. The relation between these two different times, where the one time has disappeared from the start, as the sensed has already disappeared in the sensing of the sensed, is diachrony. Since the saying to which the said-saying correlation can be reduced can only thus be held in self-evidence outside of time or in two times, the only way that this can take place in speech, governed as it is by the linearity of time, and which therefore "espouses the forms of formal logic," is as follows: "The otherwise than being is stated in a saying that must also be unsaid in order to thus extract the otherwise than being from the said in which it already comes to signify but a being otherwise" (7). Thus, to be able to be *convinced* that there is meaning and truth to the otherwise ridiculous phrase otherwise than being means that one must have set aside, for this purpose, the requirement of identity, of simultaneity, that governs the notions of truth "espoused by formal logic" and thus not require a "*simultaneity of saying and being unsaid.*" (7) It requires that one not brush aside with a-temporal logic the skeptic's a- and antilogical claim, while rigging the game against him by requiring that all truths be held within simultaneity. The *process* of the reduction of the saying-said co-relation to a preoriginal Saying, one might say once-and-for-all, will thus *exhibit or perhaps perform* the structure of the diachrony that it both presupposes and aims at, without being ever able to fully say.

A third reason for the transposition has to do with the need, not simply to negate Heidegger's late philosophy, but, especially as it pertains to language as the "house of being" and as that which "speaks man," to go beyond it. As Levinas says, he does not "disdain being," or treat it as a fall from a higher order (*OTB,* 16). This should be taken to include a nondisdain for Heidegger's thinking of being, but perhaps a certain disdain for where that thinking stops. If, as we have seen, Heidegger's late philosophy for Levinas ends up ironically as a repetition of "rational theoretical consciousness in its purity" the same or a similar movement will take place in the way fundamental ontology would see the *relation* of the Saying to the Said. Essentially for Levinas, the late Heidegger's understanding of the relation of language to being goes beyond Husserl in that Heidegger, by way of the amphibology of Be-ing and beings, is able to reduce all nouns within language to verbs. Thus, unlike Husserl, he does not quite entirely "exclude from time the irreducible diachrony" that Levinas means to bring to light. And unlike Husserl, language as verb-al means that "language is thus not reducible to a system of signs doubling up beings and relations," which it would be if it were reducible to nouns. Instead, language for Heidegger "seems to be an excrescence of the verb. And qua verb it already bears sensible life — temporalization and being's essence" (35). This would suggest that temporalization is not, as Husserl would have it, essentially in the service of representation and identification. For Heidegger, "The verb to be tells the flowing of time as though language were not unequivocally equivalent to domination" (34). If language speaks, and if it is verb, if it is Saying that in saying effaces and/or hides itself so that entities might appear, and thus appears as its own dis-appearance, then the subject *as* the free, spontaneous, power of identification, as transcendental ego, would or should also disappear.

But language, as reducible to the verb form, is not free from its own amphibology. In all cases, according to Levinas, the verb to which the noun can be reduced is itself not so much reducible to a noun, as subject to the possibility of appearing as a substantive. Thus, "There does not exist a verb that is refractory to nominalization" (42). Language is thus always "also a system of nouns." Within this system "the word identifies 'this as that,' states the ideality of the same in the diverse." This is not something that can be dispensed with while meaning is retained. Therefore, "In their meaning entities show themselves to be identical entities." And in, or along with, the reversibility of verb and noun the verb-al dimension is submerged in an "already said." Consequently, "the 'this as that' is not lived; it is said" (35). The nominalization function, without which language itself could not function, implies that within language the sensible, and especially the sensing of the sensed, diachrony, the lived, is imperceptibly lost to sight.

> In analyzing the sensible…we have found it already said. Language has been in operation, and the saying that bore this said, but goes further, was absorbed and died in the said…across time the same finds again the same modified. Such is consciousness. These rediscoveries are an identification — of this as this or as that. Identification is ascription of meaning. Entities show themselves in their meanings to be identical entities. They are not first given and thematized and then given a meaning: they are given by the meaning they have. But these rediscoveries by identification occur in an already said. (*OTB,* 36)

Due to "the hold the said has over saying" (*OTB,* 5), the "lived," the *diachronically* unidentifiable *sensed* of the sensing of the sensed *and* the diachronically preoriginal *sensing* of the sensing of the sensed are both and each progressively absorbed into temporalization and identification. The "pre-original saying" does not move unobscured into language (6).

It seems that, for Levinas, Heidegger's late philosophy, even though it attempts to uncover, by linking saying "teleologically" to the "*kerygma* of the said," and succeeds in making manifest the reducibility of the said to the saying, in a sense is brought up short before the verbal sense of language, before it can get to the preoriginal, to diachrony. By stopping the reduction in the co-relation of saying and said, the saying Heidegger discovers will have already been absorbed in the said to the extent of "having been forgotten in it" (*OTB,* 37). Heidegger will therefore turn to art in order to rescue the Being of beings: "Art is the pre-eminent exhibition in which the said is reduced to a pure theme, to absolute exposition...the Said is reduced to the beautiful, which supports Western ontology. Through art essence and temporality begin to resound with poetry and song. And the search for new forms, from which all art lives, keeps awake everywhere the verbs that are on the verge of lapsing into substantives" (40). Yet the continuous effort to keep awake the verb-al, in art or in the thinking of being, does not amount to a full reduction of the said to saying. Though firmly replacing the said in the service of the saying, Heidegger nevertheless subordinates the saying of the subject to Being, which ever and again and always, in its very be-ing, as opening for the light, loses itself in the said. Although the subject as the spontaneously free power of identification, the transcendental ego, the pure chooser of liberalism, is here cancelled in the piety of accepting the role given to it to re-say the saying of the said, it is to be identified by its subordinate role in the play of the power of identification itself. If, then, there is to be any meaning to a subjectivity that is "otherwise than being or beyond essence" this will require a reduction of a different sort.

Levinas's reduction, the central philosophical step of *Otherwise than Being,* is thus not in essence methodologically distinct from either Heidegger's or Husserl's reductions. They are all of a species and Levinas is completely indebted to *both*. Where he differs essentially, however, is in outstepping the adventure of cognition itself to which both Husserl and Heidegger remain committed. Whereas Heidegger arrives at the co-relation of saying and said,

Levinas will take this as the object of a further reduction, but one that goes so far as to lose all but a negative, though not privative, reference to the noesis-noema schema.[16] According to Levinas in "The Argument," the "methodological problem" of *Otherwise than Being* revolves around the question of whether the "subordination of the saying to the said," the "betrayal" of the former in the latter, can be reduced (*OTB,* 6). Reduction, here, has an evident triple meaning. It refers in the first place to a diminution: can there be less betrayal of saying in the said, less betrayal, for example, of ethics in being and in politics? It also refers to the methodological issue of the extent to which, or the way in which, the saying that must be said in the said can be a said saying or a saying said. But third, it also refers to the phenomenological question of whether the subordination of the saying to the said can be further reduced within a horizon to which *it* belongs. Although all three meanings are related, it is worth keeping the three dimensions of the issue at least analytically separate. The reduction that takes place in chapter 2 of *Otherwise than Being,* entitled "Intentionality and Sensing," has mostly to do with the last aspect of the question.

For Levinas, Heidegger's late philosophy, though still indebted to phenomenology, has not been phenomenologically radical enough. For Heidegger, saying remains strictly "correlative with the said"; saying, the verb, has "no other *meaning*" than the enunciating of the said, which is itself "the birthplace of ontology" (*OTB,* 43, 42; emphasis added). And "it is only in the said…that the diachrony of time is synchronized into a time that is recallable" (37). Heidegger's late reduction of the said to the saying, although it dethrones the Subject in its sovereignty, makes sovereign the correlation of said and saying. In doing so, it betrays the betrayal of the saying in the said. If a strict correlation of saying with the said is the case, says Levinas, then the subject is dependent on Being, and Being refers to the subject. But Levinas subjects *this correlation* to a further reduction: "We must go back behind this correlation" (43) because the "the subjective and its Good cannot be understood out of ontology" (45).

Levinas's reduction is often simply understood as a reduction of the said to the saying.[17] And it is also that, or allows for that. But to understand the reduction simply in these terms is to miss the essential difference from Heidegger (and Husserl), the further reduction of the said, beyond the said-saying correlation to the ultimate horizon of the said in a saying that signifies "otherwise than as apparitor presenting essences and entities" (*OTB*, 45). This signifying otherwise, it is important to note, is not yet another correlation, nor like the noesis-noema scheme in its synchronizability. Without the discovery of diachrony in the sensing of the sensed there would be no conceptualization of this signifying otherwise. Levinas's reduction is the answer to a quite specific question, that can perhaps only be raised, or at least has only been raised by Levinas by way of an unrealized implication in Husserl, in the context of Heidegger's thinking of being: "Is the power to say in man, however strictly correlative to the said its function may be, in the service of being? If man were only a saying correlative with the logos, subjectivity could as well be understood as a function or as an argument of being. But the signification of saying goes beyond the said. It is not ontology that raises up the speaking subject; it is the signifyingness of saying going beyond essence that can justify the exposedness of being, ontology" (*OTB*, 37–38). That there is a saying that signifies "otherwise than as apparitor," a saying that signifies "before signifying a said" is, for Levinas, one of his "central theses" (46). And saying in this sense, once the right questions are asked, is not something subtle, arcane or mysterious — even though its description in its reduced form will require certain logical and rhetorical contortions in the said. It was already there, so to say, all along. It is something quite concrete, out of which the radical phenomenological reduction is performed. And it can appear "in self-evidence," even though the structure — if it is one — of its essence — if it is one — defies the identifying terms of logic.

The saying that signifies prior to essence or identification (*OTB*, 45) is simply the same saying, or even "the Same, saying," now brought back to the horizon in which it may be perceived that saying states and thematizes, "but to the other, a neighbor, with a signification that has to be distinguished from that borne by words in the said. This signification to the other occurs in proximity. Proximity is quite distinct from every other relationship" (46). It is from this point on that Levinas will, in *Otherwise than Being,* progressively unfold the character, the distinct difference of the relation of proximity to every other relation, in an interlocking and dizzying cascade of its profiles, any of which, leading to the others, might be thought of, in the said, as "moments" of a subjectivity subject to diachrony, which is itself an "other in the same" different from the "other in the same" proper to knowledge.

At this point, though, it might be worthwhile to pause briefly, and simply note that the saying-said correlation is therefore not ultimate, that before it always, as the horizon from which it lives, is saying-to. It is also not unimportant from the start, to observe that saying-to is not the spontaneous activity of a subject understood as a free substance. Saying-to is passive, but "radically" passive, without needing to be assigned exclusively to either side of the activity/passivity duality: its activity is a passivity and its passivity is an activity. In these senses the meaning of saying-to must be kept distinct from the subjectivity of intersubjective communication: "Saying is communication, to be sure, but as a condition for all communication, as exposure. Communication is not reducible to the phenomenon of truth and the manifestation of truth conceived as combination of psychological elements" (48).[18] The radical passivity of saying-to must also be kept distinct from the role subjectivity might assume in the revealing of Being. Therefore, for Levinas, "It is not the discovery that 'it speaks' or that 'language speaks' that does justice to this passivity" (*OTB,* 47).

Subjectivity as Responsible Sense

The reduction of the co-relation of Said and Saying to saying-to in proximity operates like a wedge that displaces and fractures the notion of subjectivity to the point that the subject may now be perceived in its independence of the adventure of cognition. Like a proper wedge, it can be insinuated into the smallest of fissures. (The fissure here being the question of who speaks the question "what?") But it opens up the possibility of a radically novel redescription of that which, under the sway of the priority of identification and cognition, appeared in its spontaneity and freedom as an independent substance, or as a function of a totality (whether or not that totality could ever be fully present to that which existed in relation to it). The reduction by itself addresses the problem of showing that there is an otherwise than being *to be described* which is not only irreducible to being, but without which not only beings, but the Being of beings, could not.... The reduction therefore desubstantiates subjectivity completely, "contrary to Western thought which unites subjectivity and substantiality...here A does not, as in identity, return to A, but retreats to the hither side of its point of departure" (*OTB,* 114).

The process of reduction, however, in itself cannot supply a mode of description for that which it opens to description. Moreover, description without identification is not possible. Nonetheless, in one sense, such "indiscretion with regard to the unsayable" is "the very task of philosophy." And the task involves both knowing and freeing the known "of the marks which thematization leaves on it by subordinating it to ontology" (*OTB,* 7). One of the principal means Levinas employs to attempt this description, this knowing of a not-a-knowing-or-a-known, involves the adoption, the borrowing, of a myriad of terms from any number of domains which are then, to borrow a Benjaminian term, *umfunktioniert* to mean something different from the negation of their opposites. Thus, radical passivity, like otherwise than being as neither being nor nonbeing, will mean something different from the opposite of activity (see also 118); being hostage will mean something different from the opposite of being free to dispose of oneself as one wills. Yet each term also preserves a link to its borrowed meaning. Radical passivity is not activity. Being hostage is not being free to be indifferent. All of these re-engineered terms, chosen and re-formed to signify otherwise than the central terms which the tradition brings to bear on subjectivity are, moreover, not themselves ordered in any way that admits of classification by species and genus. No one of them, not "proximity," or "sensibility," even "substitution," should or can be taken to refer to some ultimate principle, or being, in relation to which the others are derivative (19). Thus, the themes of *Otherwise than Being*'s redescription of subjectivity, beyond the reduction, do not, according to Levinas, lend themselves to linear exposition. "All" of the concepts used to try to state transcendence "echo one another" (19). Thus, Levinas is not explaining subjectivity (as he might appear to have been doing in *Totality and Infinity*); nor is he positing subjectivity as a first principle that might be used to explain a varied array of phenomena. He is instead describing what it means to be subjectivity, or what otherwise than being means.

Following from the reduction, the first note to sound for this metaphenomenologically redescribed subjectivity, a note that echoes with all of the other notes that will be sounded, is that saying-to is not the simple intention to address a message. It is not a giving of signs, inasmuch as that would that the relation with another would imply an extension of intentionality out of a subject posited in itself, and "disposed to play." The subject of saying "does not give signs, it becomes a sign, turns into an allegiance" (*OTB,* 48–49). Not being an agent, not having the status of a substance, exposed to another before it is "there" to be something subject to exposure, stripped "of every identical quiddity, and thus of all form" (49), subjectivity as "extreme passivity of exposure to another" (47) is already in proximity to the whom of saying-to. Why this qualification of "extreme" passivity in the exposure to another? Surely we all already knew that as *finite* beings we were vulnerable, as we also knew that as finite *beings* we could ward off threats, maintain ourselves, if only temporarily, as beings in being? Extreme passivity only because, again, it is not as though passivity is an attribute of subjectivity, but that subjectivity *is* this extreme passivity that, *as* subjectivity, it cannot avoid. It *is* this diachrony, or relation to a past older than the time-consciousness within which alone past, present, and future make sense and *make* sense.

Proximity, a spatial concept that in everyday parlance connotes a state in which at least two entities are relatively close to one another, but whose relative closeness is accidental to either one of them, now, as a dimension of the extreme passivity of saying-to implies, or is recast to mean both a relation and the term of a relation that is neither an accidental event transpiring between two independent entities, nor the negation of their separation in some form of fusion. The co-relative terms of substance and accident do not apply. The subject is not an entity capable of proximity to another entity. Its subjectivity is its proximity, but not in the sense of a state: "Proximity is not a state, a repose, but a restlessness, null site, outside of the place of rest....Never close enough, proximity does not congeal into a structure, *save when represented in the demand for justice as reversible*" (*OTB,* 82; emphasis added). The subject, says Levinas, "is in proximity; not prior to it" (84).

But proximity, not being a state, even though in the semantics of ordinary speech it should be one, now seems to have the properties of a force, or at least a direction: "Proximity, as the 'closer and closer,' becomes the subject. It attains its superlative as my incessant restlessness, becomes unique, then one, forgets reciprocity, as in a love that does not expect to be shared" (*OTB*, 82). As this forgetting of reciprocity, proximity places itself/is placed outside of all possible systems of spatializable coordinates that might allow it to insist on or even conceive of some form of reciprocity or belonging. Proximity seems to be a movement not only towards the other, but for the other. It does not expect to be shared. It is therefore not amenable to having in it a goal of union, unity or fusion with that which it is for. As response to the other before it will have had consciousness of the before and after, it is "the fine risk of approach qua approach" (94).

Even the *re-engineered* term proximity remains a term congealed in the said, and as such, no matter how much it twists and falls back against the meanings already given in what Levinas calls *the already said,* it cannot identify what it conveys. Yet it manages to convey what it cannot identify, but only by exceeding itself as it goes along, as what it refers to also does by burning without being consumed. The terms of the said and the already said, as identifying nouns and verbs all, would place proximity into the domain of objectivity. But proximity in saying-to, as quite distinct from the relation in consciousness-of, is necessarily a relation of which one cannot become fully conscious. This is so because proximity "throws me outside of the objectivity characteristic of relations." Thus, proximity itself makes itself unknown; it "cannot consist in a becoming conscious of this situation, which would annul the non-indifference or fraternity of proximity. Is not a conscious subject one that has no alliance with that of which it is conscious? Does it not feel that any kinship with that of which it is conscious compromises its truth?" (*OTB*, 82). To some extent this very weakness, this lack of ability of proximity to make itself present to the order of consciousness and reason even explains its relative absence from not only the philosophical, but also the naïve awareness of humankind: "Not to turn into relations that reverse, irreversibility, is the universal subjectness of the subject. The ignorance of it by the subject bears witness not to the naivety of a humanity still incapable of thinking…nor to the everydayness of man…but to the pre-originary hither side of abnegation…. [I]n this 'not-thinking-of-it' is announced, on the hither side of the 'state of nature' (from which nature itself arises), the one-for-the-other, a one-way relation…the immediacy of the other" (84). With this passage Levinas also indicates that it is not the native perversity of the West or its philosophy that has subjected ethics to ontology. With respect to any rational order at all, proximity is "an exception." Subjectivity as proximity "is both the relation and the term of the relation. But it is as subject to an irreversible relation that the term of a relation becomes a subject" (85).

The subject as the structure of saying-to, as distinct from the structure of consciousness-of, may be indicated or said as the relation of proximity. But any term or concept, no matter its having been re-engineered, will not suffice to fully expose, let alone identify "Saying saying saying itself" in all of its profiles, nor will it expose the relations among its profiles considered separately. In fact Levinas does not even attempt to consider them separately but runs them all together as though the whole structure insisted monadically in each one. Thus, from the very start, it is about to become evident that the saying of a said already monadically refers to a proliferating set of implications. But implications is the wrong word, inasmuch as it connotes that the relations among the evident and not-yet-evident sides are inferences. Thus, "the predicative statement…stands on the frontier of a dethematization of the said, and can be understood as a modality of approach and contact" (*OTB,* 47). The predicative statement, as approach and contact is, moreover, already responsibility, which is substitution (47). In the course of the two pages (*OTB*, 46–47) devoted to the reduction itself, Levinas already includes at least a foreshadowing of all of the lineaments he will draw out of subjectivity as ethical. This means that saying-to or proximity is immediately to be perceived in self-evidence as responsibility. Not only distinct from every other relation it also "has to be conceived as a responsibility for the other; it might be called humanity, or subjectivity, or self" (46). This already means, as he will begin to list on the next page, all of those profiles that echo one another as the book progresses up to its return to the relation of subjectivity to theory and ontology with the remembrance of the third.

What distinguishes responsibility, in the relation of proximity, from objectifying notions of responsibility (like the liberal idealist notion of responsibility, which makes me responsible because I could always have chosen something else inside the structure in relation to which I stand at a distance outside) is that, since proximity pertains to a relation in which reversibility does not obtain, it has no limit or measure (*OTB*, 47). It is inordinate and infinite. Limited, measured responsibilities can only pertain to a subject that sees itself as included at one level in the structure that it sees, at another level, from outside. But proximity never simply congeals into a structure. As he says when discussing responsibility again in the context of the notion of substitution, from which it cannot even be analytically separated, "responsibility for another is not an accident that happens to a subject, but precedes essence in it, has not awaited freedom.…I have not done anything and already I am under accusation — persecuted" (114). My responsibility is unidirectional, "goes from me to the other" (138). And it can therefore not be limited by her or anyone else's actual irresponsibility or even their other responsibilities. Thus, "Peace with the other is first of all my business" (139). Moreover, "The self is a sub-jectum; it is under the weight of the universe, responsible for everything. The unity of the universe is not what my gaze embraces in its unity of apperception, but what is incumbent on me from all sides" (116).

The subject, saying-to already subjected in its responsibility to what is incumbent from all sides is not some thing, either simply a unity or a relation, even a positive dialectical relation that, remaining in itself, can unfortunately experience suffering. On the contrary, "The subjectivity of the subjection of the self is the suffering of suffering" (54). It is radically sensibility, the sensing of the sensed; no subjectivity without the suffering of suffering. This means that suffering is not simply a possibility that may or may not strike a subject whose essence[19] is not the suffering of suffering. This is because "Sensibility, all the passivity of saying cannot be reduced to the experience that a subject would have of it, even if it makes possible such an experience" (*OTB*, 54). As the suffering of suffering, subjectivity is sensibility for the other, *both pain and enjoyment* in, for and by the other (90). Even the pure enjoyment of the other or joy in the other's joy is a suffering of suffering. Subjectivity is thus inseparable from patience and pain. Without this possibility of pain in the suffering of suffering, which Levinas calls a "possibility of pure non-sense invading and threatening signification," a "folly at the confines of reason... [,] the one would take hold of itself... and recommence essence." The possibility of pain that is inseparable from the suffering of suffering is therefore an "adversity" that is "ambiguous": "It is only this way that the for-the-other... is kept from being for-oneself" (50).

It is not that I must or ought to feel pain for the other or feel the other's pain, but that the suffering of suffering, in its permanent possibility of pain *even in enjoyment,* is my radical sensibility, radical because it cannot be summed up in a thought, cannot recommence essence. Thus, the sensation in the suffering of suffering "is not reducible to the clarity of the idea derived out of it.... It is vulnerability, enjoyment and suffering, whose status is not reducible to the fact of being put before a spectator subject" (63). Sensibility is the affective that does not remain an information for the subject that even *phenomenological* idealism would make sovereign (66). Beyond phenomenological idealism,

Heidegger's "faint materialism" cannot situate sensibility, what for it would be this "residue" from the gnoseological, inasmuch as what signifies in the sensible is neither "what shows itself, nor the disclosure itself" (67). Sensibility, as diachronic, is the breakup of identity, "a defecting or a defeat of the ego's identity...pushed to the limit" (15).

Saying-to in its diachronic relation to the other *as* proximity and responsibility, which *are* vulnerability and the immediacy of the sensible is also, therefore a "coring out," a "denucleation" of the ego. But this does not imply that the ego was there from the start to be the core that can be cored out by a superior force. The coring out *is* the ego or subject itself, the core, a "psychism" that in sensibility is a "peculiar dephasing, a loosening up or unclamping of identity: the same prevented from coinciding with itself" (*OTB,* 68), an other in the same different from the other in the same of cognition. Such a dephasing of the same with and within its own sensibility, a nonidentity that is not a relation to nothing or a nonrelation, would be neither "a deception nor truth, but the preliminary intelligibility of signification" (69). Such a psyche, inseparable from an "original" diachrony in its being the sensing of the sensed, which is "the signifyingness of the one-for-another," the psyche that animates perception, hunger, and sensation, must be kept distinct from the meaning of psyche "in the linguistic system," where it becomes, rather than other-in-the-same, soul in relation to body, other in relation to same. These latter sets of terms "mark two Cartesian orders," which are "cloven when thematized" but which are "in accord prior to thematization" (70). The psyche, in this sense, can never, as it is when conceived as theoretical or knowing, be "neutralized into serenity" (71).

Since the psyche is restlessness in proximity, signification, the one-for-the-other, it "is not an ordinary formal relation, but the whole gravity of the body extirpated from its conatus. It is a passivity more passive still than any passivity that is antithetical to an act" (*OTB,* 72). Such radical passivity goes beyond the receptivity which "for philosophers" is the ultimate model of passivity for a subject (48). Radical passivity does not receive into itself something other. It is more than a welcome. Receptivity, on the other hand, already posits the agent doing the receiving. But radical passivity *is* the agent who responds to what cannot be fully received, before the agent is there to do the receiving. This is what it means to occupy a null-site. Radical passivity is not radical in the sense that in it activity — restlessness, giving, saying-to is impossible. Passivity is *radically* passive where inactivity, indifference, nonresponsiveness is not an option. It acts passively. The most radical passivity is the passivity that cannot *but* act, but acts in relation to what it cannot include in the same and by including make into its own, rationally, peacefully — and violently — by way of a third term. Radical passivity acts, it does something, but by and for the other, not by and for itself. In radical passivity "Impassively undergoing the weight of the other...subjectivity therefore no longer belongs to the order where the alternative of activity and passivity retains its meaning" (118). In radical passivity the other (and the self) cannot enter into any calculations. Thus, the subject who says-to "lies as it were on the underside of the active ego...a lassitude, a passive exposure to being which is not assumed" (54).

The radical passivity of responsible proximity also implies a limit to the distance achievable in all forms of reflexive self-critique: "The ego, in consciously reflecting on itself...escapes its own critical eye by its spontaneity, which permits it to take refuge in this very eye that judges it. The negativity in which the ego is detached from itself to look at itself is, from all points of view, a recuperation of the self" (*OTB,* 92). This is the self-recuperation that Adorno's negative dialectics acknowledges in its referring its own possibility back to that "drastic guilt" from which the preponderance of the object might follow. According to Levinas, radical passivity, beyond the passivity of being the object of self-critique, does not contain any reference, positive or negative, to a prior will (51). Responsibility, as not an act on the part of the subject, but a restlessness in proximity, is not something that can be assumed, not a free commitment (51), but takes place "despite oneself" with a "despite" that is not opposed to will, wish, or nature (51). Radical passivity is not self-negation or acceptance of the negation of the self by another, not a negation of essence "but a disinterestedness that turns into a burning for the other." This is anything but the disinterestedness of the good will in the form of a categorical imperative of pure practical reason, because it "has the form of a corporeal life devoted to expression and giving" (50).

Not coming from a free commitment, not coming, that is, from the present, disinterestedness, the despite oneself or radical passivity "is thus in a time without beginning" (*OTB*, 51). Saying-to or saying from beyond the co-relation of the saying and the said thus returns to the diachrony in sensibility for which it is yet another name:

> Proximity, suppression of the distance that consciousness of... involves, opens the distance of a diachrony without a common present, where difference is the past that cannot be caught up with, an unimaginable future....This difference is my non-indifference to the other. Proximity is a disturbance of rememberable time.
>
> One can call that apocalyptically the breakup of time. But it is a matter of an effaced but untameable diachrony of non-history, non-said time, which cannot be synchronized in a present by memory and historiography where the present is but the trace of an immemorial past. (*OTB*, 89)

Sensibility, as the sensing of sensation, thus "attests to a different time than that which scans consciousness," one in which "my reaction misses a present which is already the past of itself" (*OTB*, 88).

Not coming from a free commitment, my responsibility marks my subjectivity as corporeality, as matter, as incarnation. Disinterestedness is not the miracle of participating in two worlds, an empirical and an intelligible world, but is "the very possibility of offering, suffering and trauma" (*OTB,* 50). But incarnate responsibility, if incarnation means sensibility, means in turn that "such a response cannot be converted into an 'inward need' or a natural tendency. The response answers, but with no eroticism, to an absolutely heteronomous call" (53). Both inward need and natural tendency would themselves presuppose a duality in which subjectivity preexisted, or existed alongside or in relation to its vulnerability and sensibility. But the for-the-other is not an affection, but an "attack made on the plenitude of complacency in oneself" (74).

Incarnate signification, saying-to bears "in fact all the gravity of an animate body, that is one offered to another, expressed or opened up!" (70). The incarnate subject is not a materialization of the nonspatial into space and into relations of contact that can be known and mapped inferentially in a priori synthetic or a posteriori analytic judgments (77). But because subjectivity is this sensibility in which sense, thanks to the "effaced but untameable" diachrony, is not an information, and because "matter is the very locus of the for-the-other," incarnation is the subject "of flesh and blood," capable "of giving the bread out of his mouth" (77). Levinas writes, "Incarnation is not a transcendental operation of a subject that is situated in the midst of the world it represents to itself; the sensible experience of the body is already and from the start incarnate. The sensible…binds the node of incarnation into a plot larger than the apperception of self. In this plot I am bound to others before being bound to my body" (76). This last sentence cannot and should not be taken to mean that for Levinas, the I, the self, psyche, or spirit is in any way separate from my body, but that my body already involves responsibility to others before it can assume or presume that position of externality to itself by which body might become an animate or inanimate thing. But it also means, conversely, that my body is *not* that which *resists the pull of the other,* her absolutely heteronomous call. The ethical relation is the energy of bodies in a gravitational field, one might say.

Otherwise than being, or to be incarnate, sensible matter subject to untameable diachrony thus also means the inescapability of the other, means that I am obsessed, despite myself, with the other. I cannot not sense, and cannot not sense the sensed, and in sensing the sensed but respond to what remains forever past, and responded to before "I" was there to respond. Obsession, says Levinas, is a relation with the outside before any act that could open up the outside (*OTB,* 110). Obsession is the subject affected without the source of the affection becoming an object of representation (101). Thematization is undone. Neither represented nor representer can be first. In obsession, the intentionless intention, the other, the object is truly and ever and again preponderant. Obsession is the ultimate condition for the "sense of contradiction" upon which any negative dialectics depends.

Here an-archy is set free in the world, but an an-archy which is neither order nor disorder (*OTB,* 101). In this lawlessness even before the state of nature *and* the laws of nature I am a hostage to the other, persecuted, but not because the other might, empirically, have a will to act against me, or a hold over me, but because I am here, saying, and in saying saying here I am. And as we already know, saying saying saying itself is infinite and inordinate. I am persecuted inasmuch as I am responsible for what someone else might be accused of doing. I am persecuted because I cannot be held to be innocent. As persecuted I am hostage, responsible for acts the other committed or omitted, not even in my name. That a "subject is a hostage…means concretely: accused of what the others do or suffer, or responsible for what they do or suffer. The uniqueness of the self is the very fact of bearing the fault of another" (112). Responsibility is this an-archy and lawlessness in which responsibilities, cannot be differentiated, apportioned, weighed, measured, assigned, distributed, and enforced.

So unfair. So *not* just. And so truly dangerous to state and economy. Untameable responsibility perhaps more dangerous than untameable eros. Why should all this be my responsibility? And there is no rational answer to the question. But also no concrete possibility of rationality without the question already having been, if not answered, then obviated in the question itself, as put to an other (see *OTB,* 117n20, 196). Truly one might want to try hard to think of ways of conceiving oneself as not hostage. Most of political philosophy and political theory have been doing that for a very long time. But the lack of reciprocity in my ethical obsession, according to Levinas, should not be taken to imply a moral imperative on the subject (*aufgegeben* rather than *gegeben,* as Kant puts it) taken to extremes: "The unconditionality of being hostage is not the limit case of solidarity, but the condition for all solidarity" (117). This would imply also that neither the long-run, enlightened self-interest of even a nonpossessive individualism, nor universalization through self-legislation, nor common belonging within a secular or sacred tradition (such as those of natural law), or within a nation or any identity at all, certainly not the tepid "communitarianism" that positions itself as a complement to liberalism — that none of them amount to that much when it comes to the grounds of human solidarity, and are certainly not its ultimate form(s). Also, to insist, as Levinas does, that the subject is persecuted as a hostage, and thus witness to the glory of the Infinite (see 140ff) is not to glorify the suffering in the suffering of suffering, "not to draw from suffering some kind of magical redemptive virtue...[but instead] to pass from the outrage undergone to responsibility for the persecutor [this does *not* mean I should either love and forgive the empirical persecutor or continue to hate him], and in this sense from suffering to expiation for the other" (111).

The self, in the accusative, obsessed, and persecuted in responsibility, hostage to the faults and misfortunes of the other, therefore the radically passive restlessness of expiation for the other, can be nothing "but a substitution of me for the others" (*OTB*, 114). Not a will to sacrifice myself for the other, but a being for-the-other despite myself. The very term substitution, however, is significant in its difference from any consciousness of unity, fusion, or common belonging. Restlessness here is not the longing for a state of nondifferentiation in which the other and myself were not yet separate from the one or within the whole, but "an exposure to the other...signification itself, the one-for-the-other to the point of substitution, but substitution in separation, that is responsibility" (54). The separation involved in substitution is, moreover, not the separation achieved by the reflexiveness of consciousness. In the reflexiveness of consciousness there is formed a recurrence, but as a shadow of substantiality for the I. In substitution, however, recurrence refers to the recurrence of "oneself" (104), not of the negating and self-negating "for-itself" of consciousness.

Parallel to the unity of the universe in responsibility, in which that unity is in its being incumbent upon me from all sides rather than the apperceptive unity of the gaze, the unity of the self, necessary for self to be involved in substitution as responsibility, is in "exposure" (105). The recurrence of the oneself, "me" in the accusative, "able" to endure the suffering of suffering through time, is not something that is self-formed, self-constituted. On the contrary, "The recurrence of oneself...is already constituted when the act of constitution first originates" (105). Thus, substitution is not the act of an I, going against itself for the other, but the self itself, but not present to itself, or even representable to itself because, diachronically, it has always already been formed, or, one should say, created: "The oneself cannot form itself; it is already formed with absolute passivity...an attachment that has already been made, as something irreversibly past" (104). It was made "in a time of...creation, of which nature or creation retains a trace" (105). The oneself in its recurrence as already subjected to the weight of the universe, "the oneself proper to consciousness...[which is] not again a consciousness...can indeed appear in an indirect language, under a proper name, as an entity, and thus put itself on the edge of the generality characteristic of all said, and therefore to essence. But it is first a non-quiddity, no-one, clothed with borrowed being, which masks its nameless singularity by conferring on it a role" (106). In its nameless singularity the oneself is "prior to the distinction between the particular and the universal. It is, if one likes, a relation, but one where there is no disjunction between the terms held in relation...a materiality more material than all matter" (108).

According to Levinas, it is "in such terms" that we must conceive "the de-substantiation of the subject, its de-reification.... It is a pure self, in the accusative, responsible before there is freedom" (*OTB,* 127). The new categorical imperative that Adorno perceives as given through the experience of Auschwitz, the experience of the possibility, and more than the possibility, of the disappearance of the possibility of murder — truly the terminus *ad quem* of reification itself — the philosopheme of pure identity as death, demands this outstepping of subjectivity as consciousness-of. The new categorical imperative requires a relation to the other as an other and as a relation that is inconceivable. The critique of ideology that is the operation of negative dialectics and critical theory can rest upon no other, precisely nonrational, foundation than this materiality of the self in radical passivity as a substitution for the other. But to rescue the metaphysical, as matter in this sense, means, first of all, as Levinas does by taking *un pas au dela* with respect to both (and in both senses of the term respect) Heidegger and

Husserl, differentiating, and then keeping in a nonprivative relation, the other-in-the-same that is knowledge and the other-in-the-same that is ethics or substitution. Negative dialectics, through its second Copernican turn installing the preponderance of the object within rational subjectivity does not quite know this differentiation. The infinitesimal that eludes the concept, the infinitesimal that must continually recur for any negative dialectic to find purchase, in other words, to effectuate the standpoint of redemption, is to be found not in yet another even ineffable quality, not simply in the nonidentity of the object with respect to the concept, but in a nonidentity presupposed by conceptual nonidentity, that nonidentity par excellence which is the relation of my substitution for the faults and misfortunes of the other. One should say that the claim of the autarky of thought is to be undone not simply through another information that exceeds the concept but in the sense that what exceeds the concept is not another, even nonconceptual information, but the other in his singular nudity and nonidentity.

Assymetry, Radical Plurality, and the Problem of Propagation

Levinas's metaphenomenological disclosure of an otherwise than being, of sensible subjectivity as substitution in proximity is an indispensable supplement to negative dialectics and therefore to critical theory. Negative dialectics, because it still conceives of the sensual along the lines of the reception of information, cannot thematize the relation with the absolutely other that commands it. Yet Adorno comes very close to this by virtue of the role assigned to mimesis in sustaining the reflexive self-criticism of reason. Adorno has based the possibility of negative dialectics on a "right intention," an intentionless intention that is an absolute self-relinquishment, and will therefore declare that "the need to lend a voice to suffering is the condition of all truth" (*ND,* 17).

Negative dialectics knows that it lives from a responsibility, from "the guilt of a life which purely as a fact will strangle other life.... This and nothing else is what compels us to philosophize" (364). Its "abiding insistently with the particular" is "the morality of thought" (*MM,* 74). But being unable to reach the otherwise than being, or perhaps being unable to discriminate being otherwise and otherwise than being, or a being-summoned from a letting-be, Adorno and critical theory were not able to disclose a relation which is not one of disclosure, that is, the ethical relation. Such a relation would be the fixed point that critique needs, without being a fixed, final or perfected form of being, or a standard or a norm. Levinas points out that such a fixed point, needed for critique, "can only be the absolute status of the interlocutor, a being and not a truth about being" (ET, 41). The fixed point for critique would be the relation with a reality infinitely distant, without distance destroying the relation or the relation destroying the distance (*TI,* 41). This would be ethical proximity, which is both a relation and the term of a relation (*OTB,* 85).

Although negative dialectics can therefore be seen to need ethics as first philosophy as more than even a clarification of its tacit grounds, this would mean something quite different, and even antithetical to the efforts to redeem the "normative deficit" of critical theory undertaken by the so-called second generation of critical theorists. It would not issue in a new version of deontological moral theory, a formal, rule-based, proceduralist ethics; nor would it involve a subsumption of the philosophy of the subject within a new progressive history of the linguistification of the sacred. For nearly all intents and purposes ethics as first philosophy, not yielding a principle, could simply underscore the operation of negative dialectics as another, a different "thought more thoughtful than the thought of being, a sobering up that philosophy attempts to say...if only in a language that ceaselessly unsays itself, a language that insinuates."[20]

The allegiance of negative dialectics and ethics as first phi-losophy may herald a critique that is at once a great refusal and a great reversal, and in these senses eminently political as well as ethical. But this is not quite the direction in which Levinas takes it. Staying with the presumption, heuristically, that the trajectory of all his later thinking departs from the problems unfolded in "Reflections on the Philosophy of Hitlerism," how far has Levinas gotten in resolving what I called earlier the conundrum of a freedom without history or a history without freedom? It is no accident that, in the language of *Otherwise than Being,* the ethical relation, substitution, is at times referred to as an alliance, an allegiance, a kinship, an attachment to a past older than history: "Here there is a relationship of kinship outside all biology, 'against all logic'" (*OTB,* 87). Yet it is not a kinship that has any resemblance to resemblance or to the logic of universal and particular: "One has to find for man another kinship than that which ties him to being, one that will enable us to conceive of this difference between me and the others, this inequality, in a sense absolutely opposed to oppression" (177). But this other kinship, which is anything but universalist, is not biological: "The concept of the incarnate subject is not a biological concept. The schema that corporeality outlines submits the biological itself to a higher structure" (109). But incarnate, sensible matter, absolutely and radically passive in saying-to, unable to assume the infinite responsibility that it is, is not an other kinship in the sense of a freedom that has no history. Its history is older than memory, but a history nonetheless. It is a "'prehistory' of the ego posited for itself [in which] speaks a responsibility" (117).

Subjectivity conceived as ethical, as a not-a-knowing cannot *have* anything, let alone the freedom attributed by Husserl to the transcendental ego presupposed by the correlation of noesis and noema. It is, as "Reflections" puts it, without yet having made the distinction between temporality and diachrony, a condition subject to finality that "forever evades man's control" (RPH, 65). There is nothing more final for a subject than its "own" diachrony. Responsibility, which binds me to others before I am bound to my body is exactly the intuition, the absolute position, both betrayed in and belied by the philosophy of Hitlerism, in which "the situation to which he is bound was not added to him but formed the very foundation of his being" (67). But the situation forming the foundation of one's being is not the being-in-the-world of a thrown *Dasein* absorbed in care, or even absorbed in one of the modalities of care, *mitsein*. Nor is the situation of incarnate proximity the response of thinking and dwelling to Being. Nor is the situation in any way a particularism of historical belonging to place and time, languages, traditions, particular life-worlds, or the particularism of any determinate life-worlds, contexts, destinies, or fates. On the very last page of *Otherwise than Being,* Levinas is intent to remind his reader that "we find the agglomerations or dispersions of peoples in the deserts without manna of this earth. But each individual of these peoples is virtually a chosen one, called to leave...the concept of the ego, its extension in the people, to respond with responsibility: me, here I am, for the others, to lose his place radically" (*OTB,* 185). Thus, the radically situated self is neither the universalized self proper to liberalism, the spectator-subject that is free to choose or even assume the right not to choose. The incarnate, exposed self, in responsibility, is anything but, or otherwise than that self doubled over by liberalism into the subject ever outside itself and thereby able to choose its destiny. But its "destiny" is to be chosen not to have a destiny, or even a destination.

The situation to which the subject belongs radically, the otherwise than being, is therefore not the same situation as that of the famous subject of transcendental idealism. Ethics as the surplus of the social does not mean a freedom without history, even if that history is not reducible to the external, therefore recuperable history of nations, tribes, even classes, even of genders, even of *homo sapiens sapiens,* even the sendings of Being. The situation can therefore not lend itself to universalization, without a crucially significant remainder. To recognize the other as another consciousness-of, to recognize the other as the freedom of the other in essential resemblance to my own(most) freedom, as belonging to the same species or concept, and thereby to submit to the universalization that puts all of our freedoms on the same plane, making possible reciprocity and equality (and also private property, commodity exchange, capitalism, the market and the state, also welfare apparatuses), is already not to respond to the other as absolutely other. Another other is not the absolutely other, only another same, the same other that I am. "Here I am" and "here are both he/she and I, and all of us" are radically distinct subjective and intersubjective situations.

But neither is the situation, as the surplus of the social, a history without freedom. The history, the past and passed, the diachrony of the prehistory of the ego, are a freedom otherwise, because the situation is otherwise, than the history of either the destiny of my kin or the fate of natural history. This becomes visible, without reverting to the status of the visible, in Levinas's descriptions of the social meanings of the ethical relation or responsible proximity. What marks the sociality of the ethical relation, and the ethicality of the social relation, and therefore indelibly marks the sociality of subjectivity, a sociality not added to it, but the foundation of its being are asymmetry — one might say assymetrical fraternity[21] — nonidentity, singularity and radical plurality. These are foregrounded more strikingly in *Totality and Infinity* than in *Otherwise than Being,* but they are all just as much profiles of saying-to as are the monadic moments that are focused upon a bit more narrowly in the newer work.

In *Totality and Infinity,* the asymmetry that characterizes the relation in which the other's distance is inflected into height, thus the inequality of the other, is described as a "kinship" that is radically different from the unity of a genus, or any coordination at all, whether "just" or "unjust." Thus, "Like a shunt every social relation leads back to the presentation of the other to the same [presentation or expression become its "trace" in *Otherwise than Being*]....When taken to be like a genus that unites like individuals the essence of society is lost sight of" (*TI,* 213). No third-person perspective at all is thus capable of describing the essential asymmetry of the social relation, especially not that third-person perspective from which universalization arises and which the distanced freedom sought by enlightened rationality presupposes. In *Otherwise than Being,* asymmetry reappears as an aspect of proximity, that "thorn in the flesh of reason, which is the shudder of subjectivity." Whereas symmetrical relations, and therefore the possibility of reciprocity and equal exchange, presuppose reversibility, "not to turn into relations that reverse, irreversibility, is the universal subjectness of the subject" (*OTB,* 84). Asymmetry even escapes the anti-identificatory operations of a negative dialectics: "In consciousness, no supplementary specific difference, no negation of universality, can extract the subject out of universality" (83).

Thus, while Adorno's new categorical imperative has the barest possible meaning of not treating the object as in any way a specimen, it does not yet quite glimpse the irreversible asymmetry of the relation it says is commanded. Thus, unlike proximity, it tends toward consciousness of, whereas

> Proximity [as a spatial relation further disclosing asymmetry] does not resolve into consciousness of...another being that it would judge to be near inasmuch as the other would be under one's eyes or within one's reach and inasmuch as it would be possible to take hold of that being, hold on to it or converse with it, in the reciprocity of handshakes, caresses, struggles, collaboration, commerce, conversation. Consciousness, which is consciousness of a possible, power, freedom, would then have lost proximity properly so called, now surveyed and thematized, as it already would have repressed in itself a subjectivity older than knowing or power. (*OTB,* 83)

If the subject is the asymmetrical relation to the other, a relation perceivable only in the height of the other, the social relation must come to be understood as a radical multiplicity rather than a numerical multiplicity (*TI,* 121, 220). As with asymmetry, radical multiplicity belongs to "the relation proceeding from me to the other [which] cannot be included within a network of relations visible to a third party. If this bond between me and the other could be entirely apprehended from the outside, it would suppress, under the gaze that encompassed it, the very multiplicity bound with this bond" (121). In radical multiplicity all individuals, not being extensions of any concept or identity at all, are each and all bound to each and all, but not to the totality that has been pursued in the thought of the West since Parmenides, where "multiplicity is taken to be the ontological fallenness of beings, mutually limiting one another in their prox-imity. Since Parmenides across Plotinus we have not succeeded in thinking otherwise" (104; see also PT, 6–11). The terms of such a multiplicity are not themselves, however, substances; they are not "congealed in isolation," not "posited as causes of themselves" (221). As "creatures" (rather than finite beings conceived in privative terms in reference to infinite Being), there-fore, they are dependent, but in a fashion that is "unparalleled": "the dependent being draws from this exceptional dependence its very independence, its exteriority to the system" (104). As radically multiple, the persons bound in separation beyond their identifiable differences and commonalities are not re-bound in any deeper participation of the sort that "philosophies of life" and of "race" propose,[22] inasmuch as such participations make the "unicity" of the subject disappear. And this is what Levinas finds to be of particular value in liberalism — insofar as its "pathos" [its own "intuition" that gets betrayed in the assertion of absolute freedom and belied as well] is "a promotion of the person...inasmuch as he represents nothing further" (120).

Radical multiplicity implies as well a different notion of the uniqueness of the person than the uniqueness that belongs to all the unique things, including individuals, that may be disclosed through ontology and thus, despite each being unique, offer themselves to the possibility of this or that form of totalization, including universalization. Everyone knows that every thing is unique, according to Levinas in *Totality and Infinity,* like the Mona Lisa or the Eiffel Tower. It is simply easier to miss the uniqueness of some things rather than other things. But what he calls "the affectivity of the I" or "inwardness" in *Totality and Infinity,* which becomes vulnerable, exposed subjectivity in *Otherwise than Being,* has a "unicity" distinct from uniqueness. Unicity means existing not as a sample of a genus, without having a genus, not as the individuation of a concept, not even as a class of one. Unicity implies an ipseity which the dialectic of universal and particular, from which Hegel begins, cannot reduce to the generality of the relation of particular and universal inseparable from thought (*TI,* 117–18). Thus, "The refusal of the concept is not a resistance to generalization by the *to de ti,* which is on the same plane as the concept — and by which the concept is defined, as by an antithetical term. Here the refusal of the concept is not only one aspect of its being, but its whole content" (118; see also 214).[23] Uniqueness, as it comes to be called in *Otherwise than Being* (*OTB,* 56, 139) or singularity is not to be placed in a privative relation with identity, but takes place on an axis or plane distinct from the plane of thought and being. The I exhibits its singularity or is "confirmed" therein, not at all in being something, but "in its incessant effort to purge itself of being the centre of gravity" (*TI,* 245). Its singularity is "a privilege and an election" (245); it is "an election in persecution," which is "the impossibility of slipping away and being replaced" (*OTB,* 56) that is of the essence of infinite responsibility. Responding to the other in radical passivity before being bound to my body, the recurrence of the oneself in persecution, makes me unique and makes the relation of me to the other radically plural asymmetrically.

But to be unique already seems to suggest an identity when it is in fact a matter always already of nonidentity, that is, by virtue of being hostage to infinite responsibility, not being this or that or these or those, but also not being nothing. Saying-to means a "denuding" of the unqualifiable one, unique and chosen, a denuding that "absolves me of all identity" (*OTB,* 50). For Levinas, "Uniqueness is without identity" (*OTB,* 57). It is a "malady of identity," the other-in-me, "only possible as an incarnation" (69). My social situatedness, the social surplus (quite radically and ironically distinct from the economic surplus of hierarchical social structures), *my historicity per se,* is therefore not ultimately to be found in any identity at all, whether it be of race, gender, age group, people, tribe, nation, class, civilization, even biological species, genus, family, order or phylum, or eco-evolutionary location. But the subject's nonidentity also does not mean an assumption of the identity of the subject belonging to that liberal universalism which claims to free the subjects of all their responsibilities except their responsibility to freely choose or not choose among all their logical possibilities (which *of course* requires the recognition of the freedom and self-mastery of the other). Such a subject has perhaps the most powerful, perhaps paranoid, and also the most bare of identities, the identity of pure freedom as achievement and performance in which he becomes unbound from the situation that forms the very basis of his being, that is, his being for the other. Levinas praises the most powerful of the "sentiments" of May 1968 for refusing this very identity, that is,

> a humanity defined by its self-satisfaction, its acquisitions and its acquittances. Over and beyond capitalism and exploitation what was contested were their conditions: the person understood as an accumulation of being, by merits, titles, professional competence

[la carrière ouvert au talent] — an ontological tumefaction weighing on others and crushing them, instituting a hierarchized society maintained beyond the necessities of consumption....Behind the capital of having weighed a capital of being. (NI, 150n9)

Yet this refusal of identity is also a radical situatedness.

Radically situated as, in, and with incarnate responsibility in asymmetrical proximity, which is both the absolute term of a relation and the absolute relation itself, the unique subject denuded of all identity, restlessly out of phase with itself in a diachronous sensibility is, in its prehistoricity, not oppressed, alienated or exploited by the other, but free. Its freedom is not a smaller version, reserved for mortals, of the infinite freedom of an eternal or omnipotent being. Its finite freedom is not infinite freedom "operating in a limited field" (*OTB,* 123). Finite freedom is not the limited freedom of a finite being but the finite freedom of a creature, a "created being."

Levinas finds in the un-Greek idea of creation *ex nihilo,* "if it is not a pure nonsense" (113), "the expression of a multiplicity not united into a totality; the creature is an existent which does indeed depend on an other, but not as a part that is separated from it [that is, totality]. Creation *ex nihilo* breaks with the system, posits a being outside of every system, that is, there where its freedom is possible" (*TI,* 104). This, Levinas's "stance," which rescues, reengineers and redeems the nonsense of the onto-mono-theist notion of creation, understands separation as absolute and not, in the manner of Greek metaphysics, as "a fall, or privation or provisional rupture of the totality" (102).[24] Creation, or the logically absurd idea of origin from nothing, is fundamentally opposed to the philosophical-ontological thought of a prior community of all things within eternity and the related notions of a common matrix from which all things arise. That notion of creation is thus well suited to express the "kinship" of beings and at the same time their "radical heterogeneity" (293).[25] Separation understood in privative reference to unity — that is, within the terms of formal logic — endlessly paraphrased by philosophical anthropology in its insistence on finitude (103), would be unable to distinguish between need and Desire, thus missing "the relation between strangers who are not wanting to one another — desire in its positivity — [which] is affirmed across the idea of creation *ex nihilo*. Then the plane of the needy being, avid for its complements, vanishes, and the possibility of a sabbatical existence, where existence suspends the necessities of existence, is inaugurated" (104).

Thus, one of the meanings of substitution — that is, of infinite responsibility in absolute separation — is finite or created freedom in which "the self is absolved of itself. Is this freedom? It is a different freedom from that of an initiative. Through substitution for others the oneself escapes relations. At the limit of passivity, the oneself escapes passivity or the inevitable limitation that the terms within relation undergo...the other no longer limits the same...the self liberates itself ethically from every other and from itself...[this] does not signify submission to a non-ego" (*OTB*, 115). Levinas is not counseling a "naïve unconditioned 'Yes' of submission." The radically passive 'yes' of created freedom which, in a sense must precede my ability to say no to my own yes, is not the unconditionality of an "infantile spontaneity," but "the very exposure to critique" (121–22). Finite or created freedom is a responsibility prior to the freedom of initiative and not a partial freedom, because the other "accuses" me, not because the other limits my freedom (*OTB*, 123–24). Neither is the freedom of responsibility in substitution "a guilt complex," or a natural benevolence, or a disposition to love or self-sacrifice. It is instead "a mode of freedom ontologically impossible...[that] frees the subject from ennui, that is from the enchainment to itself, where the ego suffocates from itself due to the tautological way of identity, and ceaselessly seeks after the distraction of games and sleep in a movement that never wears out" (124). Such freedom does not belong to any order where accountability of each to the other can be made symmetrical, reciprocal, and conditional; no bookkeeping would be possible, where bookkeeping means "an order where my responsibilities correspond exactly to liberties taken." As a result, "Freedom in the genuine sense can only be a contestation of this bookkeeping by a gratuity" (125). Created freedom would therefore mean the exact opposite of any rule requiring sacrifice: "To say [even] that the other has to sacrifice himself *to the others* would be to preach human sacrifice" (126). For to require of any other a sacrifice would be impossible when "no one can substitute himself for me, who substitutes myself for all" (126).

Whatever else it might mean, then, the finite freedom of a creature is opposed radically to both the liberal notion of the freedom of the spectator subject, able to initiate its choices (or not) from nowhere, and also opposed equally to the destining of a self submerged in its historicity, for whom freedom would mean the fully conscious acceptance of its fatality as its unconditional responsibility to its own, sacrifice to its own others. Forty years after "Reflections" Levinas has, one might say, come close to divining fully the meaning of the intuition of "identity between self and body" revealed in the "impasse of physical pain," the "absolute position" disavowed by the theology and philosophy of the West in their flight into absolute freedom and betrayed by Hitlerism when it turned the being bound to one's situation as the very basis of one's being into the spirituality of blood, *Volk,* and history. At the deepest and most concrete level of the human social relation what takes place, "effaced but untameable," is neither a freedom without history, nor a history without freedom. If one were to ask for a formula to indicate how it might be otherwise, such a formula might be a prehistory of created freedom.

But this still leaves at least one very large problem, also prefigured by the "Reflections" essay. Let us call this, as Levinas did then, the problem of propagation and propose that the process of propagation has both a vertical, intensive dimension and a horizontal, extensive dimension. In "Reflections" Levinas deals with both dimensions without differentiating them. The contrast is in the way that liberalist ideas of universalism (from Christianity onwards) propagate themselves as opposed to particularist-historicist positions. And the contrast he draws is between, on the one hand, the expansive propagation of a physical force enlarging the particular agent and subordinating the rest, and, on the other, the propagation of a universalist idea in which there is the "disappearance" "among those *who submit* to it" (70; emphases added) of physical force. The one process of propagation gives us the idea, and the institutions to go with it, of masters and slaves. The other, the idea at least, of a society instituting equality among masters. The first thing of which to take note is the subtle but studied ambiguity surrounding the *disappearance* of physical force *after submission.* Levinas is, in this essay, not saying that one *should* submit to the universalist idea because in it force disappears as a universalist hence truly ethical, arrangement is achieved. He is also, or he may be, implying that the — only apparent — disappearance of the physical force and the relation of mastery-slavery depends upon a prior but henceforward sustained submission on the part of those subjected to the propagation of such an idea.

It is not as if fascism were simply a force without an idea, and liberalism simply an idea without force, the unforced force of the better argument, as it were. I believe Levinas is implying, despite his obvious relative preference for liberalism over fascism, that liberalism could be much better at forgetting, hiding, veiling, rationalizing, and institutionalizing the violence upon which it depends for its propagation, but that it does depend upon a continuous violence. Once we have been conscripted into, and have submitted to, the force of the position reserved for us, within a totality of "rational peace," a position of at least formally equal mastery, everything seems to be all right and on the up and up. But does the force therefore disappear? This essay engages the fascist idea in order to point out the radical shortcomings of the liberal idea of freedom without history as much as it points out the dangers of fascist history without freedom. And there is little in the work that follows, up through *Otherwise than Being* and beyond, to indicate that either Levinas himself, or the Levinasian idea of the ethical relation itself, lends itself to that famous transcendental subject of idealism, that "thinks itself free" (RPH, 63), or that self-owning subject of materialist liberalism, or its forms of ethics or freedom.

If we may postulate, then, that *both* liberalism and fascism not only miss, betray and belie the ethical relation but, in so doing, propagate as both force and idea and, that for the ethical relation both are, though asymmetrically, therefore radically inadequate, and that Levinas knows this, what then are the possibilities for propagation of the ethical relation itself, for the propagation of subjectivity as substitution? It is safe to assume that the question goes beyond a mere economy of violence. What are the forms of mediation, for mediation there *must* be, and must be according to an *ethical* necessity, between what takes place at the level of sensibility and what might take place at the levels of the ego, its needs, the will, theory, action, institutions, history and politics. Such a question would be the most urgent question for ethics itself. For Levinas himself these are *the* questions of knowing that have their "latent birth…in proximity" (*OTB*, 157). The third party, never actually absent from the relation, by putting distance between me and the singular other, always and forever makes such questions an integral part of the urgency of responsibility itself. It is "not by accident" after all that the order of truth and essence which Levinas claims "to hold to" is "of the first rank in Western philosophy" (156–57). It is not of the first rank because it grasps a first principle, or achieves its aims as first philosophy, but because it is not only justified by but also needed by ethics.

The ethical relation, substitution, is not something that can replace being or come into being from nonbeing; nor can its propagation be conceived as the realization of an objective potentiality within being. Its propagation would be unlike the propagation of either a force or an idea. But neither is propagation, and therefore a mediation of ethics with ontology, eschatology with history, alien to the ethical relation. My responsibility cannot be infinitely increasing without propagation belonging to substitution. The propagation of substitution in the order of truth and essence would have something like the structure of the other-in-the-same that is substitution itself, rather than the other-in-the-same that is knowledge. Yet substitution itself is radically distinct from the entire order of truth and essence grasped in ontology. Substitution, responsibility, proximity "are not events that happen to an empirical ego" (*OTB,* 115). They belong to its "pre-history" (117). Diachronous proximity "recognized as signification or goodness, allows us to understand goodness in another way than as an altruistic inclination to be satisfied" (137–38). It is "not the psychological event of compassion or intropathy in general, but makes possible the paradoxical psychological possibilities of putting oneself in the place of another" (146). Levinas writes, "All the transfers of feeling, with which the theorists of original war and egoism explain the birth of generosity…would not succeed in being fixed in the ego if it were not with its whole being, or rather with its whole disinterestedness, subjected not, like matter, to a category, but to the unlimited accusative of persecution" (118). The psyche, as substitution, "not an anodyne formal relation, but all the gravity of the body extirpated form its *conatus essendi* in the possibility of giving," although it may have its goodness effaced, is untameable, "is a seed of folly, already a psychosis" (142). Substitution is "for the order of contemplation…something simply demented" (113). The relation between substitution and being cannot be negotiated through the normal channels of conceptual mediation because substitution and being are not separated moments of a totality. The normal channels of analytical or even dialectical reason will not do, because substitution and being are not even internally opposite to each other. They cannot be unified and each is irreducible further (because although ethics is prior to being, being cannot be reduced to ethics — only justified ethically). But they cannot remain separate.

This brings us back to the beginnings of our investigation. Substitution and essence are always already implicated in a structure of betrayal. As we have already seen in chapter 1, Levinas himself, although he continues to raise the question of propagation in terms of the relation of goodness (sometimes justice) to comparison, calculation, money, justice, the state, politics — either does so in terms of a double amphibology, a simultaneous acceptance and rejection of whatever justice there is; or, as the impasse into which liberalism leads, in the exteriority of my consciousness to itself in works, the inhuman requirements of realizing rights, following from the ontological alienation which in the real society institutes history; but finally also in the form of a bare question, the problem of a third way, an imperative to build a world that suppresses the occasions for betrayal or the injunction that we must use ontology for the other. But what Levinas does not do is take the next steps that might be useful for taking ontology for the other beyond the impasse of liberalism. Perhaps the propagation of a radically plural sociation still requires some negative, and positive, support from something in materialism which he might have overlooked in assuming the fine risk of exaggerating Husserl's method to the point it turns against itself in the subsumption of the transcendental ego in incarnate socio-sensibility to the trace of the other.

Six

The Sense of Hope

From the Surplus of the Social to Surplus Morality

Negative Dialectics, as we have seen, conveys the impression that a changed philosophy calls for a new categorical imperative, that receptivity to the preponderance of the object implies not only the failure of the power of identification, but my guilt of what I am thinking. But we have also seen that it would be more accurate to think the possibility of negative dialectics as arising from the presumption that the extreme development of natural history (issuing in, for example, Auschwitz) gives the experience of *Schuld,* making that guilt/responsibility/debt radical enough to allow for the possibility that the dialectic of enlightenment might come to consciousness. How else could identity come to a determinate negation not of this or that scheme of identification, this or that rationality, but of itself? Does identity not need an object lesson *in extremis* to recognize itself for what it is? Yet negative dialectics remains ambiguous with respect to the question of whether the subject is to be removed from its throne by its continuous failure, according to its own criteria, to constitute through identification, or by the appeal of the absolutely external in the surplus of the social relation. Negative dialectics all but knows yet cannot say that it must look beyond the preponderance of the object, to the relation with the Other, if identity is not to recover itself, if the Same is not to reinstitute its freedom through identification. Thus, negative dialectics remains ambiguous in aiming at a knowledge of the absolute which is not an absolute knowledge.

On the other side, that of the surplus of the social, the self-transcendence of the separate being in substitution, is not only the necessary condition, as Levinas says, for the difference between truth and ideology (*OTB,* 177–78), but *realizes itself* in the matter of justice — and thus necessarily demands the operations of the Same, identification, reason, calculation, comparison, and so on. But the question of justice ought not and need not issue in an amphibology of ethics and eschatology versus the State and Universal History. In that amphibology the state and history are radically disturbed, but even this radical disturbance continuously reinstates the state it disturbs. The use of ontology for the sake of the other seems to imply both an acceptance and rejection of whatever justice there is, both a confirmation and a denial of its own instantiations, without respite, without escape and without transcendence. The identification, totalization and thus injustice required by justice, by the third party, are not differentiated from the identification, totalization, and injustice required by the natural history of domination and the domination of natural history.[1] As Adorno puts it in one formulation, "what is done to all by the few always occurs as subjection of individuals by the many" (*DE,* 21–22). The injustice of justice appears to be unquestionably a social necessity and, in appearing so, both justice and injustice succumb to the principle of immanence. The question whose answer is supposed to realize justice becomes a piece of natural history, repeating itself *ad infinitum,* and in the same form.

In the Levinasian amphibology the dialectics of justice is at a standstill. The question of justice need not, however, issue in this amphibology if that very question includes, or can and should include, the possibility of differentiating between the requirements of the third per se and the past historical forms through which these requirements have been concretely mediated. Has there been a surplus justice, calculation, comparison, or identification over and beyond what the third party ethically requires, a surplus not of the social, but a surplus subtracted from the social in domination? Would the critique of natural history, resting as it does on such a differentiation, also imply that the justice required by the third party might signify a social relation in which the relation of each and every Other-to-the-Same would take a form other than the forms mediated by identification? *The* question according to Levinas — the ethical demand that institutes and regulates the development of ontology: what do I have to do with justice? — this very question ought to include the question of natural history, the construal and denial of universal history. If the question of justice avoids or evades this question it cannot do justice to the very question of justice. If it cannot include this question it will inevitably and fatally confirm every form of domination as necessity, despite ethics.

It is one of the relative strengths of Levinas's philosophy that in it this question within a question all but begs itself to be put. Levinas can bring the conscience or consciousness which is already unhappy back to this question and, perhaps newly, as a question *of* conscience. It is the main point at which the very drive for philosophical unity and comprehensiveness in his thinking breaks apart, in which the preponderance of the Other shows through. It is also one of the relative weaknesses of Levinas's philosophy that his meta-phenomenology, perhaps in overreaction to philosophies of universal history, abstracts from all historical mediation. As we have seen, although Levinas accounts, and in great structural detail in *Totality and Infinity,* for the possibility of the development of the Same, for representation, possession, labor, economy, war and the state, this account is limited precisely in terms of being what Adorno, criticizing Heidegger in "The Idea of Natural History," called a structural totality. The critique of natural history implies, on the other hand, an exquisite awareness of the development in the very repetition of the Same in the Same. And an exquisite awareness that within this development in stasis and stasis in development there is the permanent possibility, as Benjamin had put it, of a completion "of the task of liberation in the name of generations of the downtrodden" (TPH, 260).

Natural history and its critique together imply that that there is a history to the Same and a history of the relation of subjectivity to the Same. Even if the ethical relation is conceived as standing outside and beyond natural history as the eschatological, even if Levinas has reached the thing itself which is a no-thing, nonidentity par excellence in the ethical relation, this does not mean that the relation of the Same or consciousness to subjectivity is of necessity always the same. Being otherwise has a crucial relevance to what Levinas indicates by that "barbarous expression 'otherwise than being'" (*OTB,* 178), and to the possibility of its propagation. It is because Levinas appreciates this that he does not try to avoid the problem that the problem of the third brings to ethics. In fact he makes this problem appear starkly, albeit briefly, and as a problem, not transparently as a quasi-transcendental aporetic structure, in *Otherwise than Being* when he asserts that "the true problem for us Westerners is not so much to refuse violence as to question ourselves about a struggle against violence which, without blanching in non-resistance to evil, could avoid the institution of violence out of this very struggle" (177). Levinas is also reasonably clear that despite a "bad peace" being better than a "good war," the bad peace of a law ensured by force is an offence "against *a dignity other than that which attaches to respect for universal laws*" (RMRO, 123). With this brief assertion Levinas declares the opposition of the ethical to the Kantian moral law, and *a fortiori* to the concepts of right and of the state that follow from it. The agent of the Kantian moral law finds a dignity to be respected, in both self and other, only in a universalizing legislation independent of all interest, in the substancelike autonomy of reason legislating by and for itself, and thus only respects the other *as the same,* as freedom of will, as essence par excellence. The offence here to the dignity, or height of the other is intrinsic to the Kantian conception of dignity as exclusively bound to free, rational self-consciousness; the offence is not simply in the fact that the empirical law of the state forces its authors to conform to the freedom that they are. Rational peace, the unity in a purely rational legislation of a plurality of free wills negating one another, does not avoid the re-institution of violence out of the very struggle against it. Nor does the fact that liberal legal-constitutional rights allow for a continuous, nonending critique of this very self-same liberal notion reduce the violence of this dignity.

In resigning himself to simply raising the problem of the repetition of violence — within the rational and reasonable struggle against it — Levinas has stayed within the boundaries he lays down by remaining "faithful" to intentional analysis, even though he "ventures beyond phenomenology" by contesting that the appearing of being is "the ultimate justification of subjectivity" (*OTB,* 183). Both the method of *Otherwise than Being* and the more existential-phenomenological method of *Totality and Infinity,* however, also require overlooking one of its dimensions, the natural-historical investigation of which might point beyond a bad peace toward the very "messianic peace" (*TI,* 22), the "sabbatical existence" he envisions for beings no longer "needy," but Desirous of one another (104). If Levinas is correct in his criticisms of Marx for not being realistic enough, the same criticism can be directed at a certain lack of realism in his own dealings with the problem of rational peace. In criticizing Kant, Levinas does not question Kant's notion of a plurality of separate wills negating each other, only the result that Kant derives from his reinterpretation of the freedom of such wills — the idea of the dignity of the person as grounded in the autonomy of reason. This lack of criticism does not imply, however, that Levinas thinks, like Kant, that empirical individuals need necessarily be a plurality reducible to an antagonistic system united by reciprocal needs.

Also, in criticizing Kant, Levinas, beyond alluding to the offense that Kantian morality actually offers to the height of the other, does not envision the thoroughly destructive effect that such a morality has upon the ethical relation itself. Kantian morality, rational peace, remains for him something like a second-best, all that the relation between being and otherwise than being allows or can sustain. That there might, however, be a rational peace of an entirely other sort, based upon a transcendence of instrumental rationality is not something that can be readily theorized out of ethics as first philosophy. Horkheimer and Adorno, on the other hand, in subjecting Kantian morality to a natural-historical critique will take a necessary step in the direction needed to argue the possibility that the law required by the third party is qualitatively other than the law required by either the few or by, at best, the fusion of the demands of the few with the third. Marcuse will take such a critique a step beyond, by arguing that not only is the abrogation of the law of the few possible, but that once, or if abrogated, the law demanded by the third would characterize the messianic peace of a sabbatical existence.

The Self-Destruction of Enlightenment Morality

According to Horkheimer and Adorno, the truth of Kantian morality is not to be found in the apparent reconciliation that would take place through a continuous approach toward a "perfect constitution," not in any asymptotic progress toward the regulative Idea of a Kingdom of Ends. Kantian morality does have such "utopian elements"; it envisions "autonomously acting individuals whose individual decisions smoothly yield the welfare of the whole." The Kingdom of Ends expresses "a beautiful vision" that "the yearning thought forms...from the unchanged elements of the present."[2] The truth of Kantian morality, however, is not to be found in Kant's explicit statements about morality. The result or meaning of Kantian morality is instead "the shocking truth" that formalistic reason "is no more tied to morality than immorality." The truth is "the impossibility of deriving from reason any fundamental argument against murder" (*DE,* 118). Such implications are not drawn by Hegelian or utilitarian or sentimentalist or, these days, moral realist critiques of Kant's moral philosophy. They are instead drawn, and theoretically performed, by those "black writers of the bourgeoisie" who, in not postulating a closer tie between formalistic reason and morality than immorality, do not attempt to ward off the consequences of enlightenment with harmonizing theories. Sade and Nietzsche especially belong to this group. Although they exaggerate, the truth is only in those exaggerations. For Horkheimer and Adorno, "The statistical account of a pogrom...obscures the essence which comes to light only in an exact portrayal of the exception, of the very worst atrocity" (118). Sade, and Nietzsche, constitute the "intransigent critique of practical reason" by drawing out the proper consequences of formalized and instrumental reason. Formal reason ends not in a Kingdom of Ends but, in the end, in the avid destruction of conscience and remorse, pity and compassion, pleasure and love (94–114).

In the destruction of remorse and conscience, Sade's Juliette is exemplary. Her enlightened revolt against Catholic mythology involves a redirection of the energies religion had devoted to the sacraments to sacrilege instead, a sacrilege inflicted on the bodies of the weak. She is, however, no devotee of the "primal behaviours" that civilization has tabooed, "under the stigma of bestiality," for the drives in those behaviors had been transformed, in their subterranean existence, into destructive forces, and Juliette practices them not as natural, but as tabooed. She thus reacts to the value judgment against them not by practicing the "primal" behaviors, although they do get repeated in distorted form, but by reversing the value judgment. What had been made bestial under the taboo becomes for Juliette a virtue, rather than a vice. Juliette therefore embodies "neither unsublimated nor regressive libido, but intellectual pleasure in regression — *amor intellectualis diaboli,* the pleasure of attacking civilization with its own weapons" (*DE,* 94). To accomplish this freedom from conscience, the realization of reason as purely formal is necessary and welcome. Her procedures are not fanatical, but "enlightened and efficient" (94); she is a "proficient manipulator of the organ of rational thought" who "preaches on the self-discipline of the criminal": "The murderer's face must display the greatest calm.... Let your features express calm and equanimity; and try to summon up an extreme degree of callousness...if you were not certain that no pangs of conscience would attack you (and you will be so assured only through constant habituation to crime)...all your efforts to control your features and gestures would be of no account" (95; Sade's Juliette quoted by Horkheimer and Adorno). Nietzsche, in *The Transvaluation of All Values,* confirms Juliette's logic when he asserts that the "weak and unsuccessful must perish; this is the first proposition of *our* philanthropy. And they should even be helped on their way. What is more injurious than any vice — the compassion of action for all failures and weaklings — Christianity" (Nietzsche, quoted in *DE,* 97). Having followed Kantian enlightenment to the end in the construal of objective reason as myth and prejudice, "Nietzsche knows of no law 'which we not only acknowledge, but acknowledge as above us.' In so far as the understanding...recognizes a law of existence, it is that of the stronger" (99).

If conscience, remorse and repentance are, according to Sade and Nietzsche, irrational ruses of the weak, then pity and compassion are "sin pure and simple." The enlightened self-destruction of objective reason is, however, by itself, they recognize insufficient to entirely remove them from what Horkheimer in an earlier essay called the "psychic constitution" of the human.[3] Thus, "Sade and Nietzsche recognized that, after the formalization of reason, pity still remained as, so to speak, the sensual consciousness of the general and the particular, as naturalized mediation" (*DE,* 101). But it is for them a womanly trait, a softness and weakness which according to Juliette, "must above all be overcome...irreconcilable with the maxims of philosophy" (Sade, quoted in *DE,* 101–02). For Nietzsche it is "'a threat to the state, takes away the necessary rigor and discipline, makes heroes behave like whimpering women'" (Nietzsche, quoted in *DE,* 102).

The radical rejection of conscience, remorse, compassion and pity is, however, not for the sake of anyone's pleasure, even for the strong. Thus, "Even injustice, hatred and destruction, are regulated, automatic procedures....The means is fetishized, and absorbs pleasure" (*DE,* 104). The absorption of pleasure in the routinization of activity as its own end, a "purposeless purposiveness" (89) is plainly portrayed in the disciplined and methodical sexual teams of *Juliette* (88). Nietzsche recognizes "an aspect of resignation" not only in compassion, but also in pleasure which "relinquishes the possible" by "paying tribute to nature." Thus, for example, in his *Nachlass,* he proclaims "'Down with all those who merely enjoy'" (106). Pleasure as an indulgence, as a weakness, is an idol subject to rational abrogation: "pleasure is self-sacrifice to another." Pleasure is an enemy to the enemies of compassion inasmuch as it always, according to Horkheimer and Adorno, contains a moment of regression, behind a forgotten civilized taboo, to an age in which there was neither mastery nor discipline. It is a dreamlike release from the pressures of mastery and discipline, and ultimately, from the bond that joins the individual "to the self" (105).

Love in its various forms — romantic, parental and the love of God — are not far behind. Sade's libertines require that "men enter into the rational, calculating relation to their own kind, that in Juliette's enlightened circle has long since passed as proverbial" (*DE,* 107–08). Romantic love is destroyed as mere illusion, "actually a disguise, a rationalization of physical impulse, 'a false and always dangerous metaphysic'" (108). But not only is the romantic illusion destroyed,[4] all of love is subjected to the operations of a reason that is neutral with respect to "natural" ends. So it is that "Dolmance provides the materialistic disenchantment of parental love: 'These bonds derive from parents' fear that they will be deserted in their old age; and the degree of care which they show us in our infancy is intended to bring them the same attention in their dotage'" (116). Every kind of universal, unconditional love, not merely romantic love or religious love, are to be denounced, "for reason displaces all love" (116).

Afficionados of Nietzsche or Sade, as well as followers of Kant, would no doubt object, each from opposing directions, that Horkheimer and Adorno are here engaged in a *reductio ad absurdum* that is itself absurd, in identifying the categorical imperative with the will to power or with Sade's libertinism. But they would be missing the point of the dialectical constellation into which they place these otherwise radically different thinkers. They are not concerned to argue that Kant, Sade, and Nietzsche are all one, but that they are all symptomatic of what happens to the ethical relation as it is subjected to the dialectic of enlightenment in thought and in social reality. Kant, Sade, and Nietzsche all share in the modern European unfolding of that dialectic, in which the antiauthoritarian principle of enlightenment turns against itself (*DE,* 93). Thus, all are still reacting to the demise of a religion that had placed "harmony and fulfillment" in a hypostatized "religious beyond" (88). The modern enlightenment in general meant, positively for the materialists Horkheimer and Adorno, the separation of fulfillment from such a world behind the scenes and its transformation into the criterion of "human aspiration" in this one, although it was through "the form of systematization." Thus, Kant's more harmonizing theory joins earlier (and later) enlightened moral teachings in being a "hopeless attempt to replace enfeebled religion with some reason for persisting in society when interest is absent" (85). Sade and Nietzsche no longer want to replace religious authority with the authority of reason, and they no longer want to associate fulfillment with harmony, but with one or another naturalistic agonism. But their fictions and exaggerations do foreshadow what will happen to enlightened morality after "the short intermezzo of liberalism" (87). In succumbing to the post-Kantian confirmation of the scientific system as *the* form of truth, the advancing totalitarian order of late capitalism, in its nonfascist as well as fascist forms, "gives full reign to calculation and abides by science as such. Its canon is its own brutal efficiency" (86). That the canon of rational morality *is* brutal efficiency is born out by Sade, whose work "portrays 'understanding without the guidance of another person': that is, the bourgeois individual freed from tutelage" (86). Nietzsche, despite his railing against Kant, turns out to be a "secret Kantian" trying to replace religion with the higher self, God with the *Übermensch*. Both the categorical imperative and the overman "aim at independence from external powers, at the unconditioned maturity defined as the essence of enlightenment" (114).[5] Sade functions as a "spur to the salvation of enlightenment" in so far as he "did not leave it to opponents of the Enlightenment to take fright at its own nature" (117).

In the Kantian moment of enlightenment, there is no fear, as yet, of the nature of formalized subjective reason. The reason of the constituting, transcendental ego, on its practical side, in the categorical imperative, in fact seems to promise the harmony of the whole out of the autonomous legislative activities of individuals, so long as they can be brought to reason, so long as their legislation remains pure of any interest and follows the "formal directive" of "a will without contradiction." The categorical imperative even holds up a certain "general law" against the "natural law" of economic advantage.[6] To be sure, this can result in a certain absence of affect.

> "Apathy (in the form of rigor)," says Kant, "is a necessary presupposition of virtue," and (not unlike Sade) he distinguishes this "moral apathy" from insensibility in the shape of insensitivity to sensory stimuli. Enthusiasm is bad. Calmness and decisiveness constitute the strength of virtue. "That is the state of health in the moral life; an emotion, even when awakened by the notion of good, is but a transient brilliance succeeded by languor." (*DE*, 96)

But certainly, our Kantians would say, a judicious calm in the process of impartially and objectively testing the maxim of an action is not to be feared as the universalization of a brutal efficiency that is its own canon. And neither Kant, nor the categorical imperative, nor the morality of enlightenment in general can be held responsible for what are after all perversions of formal rationality. But this is not exactly Horkheimer and Adorno's argument. They are not, strictly speaking, concerned with whether Sade's and Nietzsche's fictions are or are not perversions of the categorical imperative, the "purest expression of the bourgeois moral concept." They are concerned with indicating that *enlightenment has no arguments against even perversions of its "proper nature"* and, that once enlightenment morality is harnessed to the dominant mode of production (which it is from the start), it abrogates its own efforts to overcome repressive social orders and confirms the brutal efficiency of totalized calculation.[7]

This reversibility of enlightenment proper with its perversions, however, *can* be seen, *in nuce,* in Kant. For Kant, enlightenment is an emergence from a self-incurred immaturity; it is the employment of the understanding without the guidance of any external authority, an understanding guided only by reason. The purpose of reason, moreover, is the organization of the individual data of cognition into a system. And system is the achievement of coherence according to a single principle (*DE*, 81). Thus "Reason contributes only the idea of systematic unity, the formal elements of fixed conceptual coherence" (82). System is, in essence, "the resolution of contradictions" (81). Systematic knowledge, enlightenment, is a subsumption of the experiential given under principles that are ultimately unified in their formally logical coherence. Anything other than systematically directed thinking is disoriented or authoritarian. All substantial goals, are thus, from the point of view of reason in its purity, one or another form of delusion (82), a regression into immaturity and external authoritarian guidance, external, that is, to reason. Any goal, end or purpose that is not unity itself, as the absence of formal contradiction, is extrarational if not irrational. When it comes to the realm of practice and the factual, such systematic understanding takes on the function of coping best with facts for the purpose of the mastery of nature. The principles of the enlightenment system are the principles of self-preservation. Immaturity is the inability to survive (83). Self-preservation is not only the constitutive principle of science, but "the soul of the table of categories." But not only the a priori categories and principles needed to establish science are tied to self-preservation, even "the ego, the synthetic unity of apperception…is in fact the product, as well as the condition for, material existence" (87).

For Kant, the fully enlightened and mature rational subject of both scientific knowledge and autonomous morals is above and beyond whatever history or contingency it must nevertheless face in the realm of empirical experience. It is, essentially, a freedom without history. Thus, it is structurally unable to recognize its own sociohistorically constituted identity, its identity as the *soi-disant* free but finite subject of identification, as itself being bound to natural history. It neither recognizes itself as bourgeois nor as bound to what it takes to be irrational forces of any kind, like remorse, compassion, pity, pleasure, or love. The closest it may come, as pure practical reason, to any such thing is a certain respect, flowing from the awe it directs exclusively to the starry skies above or its own moral law within. But here, in laying down these very conditions of respect, it actually announces its own affinity with and for power and domination, the power of that which is absolutely unreachable, of that which is insensible.

Kant's mature subject would not even have needed to be bound to the mast in order to hear the song of the Sirens and pass them by. In asserting its identity as freedom, it disregards its (non-)identity as what Levinas would describe as subjectivity, radical passivity, obsession, and so on. In this very freedom, in the autonomy of formal reason, however, it also begins to find in itself its own opposite. According to Horkheimer and Adorno, "so long as the identity of the user of reason is disregarded, the affinity of reason is as much to force as the mediation…it permits peace or war, tolerance or repression. *Since it exposes substantial goals as the power of nature over mind,* as the erosion of its self-legislation, reason is — by virtue, too, of its very formality — at the service of any natural interest. Thinking becomes an organic medium pure and simple, and reverts to nature" (*DE,* 87; emphasis added). In removing freedom from any bond that could be described as interhuman or social, in making freedom self-limiting only according to the principle of formal noncontradiction, Kantian morality points to the radicality of the modern enlightenment. Horkheimer and Adorno point out that the modern enlightenment became radical as it "banished any form of devotion which claimed to be objective and grounded in actuality. All previous obligations therefore succumbed to the verdict which pronounced them taboo — not excluding those which were necessary for the existence of the bourgeois order itself" (92–93).[8]

All affects are equally removed from reason as it declines the right to posit any substantial goals (*DE,* 89). But this is not, on Horkheimer's and Adorno's part, either a Hegelian critique of Kant, or a critique (or an endorsement) of moral relativism. They are not criticizing Kantian morality from the vantage point of the historical achievement of rational *Sittlichkeit,* whether actual or potential. Nor is their critique the obverse of any tacit claim that some new form of objective reason, one that could set absolute moral standards, is either possible or desirable. Earlier on, writing alone, Horkheimer had made this clearer in "Materialism and Morality," in the rather blunt conclusion that what "separates materialism from the idealist currents of philosophy," is "the insight that morality cannot be proven, that no single value admits of a purely theoretical grounding," whether this grounding be "by means of intuition...[or] of argument."[9] Their critique of Kant's moral doctrine, and by extension of the modern enlightenment's understanding of morality in general, is that it was from the start a sublimated but mimetic repetition of pure power and authority. And it was so because it aimed at the radical separation of the freedom of the subject from the human, shall we say "capacity" for objective devotion, or obligation, or for what Horkheimer in "Materialism and Morality" calls a "psychic constitution" which he thinks is only poorly prefigured in the Kantian notion of a specifically moral sentiment — for a psychic constitution that has in it the possibility of "groundless," noninstrumental love.[10]

The morality of the enlightenment, however, in following through, with absolute formal rigor, the rational destruction of the myth of the substantiality of devotion (shall we say to an "Other"?) turns out to be subjection to the power of power itself — that is, myth (or, in Levinas's terms, being or essence). Horkheimer and Adorno write, "In order to escape the superstitious fear of nature, it wholly transformed objective effective entities and forms into the mere veils of a chaotic matter and anathematized their influence on humanity as slavery, until the ideal form of the subject was no more than unique, unrestricted, though vacuous authority" (*DE*, 89). In carrying through the program of enlightenment beyond the restrictions even Kant laid on himself — that critique left room for a rational faith in God, in freedom and in immortality — Sade and Nietzsche theoretically perform the self-destruction of the antiauthoritarian principle of enlightenment. The Kantian distinction between *Wille* and *Willkür* is effaced to the point of disappearance. Pure power becomes its own justification for existence. All this means that "The abrogation of everything inherently binding, which it brings about, allows domination to ordain as sovereign, and to manipulate whatever bonds and obligations prove appropriate to it" (93).

There is even a telling affinity between moral enlightenment and domination. Perhaps the one thing above all else that the morality of enlightenment cannot abide is weakness, always seen in Western philosophy as the vice of the many. In Kant this is clear enough in the formal structure of the subject of pure practical reason, in his stoical *apatheia*. In Sade and Nietzsche, it becomes the exaggerated celebration of power that seems to need to find a transvalued fault in weakness, or even in sympathy for weakness. Perhaps there is something of which to be suspicious here. Horkheimer and Adorno suggest that fear and weakness "enrages the strong, who must pay for their strength with an intense alienation from nature, and must always suppress their fear." Fear and weakness, in another or oneself, signal the radical bond of the self to nature, a bond made real and visible in those who have had it produced in them through "perennial oppression," in those "who have not ruled for thousands of years" — women, Jews, other others. Their "greater affinity to nature" becomes for them "the very element which gives them life," even though they "could be exterminated." The strong, not just enraged, but outraged by the survival of the weak, get to identify unconsciously with the nature, against which they must be radically other, when they hear the cries of their victims which they cannot themselves emit (*DE*, 112).

Transcending Natural History: Agape Is Eros

The self-destruction of enlightenment morality is not, of course, the doing of Kant or Sade or Nietzsche. Both that morality and its self-destruction are, for Horkheimer and Adorno, aspects of the social logic of natural history. Kantian rational peace reproduces violence out of the very struggle against it precisely because, in radically separating duty from interest, and in making duty an expression of a purely formal noncontradiction, it necessarily places all interests on a par while presuming that all interests are contradictory with each other. It cannot conceive or imagine the transformation of interest, or the noncontradiction of interests.[11] In Levinas's terms, enlightened morality has no concept of Desire, only needs and rational abstraction and distance from needs, a rational abstraction and distance which are not at all Levinas's disinterestedness. Kantian rational peace thus expresses, but cannot transcend the practical predicament of the bourgeois form of natural history. Natural history reproduces again and again the law of the stronger as the law of all, or the law of the few as the law of the third. Radical enlightenment does not bring this to an end, but brings it to a head, to an extreme. As Sade and Nietzsche will point out, the interest of devotion to an Other is no better than the interest in the domination of the Other. In fact it is worse, a rationalization of weakness. What matters to the enlightenment's conception of autonomy is strength, freedom from the Other.

The problem that Horkheimer and Adorno leave in abeyance is the problem of how to conceive and imagine a law that will not be the law of third fused with law of the few, how to conceive and imagine a transcendence of natural history. Despite many terse formulaic suggestions concerning what could or would be beyond natural history, they remain more wedded to a rigorist program of determinate negation, a stricter adherence to the "ban on the Name" than does Marcuse. But the problem all three share, beyond methodological similarities and differences, is a common inheritance from Marx: it is the problem of the last revolution, of the social transformation that in abolishing domination will, exactly, not reproduce oppression out of the struggle against it.

It is important from the outset to slough off any presumption that this problem is the same as the problem of the abolition of pain, suffering, want, conflict, death, or finitude in general. Those who would falsely conflate these two dimensions will have little trouble, after that conflation is tacitly accepted as both common sense and ontologically self-evident, in demonstrating that any notion of a final revolution is a merely infantile and potentially dangerous utopian wish to bring a false heaven down to earth, a wish that when it turns fanatical, as it no doubt must, will issue in the worst violence. Or they may, out of fear of such violence, insist so rigorously, and therefore dualistically, on a messianicity without messianism, that such messianicity will become all but indistinguishable from a mild reform of the presently given order of rational peace. All their prayers and tears will be for naught. When Levinas says that if history is not to have the last word, then the invisible must manifest itself, but that this does not mean its passage from the status of the invisible to the visible, he is rightly contesting the Hegelian conflation and identification of history with eschatology. And insofar as Marx remained Hegelian enough to leave open the possibility of thinking that historical materialism is an ontology that discovers a different universal-historical logic, but one parallel to the Hegelian system, he is vulnerable to the same criticism. But Marcuse is, as are Adorno and Horkheimer, definitely not repeating this Hegelian algorithm. The subject of natural history is not consciousness, or social labor across a logically necessary succession of modes of production. Adorno, Horkheimer, and Marcuse, rather than following Hegel in this respect, are each and all tacitly subscribing to Benjamin's allegory in the "Theologico-Political Fragment," which makes a crucial distinction between the messianic kingdom and the divine kingdom. The messianic redemption of human society is not the achievement of divine perfection.

Marcuse's theorization of the possibility of a transcendence of natural history, mostly in *Eros and Civilization,* but very much present in other works as well, leans heavily on and borrows liberally from the determinate negation or immanent critique in nonsystematic form that will achieve its fullest self-reflexive elaboration later in *Negative Dialectics. Negative Dialectics,* as we have been at some pains to point out, is a philosophical elaboration of allegory as the lens proper to the analysis of natural history. In other words, *Eros and Civilization,* without referring to itself explicitly in such terms, is a also a thinking in constellations. In this constellation some major figures are more apparent than others. Some of these figures are aspects of entire traditions of thought. The major figures are Freud, Marx, the idealist notion of reconciliation of subject and object from Aristotle to Hegel, Nietzsche, idealist aesthetics from Kant to Schiller, the Greek myths of Orpheus and Narcissus, and Benjamin. The explicit presence especially of Freud throughout, and of Benjamin punctually and more tacitly, are themselves indications that Marcuse will be giving a greater weight and function to remembrance, and particularly to the remembrance of the archaic, than Horkheimer and Adorno generally do. Going back all the way to Adorno's "Idea of Natural History," Marcuse tacitly agrees that what is new in history actually presents itself as the most archaic.

Marcuse makes elaborate strategic use of the most archaic and archaicizing aspects of Freud's writings, primarily the anthropological speculations on the "primal horde" in *Totem and Taboo,* and the metaphysical speculations on the nature of living processes, that is, on the fundamental dynamics of the "instincts," in *Beyond the Pleasure Principle.* These are works that conform least to Freud's own cherished perspective as a child of the modern scientific enlightenment, and the amount of attention Marcuse devotes to them has often puzzled his readers. But they contain in either mythical or metaphysical form insights into natural history and into the potentially transformative implications of psychoanalysis that are not available from the rest of Freud's work.

Freud's myth of the primal horde turns out to have allegorical historical value. The myth analyzes the dynamic of the repetition of domination that has occurred in the course of all past efforts at a revolutionary transformation of the Law. In the reestablishment of the Law of the Father out of the panic felt by the murderous brother clan, Freud has produced an allegorical account of the repetition throughout history of the primal crime, which is perceived to be a crime against the reality principle, against civilization, law, justice, society, and humanity itself and of the redemption of that crime through ever more rationalized domination. The revolt, expressing at some level the most basic demands of the pleasure principle for what Marcuse calls "integral satisfaction" (*EC,* 11), through the internalization of the Father in the form of the Law of the Brothers, the law of equality, has as its consequence an "ever 'better' domination." Thus, "The crime against the reality principle is redeemed by a crime against the pleasure principle: redemption thus cancels itself" (68).

Throughout history the primal crime and its consequences get repeated (69). This takes place in the development of religion, in, for example, the transubstantiation of the ("heretical") Jesus, the "Redeemer in the flesh," by Augustinian orthodoxy into the deified Son beside the Father, "the denial of the liberation in the flesh." Christianity surrenders the "gospel of Agape-Eros again to the Law" (70). The suppression of the revolt, along with the revolt itself, is expressed in "all the bloody wars against the Christian revolutions which filled the Christian era...the cruel and organized slaughter of Cathari, Albigensians, Anabaptists, of slaves, peasants and paupers who revolted under the sign of the cross, the burning of witches and their defenders.... The executioners... fought the specter of a liberation which they desired but which they were compelled to reject" (71). With the passing of the religious idiom this dynamic has not failed to repeat itself. Ontogenetically, the primal revolt is "contained" in the normal, though "catastrophic" outcome of the Oedipal conflict (75, 90). But phylogenetically, or historically, each revolution "from the slave revolts in the ancient world to the socialist revolution," although containing moments that "overshot" the "conscious effort to replace one ruling group by another," efforts, that is, to abolish domination and exploitation, also had within them elements of "self-defeat." To some significant extent "every revolution has also been a betrayed revolution" (90–91).

Freud's hypothesis on the origin and repetition of guilt feeling elucidates this social dynamic in psychological terms. The revolutions reach their Thermidor and/or devour their own children inasmuch as an identification with power is needed and called up by the anxiety that issues from the revolt *seeming* to be not simply against oppression, but a revolt against the reality principle itself involving the loss of all stability and order, the threat of a regression behind civilization itself, and even the human. This is so all the more in an age of administration where "the dominion of the father has expanded into the dominion of society" (91). A revolt that called up and remembered the supreme demands of the pleasure principle for integral satisfaction would feel its guilt to be fatal to the extent that the law has become the law of the life of the generality.[12]

This is one way in which Marcuse implicitly criticizes Marx, via Freud, for not being realistic enough. Marx's materialism, his social ontology, rests on a conception of subjectivity that, inverting Hegel, makes "sensuous human activity," as Marx puts it in the "Theses on Feuerbach," essentially a process in which the human subject reconciles subject and object through conscious identification. The subject of the Marxian revolt is essentially "free conscious activity" ultimately realizing its powers in its ability to rise to a differentiation of objectification from alienation, both theoretically and practically. Marx is not realistic enough, for one thing, in his abstraction of even nonalienated labor from the fundamentality of the libidinal and erotic relation of the subject to its sensuous reality in all of its dimensions. Production in accordance with the laws of beauty does not go nearly far enough in making sensuous activity sensuous. Thus Marx, though he can anticipate a proletarian revolution that might simply fail, or that, in not occurring, might simply succumb to capitalist barbarism, cannot raise the prospect of a proletarian revolution that would possibly *betray* itself through an identification with power that takes place sensuously, in images in the unconscious, long before it reaches its rationalization in forced industrialization and in the doctrines of the Comintern. Freud's conception of sensuous human activity begins to make that possibility comprehensible because the libidinal-erotic subject is bound to his situation in such a way that the situation is not added to him but forms the very foundation of his being. The erotic relation to the other is a relation that, like the ethical, cannot and ought not be conflated with knowledge, understood as identity.

But this does not mean that Marcuse is replacing Marx with Freud. And it certainly does not mean that Marcuse is giving up on the possibility of a revolution to end all revolutions. Marcuse focuses on Freud not only because the psychology is useful in accounting for the failures of the revolutions, and not only because the metapsychology adds layers to the materiality of the subject, but because Freud supplies the most powerful argument in favor of that view which conflates the law with the law of repression. Freud's theory presents simultaneously the most uncompromising indictment and defense of Western civilization (*EC,* 11). To the extent that the indictment is taken seriously and the defense is vulnerable to immanent critique, the dimension of added realism that Freud brings can be transmuted into hope — although not necessarily into optimism.

In his simultaneous defense and indictment of Western civilization Freud both construes and denies universal history, but ends by denying the denial. This universal history, moreover, takes place in both ontogenesis and phylogenesis, and in the relation between them (*EC,* 20). Freud's psychology is in essence social psychology (16). It is not *simply* the case that civilization is based upon a permanent subjugation of the instincts, (3) but that it is, in Freud's account, necessarily bound up with *increasing* unfreedom (4). In his analysis of civilization and its discontents Freud, like Sade and Nietzsche in relation to Kant, begins to bring the dialectic of enlightenment into consciousness. Consequently, "His work is characterized by an uncompromising insistence on showing up the repressive content of the highest values and achievements of culture. In so far as he does this, he denies the equation of reason with repression on which the ideology of culture is built" (17).

The development of civilization is due to the decisive role of the sense of guilt. But the connection of civilization to the sense of guilt, the necessary human development of an introjection of repression in the form of the superego, is not a static relationship. It acquires, for Freud, a dynamic of its own. There is "a correlation between progress and *increasing* guilt feeling" (78).[13] Moreover, Marcuse stresses that in Freud's analysis the increasing guilt feeling is not simply the result of some independent societal drive toward progress, but that Freud goes beyond his own individual-therapeutic analysis of a pathologically punitive superego in attributing the very drive toward progress to a dynamic logic of intensifying repression rooted in the structure of the socially mediated psyche. The dynamic of the excessively severe superego *is* the dynamic of civilization. The introjection of repression, as mediated by the dynamics of the relation of superego to id and ego, leads to a struggle "against freedom," that is, a struggle against the potentiality of the drives toward their nonsurplus-repressive development. For Marcuse, "It is this mental dynamic which Freud unfolds as the dynamic of civilization" (16; see also 54, 78–80).

The dynamic of the civilizational process not only involves increasing unhappiness, it also impels increasing "fatality and futility" (*EC,* 80). It means that "Freud's metapsychology comes face to face with the fatal dialectic of civilization: the very progress of civilization leads to the release of increasingly destructive forces" (54). This takes place not only within individuals in the form of "inner-directed destructiveness" or pathological melancholia, or through an increase in neurotic as distinct from normal suffering, it threatens the balance of life and death instincts, both within and without the individual psyche (53).

The main sphere of civilization is in the sublimation of erotic and aggressive drives in work, but sublimation, by demanding a desexualization of the drives weakens eros, "the builder of culture." To bind the aggression intensified by civilized unhappiness, a strengthening of eros is necessary, but this is exactly what civilization is incapable of doing because it depends on extended regimentation (80; see also 43). Ultimately, civilization is threatened by a "de-fusion" of the life and death instincts, (83) which defusion, along with the weakening of eros, allows for the realized and not-yet realized terrors of the twentieth and twenty-first centuries. Although Freud himself does not put it this way, perhaps Benjamin expressed this process of impending de-fusion best in his characterization of the wish through which Fascism encourages the mass to express itself without a transformation of the order of property: the "self-alienation [of mankind] has reached such a degree that it can experience its own destruction as an aesthetic pleasure of the first order."[14]

According to Marcuse, Freud's defense of the law of repression is also its radical indictment; the universal course of civilization is both construed and denied, the dialectic of civilization is left at a standstill. But, in fact, the denial is also denied, and Freud is left "haunted" by the "sinister hypothesis that culture...stands under the rule of the Nirvana Principle" (*EC,* 108). His denial of the equation of reason with repression is also denied. If irrational guilt is necessary for civilized progress, then irrational guilt is for Freud rational. In Freud's quantitative analysis of guilt, its growing qualitative change into a more extreme irrationality[15] disappears because of his sociological position. For him there is "no higher rationality against which the prevailing one could be measured" and potentially replaced (80). But in order for this to take place, not only must Marx be brought back into the constellation, it must be a changed Marx who has learned something more about the subject from out of the direction that Freud's re-sensualization of the subject helps make possible.

Although Marcuse is working under the ban on the name of Marx, a name that does not even appear in the index to the second (1966) edition of *Eros and Civilization,* he is very much working with the Marxian perspective on the historicity of whatever is taken to be and might be human nature. For Freud, the law of repression, the justification for the repressive modification of the instincts, the antagonistic relation between the pleasure principle and the reality principle, is based upon the assumption that Scarcity, Necessity, *Ananke* are eternal (*EC,* 16–17). But Freud mistakes the consequences of a specific organization of scarcity, an organization in the interests of domination, for the consequences of the brute fact of scarcity (36). Freud's psychological theory is based upon and follows the substantial mutability of the instincts, but does not introduce such mutability into the sociohistorical world that shapes those instincts (12).

In Freud's theory there is an inevitable conflict between the pleasure principle and the reality principle, a conflict that lies at the foundation of the dynamic of repression, guilt and civilized progress. Marcuse will not contest either the historical fact of this antagonism or that there must be some tension between pleasure principle and reality principle. But the development of the *relation* between the two principles is seen by Freud as inevitably anatagonistic and fateful only because *Ananke,* "Lebensnot," the struggle for existence, is seen as inevitable and static. Yet there are, according to Marcuse, and even Freud (for whom there is no "instinctual structure 'outside' the historical structure") (*EC,* 132), two levels to the history of the instincts: a phylogenetic-biological level and a sociological level. Marcuse will point out that "factors generated at the second level are exogenous to the first and have therefore a different weight and validity" (133). By not allowing for the possibility of an historical overcoming of a scarcity which is not absolute — an overcoming that does not necessitate an abundance for all, but simply a sufficiency (151) — and especially by not factoring into the dynamic the distinction between scarcity and the historical distribution of scarcity, Freud allows "an extraneous fact...[to obtain] the theoretical dignity of an inherent element of mental life, *inherent even in the primary instincts"* (134; emphasis added). The dynamic of civilized progress thus becomes for Freud a natural history (34–35) of eros and thanatos locked in a struggle in which thanatos increasingly gains the upper hand and in which no essential transformation of the law of repression is possible.

But if the relation between pleasure principle and reality principle is affected not only by phylogenetic-biological factors, but also by historical-sociological factors, the possibility of a differentiation in the law is opened up: "This difference in the origin of instinctual modification underlies the distinction...between basic and surplus repression; the latter originates and is sustained at the sociological level" (*EC,* 133). If the "nature" of the instinctual dynamic is not identified with its historical forms, if the "performance principle" and other historical forms of surplus repression are seen as specific and mutable, Freud's theory of the *dynamic* between eros and thanatos is also affected and loses its finality (130). Surplus repression is that mode of repression necessitated not by scarcity and need as such, but by the hierarchical distribution of scarcity in social domination (37). The surplus repression in civilized, liberal-capitalist modernity is mediated through a specific historical form of the reality principle, the performance principle, the "principle of an acquisitive and antagonistic society in the process of constant expansion" (45), under which body and mind are made into instruments of alienated labor (46ff). Basic repression,[16] which could be effected under a different form of the reality principle, would be that form of repression needed only to transform the human animal into the *animal sapiens*. As repression, as, therefore, a law including the inclusion of the third, and all the other parties, now separated from their mediation in the form of a hierarchized totality, basic repression cannot be conceived as an attempt to undo individuation, or what Levinas calls "separation" and "interiority," but would be "the privilege and distinction of man" because it in fact breaks "the compulsion of nature" and in doing so "increases rather than reduces gratification" (38; see also 227).

It is the fundamentally Marxian understanding that historically specific yet dynamic modes of production reach all the way down into the development, indeed the nature of the instincts themselves — through the social forms in which reality and pleasure principles are mediated to each other — that allows Marcuse not only to differentiate between a law of the third and the law of the few, but to raise the possibility of a development of the law of the third, beyond the law of the few, in which the former does not succumb to the amphibology of ethics and totalizing ontology. But the analytic distinction between basic and surplus repression is not by itself sufficient to establish this as a real possibility. More is needed in the constellation than the tacit exchange between Freud and Marx.

In *Eros and Civilization* Marcuse restricts his critique of Marx to the tacit implication that Marx has left undeveloped the notion of the sensuous side of human sensuous activity, and in particular the implications for the concept of rationality that a possible development of this sensuous activity might have. But some years later, in *Counter-Revolution and Revolt,* Marcuse will state quite explicitly and forthrightly that, to its misfortune, the moral and aesthetic qualities of socialism have been minimized in Marxian theory (*CRR,* 31). In Marxism, nature is predominantly an adversarial object (62), and Marx's notion of the "human appropriation of nature" retains something of the hubris of domination (68–69). This is so despite Marx's suggestion in the *Economic and Philosophic Manuscripts* that an emancipation of the senses might help generate new social relations (64). He asserts that the socialist universe is also a moral and aesthetic universe and that in it moral and other faculties would "become factors in material production itself" (land, labor, machinery, beauty, and ethics) (3). Capitalism itself is creating transcending needs which it cannot fulfill, moral, and aesthetic needs that are becoming vital basic needs, and which drive toward new social relations that point toward freedom in the fulfillment of needs that are "sensuous, ethical and rational in one." The repression of aesthetic and moral needs is a vehicle of domination (17).

In the present context, what is most significant is Marcuse's attempt in *Counter-Revolution and Revolt* to link desire, morality, and sensuousness, and all of the above to a transformed use and self-understanding of reason, one that goes beyond the limits of critique as determinate negation. Marxian determinate negation, although it depends upon it, is lacking in *remembrance,* is deficient in the recollection that has become, more and more, exclusively the function of art, a recollection that "appeals to a pre-conceptual experience and understanding which re-emerge in and against the context of the social functioning of experience and understanding — against instrumentalist reason and sensibility" (*CRR,* 99). Such radical recollection, which can sometimes find expression in art, lends its voice to "ultimate states of sensibility" (100).

In *Eros and Civilization,* the question about basic repression, about the possibility of a law of the third that is not the law of the few, is referred behind the alienated, instrumental rationality of the dialectic of enlightenment, to a remembrance of ultimate states of sensibility, states that are accessible to reason only in forms of remembrance of what appears as the most archaic. Memory, including psychoanalytic memory, has not only a therapeutic value, but a social truth-value in giving way to a re-cognition that reason denies. As a result, "The recherche du temps perdu becomes the vehicle of future liberation" (*EC,* 19). And "the restoration of remembrance to its rights is one of the noblest tasks of thought" (232). The question of the substance of a nonsurplus-repressive reality principle — will it break from natural history in not reproducing violence out of the struggle against it? — cannot be answered by Freud's methods alone. And remembrance requires a "regression" to archaic, other than exclusively rational modes of mentation: metaphysical speculation, aesthetic judgment, art, and myth which, all together, will speak something about ultimate states of sensibility which is little heard.

Fully one third of *Eros and Civilization* is given over to an attempt to probe into the repressed meaning and import of thoughts that in an increasingly enlightened world are at best considered to be conceptual poetry, usually harmless, perhaps edifying and pleasant ornaments to the serious business of the real mastery of nature. What Marcuse seeks in them, even beyond their critical function as a refusal to forget what can be (*EC,* 149), is their truth-value in indicating and expressing the direction and potentiality of the drives, of the ultimate states of sensibility, a direction and potentiality repressed and forgotten in the constitutive activity of a transcendental ego whose relation to its senses remains one of radical abstraction. The difficulties not only for us, but for Marcuse, of interpreting, ordering and systematizing these meanings is reflected in the almost freely associative texture of the chapters devoted to them, and to the nonsystematic associative relation among these chapters themselves. What can be constructed is an image, along Benjaminian lines, an enormous abridgement, a monadic indication of ultimate states of sensibility, where thinking as systematic classification and unification "suddenly stops." These reflections on metaphysics, art, fantasy, aesthetics and myth do not amount in and of, and by themselves to an adequate representation of a nonsurplus-repressive order. But they are all signs and expressions, or symptoms — allegories for a nonantagonistic mediation of the reality and pleasure principles. All represent sensuousness, the erotic subject whose flesh is not added to him but forms the foundation of his being, as bearing the potentiality for a nonsurplus-repressive order, for a law of nontotalization, for a nonantagonistic, hence asymmetrical relation to the object, to the Other and exteriority. In fact, were they to presume more than this, they would be either identity theory on the one hand or, on the other, art. As a Benjaminian dialectical image, or discursive analog thereto, they amount to neither. Marcuse wants here, in these reflections, to draw from art while avoiding it. This avoidance follows from the dual function of art: art recalls the repressed and, in its necessary commitment to appearance, illusion, to *Schein,* represses it again (144–45).

The history of Western metaphysics, according to Marcuse, bears a similar dual function. It develops reason first out of the conquest of the "lower" faculties; its very function is repressive with respect to the receptive faculties (*EC,* 110–11). Aristotle's formal logic had already become mastering reason. The development of Western philosophy has expressed and allowed the will to power over nature to shape "the predominant notion not only of the ego, the thinking and acting subject, but also of its objective world — the notion of being as such" (111). But this very same philosophy does not leave its own logic of domination unchallenged (112). It recurs again and again to notions of reconciliation of subject and object in which receptivity, contemplation, and enjoyment are essential, albeit only in the highly sublimated form of a pure mentation: in, for example, Aristotle's *nous theos*.

Western metaphysics, in its consummation with Hegel, repeats this same affirmation and/in denial. The *Phenomenology* "unfolds the structure of reason as the structure of domination — and as the overcoming of domination" (113). It unfolds the structure of reason as domination because Hegel moves from simple consciousness to self-consciousness only through the negation of the other. Self-consciousness arrives at being-for-itself only through the negation of all otherness. Nevertheless the final form of freedom for Hegel does not derive from the antagonistic relation to the other. It has a different "ontological climate," in which true freedom is a "coming to rest in the transparent knowledge and gratification of being." Mutual acknowledgement and recognition on the part of antagonistic self-consciousnesses remain essential to freedom, but "the terms are now forgiveness and reconciliation" (115). Yet these, along with the form of remembrance they require, are attained and attainable only "in the idea…as a spiritual event." Although "philosophy testifies not only to the reality principle which governs the empirical world, but also to its negation," it represses what it recalls of the ultimate state of sensibility by virtue of the restriction of receptivity and enjoyment only to highly sublimated and non-sensuous activities. Thus, "The repressed liberation is recalled: in the idea and in the ideal" (118). A nonsurplus-repressive rationality is denied in its very construal.

One reason Marcuse separates his consideration of Western metaphysics and ontology from his consideration of Idealist aesthetics in Kant and Schiller is because the latter, in taking up a post-Classicist notion of art, are necessarily drawn to embrace the rationality of the sensuous. And in doing so they go beyond the metaphysical tradition in two essential ways: first, they explicitly assign to sensuousness in its aesthetic form a rationality, an order, a relationality of Subject to Object that is different in kind and autonomous with respect to the rationality (and the reconciliation) developed in the metaphysical tradition from Aristotle to Hegel; and they begin to develop what might be thought of as principles descriptive of such an order. Second, they both assign to this sensuous rationality a status that is higher and better than the rationality that depends on formal logic and identity (as even dialectical logic does). By doing so, or to the extent that they do so, they bridge idealism and materialism, even if unbeknownst to themselves. They recollect the potentiality of ultimate states of sensibility. Such recollection, the rediscovery of the true forms of things, is, according to Marcuse in *Counter-Revolution and Revolt,* "the perpetual materialistic core of idealism," whereas the imagination of a real beyond the given is "the idealistic core of dialectical materialism" (*CRR,* 69). In Schiller's case, according to Marcuse, the thought of receptive sensuous activity even begins to lose the repressive aspect of the dual function of the recall of the repressed.

The central "notion" of classical idealist aesthetics is, according to Marcuse, the idea that the "truth of art is the liberation of sensuousness through its reconciliation with reason" (*EC,* 184). The rationalist metaphysical tradition had either insisted on the suppression of sensuousness for the sake of cognition or, at most, had allowed to the senses the role of furnishing the "mere stuff, the raw material for cognition, to be organized by the higher faculties of the intellect" (180). Rationalism, broadly speaking, assigned sensuousness only a subordinate role in cognition insofar as it found in the senses a mixture, a confusion of the appetitive and the cognitive (183–84). As confused and passive, sense cognition remained unsuitable to the reality principle unless given form and coherence by the intellect. Consequently, "And in so far as philosophy accepted the rules and values of the reality principle, the claim of sensuousness free from the dominance of reason, found no place in philosophy; greatly modified, it obtained refuge in the theory of art" (184).

With Kant's consideration of the aesthetic judgment of beauty in the *Critique of Judgment,* philosophy for the first time more than tacitly grants to the *sensuous* an autonomous cognitive value and principles of its own. But not only is the aesthetic judgment for Kant a third irreducible dimension and faculty of the mind, it even becomes the "center, the medium through which nature becomes susceptible to freedom, necessity to autonomy" (*EC,* 174). The aesthetic dimension is given the new function of allowing for and suggesting an ultimate reconciliation of freedom and necessity, the fundamental demand of the pleasure principle. The central position aesthetic judgment occupies is in its mediating role "between sensuousness and morality" (176). Morality is symbolized by the beautiful in that "[it] demonstrates intuitively the reality of freedom. Since freedom [for Kant] is an idea to which no sense perception can correspond, such demonstration can only be 'indirect,' symbolical, *per analogiam*" (174). If beauty symbolizes, represents, makes sensual, the unperceivable reality and necessity of morality as freedom, if it brings together the otherwise irreconcilable domains of freedom and necessity, this is because it contains according to Kant, principles that are valid for both realms (176). Autonomously mediating the apparently irreconcilable domains of freedom and necessity, aesthetic judgment bears and generates categories and principles of its own: "purposiveness without purpose" and "lawfulness without law," which, for Marcuse, "circumscribe, beyond the Kantian context, the essence of a truly non-repressive order." He adds the decisive qualification "beyond the Kantian context" inasmuch as "Kant develops these categories only as processes of the mind" (177).

Beyond the Kantian context these categories may represent new *relations* that symbolize, evoke, project a human existence in which pleasure and reality principles are not gripped in the fatal dynamic that Freud made inherent even in the primary instincts. Such new relations symbolized in the philosophy of the aesthetic would be desirous, sensuous and moral in one. Purposiveness without purpose indicates a relation in which the object is not represented (known and related to) in terms of either its usefulness *or even* "its 'internal' finality and completeness," an experience utterly different from both the pragmatic and the scientific, a relation in which "all links between the object and theoretical and practical reason [in their Kantian senses] are severed, or rather suspended." In such a relation, the object, when represented, is represented as "freely being itself." A "new quality of pleasure" results from "the form in which the object now reveals itself." Lawfulness without law indicates that the order of beauty "is in conformity with laws, but laws that are themselves free: they are not superimposed and they do not enforce the attainment of specific ends and purposes; they are the pure form of existence itself" (178–79). The possibility of a new relation to the object, the central and mediating role of the aesthetic function, depends not upon the function of identity in the concept, but takes place through the intrinsic and essential link of aesthetics to sensuousness. As Marcuse puts it, "The basic experience in this dimension is sensual rather than conceptual; the aesthetic perception is essentially intuition, not notion. The nature of sensuousness is 'receptivity,' cognition through being affected by given objects" (176).

Even though Kant's reflections on aesthetic judgment begin to recollect the liberation of sensuousness via its reconciliation with reason, and might also imply the need for a desublimation of reason as a condition of that reconciliation, Kant will not go so far. Kant may recognize "a reality with quite different standards" than those constituted by a pure transcendental ego, quite different than standards of natural necessity and standards of universalizing self-legislation, but since "this other, 'free' reality is attributed to art, and its experience to the aesthetic attitude, it is non-committing and does not engage the human existence in the ordinary way of life; it is unreal" (*EC,* 185). Schiller, starting where Kant left off, attempts to go beyond such unreality by making the principles of aesthetic experience the principle of material existence, by making of them a political project for a new civilization that would heal the wounds that modern civilization had dealt, a wound felt in the antagonism between sensuousness and reason, matter and form, nature and freedom, particular and universal (186). For Schiller this means that the practical reconciliation of sensuousness and reason must come about not through the creation of a separate realm of aesthetic reason, but in the undoing of "the sublimation of the aesthetic function" (185), through its translation into the "play impulse," the mediation of the sensuous and form impulses that underlie culture as such (186). For Marcuse, the "idealist and aesthetic sublimations which prevail in Schiller's work do not vitiate its radical implications" (192). His ideas "represent one of the most advanced positions of thought" (188) because he seeks freedom "in the liberation of sensuousness rather than reason and in the limitation of the 'higher' faculties in favour of the 'lower.'" He "aims at basing morality on sensuous grounds" (190), and recognizes that this is accomplished only where " 'the will of the whole' fulfills itself... 'through the nature of the individual'" (191). In his demand for the transformation of toil into play, for the self-sublimation of sensuousness and the desublimation of reason, and for "abolishing time in time," the elements of Schiller's prescription are "practically identical with those of a reconciliation between pleasure principle and reality principle" (192–93).

If idealist metaphysics and classical idealist aesthetics betray something of the ultimate state of sensibility in its potentiality for a being otherwise, they are nonetheless not sufficient for Marcuse in delving into the recollection of sensibility in its original direction. In Aristotelian terms, they *indicate,* without systematizing or making fully visible, the final and formal, but not the material and efficient causes of a nonsurplus-repressive social reality. And it is for this reason that Marcuse turns toward the myths of Orpheus and Narcissus. The Orphic-Narcissistic images "refer to the aesthetic dimension as the one in which their reality principle must be sought and validated" (*EC,* 171). But the nonrepressive reality given rational expression in the philosophy of the aesthetic dimension draws from and draws out of the "deepest layers of the unconscious" which remain the preserve of phantasy, myth and imagination (*EC,* 140–42). Consequently, "In and against the world of the antagonistic *principium individuationis,* imagination sustains the claim of the whole individual, in union with the genus and the 'archaic' past" (143).

In trying to present the materiality of the ultimate state of sensibility by reference to these Orphic-Narcissistic images, Marcuse must be, and aims to be, at his least discursive. Their meaning is not presented through a logical derivation or an empirical induction, or through reflexive critique. In order to suggest what these myths preserve he instead cites not only our knowledge of the original Greek stories, but also, at some length, the work of modern poets: Rilke, Valéry, Beaudelaire — even Gide's prose poetry. When the attempt is made, under the reality principle, to translate these images into meaningful "messages," Orpheus and Narcissus "mean" something like "one cannot defeat death or forget and reject the call of life in the admiration of beauty."[17] But in fact "such moral messages are superimposed upon a very different content" (165). The Orphic-Narcissistic images refer to a climate in which eros and thanatos are reconciled, and are reconciled in their experience and expression of the Nirvana Principle "not as death but as life," as a "static that moves in its own fullness" (164). Although Orpheus and Narcissus seem committed to the underworld and death (165) they recall and preserve "the experience of a world that is not to be mastered and controlled but to be liberated" because they face powers ("internal" and "external") now "conceived not as destruction but as peace, not as terror but as beauty." Beaudelaire reveals such a world in two lines: "La, tout n'est qu'ordre et beauté / luxe, calme et volupte." Such images are committed to a dimension, a relation to being, a being otherwise, circumscribed by "the redemption of pleasure, the halt of time, the absorption of death; silence, sleep, night, paradise" (164).

The images of Orpheus and Narcissus are unreal and repulsive to the performance principle because they are "a refusal to accept separation from the libidinous object (or subject)." And such a refusal is also a liberation inasmuch as it releases the one who refuses such separation from the need and project of mastery and discipline. Thus, it will appear immoral or amoral and weak to enlightened morality. But Orpheus is the poet of redemption, "pacifying man and nature, not through force but through song" (170). The Orphic-Narcissistic attunement to life in death and death in life experiences being "as gratification." But the significance of this gratification is not the fulfillment of the hedonist program for happiness, or the eudaemonist program for that matter. Because, one might say, "timeless" gratification "unites man and nature" it is possible that "the things of nature become free to be what they are" (166). The destruction of the denigration of pleasure is not here the apotheosis of pleasure. The significance of pleasure here is not to be the good in itself. Pleasure acquires its full significance as the possibility for the release of goodness in the relinquishment of allergic separation, mastery, autarky, and domination, in a relinquishment that normally *appears* as death, as the overwhelming power of the negative other, but *is* peace.

The Orphic-Narcissistic images convey the world of the Nirvana Principle not as death but as peace. This has decisive significance with respect to Freud's theory of the dynamic of the law of repression. According to Marcuse, Freud indicates that the transformation of the pleasure principle into the reality principle, "the great traumatic event in the development" of the human (*EC,* 15), does not mean the simple denial of the pleasure principle but its "dethronement" *and* "safeguarding." This safeguarding, however, means not only a change in the form and timing of pleasure, but a change in its "substance" (13), a "transubstantiation" (14). The transubstantiation of the pleasure principle is not only a reorientation from total and immediate gratification to partial (and sublimated forms are included under partial) and delayed gratification, but a relinquishment even of the wish for the immediate identity of freedom and necessity that "is" the unconscious, that "is" the demand for integral satisfaction (18). By way of the introjection of aggression in the form of the superego, the dynamic is set in motion that, even though it initially sustains eros and the pleasure principle, eventually leads not only to the de-fusion of eros and thanatos but also to the near-complete forgetting of the Nirvana principle and its meaning. When it is "remembered" in Freud's late theory of the instincts in *Beyond the Pleasure Principle,* it is linked to the "frightening" discovery of a "fundamental *regressive* or conservative tendency in all instinctual life." Freud worries over but cannot resolve the question of whether this fundamental principle, the Nirvana Principle, is anti-erotic and anti-vital, in Freud's own words, "a compulsion inherent in organic life to restore an earlier state of things which the living entity has been obliged to abandon under the pressure of external circumstances" (Freud, quoted in *EC,* 24). Yet despite his apparent turn toward the hypothesis of a "monism of death," Freud, according to Marcuse cannot discover anything in the primary instinctual structure "that is not Eros" (28). Theoretically there is a stasis and contradiction: on the one hand, there is the notion of a common conservative nature to both life and death instincts in that both have as their ultimate direction "earlier states of the living substance" (Freud, quoted in *EC,* 26); on the other, militating against it, is the dualistic conception of the instincts that seems to be necessary to avoid a monism of death (28).

The Orphic-Narcissistic experience of the Nirvana Principle as peace, an expression relegated to the remotest regions of mythic-poetic fantasy, on the other hand vindicates Freud's inability to relinquish the monism of "sexuality," despite the formal contradiction this introduces into his late theory of the instincts. This inability to reconcile the contradiction on Freud's part is, according to Marcuse, the "very token of the truth" (*EC,* 28). Thus, "Never before has death been so consistently taken into the essence of life; but never before has death come so close to eros" (*EC,* 28–29). Freud had made a decisive step in the direction of asserting the common origin of the two basic instincts. They find their common origin in a tensionless state without want, integral satisfaction, an identity of freedom and necessity (*EC,* 28). But this means that the de-fusion of eros and thanatos that menaces civilization from within is a threat that can in principle be defused. The increase in and release of aggression (whether inward or outward) is not a function of the primary instincts themselves, which instincts therefore need not be linked in the futile logic of increasing repression and rational irrationality that has characterized all of previous history, that is, natural history. According to Marcuse, "If the Nirvana Principle is the ground of the pleasure principle, then the necessity of death appears in an entirely new light. The death instinct is destructiveness not for its own sake, but for the relief of tension. The descent toward death is an unconscious flight from pain and want. It is an expression of the eternal struggle against suffering and repression" (29).

Under the rule of the Nirvana Principle the nature of the instincts is itself and in their internal relations subject to change. And a qualitative change in the form in which sexuality is developed would alter the manifestations of the death instinct, which only operates in fusion with the erotic instincts (139). If the death instinct operates under the Nirvana Principle, which is a striving for a tensionless state without want, this "implies that its destructive manifestations would be minimized as it approached such a state...the conflict between life and death is the more reduced, the closer life approaches the state of gratification" (234–35). The lifting of surplus repression would not mean the release of the forces of aggression, but their pacification. This ultimate state of sensibility, which idealist aesthetics conceives as a creative receptivity, as a "cognition through being affected" could make possible a development in which the appeal of all the others would be the law, not simply the ground of a law in which all others and myself must be reduced to the same.

The notion of a nonsurplus-repressive reality principle, a law of the third that is not the law of the few is, according to Marcuse, derivable from Freud's theory itself. By placing Freud within the constellation that now includes not only Marx, but the other figures mentioned, its real possibility begins to emerge. The fusion of basic and surplus repression that characterizes all previous history to varying degrees is a function not of the dynamic of the instincts themselves, but of exogenous historical-sociological factors that are in principle mutable. The existence in the subject of the death instinct does not mean that its destructiveness is a primary and independent force (*EC,* 131). The ultimate direction of the ultimate state of sensibility is indicated, in the forgotten and bypassed truths of art, metaphysics, and aesthetics, to be peace above self-preservation, a peace that takes shape in the form of *relations* that though rational, defy the terms of identity and totality (139).

A nonsurplus-repressive reality is not a utopian concept, but a real possibility. Under the performance principle, this possibil- ity must evoke a strengthening of controls in proportion to the maturation of the possibility that surplus repression itself does not cease from producing and repressing (3, 5, 93ff, 150). The more the law of the few is unnecessary, the more necessary it is made to appear, and to appear as the law as such. But the primary obstacle is not an independent aggressivity to be met within the terms of rational peace. The rationality of such peace is the rationality of the aggressor. The primary obstacle is the repression of the possibilities for the *development* of eros outside of the requirements placed on it — and on reason — by domination.

Thus, Marcuse will not simply reject the law. He accepts from Freud that eros has in itself both constructive, uniting connotations and possibilities, and explosive ones (*EC,* 43). Eros is not only a striving toward greater unities "so that life may be prolonged and brought to a higher unity" (211), Eros under the pure pleasure principle remains equivocal, the most "disorderly" of the instincts (199). Moreover, "instinct itself is beyond good and evil, and no free civilization can dispense with this distinction" (226). But the development of eros to date is not the measure of its possibilities. Those possibilities would be quite different if both the ultimate state of sensibility is the desire for peace and if the abolition of domination meant the lifting of surplus repression.

Not only is the past history of eros not the final measure of its possibilities, the character of eros cannot be measured by the demands of the superego. The superego is the representative of the *established* morality (32–33), and not of the ethical relation per se. Such "morality" has been entwined for eons with the experience and demands of domination. The "mature sense of guilt" in civilized domination is out of proportion with the once dangerous impulses it controls, which it represses and in its repressiveness fixes in their undeveloped state (56). Because the superego enforces the demands not of reality per se, but of past natural-historical reality, because it is the introjection of external controls that are themselves representatives of the introjections of past generations, the "mature," civilized superego is a lag and retardation on the development of erotic social relations (32–33). The mature sense of guilt of the subject of domination is an arrested development toward an erotic ethic. Freud's therapeutic practice puts this arrested development, and the reduction of the demands of the superego, at its centre, but lacking in a notion of rationality beyond the instrumental, it cannot transcend the natural history it suffers. Freud's theory remains manifestly adaptive, though latently transformative.[18]

With the lifting of *surplus* repression what is therefore to be hypothesized and expected is not a regression from ego, subjectivity, to an uncivilized, immoral and irrational rule of It, a sensibility inherently insensible to the other, but a development of subjectivity in which the drives, by virtue of their own dynamic (a dynamic enhanced rather than inhibited by basic repression) generate lasting erotic relations among mature individuals (*EC*, 199). Liberation from the surplus repression of domination "would not simply re-activate…infantile stages but would also transform the perverted content of these stages" (203). It would involve not only a release of erotic energy but, quite differently from the explosive release of constrained sexuality within the institutions of the performance principle, a spread of such energy over the body and over society, that is, the other and the third. It would "minimize the manifestations of mere [genital reproductive] sexuality by integrating them into a far larger order, including the order of work" (201–02). Ultimately, the realization of the direction inherent in the ultimate state of sensibility would imply a "fundamentally different experience of being, a fundamentally different relation between man and nature, and fundamentally different existential relations" (5). Moreover "A new basic experience of being would change human existence in its entirety" (158).

Such a being otherwise would even extend to the temporalization of time. The "abolition of time in time," which is one

of the main elements for the reconciliation of pleasure principle
and reality principle, is for Marcuse, anything but the quest for
eternity. Eternity, the effort to "halt the flux of time," points to
a remembrance of the claims of the pleasure principle, but also
to the alliance between time and the order of repression. It is
that alliance of synchronizable time, necessary for the same to
persist in being, but destructive of eros, that "motivates" its
opposite, the desire for eternity, the hunt for perfected identity
within the same (233). The lifting of surplus repression would
thus undermine the still-standing dialectic of temporalization
and eternity. In a world beyond mastery and the discipline it
requires, even death would not refute the possibility of liberation
inasmuch as the transience of existence and enjoyment need not
be felt as their destruction. Humans "can die without anxiety
if they know that what they love is protected from misery and
oblivion. After a fulfilled life they may take it upon themselves
to die — at a moment of their own choosing" (236).

The lifting of surplus repression also implies the lifting of
surplus morality. But the idea of a surplus morality would not
propose that there is too much morality, or that morality is
destructive of pleasure, or of happiness, and that therefore we
should be less moral. A surplus morality would be that morality
required by surplus repression and domination, required in the
present by a society that absolutely needs and produces subjects who are capable of (if not eager for) exploiting and being
exploited, and whose framework for experience is limited by
such an identity, who experience the absolutely other, but only
in reified form. The enlightened morality of rational peace is
one such surplus morality, surplus by virtue of the fact that it
not only confirms the ontological status of individuality as the
possessive attainment of individual self-consciousnesses who can
be for the other only by allowing/forcing the other to be for
himself — that is, on the basis of an equality of rights — but
also because it reduces the sensibility and materiality of being

for-the-other to the freedom of a pure practical reason free from materiality; hence it is a reduction to identity within a totality. Even the Kingdom of Ends is such a totality.

Although Marcuse does not explicitly make use of a concept of surplus repressive morality, such a notion is implicit in his critique of the superego as the agent of past forms of domination within the self (a domination, we might add, that is *strengthened* by the fact that the superego *also* would have been the intrapsychic mediation of the ethical relation), and by three other suggestions. There is the notion, first, that a "sensuous rationality contains its own moral laws" (*EC,* 228), a notion suggested by Freud's observation that full satisfaction demands arrest, delay and detour (226). Sensuous rationality is prefigured in the aesthetic receptivity of lawfulness without law and purposefulness without purpose. These are not so much qualities of the object, but structures of the relation to it. It is suggested second, by the idea of a "maternal superid" as correlative to a nonsurplus-repressive reality principle (228–29); such an agency would extend the erotic (rather than aggressive) resources in the id, not to engulf the ego, but to bring it to the other. Third, Marcuse suggests the notion "that Eros and Agape may after all be one and the same — not that Eros is Agape, but that Agape is Eros" (210). And when a negative dialectician suggests that it is not the case that A is B, but that B is A, he is affirming that neither can be reduced to the other, but that both refer to a nonidentity. We will return to this question in our final considerations.

One of the worst possible misreadings of Marcuse (and critical theory in general) would be one that attributed their views on morality to the priority of an economic, economistic or hedonistic program, or to the logic of universal history. The opposite would be much closer to the truth. A nonsurplus-repressive, hence *ethical* society depends upon a breaking of the compulsion of "nature" within the productive relations subjected to the principle of the economy of the same. New needs that are sensuous, ethical and rational in one — and we can no longer be thinking of such needs as referring to a lack which when filled will restore a lost identity — depend for their emergence and propagation on the pacification of the struggle for existence, a struggle which, if it ever was, is no longer determined entirely by nature. Only such pacification could "affect the very structure of the psyche, alter the balance between Eros and Thanatos, reactivate tabooed realms of gratification and pacify the conservative tendencies of the instincts" (*EC,* 157). No such pacification of the struggle for existence can take place without the reduction of the sphere of toil and alienated labor to a minimum.

With the reduction of necessary labor time to a minimum, the antagonistic relation between pleasure principle and reality principle collapses, releasing erotic-ethical potentials "to an unprecedented degree" (153–54). And there can be no reduction of necessary labor time to a minimum without *both retaining and canceling* the comparison and calculation that belong to the law of the third. The law of the third and the ethical relation cannot be synthesized in a final and ultimate form. But now, under such conditions, under the conditions of the abolition of the commodity fetish and the law of value, under the condition in which a realm of freedom that is both creative and created is given over to expression among human singularities, the development of the law of the third is *not* a detraction from the ethical relation. The ethical relation is expressed also and much better in that law, without being traduced. Betrayal becomes loyalty in the subjection of the law of the third to the appeal of the Other, a subjection that can only take place in the gift to the Other of ontic enjoyment, that is, freedom from toil. The wish for paradise is recollected and mediated in a sabbatical existence by a peace that is eschatological, that breaks with the totalization of totality.

And Eros Is Agape

Marcuse's vision of a sabbatical peace is, from Levinas's point of view, not yet a translation of the law of the third into the terms of the ethical relation. It remains residually framed in the terms of the knowledge relation, even as the knowledge relation is, in the aesthetic dimension, transcended in sensuous receptivity. The face to face, the ethical relation per se has to be presented as radically different from the exteriority of subject and object to each other (*TI,* 290). There remains a tension between the law of the third and the radically plural asymmetry of the ethical relation. But Marcuse breaks with all previous forms of rational peace. His is not the unity in reason of existents allergic each to, but needing the other. Rationality, as inherently erotic, now becomes self-limiting in its function of identification: the function of identification becomes the reduction of the sphere of identification, the sphere of functioning in relation to a purpose, and the reduction of totalization, the realm of necessity, to providing the foundation for a realm of freedom that Marcuse conceives/imagines as both Eros and Agape, both creative and created freedom. And what could this indicate but a sensuous being for the other? The ideas of beauty as lawfulness without law and purposefulness without purpose, these formally logical impossibilities, formally oxymoronic but no less sensuously real for all that, are indicative of a subjectivity loosened from the intentionality of the Same, of the noesis-noema scheme. History bears the possibility of a radically different relation of subjectivity to the Same.

Although a tension between a just law and ethics remains, it is possible to advance the notion that the tension is now radically, qualitatively different.[19] This being otherwise changes the relationship of otherwise than being to being. Ethics does not simply radically disturb the State, supply it with a bad conscience. Ethics, if it is ethics, does something in and to the public sphere; it makes the State wither away. And neither is ethics ensnared forever in an amphibology in which it sustains what it destroys. Ethics is freed from its natural history. The coordinating functions of the State and Economy are reabsorbed into *and subordinated by* the social relation, conceived as moral, sensuous and rational in one. An erotic (hence agapic) ethic legislates the reduction and transformation of the sphere of law and, in so doing, the propagation of an ethico-social-erotic sphere. The sphere of nonalienated labor is not simply one in which activity is pleasurable because it flows from the self and is not captured by the other; it is also one in which activity flows from the self to the other gratuitously. Work as play merges with speech and expression.

It may not be necessary, as it was for Marcuse in relation to Freud, but it is possible to find in Levinas himself additional grounds for imagining the convergence of a negatively dialectical critique of natural history with ethics. Such grounds follow from the fact that although for Levinas the ethical relation is not the intentional relation of knowledge and must be kept separate from knowledge, even or especially in its being brought to knowledge, the ethical relation is a relation that is sensuous. It is sensuous, and may be conceived as sensuous, as sensibility, so long as sensuousness and sensibility are themselves not understood as simply vehicles or media for the reception of information about a knowable or even unknowable other, as inferior forms of theoretical knowledge (*TI,* 135). Thus, for Levinas the ethical subject is a fully embodied subject. Its relation to the other is no anodyne formality. Because ethical subjectivity is conceived as transcendence even to the point of the destruction of the Same, the ethical subject is incarnate. Incarnation is far from the transcendental operation of a subject situated in the midst of a world that it represents to itself (76). Thus Levinas asserts that "Matter is the very locus of the for the other" (77). Otherwise than being is not nonbeing. Thus, when Levinas himself attempts to envision the form of the propagation of the ethical relation it is to the weak and intimately interrelated forces of enjoyment, eros and fecundity that he recurs.

As is well known and well documented, Levinas begins his phenomenology of ethical subjectivity in *Totality and Infinity* with the effort to leave the atmosphere of Heidegger behind. But this does not mean going behind Heidegger and beginning with a subject who is not his own relation to his situation, a subject who is not his being-in-the-world. At least this much of Heidegger's revision of Husserlian phenomenology is accepted. But Levinas does not begin with a being-thrown into a condition of care that bifurcates into the average everydayness of "das Man" as opposed to the anxiety of mortal finitude leading to the inherently totalizing project of authenticity consciously taking on its fatedness. Levinas begins instead with the radical separation of the subject from the totality in the relation of enjoyment. Enjoyment is not a nonrelation, even though, as interiority, it is radical separation from the totality (147). It is, he asserts, "an ultimate relation with the materiality of being" (133). In a way, like "primary narcissism," the absolute separation effective in enjoyment is purely subjective and, at the same time, the pure, the ultimate state of sensuous subjectivity. It is innocent, neither against the other nor for-myself (134), prior to reason, yet enacting separation (139). It is not a representation, a thought making its way outward, but a sensibility and an affectivity that does not constitute, and in which the "egoism of the I pulsates" (135). Enjoyment is not negated by need, but lives from its needs, not beyond pain or discomfort, but beyond anxiety for itself or for the morrow. It is a love of life that includes need, pain, and so on. (145).

The persistence of enjoyment is, for Levinas, absolutely crucial to the possibility of transcendence, that is, to the possibility of the ethical relation. It is not simply a stage or a level that is destroyed or left behind. It is for him extremely important that the noesis-noema structure, arguably still at the centre of Heideggerian "care," is not the "primordial structure of intentionality" (*TI*, 294). Enjoyment has a "different intentionality" than the intentionality of the noesis-noema structure, one which "holds on" to the exteriority that transcendental method suspends (127). *The ultimate moment of separation and interiority is in the refusal of separation in enjoyment.* Here, alterity enters into the same differently than in representation. In representation alterity comes and is represented as the inconceivability of the particular, but in enjoyment "the movement of constitution is reversed" (129).

The body's need affirms exteriority beyond all constitution on the part of the subject (127). Things come as essentially unpossessable, hence as elemental, enveloping without being able to be enveloped (131). If there is to be a subjectivity beyond pure enjoyment, it will have had to develop a different relation to exteriority than the one that "holds on" in absolute separation from the totality. And when it has discovered the impersonal menace of the elemental in disquiet over concern for the morrow, a disquiet that comes from the fathomless depth of the element, the mythical depth of a primordially uncertain future (142–50), subjectivity will be required to become a recollecting, dwelling, constituting, representing, negating, laboring, possessing, historical being. But enjoyment itself is and remains "already beyond being" (120). Its solitude, which "radically breaches" the totality (119) is a force essential to transcendence, to the ethical relation, even though enjoyment is "anonymous" (132) and is capable of killing for a crust of bread (118). Desire is not, according to Levinas, "produced" by enjoyment, but the egoism and separation of subjectivity are necessary for Desire (148), necessary not because one only scores moral points by self-sacrifice, but because Desire must be a force that cuts through all totalization.

Thus, in the conclusion to *Totality and Infinity,* Levinas will return to his insistence on enjoyment as necessary to separate and liberate the I from the totality (298). And in *Otherwise than Being,* despite his abandonment of the quasi-developmental schema of *Totality and Infinity,* he will reiterate that enjoyment is "an ineluctable moment of sensibility." Without enjoyment one would not be able to give with one's heart, "to give oneself in giving it" (*OTB,* 72; see also 64, 80). Thus, "Only a subject that eats can be for-the-other" (74). He will even, if only for a moment, suggest that although enjoyment does not produce Desire, the satisfaction of need, which has something to do with enjoyment, allows a turning to Desire (*TI,* 117). In doing so, he is converging with Marcuse, and with Adorno when the latter says that "only if the physical urge were quenched would the spirit be reconciled and would become that which it only promises while the spell of material conditions will not let it satisfy material needs" (*ND,* 207).

In *Totality and Infinity,* Levinas presents an account of subjectivity that not only leads up to the possibility of the face to face relation, to the revelation of height and asymmetry in the face, to the expression, speech and teaching of the absolutely Other, to the possibility of the I being murderous. The account, in section 4, goes beyond the face and into the phenomenology of erotic and fecund relations. Eros and fecundity go beyond the face in order to bring the eschatological dimension into relation with history. The subject who moves into and through enjoyment to disquiet, dwelling, recollection, representation, economy, labor, possession, and the possibility of war and exploitation, will have also entered into a history of the Same, into totalization, politics, and the state. Eros and fecundity, however, represent a parallel, even alternative dimension in which the eschatology of messianic peace transports the subject beyond the operation of the Same, to a "plane" where the subject, although it will die, "bears itself beyond death" (*TI,* 252–53).

What marks the erotic and fecund relations as outside of historical and even biological time is their *return to the refusal of separation,* a refusal that suffuses enjoyment. Enjoyment establishes absolute separation from totality by refusing separation from the elemental. But separation, in eros, after the entrance of the face, is now refused not in relation to the elemental, or to the later thing, or world of representation, which requires an assumption of separation. Eros refuses separation in relation to the Other while, simultaneously, impossibly and a-logically acknowledging the absolute Otherness of the Other. Thus, eros becomes the basis, though not yet sufficient, for an ethical relation to an infinite plurality of radically separate Others, radically separate but nonseparate, even in time. Eros and fecundity abolish time in time, in a grand abridgement. The model for this — in the sense of the concrete instance out of which the structure is phenomenologically developed — but not the telos of eros, is the generational relation.

Inasmuch as love refuses separation it, like enjoyment, is not a knowledge mixed with affective elements. It is, Levinas says, a model of being irreducible to intentionality, a "pure experience which does not pass into any concept" (*TI,* 260–61). The erotic caress, which one might say is a purposiveness without purpose, is, according to Levinas, not the intentionality of disclosure. Although a hunger, it is, he says, like Desire in that it does not seek to dominate a hostile freedom, but seeks a future not open to anticipation. In tenderness, the subject leaves its position as subject (259). "Being" in the caress is "incessant recommencement" (270). And nothing is further from eros than possession. It is anything but a "taming," "objectification," or "reification" of the Other. It aims at the beloved's "freedom untamed which I nowise desire objectified." The Other is not only sensed, but in the sensed is affirmed as sentient, as though there were one same sentiment (one might say: a lawfulness without law). Being beyond, but not annihilating the separation of self and other, the being of eros is "voluptuosity": "In voluptuosity the other *is* me and separated from me" (265; emphasis added). Thus, voluptuosity "transfigures" the subject himself. Identity here is not derived from power, but from love received. It is a "reversion" of the virile and heroic I (270). Thus, eros aims at the frailty of the Other; it is to fear for the Other, to come to the assistance of his frailty and is therefore a vulnerability (256).

Thus, eros is the transcendence of identity and identification. In its refusal of separation from the Other it "arrests the return of the I to itself." It "goes toward a future which is not yet and which I will not merely grasp, but I will be — it no longer has the structure of the subject which from every adventure returns to its island, like Ulysses." It "finds itself the self of another" (*TI,* 271). But the erotic relation, although in one sense fully ethical, is in another sense equivocal as transcendence. It is equivocal, because in its urgency to go beyond the I back to the pure refusal of separation in enjoyment, it also goes beyond the face of the Other to disappear into the one same sentiment of boundless love. It is not a desire for recognition, but a "trans-substantiation" (266), a transcendence of the virile and heroic I of representation, because it is a transcending search to be "divested of all transcendence," a movement that seeks what a being was bound to before it started the search (254). In aiming to lose itself completely it moves beyond the face to meet what is neither the thing nor the element; it is thus still expression, but expression of the clandestine, the mysterious, the expression of an expression that, in its own search for one same sentiment, "expresses the refusal to express" (260). Thus, "in love transcendence goes both further and less far than language" (254).

Eros is more and less than ethical because it expresses transcendence in the profane. The desired freedom of the Other is not desired in the clarity of his face, but "in obscurity" (*TI,* 265). It is only when the face of the Other expresses the refusal to express, when the face of the Other also recurs to enjoyment and enjoyment's refusal of separation, that erotic love loves.

Thus, on both sides, because both are both lover and beloved, to love is to love not only the Other, but also to love oneself in love. Thus both, in ef-facing themselves, by expressing the refusal to express, can bring themselves and the Other back to enjoyment, the refusal of separation. Thus, although eros does arrest the return of the I to itself, it is also a return of the self to the self (266). Eros is thus transcendence as "equivocality par excellence" (254). The tender is a way of "remaining in no-man's land" between being and nonbeing. And voluptuosity, although a fear for the other, is also "a pity that is complacent, a pleasure, a suffering transformed into happiness." In eros not only the said, but the saying is equivocal (260). From out of its "too great audacity" in leaving behind the I it remains a relation that turns into need, even though this need presupposes the totally transcendent exteriority of the Other (254). It is a "simultaneity of need and Desire, concupiscence and transcendence" (255).

If what distinguishes the relation of enjoyment is the holding on of a sensuous being to exteriority, then what distinguishes the erotic relation is the holding on by a sensuous being to the enjoyment that holds on to exteriority. The first is an innocent refusal of separation. The second, the erotic relation, is the accomplishment of a being who has already, in dwelling, recollection, representation, labor, possession, and the ethical encounter, achieved a separation concerning which he now expresses the refusal to express. Eros is a drive for trans-substantiation, hence a transcendence, not needed by or even relevant to enjoyment. But because eros is the holding on to nonseparation by a now separate being, it must remain equivocal as transcendence. The fecund relations of a sensuous being go a decisive step further in transcendence. But the separation they express is anything but indifference. They hold on to the holding on to the holding on to exteriority. If eros recurs to enjoyment, fecund relations recur to eros. But fecund relations do not express any refusal to express. They always maintain separation in Desire, unlike identity, representation, or rational peace, which always maintain unity in differentiation. Fedund relations are neither innocent, nor equivocal, but responsible.

In the last section of *Totality and Infinity,* Levinas appears to propose a highly idealized version of the family and of procreative relations as some sort of social alternative beyond the State. And his treatments of procreation and paternity could in fact even lend themselves to a traditionalistic and repressive celebration of the traditional family and to the glorification of paternity. But if this is going on here, it is not the only thing going on. And it is no longer going on in *Otherwise than Being,* or any of his later writings. Levinas is not only rhetorically obsessed with hyperbole, but with the synecdoche that goes along with it, in which the particular and the general are interchangeable, as in a dream logic. Once again Levinas is philosophizing out of the concrete phenomenologically, in order to reach the intuition of the structure of a relation. And this structure, although generalizable, presents itself not simply in paternity, or also or better in maternity, but in the generational relation. Thus, at least three times Levinas will distinguish fecundity from biology: "The notion of fecundity does not refer to the wholly objective idea of the species to which the I comes as an accident" (*TI,* 272); "The biological origin of this concept nowise neutralizes the paradox of its meaning, and delineates a structure that goes beyond the biologically empirical" (277); "In the biological fact of fecundity are outlined the lineaments of fecundity in general as a relation between man and man and between the I and itself not resembling the structures constitutive of the State" (306).

The relation of fecundity has the structure, the lineaments, in which "he is me a stranger to myself" (*TI,* 267). In spatial-mathematical terms, the fecund relation "evinces a unity that is not opposed to multiplicity, but in the precise sense of the term, engenders it" (273). It is a unity, still a holding on to exteriority, that *engenders multiplicity,* that does not equivocate by expressing the refusal of expression, that has Desire for the other beyond need for the desire of the other, that finds itself again, not in its island but impossibly, in the being of the wholly separate other. Fecundity is "the sole relation possible with the very unicity of another" (279). The parent-child, child-parent relation synecdochizes this; "The I is in the child an other" (267). And conversely as well, inasmuch as filiality, the child-parent relation, is a rupture and a recourse at the same time (278).

In temporal terms, the fecund relation establishes a *relation* with an "absolute future," that is, another future still *my* future which is not the future of the Same (268). It "articulates the time of the absolutely other" and "alters the very substance of him who can" (269). The fecund relation is the diachrony of the future, in which the Other's time is and is not my own. The diachronous future of the fecund relation puts a halt to the tedium of repetition, the repetition of me in Protean forms (268). It evinces the true discontinuity of time, where "the definitive is not definitive" (282), where infinite resurrection "constitutes the principle event of time," where "one instant does not come out of another...by an ecstasy" (284). Thus, a fecund being is not a being who produces or reproduces something out of him/herself, who replicates, multiplies or objectifies him/herself, who simply has an effect, leaves a mark, founds a polis, creates or originates an action or a thing that is immortal. It is "better" than eternal life, which it does *not* bring. Instead, "a being capable of a fate other than its own is a fecund being" (282). Such a being "accomplishes goodness." It does not fulfill a need, nor does it ask for recognition, but inverts, turns inside out, both the orders of need and recognition. It goes even beyond forgiveness and reconciliation in not only not desiring the desire of the other, but in being a Desire that "desires another Desire" (269). In *Otherwise than Being,* this "capability" is called the radical passivity and proximity of substitution, and substitution, like fecund being, "opens an order in which death cannot be recognized"

(*OTB,* 115). A being who can substitute herself, a being in the recurrence of fecundity, "is human fraternity itself" (116).

In *Totality and Infinity,* Levinas brings Freud to task for one thing only, whether correctly or not. Freud, according to Levinas, makes the mistake of reducing sexuality to the search for pleasure. Freud seems to abstract from sexuality something of crucial significance in voluptuosity, an aspect of it that is irreducible to pleasure and seemingly unsuspected by Freud. For Levinas "Sexuality is in us neither knowledge nor power, but the very plurality of our existing" (*TI,* 277). What remains unrecognized by Freud is that the erotic "analyzed as fecundity, breaks up reality into relations irreducible to the relations of genus and species, part and whole, action and passion, truth and error; that in sexuality the subject enters into a relation with what is absolutely other, with an alterity of a type unforeseeable in formal logic, with what remains other in the relation and is never converted into 'mine,' and that nonetheless this relation has nothing ecstatic about it, for the pathos of voluptuosity is made of duality" (276). It is worth noting that in this disagreement with Freud, there is no denigration of pleasure. The protest against the forgetting of radical plurality is not a moralizing against pleasure. It worth noting, even more, that sexuality here, analyzed as fecundity is the model of and for a transcendence which maintains the I in its substantial transcendence. Transcendence, according to Levinas, as classically conceived, is self-contradictory. Either the classical concept reduces transcendence to a change of "properties, climate or level"; or, if it commits "the very identity of the subject" to transcendence, it conceives such transcendence as "the death of its substance" (274). Sexuality as the voluptuosity of the radically plural, on the other hand, gives the structure of a transcendence that both maintains and radically changes the I. The I is paradoxically maintained in no longer being a substance. Its (non)identity is in its capability of a fate other than its own.

Although Levinas never uses the term *agape,* it is difficult not to see in his constructions of eros, voluptuosity, and fecundity in their relation to enjoyment, and in the significance he draws from them, a marked convergence with Marcuse's notion that, *pace* not only Plato, but Freud as well, agape is eros. For Marcuse, agape is eros when eros finds its own route from primary narcissism toward a letting be of the other, implicitly a radical plurality within the libidinal rationality prefigured in the aesthetic relation, or when basic repression results in the "self-sublimation" or nonsurplus-repressive sublimation of eros. Marcuse never imagines that this self-sublimation can occur without the interruption of primary narcissism. For Levinas, agape, the otherwise than being that is *being* for the other, is never immaterial, has never left behind enjoyment, the sensuous holding on to exteriority that always characterizes subjectivity in its separation from the totality and its demands. Neither fecundity nor substitution abolish enjoyment. They, in a sense, establish enjoyment in the only way that is both justified and possible in relation to the absolutely other.[20] This notion of eros as agape and agape as eros suggests in Marcuse and in Levinas something like a common weakness. They both have a weakness for the other, a weakness that is not a yielding to the opposite of goodness, but an active yielding to the beauty and/or height of the other, a memory of the trace of the other.

Critical theory and Levinas also converge in their notions of the realization of an historical freedom even beyond that of Marx. Marx conceived of freedom not, of course, as the abolition of the realm of necessity, but as its separation from a possible realm of creative freedom, a separation which could emerge on the basis of the abolition of alienated labor. Necessity would be limited by freedom, while remaining necessity. The alienation of labor could be abolished through the conscious and rational reappropriation by the associated individuals of their social labor power in such a way as to reduce the realm of necessity to a minimum.

But even though, beyond the realm of necessity, activity could become freely creative, activity and existence within the freely administered realm of necessity would remain a limitation on freedom. Marcuse goes further in maintaining that not only is the liberation of eros from surplus repression necessary for the separation of necessity and freedom, for the abolition of alienated labor, and therefore for the establishment of the realm of freedom conceived by Marx, but that, upon its abolition, there would be a change in character in both realms, even in the realm of necessity, because a nonsurplus-repressive civilization would enable a fundamentally different experience of being, of nature and of existential relations. Even the reduced realm of necessity (and only when reduced) could begin to resemble the realm of freedom (see *EC,* 5, 158, 188–90, 195–96). The liberation of eros and the abolition of alienation go hand in hand, are each the condition of the other, and in their mutual interplay refer to Benjamin's premonition of a "kind of labor which, far from exploiting nature, is capable of delivering her of the creations which lie dormant in her womb as potentials" (TPH, 259). Such a change in the character of necessity would mean the release from natural history, from the dialectic at a standstill which is natural history, from the dialectic of freedom and necessity in which subjective freedom is continuously turning into its opposite because it wants above all to be its opposite, the power of necessity stored up in identity.

Levinas goes beyond Marx's conception of the realization of freedom in his conception of a sabbatical existence. A sabbatical existence does not refer directly to the liberation of the subject from toil, or alienated labor, but to a release of the subject from the order of necessity in which subjects are placed inside a social totality. Within the totality it is the need, rather than the Desire of social beings that brings them into and maintains them in the relation. Freedom, the freedom of creation *ex nihilo,* created freedom, the ethical relation all express "a multiplicity not united into a totality; the creature is an existent which indeed does depend on another, but not as a part that is separated from it. Creation *ex nihilo* breaks with the system, posits a being outside of every system, that is there where its freedom is possible" (*TI,* 104).[21] In the order of Desire "in its positivity…the plane of the needy being, avid for its complements, vanishes, and the possibility of a sabbatical existence, where existence suspends the necessities of existence, is inaugurated" (104). A sabbatical existence is not meant by Levinas to refer to a simply spiritual or to a private realm. It is to be generalized to the social relation publicly and materially. Thus, he will assert in one of the talmudic readings that "revolution takes place when one frees man, that is revolution takes place when one frees man from economic determinism…. To affirm that the working man is not negotiable, that he cannot be bargained about, is to affirm that which begins a revolution" (JR, 102). The separation of freedom from necessity, needed to transcend natural history, the reappropriation of social labor by the associated producers, which is itself the condition of possibility for the abolition of surplus repressive civilization, can only be accomplished by ethical subjects who as social beings are radically plural in having no identity. The *separation* of the realm of necessity and the realm of freedom, and thereby the *reconciliation* of freedom and necessity beyond natural history, would depend on the priority of *created* freedom.

In the end, ethics as first philosophy and critical theory not only critically supplement each the other. They converge. But I would like to see this convergence not as a weak form of an identity of perspective or of judgment, although that also occurs. Convergence might be seen as analogous to the way in which Benjamin's two arrows relate to each other. Benjamin recognized an antithesis between the messianic "spiritual *restitutio in integrum,*" the "intensity of the heart," and the order of the profane. Yet the profane in its dynamic quest for the happiness of a free humanity assists the messianic "in its quietest approach." And what allows the profane to assist in this approach is the allegiance of the profane, of happiness, to "the rhythm of this eternally transient worldly existence" (312–13), an allegiance sometimes despite, but always beyond the allegiance of reason to the One.

Notes

Notes to Introduction

1. Richard Cohen, foreword to *OTB,* xi.

2. See Asher Horowitz, "'How Can Anyone Be Called Guilty?' Speech, Responsibility and the Social Relation in Habermas and Levinas," *Philosophy Today* 44, no. 3 (Fall 2000): 295–317.

3. Max Horkheimer, "Materialism and Morality," in *Critical Theory: The Essential Readings,* ed. David Ingram and Julia Simon Ingram (New York: Paragon House, 1991), 187.

4. The most sophisticated and a remarkably insightful examination of Adorno's negative dialectics as the morality of thought is to be found in J. M. Bernstein's monumental study, *Adorno: Disenchantment and Ethics* (Cambridge: Cambridge University Press, 2001). It is one of the very few studies of Adorno that should be made required reading for anyone who wishes to pronounce upon the latter's thinking. It is hard to think of another work that has reached this level. Bernstein's is too complex and elaborate an argument to be engaged with here. If I have an argument with Bernstein with respect to his interpretation of Adorno, it would follow from two strategic moves that orient and structure his work. First, in order to bring out the meaning of negative dialectics and make it palatable to the ethos and methods of contemporary analytic philosophy, Bernstein tends to assimilate Adorno to the tradition of moral realism, both ancient and modern, inasmuch as he uses this tradition to expertly unpack the implications of negative dialectics. He does this primarily by elaborating on Adorno's effort to include the simple concept within a larger positive model of the complex concept as already harboring the structure of moral insight elaborated by current theories of moral realism (for example, Henrich, McDowell). The logic of moral insight is the unfolded logic of

the complex concept (321). Ethicality becomes "an historically emergent configuration of conceptuality as such" (322); "the structures of moral insight are nothing other than the elaborations of human conceptuality as such" (34). Bernstein, in this and in other ways, actually comes close to Levinas's position that ethics is the condition of possibility of more narrow and instrumental modes of cognition (231, 279). But in doing so, Bernstein must at least begin to make of negative dialectics an alternative ontology (see 226). By all but fusing Adorno with moral realism, Bernstein makes what Adorno claims is not an ontology into something ontological, for the sake of revivifying "material inference structures" destroyed by theoretical and cultural disenchantment. For Bernstein, Adorno wants to derive the ought from an expanded is, or practical material inferences from assertoric statements (275). My own reading of Adorno has him, like Levinas, quite consciously shying away from making ethical insight and action ontology-dependent. I also find the notion of a material inference to be only similar to what Adorno has in mind in terms of his "thinking in constellations," rather than homologous with that thinking. Second, Bernstein tends to make Adorno into something of a pure Weberian struggling with disenchantment whereas Adorno, should in my opinion, be seen as a Marxist actively struggling with Weber's political conservatism after having absorbed the import of the Weberian construal of disenchantment. By making Adorno into more of a Weberian than he is, and by dropping Marx almost entirely out of the Adornian picture, Bernstein assimilates Adornian "pessimism" to his own Weberian pessimism, which is one that might outdo Weber himself. Adorno would never have allowed himself to say that revolutions always have their Thermidors (441–42) and would never have forgotten the imbrication of disenchantment in social domination. In what follows I will turn Adorno toward Levinas because moral realism tends strongly towards turning sensibility into another type of information. For Levinas it is clear that ethical sensibility is other than information. And it seems to me that in the case of Adorno the morality of thought is not morality itself.

5. Jürgen Habermas, *The Theory of Communicative Action,* vol. 1, *Reason and the Rationalization of Society,* trans. Thomas McCarthy (Boston: Beacon Press, 1981), 374.

6. Josh Cohen in *Interrupting Auschwitz: Art, Religion, Philosophy* (New York: Continuum, 2005), points out deftly how, according to Adorno, some examples of modern art, in their form of "impossibility," are able to approach truth without traducing it. For Cohen, art thereby becomes the "priviledged executor" of Adorno's "new categorical imperative because in it alone does the figure of utopia converge with its unrelenting renunciation" (63). Adorno doubtlessly approaches art with such a

functionless function in mind (see chapter 4 below), and in this sense it is privileged as a form of thought. But to suggest that art thereby becomes the "executor" of the new categorical imperative simply abstracts from and forgets Adorno's unending commitment to the practical transformation of fundamental sociopolitical institutions like commodity production and the division of labor.

7. Levinas, "The State of Caesar and the State of David," in *Beyond the Verse: Talmudic Readings and Lectures,* trans. Gary D. Mole (Bloomington: Indiana University Press, 1994), 181.

8. The Frankfurt School was therefore the first to feel what Suvin describes in the following: "We may echo the famous quip that the whole of Russian literature emerges out of Gogol's *Overcoat* by saying that all radical left intellectuals and thinking today emerge out of Benjamin's attempt to understand catastrophic history. This is a major reason for his posthumous fame." Darko Suvin, "The Arrested Moment in Benjamin's 'Theses': Epistemology vs. Politics, Image vs. Story," *Neohelicon* 28, no. 1 (2001): 191.

9. Which is not to say that having many more such studies as acute as that, for example, of Catherine Chalier's *What Ought I to Do? Morality in Kant and Levinas,* trans. Jane Marie Todd (Ithaca: Cornell University Press, 2002) would not be extremely useful.

10. One of the ways in which this work is marked as not comprehensive or systematic, but as a quite specific interpretive constellation, is by the intentional omission, except for two of the briefest citations, of Levinas's so-called "Jewish" or "confessional" writings, primarily several of his "talmudic readings" that bear on the relationship of ethics to justice and the state. In doing so I am first of all respecting Levinas's own wish to separate his writings on Judaism and Jewish topics from his phenomenological investigations. I believe he was quite right to do this inasmuch as his phenomenology of the ethical relies on phenomenological evidence for whatever import it has, rather than on any traditional texts, no matter how much they in turn might bear on the topics and issues uncovered by the phenomenological investigations. This should remain the case even if the traditional texts were at some level inspiration and even guidance for the phenomenological investigation. Secondly, despite the fact that a number of commentators see in the talmudic readings an attempt on Levinas's part to negotiate the tensions between ethics and politics (see, for example, Cohen, *Interrupting Auschwitz,* 97–103), it is my belief that in none of the talmudic readings does Levinas get any further than he does in his non-Jewish writings in going beyond what in chapter 1 is described as the amphibology at which he arrives. In fact, one of the important things that Levinas attempts to draw out of certain Jewish

traditions is precisely an awareness of the difficulties of remaining in the situation I will claim produces the amphibology. The point of bringing the Frankfurt School into a constellation with this problem in Levinas is precisely not to remain there.

11. As for example in one study that purports to relate Levinas with critical theory in general: C. Fred Alford, *Levinas, the Frankfurt School and Psychoanalysis* (Middletown, Conn.: Wesleyan University Press, 2002). Alford's study seems rather to be more of an external critique of Levinas from the assumed standpoint of psychoanalytic object-relations theory.

12. There are two valuable extant treatments of Adorno and Levinas together, though not of Levinas and the Frankfurt School more generally: Cohen, *Interrupting Auschwitz,* and Hent de Vries, *Minimal Theologies: Critiques of Secular Reason in Adorno and Levinas,* trans. Geoffrey Hale (Baltimore: The Johns Hopkins University Press, 2005). Despite many points of possible interpretive agreement and contention in relation to them, the present study differs from them substantially not only in scope, but in method and aim. Methodologically, both Cohen and de Vries relate Adorno and Levinas to one another by way of each belonging to a third term. In the case of Cohen, both Levinas and Adorno illustrate in different ways the structure of impossibility (in which the possibility of relating to an absolute is predicated on the recognition of the impossibility of attaining it), a structure that Cohen sees as the only genuine form of religious experience after Auschwitz. For de Vries, both Adorno and Levinas exemplify evolution towards attaining a "minimal theology" in which reason's other is approached through one or another rational practice of performative contradiction. Although neither are presented as theologians, their works supply complementary resources for the only form of rational theology that would be acceptable after thoroughgoing enlightenment, after Kant. Although de Vries suggests that a certain "cross-pollination" is possible between them that would allow them together to express what they cannot separately articulate (559), the relation explored here is different in being closer to an Adornian constellation in which a variety expressions both criticize and supplement one another. With respect to aims, both Cohen and de Vries approach the relation between Levinas and Adorno for broadly speaking theological purposes. The aim here, on the other hand, is to at least set the stage for an advancement of the critical social philosophy missing but somehow pregnant in Levinas, amply present but still underdeveloped in its ethical dimension in the Frankfurt School. In the sorts of treatments given by de Vries and Cohen, emancipatory social theory and the political projects it conveys are first of all orphaned. They are not recognized to be or made central to the theories being investigated. Their being orphaned is not simply a matter of Cohen or de Vries not

recognizing the essentiality to the Marxian Adorno of the mediation of the ideational by historical-social categories. Both de Vries and especially Cohen tend to see anything more than an attempt to maintain or enliven the necessary friction between ethics and justice in transformative political projects as reassertions of a dogmatically given absolute. The aim here is precisely in the supplementation of Levinas by the Frankfurt School, and vice versa, to rethink the possibility of an emancipatory politics that goes beyond a reveling in the aporetic or, in fixating on the aporetic, conflates what we might in Marcusean terms call a basic aporetics which would recognize the permanent tension between ethics and politics, with a surplus aporia, not properly aporetic, not necessary within being, which, when conflated with the basic could become complicit with domination. On the need to make a Marcusean, even "Sabbatian" distinction see Gad Horowitz, "Aporia and Messiah in Derrida and Levinas," in *Difficult Justice: Commentaries on Levinas and Politics,* ed. A. Horowitz and G. Horowitz (Toronto: University of Toronto Press, 2006), 307–30. The social-theoretical import of the relation between Adorno and Levinas in minimal theology or impossibility is not completely shut out, but it is treated idealistically. Domination is comprehended essentially as a failure of self-reflection.

13. I am borrowing this understanding of Derrida's notion of the supplement from Silvia Benso in *The Face of Things: A Different Side of Ethics* (Albany: State University of New York Press, 2000), 128–29. In this book Benso tries to establish a relation of supplementarity between Levinas and Heidegger.

Notes to Chapter 1

1. I am using the term "against" here in the sense that John D. Caputo uses it in *Against Ethics: A Contribution to a Poetics of Obligation with Constant Reference to Deconstruction* (Bloomington: Indiana University Press, 1993). For Caputo, against signifies being up against, attached to but opposing; contesting, but cleaving to.

2. Here we might note that the order of commodities does not presuppose persons per se, but only persons insofar as they are contractors; and that the relation between contractors, at least in a capitalist market society, by virtue of the fetishism of commodities, comes to perform only the alienated form of the relation between persons. The person presupposed in the contract becomes the person reduced to the contractor.

3. The best treatments of Levinas's relation to Rosenzweig are to be found in Robert Gibbs, *Correlations in Rosenzweig and Levinas* (Princeton: Princeton University Press, 1992), and Richard A. Cohen, *Elevations: The*

Height of the Good in Levinas and Rosenzweig (Chicago: University of Chicago Press, 1994).

4. This is expertly handled in Robert John Sheffler Manning's reading of Levinas against the Heidegger of *Being and Time,* namely, *Interpreting Otherwise than Heidegger: Emmanuel Levinas's Ethics as First Philosophy* (Pittsburgh: Duquesne University Press, 1993).

5. For an extremely useful reading of Levinas that stresses the always-already character of the sociality of subjectivity conceived as both the relation and the term of the relation, see Jeffrey Dudiak, *The Intrigue of Ethics: A Reading of the Idea of Discourse in the Thought of Emmanuel Levinas* (New York: Fordham University Press, 2001).

6. Levinas, "Ethics of the Infinite," in *Dialogues with Contemporary Continental Thinkers,* ed. Richard Kearney (Manchester: Manchester University Press, 1984), 66.

7. Ibid., 64.

8. Ibid., 66.

9. Adorno, *Aesthetic Theory,* ed. Gretel Adorno and Rolf Tiedemann, trans. Robert Hullot-Kentor (Minneapolis: University of Minnesota Press, 1997), 83.

10. It is, of course, also possible to be a left anti-Levinasian. The most prominent example would be Howard Caygill in *Levinas and the Political* (New York: Routledge, 2002). Left anti-Levinasianism, as exemplified by Caygill, seems most of all to be offended by Levinas's Zionism and tends to see Zionism not simply as a particularly difficult case for the difficult relationship between ethics and politics that Levinas's ethics as first philosophy constructs, but as the secret protocol of his ethics. For Caygill, Levinas wants to effect a Christian-Jewish alliance against not only paganism (à la conservative German nationalism), but pagan peoples (which seems to eventually include Arab Moslems and Asian Hindus and Buddhists). But given his Judaism and Zionism, a simple universalism (of the Christian sort) is not enough. What Caygill takes to be Levinas's actual particularist, if not at least borderline racist politics seems to get reflected for him in Levinas's construal of the relation between self, other, and the third. Caygill, however, misreads this relation as a relation between my identity, an identity I share with an other who is other (but in our shared identity closer to me), and a third (that is, a second other) who claims a different identity, and whom I will therefore side against in any conflict with the other who is closer (through shared identity). Thus, Levinas (the non-Israeli Jew) sides with the Israeli (Jewish Zionist) against the Palestinian and rationalizes away the ethical offence committed by the Israeli at Sabra and Shatilla. For Caygill there seems to be

no third way beyond universalism and particularisms. Moreover, Caygill seems to leave no alternative to the Jew but to be stateless in what is still a world of nation-states. Anything less would be to abandon the prophetic mission apparently claimed by the chosen people. For the Jew to have a state under which war crimes could possibly be committed is, for Caygill, in fact to be a pagan, but a hypocritical one. One supposes that this form of post-Christian universalism (because it does seem to be one) is at least an advance over traditional Christian anti-Semitism and assimilationism because it seems to imply a place for the Jew dispersed among the universalist nations of post-Christendom. We will tolerate them as long as they choose to be the chosen stateless people they claim to be. Nonetheless Caygill does point in the direction of the amphibology discussed earlier in this chapter when he asserts that Levinas's correction of proximity by ontology potentially leaves a state in place that is unjust (142), and that therefore Levinas does not guard himself against surrendering the possibility of justice in the worldly human city (143). He laments the fact that it is extremely difficult to imagine the coexistence of ontology and ethics. And it is. But this is precisely the sort of question taken up in different form by the Frankfurt School. And it is the sort of question that Levinas, in some of his "Jewish" writings, does not answer, but raises again from out of his particular tradition.

11. See for example, Richard A. Cohen, "'Political Monotheism': Levinas on Politics, Ethics and Religion," in *Essays in Celebration of the Founding of the Organization of Phenomenological Organizations,* ed. Cheung, Chan-Fai, Ivan Chvatik, Ion Copoeru, Lester Embree, Julia Irbarne, and Hans Rainer Sepp (The Organization of Phenomenological Organizations, 2003), http://www.o-p-o.net/pragueessaylist.html. For Cohen the Levinasian state is "essentially classically liberal" (35) and Levinas is brought intimately close to Locke (7) and even Hayek (38). Others who read Levinas as an endorsement of the liberal political state would include Susan A. Handelman, *Fragments of Redemption: Jewish Thought and Literary Theory in Benjamin, Scholem and Levinas* (Bloomington: Indiana University Press, 1991); and William Paul Simmons in "The Third: Levinas's Theoretical Move from An-Archical Ethics to the Realm of Justice and Politics," *Philosophy and Social Criticism* 25, no. 6: 83–104, and in *An-Archy and Justice: An Introduction to Emmanuel Levinas' Political Thought* (Lanham, Md.: Lexington Books, 2003). It is also, of course, possible to mount a liberal critique of Levinas, such as the one given by Samuel Moyn, *Origins of the Other: Emmanuel Levinas Between Revelation and Ethics* (Ithaca: Cornell University Press, 2005). In an otherwise interesting contextualization of Levinas's philosophical development, Moyne

seems to assign him the task of finding the nonbiblical, rational-moral foundations for liberalism that it still lacks, and then finds him wanting because what he offers to liberalism is a "crypto-theology."

12. Dudiak, *Intrigue,* 247.

13. Adriaan Peperzak, "Some Remarks on Hegel, Kant and Levinas," in *Face to Face with Levinas,* ed. Richard A. Cohen (Albany: State University of New York Press, 1986), 214.

14. Ibid., 215.

15. Ibid., 216.

16. Robert Bernasconi, "The Third Party: Levinas on the Intersection of the Ethical and the Political," *Journal of the British Society for Phenomenology* 30, no. 1 (January 1999): 83.

17. Ibid., 84–85. In an article some ten years later, "Levinas and the Struggle for Existence," in *Addressing Levinas,* ed. Eric Sean Nelson, Antje Kapust and Kent Still (Evanston: Northwestern University Press, 2005), 170–84, Bernasconi correctly points out that "Levinas formulates his thought as a radical alternative…to all philosophies based on the struggle for existence" (171) going all the way back to Heraclitus. Heidegger importantly becomes a late representative of such a tradition. For Bernasconi, Levinas's point is not to deny the being of such a struggle but, again, to interrupt it. Levinas falls radically short by failing "to take his philosophy to the point of a philosophy of institutions" (180). My point is that without addressing the historicity of the struggle for existence, such a political philosophy of institutions will not be capable of getting beyond the impasse of liberalism.

18. Gibbs, *Correlations,* 242.

19. Ibid., 244.

20. Ibid., 252.

21. Ibid., 251.

22. The need to move beyond liberalism for the sake of a Levinasian politics has, of course, since Gibbs's call, been felt by others. Thus, Annabel Herzog, "Is Liberalism 'All We Need'? Levinas's Politics of *Surplus,*" *Political Theory* 30, no. 2 (April 2002): 204–27, hopes to reject the liberal appropriation of Levinas and wants to go beyond Derrida and Critchley (205–06) directly to utopian goals as a "now" (215). She conceives of Levinas's aim as "no less than a radical reversal of the idea of the state" in which it would be for the weak, absent and nonrepresented (219). Not only is politics concerned with justice for the third party, but it necessarily has a second utopian dimension in which "I have to care for dessert for the poor" (221–22) in which the state provides in abundance for those who "cannot provide the state with anything" (223). But it is hard to see

how this addition of generous public charity to liberal politics-as-usual is anything more than a more liberal liberalism. As political thinking this leads straight back to John Rawls. At least Marxism has gone significantly beyond thinking of "the poor" as always with us. For Herzog, the fault of Marxism is that although it is "concerned with the Other," it is "exclusively based on the *conatus essendi*" (221). But please do not ask me how it is possible to be *exclusively* based on the latter yet still be concerned with the Other. A more promising direction is undertaken by John Drabinski in "The Possibility of An Ethical Politics: From Peace to Liturgy," *Philosophy and Social Criticism* 26, no. 4 (2000): 49–73. Drabinski sees the need to go beyond Levinas for the latter's own sake. This is needed inasmuch as Levinas, in failing to practice a *radical* phenomenology, fails to question the roots of politics in the particulars of concrete, factical, particular contexts, and thus builds into his thinking a conservative bias (58–61). It would be necessary to recognize that the "accusing Other and third accuse me simultaneously as singularities and as raced/classed/gendered bodies. The effect of this signification is a ruining of the neutrality and universality inherent in the *conservative* [read: liberal] construal of law" (64). But, despite the welcome Drabinski offers to the project of a "rapprochement between Levinas and Marx" (69), his liturgical politics is simply a call for a responsive transformation of political institutions so that power may be given to minorities and for a redistribution of capitalist wealth (66). In a subsequent article, "Wealth and Justice in a U-topian Context," in *Addressing Levinas,* 185–98, Drabinski reiterates his perceptive critique of the conservative bias that Levinas builds into law, and criticizes it as insufficient to the very "u-topia" also indicated by Levinas's ethics. The way forward for Drabinski, rightly in my view, would go beyond "the character of the *a-venir*" (196). But Drabinski assigns to law (and therefore, it appears, to the state) the political responsibility to "unsettle the work of universal law" so that "the rights of the human must find the character of generosity and sacrifice" (174). The state would will generosity and sacrifice through redistribution and reparation. Such a view might, in political terms, be characterized as ethically militant redistributive reform liberalism. It counters the conservative bias of legal universality with an opposing bias which would end up leaving the fundamental structures of market-state in place. It still does not address the machinery of domination in natural history which Marx began to unearth as early as in "On the Jewish Question." And from Drabinski's own Levinasian perspective it veers toward a recommendation for the legitimacy of "human sacrifice" (an inversion of reciprocity rather than asymmetry), something with which Levinas's ethics should arguably not coincide. But perhaps the problem, as Dussel clearly sees, is that it is the vast majority across the globe who have been rendered powerless. And that a redistribution of capitalist wealth will never undo massive destitution and universal alienation.

23. Ibid., 254. For Gibbs the task of relating these two falls on others who find social thought in need of such a positive combination. He indicates that a "space for liberation must be freed from Hegelian totalizing dialectic" even more than in Levinas and Marx in order to do so (252). In order to develop such a non-Hegelian space, Gibbs refers back to Cohen and Rosenzweig. It is my intention to refer to the negative dialectics of the Frankfurt School in order to effect a similar positive combination.

24. Enrique Dussel, *Philosophy of Liberation* (Maryknoll, New York: Orbis Books, 1985), 173. Indeed, the very first chapter of this work is entitled "History."

25. Ibid., 170.

26. Ibid., 44, 18–21.

27. Ibid., 69, 71ff.

28. Ibid., 64–65.

29. Ibid., 99.

Notes to Chapter 2

1. So, for example, in *Totality and Infinity,* in his discussion of separation, Levinas is clear that the dialectical constitution of the separated sentient being would destroy the exteriority of the absolutely other; hence "we are outside of the dialectical conciliation of the I and the non-I" (*TI,* 148). A few pages later: "The whole of this work aims to show a relation with the other not only cutting across the logic of contradiction, where the other of A is the non-A, but also across dialectical logic, where the same dialectically participates in and is reconciled with the other in the Unity of the system" (*TI,* 150).

2. This is obviously an inadequate estimation of Marx's thinking on the subject. For Marx, the possibility of shaking off social bewitchment is not so much an abstract possibility of individual consciousness as a function of historical development mediated by class conflict, the maturation of a specific form of social contradiction that would allow for/demand it. Yet there is a large grain of truth in this understanding of Marx inasmuch as Marx makes use of an historical ontology which grounds the possibility of historical social development in freedom as the negative moment in labor.

3. For an analysis of this essay that emphasizes the truth value, for Levinas, of the Germanic conservatism of which the philosophy of Hitler-

ism was a part see Asher Horowitz and Gad Horowitz, "Is Liberalism All We Need? Prelude Via Fascism," in *Difficult Justice: Commentaries on Levinas and the Politics,* ed. Asher Horowitz and Gad Horowitz (Toronto: University of Toronto Press, 2006), 12–23.

4. For a critical account of Habermas's communicative ethics from a Levinasian perspective see Asher Horowitz, "'How Can Anyone Be Called Guilty?' Speech, Responsibility and the Social Relation in Habermas and Levinas," *Philosophy Today* 44, no. 3 (Fall 2000): 295–317.

5. The argument for such an indestructible interiority as the source of freedom may also all too easily become an excuse to accept authoritarian ideologies and regimes. See Marcuse in "A Study on Authority," in *Studies in Critical Philosophy,* trans. Joris de Bres (Boston: Beacon Press, 1972), 51–155.

6. There are a number of fairly substantial treatments of Benjamin's "Theses" that each have important insights to offer: Rolf Tiedemann, "Historical Materialism or Political Messianism? An Interpretation of the Theses 'On the Concept of History,'" in *Benjamin: Philosophy, Aesthetics, History,* ed. Gary Smith (Chicago: University of Chicago Press, 1989), 175–209; Peter Osborne, "Small-Scale Victories, Large-Scale Defeats: Walter Benjamin's Politics of Time," in *Walter Benjamin's Philosophy: Destruction and Experience,* ed. Andrew Benjamin and Peter Osborne (London: Routledge, 1994), 59–109; Irving Wohlfarth, "Smashing the Kaleidoscope: Walter Benjamin's Critique of Cultural History," in *Walter Benjamin and the Demands of History,* ed. Michael P. Steinberg (Ithaca: Cornell University Press, 1996), 190–205; Michael Loewy, "'Against the Grain': The Dialectical Conception of Culture in Walter Benjamin's Theses of 1940," in *Walter Benjamin and the Demands of History,* 206–13; as well as treatments in book-length studies of Benjamin, the most notable of which are in the introduction to the revised edition of Richard Wolin's *Walter Benjamin: An Aesthetic of Redemption* (Berkeley and Los Angeles: University of California Press, 1994), and in chapter 7, entitled "Is this Philosophy" in Susan Buck-Morss, *The Dialectics of Seeing: Walter Benjamin and the Arcades Project* (Cambridge, Mass.: MIT Press, 1989). What characterizes most, if not all of these treatments is the understanding of the theses as a methodological or quasi-methodological attempt on Benjamin's part to ground the notion and practice of dialectical images and to bring dialectical images in line with a messianistic revision of Marxism which, because of its theological inheritance, fails to cohere with the Marxism it would like to reformulate and revivify. According to Tiedemann, for example, Benjamin does not really need to employ the language of theology again in order to do this because Marx had already

inherited the thoroughgoing secularization of theology from "great philosophy"; see "Progress," in *Critical Models: Interventions and Catchwords,* trans. Henry W. Pickford, 143–60 (New York: Columbia University Press, 1998), 187. My concern here is to attempt a different sort of reading of the Theses, one that blasts this specific work out of Benjamin's lifework and the lifework out of the era. I wish to follow Benjamin's own description of the activity of the historical materialist in my relation to and reading of Benjamin's own work on historical materialism and to place this work in a constellation with some of Benjamin's other writings and those of the Frankfurt School.

7. Thus, I am agreeing with Adorno ("Progress," 145) that Benjamin's critique of progress did not want to eliminate progress "from historical reflection" but that "progress" would mean the "very establishment of humanity in the first place."

8. In N, the convolute of Benjamin's notes for the *Arcades Project* that includes the materials from which TPH was composed, he quotes from a letter from Horkheimer of March 16, 1937 to the effect that "past injustice has occurred and is completed. The slain are really slain.... If one takes the lack of closure entirely seriously, one must believe in the last Judgement" (471).

9. Levinas goes on, with respect to the representation of the past that "to represent is not to reduce a past fact to an actual image but to reduce to the instantaneousness of thought everything that seems independent of it; it is in this that representation is constitutive" (*TI,* 127). This remark makes a wonderful bridge between Benjamin's empty homogeneous time and Adorno's critique of identity theory.

10. At least according to Howard Eiland and Michael Jennings the editors of *Walter Benjamin: Selected Writings, Vol. 3, 1935–1938* (Cambridge, Mass.: Harvard University Press, 2002), 306 n. 1.

11. Benjamin, "Theologico-Political Fragment," in Reflections, ed Peter Demetz (New York: Schocken Books, 1986), 312.

12. Ibid., 313.

13. Ibid., 312.

14. Ibid., 312–13.

15. Ibid., 313.

16. In the case of Scheler, however, dualism reasserts itself in that he reproduces a "basic tension between the meaningful and essential that lies behind the historically manifested and the sphere of history itself." This is because "in the origins of phenomenology there is a dualism of nature and history" (INH, 113).

17. Not Heidegger's project of ontology, but the project of historicity.

18. For Adorno a telling example of the possibility of a marriage of idealism with nonrationalism is in Schopenhauer's philosophical development: "I only need to point out that a philosophy like Schopenhauer's came to its irrationalism by no other way than by strict adherence to the fundamental theme of rational idealism — the Fichtean transcendental subjectivity. To my mind this is evidence of an idealism with irrational content" (INH, 116).

19. I will leave to others who may care to do so any treatment of the question of whether Heidegger's work after the turn addresses in any way the criticisms Adorno raises here. On the general relation between Adorno and Heidegger, see Samir Gandesha, "Leaving Home: On Adorno and Heidegger," in *The Cambridge Companion to Adorno,* ed. Tom Huhn (Cambridge: Cambridge University Press, 2004), 101–28.

20. According to the translator of the article, Robert Hullot-Kentor, in a helpful note (INH, 120 n. 10).

21. In this connection it may be worth noting that transience is not identifiable with flux. The former at least connotes the vanishing, the passing away, of a singularity, with or without a trace; the second at least connotes the continual modification of an identifiable or nonidentifiable substance.

22. "Of" in both the possessive and partitive senses of the genitive.

23. In an excellent analysis of the Benjaminian image that is at once literary-theoretical and political-historical, Darko Suvin, in "The Arrested Moment in Benjamin's 'Theses'," expresses the problematic that Adorno was tacitly addressing in approaching natural-history in *Negative Dialectics.* For Suvin "the price of Benjamin's refusal of a complex interaction between present, past, and future is very high, and may be seen in the difference to Marx's dialectics which 'understand each form in the flux of movement'.... Benjamin tried to forcibly yoke together Marxian dialectics and his 'image space' in the new term of a 'dialectical image.' This term...seems to me aporetic. The temporality of an image is frozen, however historically flowing its coming about and its effects may be and whatever tensions might be contained within its arrested balance, while the temporality of dialectics is, from Plato to Hegel to Marx and Bloch, unthinkable without a playing out of contradictions in time. Therefore to base the understanding of historical time exclusively in and on the 'fulgurant Now'...seems to me an exemplary case of reduction of politics to epistemology" (189). Such a reduction prevents Benjamin from thinking any further: "The absence of even a clear set of preconditions for the messianic horizon then in turn structures the whole...text" (192). I do not think that Benjamin bases the understanding of historical time

exclusively on the now-time, but it is just this conundrum of the relation of the now-time, messianic time of which dialectical time is shot through with chips, that Adorno wishes to address and think further.

24. For an example of that antinomianism indicating that for Adorno, "law is the primal phenomenon of irrational rationality" (*ND*, 309). Neither will Adorno allow that the principle of equity and practices that allow its application do anything to remedy the situation. See *ND*, 311–12.

25. As Adorno notes in "Progress," 146–47. According to Adorno the greatness of the Augustinian doctrine lies in the fact that "in Augustine one can recognize the inner constellation of the ideas of progress, redemption and the immanent course of history, which should not dissolve into one another, lest they reciprocally destroy each other. If progress is equated with redemption, as transcendental intervention per se, then it forfeits, along with the temporal dimension, its intelligible meaning, and evaporates into ahistorical theology. But if progress is mediatized into history, then the idolization of history threatens."

26. Adorno, "Education After Auschwitz," in *Critical Models: Interventions and Catchwords,* trans. Henry W. Pickford (New York: Columbia University Press, 1998), 201.

27. Ibid., 203.

28. On this inversion, and its relation to temporality, the work of John Drabinski is particularly helpful, beginning with "The Status of the Transcendental in Levinas' Thought," *Philosophy Today* 38, no. 2 (Summer 1994): 149–58, through "From Representation to Materiality," in *International Studies in Philosophy* 30, no. 4: 23–37, to *Sensibility and Singularity: The Problem of Phenomenology in Levinas* (Albany: State University of New York Press, 2001).

29. Adorno, "Subject and Object," in *The Essential Frankfurt School Reader,* ed. Andrew Arato and Eike Gebhardt (New York: Urizen Books, 1978), 511.

30. For an example of a reading of Levinas that emphasizes his movement out of the concrete see Robert Bernasconi, "Strangers and Slaves in the Land of Egypt: Levinas and the Politics of Otherness," in *Difficult Justice: Commentaries on Levinas and Politics,* ed. Asher Horowitz and Gad Horowitz (Toronto: University of Toronto Press, 2006), 246–61.

31. Adorno, "Why Still Philosophy?" in *Critical Models: Interventions and Catchwords,* trans. Henry W. Pickford (New York: Columbia University Press, 1998), 17.

Notes to Chapter 3

1. According to Benjamin a wish is a form of experience, a form that "accompanies one to the far reaches of time, that fills and divides time." And a fulfilled wish "is the crowning of experience." Unlike the fateful repetition of the gambler's reduced experience, which can be symbolized by the ivory ball in the roulette wheel, a fulfilled wish finds its folk symbol in the "shooting star," which in a sense fills and divides time. Quoting Joubert on the nature of the period of time of the shooting star, Benjamin adds: "Time...is found even in eternity; but it is not earthly, worldly time.... That time does not destroy; it merely completes. It is the antithesis of the time in hell, the province of those who are not allowed to complete anything they have started" (SMB, 179).

2. In this connection it would be interesting to compare and relate the traditions bound to the story with Benjamin's suggestions about their transformation in "Paris, Capital of the Nineteenth Century." Where the community of storyteller-listeners solidifies into the rituals that bear traditions of counsel, capitalist modernity substitutes the "world exhibition" for "the popular festival" that would be such a ritual. The world exhibitions are the "sites of pilgrimages to the commodity fetish." Out of such exhibitions luxury can be extended to the masses in the form of fashion, which "prescribes the ritual according to which the commodity fetish wishes to be worshipped." "Paris, Capitol of the Nineteenth Century," in *Reflections,* ed. Peter Demetz (New York: Schocken Books, 1986), 151–53.

3. Benjamin's later treatment of the aura, in "The Work of Art in the Age of Mechanical Reproduction," stresses the historic connection of the aura to the cultic, magical and religious functions of art. There, the destruction of the aura that is a result of the introduction of forms of mechanical reproduction is related to an emancipation of art from a parasitic dependence on ritual. The destruction of the aura seems to be the necessary condition for the reversal of the function of art from one based on ritual to one based on politics. Benjamin illustrates the meaning of the aura of art objects with a characterization of the aura of natural objects: "a distance, however close it may be." "The Work of Art in the Age of Mechanical Reproduction," in *Illuminations,* ed. Hannah Arendt (New York: Schocken Books, 1969), 223. Benjamin's concerns in SMB are different, and his overall position on the relation between art and progressive politics may have moved substantially away in "The Work of Art," composed during a period when Benjamin put himself in very close association with Brecht and Brecht's epic theatre.

4. The meaning of spleen time remains obscure.

5. Levinas, "Freedom and Command," in *Collected Philosophical Papers,* trans. Alphonso Lingis (Pittsburgh: Duquesne University Press, 1998), 16.

6. Ibid., 19.

7. Ibid., 22.

8. This does not mean that the critical deviations are either nonexistent or futile or, that even if they were futile, they would be wrong.

9. Thus, Marcuse refers to a change in the philosophy of physics, after the work of figures such as Born and Heisenberg, in which "the mathematized nature, the scientific reality appears to be ideational reality." The scientific subject comes to be seen in its constitutive role. In the face of the desubstantialization of the object, there is a shift away from theoretical emphasis on metaphysical questions in favor of practical certainty free from commitment to any substance beyond the operational context (*ODM,* 148–51).

10. For a more detailed account of Marcuse's view of Husserl's accomplishments in this regard, and several critical remarks, written only a year after *ODM,* see "On Science and Phenomenology," in *The Essential Frankfurt School Reader,* ed. Andrew Arato and Eike Gebhardt (New York: Urizen Books, 1978), 466–76, esp. 470–73, 475.

11. And this repugnance is voiced not only from the left, but also from the right.

12. For a thoroughgoing analysis of the meaning for Adorno of the penetration of culture by the commodity form refer to Shane Gunster, *Capitalizing on Culture: Critical Theory for Cultural Studies* (Toronto: University of Toronto Press, 2004), esp. chapters 1 and 2.

13. Horkheimer and Adorno are perhaps here drawing upon Benjamin's understanding of Greek tragedy, especially if one substitutes "society" for "god" in the following:

> It was not in law but in tragedy that the head of genius lifted itself for the first time from the mist of guilt, for in tragedy demonic fate is breached. But not by having the endless pagan chain of guilt and atonement superceded by the purity of man who has expiated and is with the pure god. Rather in tragedy pagan man becomes aware that he is better than his god, but the realization robs him of speech, remains unspoken....Guilt and atonement it does not measure justly in the balance, but mixes indiscriminately. There is no question of "the moral world order" being restored; instead, the moral hero, still dumb, not yet of age...wishes to raise himself by shaking that tormented world. The paradox of the birth of genius in moral speechlessness, moral infantility, is the sublimity of tragedy.

Benjamin, "Fate and Character," in *Reflections,* ed. Peter Demetz (New York: Schocken Books, 1986), 307.

14. This should be clear enough from Adorno's assessment and understanding of the great works of "high modernism" which negatively refer to the aura in its destruction. *Aesthetic Theory* is in large part devoted to exploring the possibility that such works represent a precarious attempt to maintain and redeem the aura in the still aesthetic reference to its absence. For a brief indication of this theme see C.

15. Adorno, "Subject and Object," 500–01.

16. Ibid., 500.

17. Horkheimer and Adorno have already made this clear two chapters before the excursus on the *Odyssey* in their treatment of the episode of the Sirens. See *DE,* 32–34.

18. It might seem that Horkheimer and Adorno are here lamenting only the loss of those "natural aims" that would belong to the sphere of need, to the *conatus essendi,* but this would be to mistake the "enthronement of means as ends" as implying that ends do not refer to ethical relations. But these are for Horkheimer, in for example *Eclipse of Reason,* clearly to be understood as ethical.

19. Horkheimer, *Eclipse of Reason* (New York: Seabury Press, 1974), 176. Written in English and for an American audience a few years after *Dialectic of Enlightenment,* Horkheimer's *Eclipse of Reason* is particularly useful as a complement to the first chapter of *Dialectic of Enlightenment.* The "disease of reason" of which Horkheimer speaks is, he says, inseparable from the nature of reason in civilization "as we have known it so far." The disease emerged from the urge to dominate nature and recovery from it depends on insight into the nature of the original disease and not on the cure of its latest symptoms. Even the concentration camps, he says, are present in germ in "primitive objectivization." Thus, the true critique of reason will go to the deepest layers of civilization and its earliest history (176).

20. Adorno and Horkheimer are not identifying the mathematical sciences with domination; nor is their critique a form of romanticism: Enlightenment's

> untruth does not consist in what its romantic enemies have always reproached it for: analytical method, return to elements, dissolution through reflective thought; but instead in the fact that for enlightenment the process is always decided from the start. When in mathematical procedure the unknown becomes the unknown quantity of an equation, this marks it as the well-known before any value is inserted. Nature, before and after the quantum theory, is that which is to be

comprehended mathematically.... In the anticipatory identification of the wholly conceived and mathematized world with truth, enlightenment intends to secure itself against the return of the mythic. It confounds thought and mathematics. In this way the latter is, so to speak, released and made into an absolute instance (*DE,* 24–25).

21. Karl Marx, *Selected Writings,* ed. Lawrence H. Simon (Indianapolis: Hackett, 1994), 100.

Notes to Chapter 4

1. Adorno includes Husserl's phenomenology among those antipositivistic and anti-idealist searches for substantiality that do not manage to avoid idealist identity: "Husserl the logician...would indeed sharply distinguish the mode of apprehending the essence from generalizing abstraction — what he had in mind was a specific mental experience capable of perceiving the essence in the particular — but the essence to which this experience referred did not differ in any respect from the familiar general concepts. There is a glaring discrepancy between the arrangements of essence perception and its *terminus ad quem*" (*ND,* 9). In this respect, Adorno's criticism of Husserl had not much changed since his *Against Epistemology: A Metacritique,* trans. Willis Domingo (Oxford: Blackwell, 1982 [1956]) or even his 1940 article in English, "Husserl and the Problem of Idealism," *The Journal of Philosophy* 37, no. 1 (January 1940): 5–18, or even from his 1931 article, "The Actuality of Philosophy," *Telos,* no. 31 (Spring 1977): 120–133, see 121–22. There is very little in the secondary literature on the relation between Adorno and phenomenology. An exception is Fred Dallmayr, "Phenomenology and Critical Theory: Adorno," *Cultural Hermeneutics* 3 (1976): 367–405, who is interested in arguing for the possibility of a convergence between Adorno and the later Heidegger in the service of the development of a critical hermeneutics.

2. Adorno, "Why Still Philosophy?" 7. Adorno, *pace* Josh Cohen, *Interpreting Auschwitz,* therefore does not use the impossibility of metaphysics simply as a new metaphysics of impossibility.

3. Levinas, "Is Ontology Fundamental?" in *Emmanuel Levinas: Basic Philosophical Writings,* ed. Adriaan T. Peperzak, Simon Critchley, and Robert Bernasconi (Bloomington: Indiana University Press, 1996), 8.

4. Levinas, "Meaning and Sense," in Peperzak, Critchley, and Bernasconi, *Emmanuel Levinas,* 56.

5. Thus, Adorno will take to task the debased theory that is implicit in the image theory of the ideological superstructure and chides Marx for

being like "a bull in the epistemological china shop" who "scarcely put too much weight on terms such as 'reflection,' where alleged supremacy is won at the cost of the subjective-critical moment." This "skipping" of epistemology "by fiat," however, led to the "revenge of epistemology" in the form of the image doctrine, a doctrine that immeasurably helped "materialism to be the very relapse into barbarism it was supposed to prevent" (*ND,* 205–06).

6. It is perhaps no accident, then, that the title of Levinas's first major work as an original philosopher, the subtitle of which is "An Essay on Exteriority," is *Totality and Infinity;* and, that despite the existentialist treatment given the subject in that work, which accounts for the possibility of idealism, the redemption of that subject does not follow from its spontaneity or even from a decision or initiative to relinquish that spontaneity.

7. Thus, Adorno will add that the "immanent critic of idealism defends idealism by showing how much it is defrauded of its own self — how much the first cause, which according to idealism is always the spirit, is in league with the blind predominance of merely existing things. The doctrine of the absolute spirit merely aids that predominance" (*ND,* 30).

8. Neither would the experimenting subject of antimetaphysical pragmatism be capable of this.

9. There is an exquisite irony in this dissolution of the image theory by way of a higher realism that thinks not in terms of the identity of the concept, but in images, or at least in imagelike constellations.

10. Adorno sometimes talks of constellations as models, which are themselves "binding statements without a system" (*ND,* 29) and of negative dialectics as an ensemble of analyses of models. Three of the chapters of *Negative Dialectics* are designated to be models. The section on "World Spirit and Natural History," analyzed here in chapter 2 above, is one such model, itself an analysis in the form of a constellation. Perhaps grouping into models is needed in order to preserve a degree of unity so that thinking in constellations does not become an amorphous mass. An ensemble of models would then be a constellation of constellations.

11. In Frederic Jameson, *Late Marxism: Adorno, or the Persistence of the Dialectic* (New York: Verso, 1993), 73.

12. It is difficult not to see the germ of Adorno's relation to Kant, and therefore the germ of much of *Negative Dialectics,* in one of Benjamin's earliest unpublished writings, "On the Program of the Coming Philosophy," (1918) in Marcus Bullock and Michael W. Jennings, *Walter Benjamin: Selected Writings* (Cambridge, Mass.: Harvard University Press, 1996), 100–10. See, for example, the following statement: "Kant's epistemology does not open up metaphysics, because it contains within itself primitive

elements of an unproductive metaphysics which excludes all others. In epistemology every metaphysical element is the germ of a disease that expresses itself in the separation of knowledge from the realm of experience in its full freedom and depth" (102).

13. Levinas, "The Thinking of Being and the Question of the Other," in *Of God Who Comes to Mind,* trans. Bettina Bergo (Stanford: Stanford University Press, 1998), 113–14.

14. Ibid., 115–17.

15. Thus, Marcuse's notion of the Great Refusal in *One-Dimensional Man,* also contains this ambiguity.

Notes to Chapter 5

1. For a brief discussion of the relation Adorno establishes between mimesis, art, and reason, see Asher Horowitz, "Mystical Kernels? Rational Shells? Habermas and Adorno on Reification and Reenchantment," in *Adorno and the Need in Thinking: New Critical Essays,* ed. D. Burke, C. Campbell, K. Kiloh, M. Palamarek, and J. Short (Toronto, University of Toronto Press, 2007), sec. 7.

2. For a masterful reading of *Totality and Infinity* along just such lines see Robert John Sheffler Manning, *Interpreting Otherwise than Heidegger: Emmanuel Levinas's Ethics as First Philosophy* (Pittsburgh: Duquesne University Press, 1993).

3. See Levinas, "Is Ontology Fundamental?"

4. The need to move beyond both is already even present at the end of Levinas's 1930 study of Husserl, *The Theory of Intuition in Husserl's Phenemenology,* trans. Andre Orianne, 2nd ed. (Evanston: Northwestern University Press, 1995), see 153–58. This need is also mentioned in Richard A. Cohen's "Foreword to the Second Edition," xxx–xxxi.

5. It is thus disappointing that the prefatory note is not included in the new translation of this essay in Emmanuel Levinas, *Unforeseen History,* trans. Nidra Poller (Chicago: University of Chicago Press, 2004).

6. For a brief description of this nexus, see Asher Horowitz and Gad Horowitz, "Is Liberalism All We Need? Prelude via Fascism," in *Difficult Justice: Commentaries on Levinas and Politics* (Toronto: University of Toronto Press, 2006), 12–23.

7. See Moyne, who links Levinas's "Reflections" to a commitment to liberalism by having Levinas argue that "antagonism to transcendental subjectivity seems to have Hitlerism as its ultimate consequence" (101).

8. And, to the extent that Marxism has not reworked its understanding of freedom to transcend the famous subject of transcendental idealism, it would have to share in that responsibility.

9. Different from Berkeley in that it does not result from a subject enclosed within itself; its subject is instead open to everything and related to everything.

10. The existence of objects outside of thought, which Idealism denies, or "affirms in thought without...in any way clarifying their significance, becomes something precise in phenomenological idealism" (WEH, 69).

11. To the best of my knowledge a proper history of the progress of this process of breaking with Heidegger has not been written, although moments of it are mentioned or dealt with in many commentaries. It would not be a matter of pinning it down to any single moment, but seeing it develop from at least 1934 through the publication of *Otherwise than Being* or the preparatory works directly feeding into the latter.

12. It has, of course, become well known, if not a commonplace, to note that Husserl himself was in the course of a development beyond even phenomenological idealism, and that the further mining of his archived writings discloses a Husserlian opening to materiality and historicity.

13. And because hyletic contents are distinct from qualities of objects, but are instead the presence of a content in a subject that is noncorrelative with a subject's intentions.

14. For an excellent and very thoroughgoing study of Levinas's debt to and transcendence of Husserl with respect to temporality, leading to the notion of a transcendental sensualism, see Drabinski, *Sensibility and Singularity*.

15. The notion of a diachrony penetrating the form of time is not present in Levinas's discussion of Husserl on temporality in "The Work of Edmund Husserl" (1940). It may be that it took the existential analyses of *Totality and Infinity* (1961), and the works leading up to it, such as *Existence and Existents* (1947) and *Time and the Other* (1947) to lead Levinas back to the Husserlian intimation of diachrony in sensibility that he is able to unearth in "Intentionality and Sensation" (1965).

16. I am taking it that Levinas implies that Heidegger's saying remains *privative* with respect to, and therefore still bound to, the noesis-noema scheme.

17. This still takes place, for example, in the otherwise highly sensitive interrelation of Levinas and deconstruction in Simon Critchley's *The Ethics of Deconstruction: Derrida and Levinas* (Cambridge: Blackwell, 1992), 7, and is what probably leads him to think of Levinas's diachrony as another form of temporality than synchrony (166).

18. This is what *radically* separates Levinas from Habermas's discourse ethics. See Asher Horowitz, "'How Can Anyone be Called Guilty?' Speech, Responsibility and the Social Relation in Habermas and Levinas," *Philosophy Today* 44, no. 3 (Fall 2000): 295–317.

19. This is perhaps the one place in which the term essence can still be used in relation to the desubstantialized subject since the essence of being subjected to everything is not to have an essence that maintains itself in being.

20. Levinas, "Thinking of Being," 209.

21. An asymmetrical fraternity would not be the equalizing fraternity of the brotherhood in revolt from the primal father.

22. And, we might add, philosophies of ecocentric ethics.

23. Even Adorno's objection to Hegel's conflation of particularity with the particular is not enough to get to the notion of unicity.

24. The single exception Levinas makes is reserved for Plato in the limited respect that "Plato nowise deduces being from the Good: he posits transcendence as surpassing the totality. Alongside of needs whose satisfaction amounts to filling a void, Plato catches sight also of aspirations that are not preceded by suffering and lack, and in which we recognize the pattern of Desire: the need of him who lacks nothing" (*TI*, 103).

25. But this radical heterogeneity is not grasped by traditional theology, inasmuch as "theology imprudently treats the idea of the relation between God and the creature in terms of ontology. It presupposes the logical privilege of totality, as a concept adequate to being. Thus it runs up against the difficulty of understanding that an infinite being would border on or tolerate something outside of itself, or that a free being would send its roots into the infinity of a God. But transcendence precisely refuses totality, does not lend itself to a view that would encompass it from the outside" (*TI*, 293).

Notes to Chapter 6

1. No one puts so clearly, tellingly, and forcefully this nondistinction between the law of the third and the law of the few in both Levinas and Derrida as Gad Horowitz in "Aporia and Messiah in Derrida and Levinas," in *Difficult Justice: Commentaries on Levinas and Politics,* ed. Asher Horowitz and Gad Horowitz (Toronto: University of Toronto Press, 2006), 307–30. No one else, in fact, has as yet pointed it out.

2. Horkeimer, "Materialism and Morality," in *Critical Theory: The Essential Readings,* ed. David Ingram and Julia Simon Ingram (New York: Paragon House, 1991), 184–85.

3. Ibid., 189.

4. A destruction in which Horkheimer and Adorno find an important grain of truth in the linkage that is thus made between bourgeois progress and the separation of tenderness from pleasure (*DE*, 109, 113).

5. Nietzsche even announces the turning of the antiauthoritarian impulse of enlightenment against itself because with him, unlike Sade, truth itself becomes an idol to be dissolved by rational critique. In Sade's case, enlightenment is not taken through "to the point of reversal" in a new mythology (*DE,* 115).

6. Horkeimer, "Materialism and Morality," 182, 179.

7. Ibid., 178, 176–79.

8. An extended discussion of this theme with considerably more historical nuance is to be found in Horkheimer, *Eclipse,* 128–61.

9. Horkeimer, "Materialism and Morality," 197–98, 189.

10. Ibid., 189–90.

11. Ibid., 178–82.

12. "The father…is resurrected, far more powerful, in the administration that preserves the life of society, and the laws that preserve the administration" (*EC,* 91).

13. It should go without saying, but let it be said anyway, that the guilt extracted by the superego is neither Adorno's sense of *Schuld* or Levinas's sense of responsibility.

14. Benjamin, "Work of Art," 242.

15. For Marcuse, its growing irrationality does not mean that it can be conceived to have been originally rational.

16. For a thorough grounding of the Marcusian concept of basic repression in the psychoanalytic literature, see Gad Horowitz, *Repression: Basic and Surplus Repression in Psychoanalytic Theory: Freud, Reich, Marcuse* (Toronto: University of Toronto Press, 1977).

17. Thus, he cautions that "any attempt to elaborate the images thus conveyed must be self-defeating, because outside the language of art they change their meaning and merge with the connotations they received under the repressive reality principle. But one must try to trace the road back to the realities to which they refer" (*EC,* 164–65).

18. The epilogue to *EC* therefore criticizes the conceptual, ideological repression of these latent transformative implications of psychoanalysis in various neo-Freudian revisionisms.

19. As Gad Horowitz suggests in "Aporia and Messiah," 320–21.

20. That the relation between eros and the ethical could be brought closer from within the framework of Levinas's phenomenology is suggested by Diane Perpich in "Sensible Subjects: Levinas and Irigaray on Incarnation and Ethics," in *Addressing Levinas,* 296–309. Here she suggests that Irigaray's ethics of sexual difference be seen as an ethics of erotic difference (307), from which Levinas is in fact not so distant (303–04). What removes Levinas from such an ethics is the need he apparently posits

for the ethical subject "of tearing [itself] up from the order of being in order to be for the other" (302). She sees, in Irigaray's appropriation of Merleau-Ponty's notion of the flesh in touch an intertwining "without synthesis" of interiority and exteriority which already implicates the subject in ethics. What she makes of Irigaray, therefore, comes close to or parallels Marcuse's speculation about the ultimate convergence of eros and agape. I believe Levinas is even closer to recognizing such an ultimate convergence than this comparison with Irigaray suggests, for reasons given in the text above, and because it seems that Perpich may have overestimated Levinas's reliance on the ego in ethical action. Levinas, after all, stresses again and again that the ethical relation is not something that I assume or initiate, that it is not I who tear myself away from being — but that in acting radically passively I am myself, in the accusative, transported beyond the I. What separates the erotic from the ethical transport is the "equivocality" of the erotic. In *fecundity in general* such equivocality is itself transcended without loss of incarnation. Perpich herself suggests that Irigaray's ethics of sexual/erotic difference "always risks falling back this side of ethics" (307).

21. The created freedom of a multiplicity of singularities not united into a totality merges precisely with Adorno's almost entirely negative notion of reconciliation: "The reconciled condition would not be the philosophical imperialism of annexing the alien. Instead *its happiness* would lie in the fact that the alien, in the proximity granted, remains what is distant and different, beyond the heterogeneous and beyond what is one's own" (*ND,* 191; emphasis added).

Index

absolute, 237–42. *See also* idealism;
spirit
acedia (spiritual weakness), 54, 57
adequation, 21–23, 120
administration, 127–28
Adorno, Theodor: aesthetics and, 75–76;
agape and, 354; amphibology and,
35–36; art and, 137; asymmetry
and, 289; Augustine and, 378n25;
Auschwitz and, 368n12; catastrophe
and, 98–99, 104–05; concept and,
155–57; constellations and, 82, 84–85;
contradiction and, 180, 187–88;
critical theory and, 80–81, 177;
critique of progress and, 376n7;
crowd and, 108; cultural experience
and, 133, 136, 138, 140, 142;
disintegration and, 190; domination
and, 320; empty homogenous time
and, 52; historiography and, 68;
Husserl and, 382n1; "Idea of Natural
History, The," 71–74, 77–80;
ideology and, 382n5; immanence
and, 150, 152–53, 160; *Juliette*
and, 311, 313–14; knowledge and,
178–80, 221, 223–24, 229–31,
234; materialism and, 319;
metaphysics and, 205–08, 215;
mimesis and, 200–204, 209–13, 226;
modern art and, 366n6; moral
realism and, 365n4; natural history
and, 127–28; nonidentity and, 185;
not-knowing and, 235; objectivity
and, 195–96; Odysseus and, 142–44;
particularity and, 89–90, 92; plurality
and, 293; reconciliation and,
388n21; reductionism and, 191–93;
representation and, 376n9; sacrifice
and, 147–48; Sade and, 316, 318;
Same and, 160, 162, 166, 169–71;
Schopenhauer and, 377n18; sense
and, 281; sensibilityand, 216–20, 228;
servility and, 124; speculation and,
183; subjectivity and, 287; surplus
morality and, 306–07; surplus of the
social and, 310; tragedy and, 380n13;
transcendence and, 101–03, 321–23;
universalism and, 86–88, 93–97.
See also specific works
aesthetics, 71, 216, 335, 361; cultural
experience and, 134; eros and,
336–39, 350. *See also* art; experience
Aesthetic Theory (Adorno), 71
affinity, 198
agape, 331–35, 341–45, 351–55, 361–64;
sexuality and, 387–88n20. *See also*
eros
Albigensians, 324
alienation, 123, 127, 147, 302; agape
and, 361–62; Hegelianism and, 27–29;
interiority and, 48, 50; liberalism
and, 372–74n22; memory and, 50;
money and, 16, 18; reconciliation and,
388n21; substitution and, 303
allegory, 77–81, 82, 97, 228. *See also*
myth; poetry
alterity, 353
Amos, Book of, 17
amphibology, 34–37, 71, 101, 267.
See also being
Anabaptists, 324
Ananke (necessity), 329–30
angel of history, 63, 67
animal condition, 27
animism, 152–53, 157
antinomianism. *See* nominalism